HOLMAN Old Testament Commentary

Job

GENERAL EDITOR
Max Anders

AUTHOR
Steven J. Lawson

NASHVILLE, TENNESSEE

Holman Old Testament Commentary

Nashville, Tennessee

978-0-8054-9470-9

Bible versions used in this book:

The King James Version

Dewey Decimal Classification: 223.7
Subject Heading: BIBLE. O.T. JOB

Job / Steven J. Lawson
p. cm. — (Holman Old Testament commentary)
Includes bibliographical references. (p.).
ISBN
1. Bible. Job—Commentaries. I. Title. II. Series.

—dc21

8 9 10 11 12 13 • 17 16 15 14 13

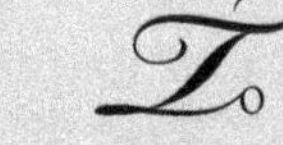

CHRIST FELLOWSHIP

BAPTIST CHURCH

Mobile, Alabama

They have been

tested by fire,

and have come forth

as gold.

Job 23:10

Contents

Editorial Preface

Today's church hungers for Bible teaching, and Bible teachers hunger for resources to guide them in teaching God's Word. The Holman Old Testament Commentary provides the church with the food to feed the spiritually hungry in an easily digestible format. The result: new spiritual vitality that the church can readily use.

Bible teaching should result in new interest in the Scriptures, expanded Bible knowledge, discovery of specific scriptural principles, relevant applications, and exciting living. The unique format of the Holman Old Testament Commentary includes sections to achieve these results for every Old Testament book.

Opening quotations stimulate thinking and lead to an introductory illustration and discussion that draw individuals and study groups into the Word of God. Verse-by-verse commentary interprets the passage with the aim of equipping them to understand and live God's Word in a contemporary setting. A conclusion draws together the themes identified in the passage under discussion and suggests application for it. A "Life Application" section provides additional illustrative material. "Deeper Discoveries" gives the reader a closer look at some of the words, phrases, and background material that illuminate the passage. "Issues for Discussion" is a tool to enhance learning within the group. Finally, a closing prayer is suggested. Bible teachers and pastors will find the teaching outline helpful as they develop lessons and sermons.

It is the editors' prayer that this new resource for local church Bible teaching will enrich the ministry of group, as well as individual, Bible study and that it will lead God's people truly to be people of the Book, living out what God calls us to be.

Acknowledgments

I have found that many times in preaching through a book in the Bible, or in writing a Bible commentary like this, God most often asks me, in a unique way, to live what I preach or write. This has certainly been my experience in writing this book. I originally began preaching through Job in order to write this commentary, but a soul-crushing storm blew into my life, one so turbulent that I was prevented from completing my preaching through Job.

Alas, God called me to experience the suffering of Job while writing on the suffering of Job. How wise of God! I suddenly became well-acquainted with Job not only in my private study but in my personal life. This book contains a message that I have been called to live, much like Job himself, only to a lesser degree. It is in the furnace of adversity that we most clearly see God's glory in the Scripture. Thus, I have written this commentary not in a cloistered ivory tower but in the real-life flames of affliction. And that is where the best study occurs.

I especially want to thank two people who have stood in the fire with me during this time. Thad Key, my personal assistant, has been a loyal and faithful supporter, one who has been indispensable in preparing the text of this book. Julie Riley has been my typist, and she has been especially devoted in seeing that this manuscript is placed in your hands. God only knows the sacrifices that Thad and Julie have made.

Finally, I must express gratitude to my wife, Anne, who has stood with me during this time. Unlike Job's wife who challenged him to curse God and die, my wife has encouraged me to bless God and live. For such a treasured gift, I am, indeed, a blessed man.

> "Now to him who is able to do immeasurably more than all we ask or imagine, according to his power that is at work within us, to him be glory in the church and in Christ Jesus throughout all generations, for ever and ever! Amen" (Eph. 3:20–21).

Steven J. Lawson
Soli Deo Gloria

Holman Old Testament Commentary Contributors

Vol. 1 Genesis
ISBN 978-0-8054-9461-7
Kenneth O. Gangel and Stephen Bramer

Vol. 2 Exodus, Leviticus, Numbers
ISBN 978-0-8054-9462-4
Glen Martin

Vol. 3 Deuteronomy
ISBN 978-0-8054-9463-1
Doug McIntosh

Vol. 4 Joshua
ISBN 978-0-8054-9464-8
Kenneth O. Gangel

Vol. 5 Judges, Ruth
ISBN 978-0-8054-9465-5
W. Gary Phillips

Vol. 6 1 & 2 Samuel
ISBN 978-0-8054-9466-2
Stephen Andrews

Vol. 7 1 & 2 Kings
ISBN 978-0-8054-9467-9
Gary Inrig

Vol. 8 1 & 2 Chronicles
ISBN 978-0-8054-9468-6
Winfried Corduan

Vol. 9 Ezra, Nehemiah, Esther
ISBN 978-0-8054-9469-3
Knute Larson and Kathy Dahlen

Vol. 10 Job
ISBN 978-0-8054-9470-9
Stephen J. Lawson

Vol. 11 Psalms 1-72
ISBN 978-0-8054-9471-6
Steve J. Lawson

Vol. 12 Psalms 73-150
ISBN 978-0-8054-9481-5
Steve J. Lawson

Vol. 13 Proverbs
ISBN 978-0-8054-9472-3
Max Anders

Vol. 14 Ecclesiastes, Song of Songs
ISBN 978-0-8054-9482-2
David George Moore and Daniel L. Akin

Vol. 15 Isaiah
ISBN 978-0-8054-9473-0
Trent C. Butler

Vol. 16 Jeremiah, Lamentations
ISBN 978-0-8054-9474-7
Fred C. Wood and Ross McLaren

Vol. 17 Ezekiel
ISBN 978-0-8054-9475-4
Mark F. Rooker

Vol. 18 Daniel
ISBN 978-0-8054-9476-1
Kenneth O. Gangel

Vol. 19 Hosea, Joel, Amos, Obadiah, Jonah, Micah
ISBN 978-0-8054-9477-8
Trent C. Butler

Vol. 20 Nahum, Habakkuk, Zephaniah, Haggai, Zechariah, Malachi
ISBN 978-0-8054-9478-5
Stephen R. Miller

Holman New Testament Commentary Contributors

Vol. 1 Matthew
ISBN 978-0-8054-0201-8
Stuart K. Weber

Vol. 2 Mark
ISBN 978-0-8054-0202-5
Rodney L. Cooper

Vol. 3 Luke
ISBN 978-0-8054-0203-2
Trent C. Butler

Vol. 4 John
ISBN 978-0-8054-0204-9
Kenneth O. Gangel

Vol. 5 Acts
ISBN 978-0-8054-0205-6
Kenneth O. Gangel

Vol. 6 Romans
ISBN 978-0-8054-0206-3
Kenneth Boa and William Kruidenier

Vol. 7 1 & 2 Corinthians
ISBN 978-0-8054-0207-0
Richard L. Pratt Jr.

Vol. 8 Galatians, Ephesians, Philippians, Colossians
ISBN 978-0-8054-0208-7
Max Anders

Vol. 9 1 & 2 Thessalonians, 1 & 2 Timothy, Titus, Philemon
ISBN 978-0-8054-0209-4
Knute Larson

Vol. 10 Hebrews, James
ISBN 978-0-8054-0211-7
Thomas D. Lea

Vol. 11 1 & 2 Peter, 1, 2, 3 John, Jude
ISBN 978-0-8054-0210-0
David Walls & Max Anders

Vol. 12 Revelation
ISBN 978-0-8054-0212-4
Kendell H. Easley

Introduction to

Job

The story of Job is one of the best known in the entire Bible yet, strangely enough, one of the least understood. No book in the Scripture is so shrouded in mystery as this ancient story. As Winston Churchill once described the Soviet Union, Job is "a riddle wrapped in a mystery inside an enigma." Tangled and troubling, its pages are veiled with the deep, perplexing issues of life. Profoundly provocative to the human mind, Job is a journey into the inscrutable ways of God. Addressed in this puzzling book are such confounding issues as: Why do the righteous suffer? Where is God when tragedy strikes? If God is all-loving, how can he allow human suffering? Does he not care? Is God worthy of worship in tough times? Or must he buy worshippers with blessings?

These are tough questions. Consequently, Job is a difficult book to grasp. The reality is that most Christians have heard about Job and his trials and many have even read about him, but few actually understand what those trials were all about. And even fewer grasp what God was seeking to accomplish through this man's ordeal. So what is this enigmatic book about?

Job is the true account of a godly man, prominent and influential, who in a matter of minutes lost all his material possessions, children, and health. His wife then told him to curse God and die. Compounding this pain, his friends used the ordeal to condemn him rather than comfort him. Still worse, God remained silent throughout this nightmare, refusing to answer Job until the very end.

What makes this inspired story so perplexing is that Job was the most righteous man on the earth, the least deserving of such tragic affliction. This raises the question: Why *do* bad things happen to good people? God was the one who initiated this entire personal nightmare for Job. This raises yet another question: Why *does* a good God allow tragedy to come to his children? It was God who removed his impenetrable protection from around Job, giving Satan virtually unlimited access into his life to bring soul-devastating destruction. Why would God be the initiator of this dark night in Job's soul? While Satan was the immediate cause of Job's troubles, God was the ultimate cause.

Throughout this entire trial, Job never did understand why he was suffering. There were no explanations from God. No behind-the-scene reports came to bolster his faith. Instead, the heavens were as brass, and this pained patriarch was forced to persevere with no answers. In the absence of any God-given insight, Job's faith was stretched to the very limits. Wracked with pain of every kind imaginable, he was forced to simply trust God. This exercise in faith came easy at first but became increasingly difficult with time. In the barren emptiness of his soul, not knowing why such trouble had come, Job was brought to the place where he could only cling to God. Did Job pass the test? Or did he soon become critical toward God? With no explanations forthcoming and no relief in sight, Job was put in the difficult position of having to rest in divine mystery.

A DIVINE MANUAL ON HUMAN SUFFERING

Here is a profoundly provocative book that addresses the weighty issues of life. Here is the inspired record of a man who was taken to the depths of despair and, by the grace of God, came forth as gold. Here is encouragement for all saints who are facing extreme difficulty and despair. Contained in the account of Job is hope for all who trust God to patiently endure the storm-tossed trials of the soul.

As you study the trials of Job, you will gain new insight into life's oldest enigmas—those dealing with sovereignty, Satan, and suffering. There are valuable life lessons waiting to be discovered in this immensely practical book. Whether you have suffered in the past and live with permanent scars, or whether you are presently suffering pain and need God-given strength for today, or whether you are trying to help someone else in their pain, here is a divine manual on human suffering. Recorded in this ancient account of God-appointed tragedies are eternal insights that will equip you to patiently endure whatever trials God calls you to endure. The person who trusts God in the furnace of life's afflictions will inevitably come forth as gold.

Before this journey through Job begins, it is essential to gain a strategic overview of this complex book.

WHAT MAKES THIS BOOK UNIQUE?

Job is truly a one-of-a-kind book in the Bible, a distinctive piece of inspired literature. Some of those unique items are:

- Job contains the longest place (four lengthy chapters) in the Bible where God himself speaks (Job 38–41).
- Job contains the longest place in the Bible where Satan speaks (Job 1–2).

- Job provides a rare insight into heaven, an otherwise unseen world, revealing a conversation between God and Satan before the angels around the divine throne.
- Job may have been the first inspired book of Scripture written, that is, if Job or a contemporary wrote the book.
- Job uses more Hebrew words not found anywhere else in the Bible, providing a rich diversity of language.
- Job involves a unique literary structure, the mixture of prose and poetry, monologue and dialogue. Thus, it is not classified in any single genre of literature. It is a *sui generis*—its own unique type of literature.
- The Book of Job specifically wrestles with these heart-wrenching questions: If God is all-loving and merciful, *why* do the righteous suffer? *Where* is God in life's trials?

WAS JOB A REAL PERSON?

Not a fictitious character or the figment of a playwright's imagination, Job was a *real* person. He was an actual historical figure, a real-life man who was married, father of ten, and a prominent businessman. He suffered one of the most devastating trials anyone has ever been called to face. The following are some substantive reasons which support this claim:

The Old Testament prophet Ezekiel spoke of Job as a historical figure, just as real as Noah and Daniel (Ezek. 14:14,20).

New Testament writers speak of Job as a real person. James, the half brother of Jesus, identified Job as a literal historical figure who was severely tested by God (Jas. 5:11). The apostle Paul quoted two times from the Book of Job—in Romans 11:35 (Job 41:11) and in 1 Corinthians 3:19 (Job 5:13). Thus, he gave credibility to the authenticity of this man Job and the account in which he is found. Unmistakably, the early apostles and disciples considered Job to be a real person.

All the many historical details of this book give every reason to believe that Job was a real individual. He lived in the land of Uz, a *real* place, and suffered *real* losses in his family, wealth, and health. The losses were carried out by a *real* foe, Satan, using *real* forces, the Sabeans and Chaldeans. Soon Job was comforted by three *real* people from *real* places and *real*, identifiable tribes. Clearly, Job was a *real* man, not a mythical character.

WHERE DID JOB LIVE?

Where did the unique events and suffering of Job take place? It is believed that Job lived in the desert lands of modern-day Arabia. The following can be concluded with certainty:

The first verse of the book identifies the home of Job as the land of Uz (Job 1:1), a large territory east of the Jordan River which included Edom in the south (Gen. 36:28) and the Aramean lands in the north (Gen. 10:23; 22:21). This was an area southeast of the Dead Sea.

In Lamentations 4:21, Uz is referred to as the same territory as Edom. More specifically, this area is the region of northern Arabia near Midian where Moses spent the second forty years of his life. This would be consistent with the attacks by the Sabeans (Job 1:15), nomadic Bedouins who lived in the area of Uz and to the south, as well as by the Chaldeans (Job 1:17) who also lived in the surrounding area.

Furthermore, Job's friends came from nearby countries. Eliphaz the Temanite most likely came from Teman, a city of Edom, east of the Jordan River. Bildad the Shuhite may suggest a relationship to Shuah, Abraham's youngest son. Zophar the Naamathite was a resident in a location probably in Edom of Arabia.

WHEN DID JOB LIVE?

Many of the details and events described in the book indicate that Job lived during the patriarchal age. This would place the events of the book some time around 2000 B.C., or the days of Abraham, Isaac, and Jacob. Various internal clues within the Book of Job indicate this early dating. Some of these evidences are:

Job lived to be well over 100 years old, a length that fits the patriarchal period. After his calamities he lived another 140 years (Job 42:16), this being after his children were fully grown (Job 1:4–5,13–19). Adding this together, Job lived to be about 200 years old, a duration of days that compares with Terah, Abraham's father, who lived to be 205; Abraham who died at 175; Isaac, who was 180 when he died; and Jacob, who lived to be 147. Obviously, the life span of people since then has been much shorter.

Job's wealth was measured in livestock (Job 1:3; 42:12), a practice that corresponds to the time of Abraham (Gen. 12:16; 13:2) and Jacob (Gen. 30:43; 32:5).

Job's leadership at home reveals he acted as the priest of his family, an indication that the Aaronic old covenant priesthood had not yet been established.

The attacks by Job's adversaries, the Sabeans and Chaldeans (Job 1:5,17), occurred while they were nomads, a practice that would not be true of them in later years when they were more settled and civilized.

The musical instruments mentioned in this book (i.e., the tambourine, lyre, and flute; Job 21:12; 30:31) are also listed in Genesis (4:21; 31:27) during the patriarchal period.

The Hebrew term for money coinage (Job 42:11) is used elsewhere in the Bible only in reference to Jacob, who was a patriarch (Gen. 33:19; Josh. 24:32).

The heirs of Job's estate included his daughters, not only his sons (Job 42:15), a practice not permitted under the Mosaic Law (Num. 27:8). This would indicate that Job lived before the giving of the law at Mt. Sinai in 1445 B.C.

The divine name *Shaddai,* or God Almighty, a name familiar to the patriarchs (Gen. 17:1; Exod. 6:3), is used thirty-one times in Job. However, this proper name for God is used only seventeen times in the rest of the entire Old Testament. Thus, it was a name used much in the early patriarchal, prelaw period, suggesting that Job probably belonged to this time.

Many of the individual and geographical names in the book were also used during the patriarchal period (Sheba and the Sabeans; Job 1:15; 6:19; Gen. 25:3), Tema (Job 5:19; Gen. 25:15), Eliphaz (Job 2:11; Gen. 36:4), and Uz (Job 1:1; Gen. 22:21).

The book contains no mention of institutions begun under the Mosaic Law (i.e., priesthood, laws, tabernacle, special religious days, etc.).

WHO WROTE JOB?

While the book itself is named after its central character, it cannot be determined with certainty who actually wrote this inspired piece of Scripture. The author of Job is unknown and can only be surmised. Several possibilities exist:

Job himself may have been the author. After all, the one who wrote this book seems to be intimately involved in the many details recorded in the book. It was not uncommon for other books in the Bible to be named after an individual (Daniel, Isaiah, Ezekiel, etc.) and to have been written by that same person. It does not seem unrealistic that the same could be true with Job. Also, it is recorded that Job lived 140 years *after* the actual events recorded in the book (Job 42:16), which was more than sufficient time to write the entire book.

Elihu, the fourth friend who spoke to Job in chapters 32–37, could have been the writer. The lengthy, detailed conversations recorded in this book suggest it may have been written by an eyewitness to all that transpired. Since

Elihu offered wise counsel to Job, if the book was written by one of his counselors, Elihu is the best choice.

Moses has been suggested by many as a possible author of this book. This position is taken by Jewish tradition. The land of Uz (Job 1:1) is adjacent to Midian, where Moses lived for forty years. It is conceivable that Moses obtained a record of the dialogue left by Job or Elihu. There are many similarities between Job and Genesis, such as a familiarity with the desert in Job, something Moses would have known.

Others have advanced Solomon as the writer of this inspired book, mainly because of the similarities among Job and Proverbs, Ecclesiastes, and the Song of Solomon about the poetic literature, Hebrew parallelism, and wisdom literature.

Still others have mentioned Ezra as the possible author. This is a feasible alternative if the time of the writing of the book dates after the Babylonian Exile.

WHEN WAS JOB WRITTEN?

The general time of the writing of this book depends upon who wrote it. There are four primary views about when this inspired book was written, each dependent on who wrote this piece of Scripture.

Many believe that Job was written in the patriarchal age, shortly after the recorded events occurred. This time of writing would be correct if either Job or Elihu were the author. If so, this would make Job the most ancient book in the Bible, predating the writing of the Pentateuch.

A second view is that Job, if written by Moses, was written in the preexodus years during the time of his isolated experience in Midian (1485–1445 B.C.). It would have been during the forty years that Moses was alone in the desert, or during the time of the wilderness wanderings (1445–1405 B.C.), a period of excruciating suffering for the nation Israel, that the book would have been written.

A third view is that the book, if written by Solomon, was written in the day of the kings, around 950 B.C.

A fourth view is that, if written by Ezra, the Book of Job was recorded during or after the Babylonian captivity. This would place the time of writing during the time of the exile (538 B.C., 458 B.C., and 445 B.C.), or shortly thereafter. However, the mention of Job by Ezekiel (Ezek. 14:14) excludes such a postexilic date.

WHAT IS JOB'S LITERARY STYLE?

The Book of Job is a mixture of various literary styles that causes it to be unique in all of Scripture. No single genre conveys the content of the entire book. Some of the literary distinctives of the book are:

The Book of Job was written in a sandwich-type format about its literary structure: prologue (prose), main body (poetry), and epilogue (prose).

The poetry section, chapters 3–37, uses the rich, figurative language of Hebrew parallelism, the skillful way of stating the same truth in different ways with striking, illustrative imagery.

Many potent literary devices were used: prose (Job 1–2; 38–42), poetry, proverbs (5:17), irony (12:2), simile (14:2), metaphor (16:13), metonymy (16:19), hymn (ch. 28), soliloquy (ch. 31), and riddle (41:1–5).

Much of the book takes the form of a lawsuit or legal disputation. Several legal terms are used by Job, his friends, and God. Some of these are: *dispute* (Job 9:3,14), to enter into litigation; *answer* (9:3,15), to testify in court; *argue* (9:14), to present a case convincingly; *judge* (9:15), one who settles a dispute; *innocent* (9:15,20,28), to be cleared of charges; *summoned* (9:16,19), to be called to court; *hearing* (9:16), a court proceeding; *justice* (9:19), an impartial hearing; *condemn* (9:20), a guilty verdict; *guilty* (9:20,29), tried and condemned; *blameless* (9:21–22), found to be acquitted; *arbitrate* (9:33), to settle a dispute.

This book contains a rich vocabulary of many Hebrew words which occur only in this book and are found nowhere else in the Old Testament. Vivid and colorful synonyms are prolific in Job as well. For example, five different words are used for lion (Job 4:10–11), six for trap (18:8–10), and six for darkness (3:4–6; 10:21–22).

The Book of Job assumes a broad knowledge of many subjects, including astronomy, geography, zoology, meteorology, oceanography, mining, travel, and jurisprudence.

WHAT IS JOB ABOUT?

Several themes emerge in this theocentric book that should be highlighted.

Sovereignty. The most prominent theme of this book is the message of the sovereignty of God. More than being a book about Job, it is, actually, a book about *God*. In the opening chapters, the reader is allowed to see into heaven's throne room where divine decisions affecting both heaven and earth are made. God controls Satan's power and man's circumstances. The book ends with God querying Job about the nature of his own right to rule his creation. This is the primary lesson learned by Job as taught in this book. God *is* God. He will do as he pleases, when he pleases, with whom he pleases, without consulting his creatures, and he will do so for his own glory and the ultimate good of his people.

Satan. In a most revealing way, Satan, the invisible foe of God and his people, is unmasked in the opening chapters of this book. Here the great adversary of God is shown to be who he truly is—the evil perpetrator behind the devastating disasters that strike Job's life. In this book the accuser of the brethren is put in his rightful place—a powerful enemy—but operating under God's sovereignty, having to request divine permission to strike Job. A real adversary armed with great power, Satan's deep hatred and animosity toward God are seen in his challenging God with accusations about Job and the devastation he unleashes upon Job's life.

Suffering. The pain and hardship endured by Job aid in answering the age-old question, *Why* do the righteous suffer? Or *why* would a loving God allow evil and pain? The righteous may ask *why,* yet God is not obligated to explain his ways to his creatures. The truth is, God's ways are above our ways. Yet he always has a purpose behind all suffering, often unrevealed to man. Job never knew why he suffered. God's answer to Job's forceful inquiry was to submit to his sovereign, all-wise counsel which is past human understanding. The oversimplified counsel of Job's friends provides no answers for the tragedies that strike the lives of the righteous.

Submission. Job serves as a good example to all believers as he humbly submits to the sovereign rule of God over his life. Job's reaction to the rapid-fire tragedies is one of reverent submission as he acknowledges God's divine discretion over all the possessions and persons in his life. This submission is understood by Job in the context of his own life when he says, "Though he slay me, yet I will hope in him" (Job 13:15).

WHO ARE THE KEY FIGURES?

There are several key figures in this book around which its unfolding drama revolves. A brief orientation to these people will be helpful in gaining an overview of the book.

Job. The primary character of this divine drama is Job, the one for whom the book is named. His name may be derived from the Hebrew word for "persecution," meaning "the persecuted one." Or it may come from an Arabic word meaning "repent," in which case his name would mean "the repentant one." Either way Job was a real person who was persecuted by Satan for his faith in God, and after self-righteousness eventually crept into his heart, he became repentant.

God. In this book the veil that separates heaven from earth is pulled back, and the reader is allowed to see into the invisible world of heaven and gain a remarkable glimpse of God. It could be argued that God himself, not Job, is the principle character of this book. Here is revealed the sovereignty of God over Satan, circumstances, and his dominion over human suffering. Likewise, his perfect wisdom, love, and grace are demonstrated in Job's life. God, who is unsearchable and inscrutable, is made known here in glorious ways. In this book we learn that everything in the universe revolves around God.

Satan. Rebellious, fallen angel that he is, Satan is also a primary character in Job, and he is revealed early in the account. He is the fiendish one who displays his accusing nature in attempting to pit God against Job and Job against God. The reader discovers the true operational style of the devil, who is entrusted with extraordinary power to wreak havoc through natural disasters, as well as removing a man's wealth, health, and family.

Eliphaz. This is the first of Job's friends to speak. Eliphaz is a Temanite, a man who was most likely a citizen of Teman, a city of Edom. Appearing on the scene after Job's second hellish attack, along with two other friends, this man challenges Job that he is suffering because of his sin. Eliphaz tends to speak as a theologian, relying heavily upon observation and experience. While the most considerate of the three "friends," Eliphaz still speaks stinging words, reasoning that only the wicked suffer. Therefore, because Job is suffering, it must be because he has sinned. Eliphaz speaks in three long discourses (chs. 4–5; 15; 22). His name means "God is gold" or "God dispenses judgment."

Bildad. This friend is the second to speak to Job. Bildad is a Shuhite, which may mean he is a descendant of Abraham through Keturah. His counsel to Job also comes in three long discourses (chs. 8; 18; 25) as he speaks as one who relies upon tradition and history. He also confides in Job the very same message that Eliphaz speaks, yet in stronger terms. His counsel is, "You must be sinning. If you would repent, God would remove your suffering." Bildad is well named; his name means "Son of Contention."

Zophar. The third friend to counsel Job is Zophar, a Naamathite, making him a resident of an unknown, surrounding location, probably in Edom or Arabia. Zophar speaks with even greater intensity than Eliphaz or Bildad and shows himself to be a blunt moralist and dogmatist. Addressing Job in only two discourses, (chs. 11; 20), Zophar is rude and curt, probably out of growing frustration, as he relies heavily on assumptions. He is the voice of orthodoxy, unbending and pointed, declaring in no uncertain terms to Job, "You are sinning and if you do not repent, your life on earth will be short-lived." With a concept of God as one who is virtually merciless, Zophar lives up to his name, which means "rough."

Elihu. A fourth counselor appears on the scene after the first three friends speak their minds. His name is Elihu, which means "he is my God." Although younger than the other three men, Elihu speaks with greater perception, applying sounder logic, and he, unlike the three friends, addresses the issue correctly. This fourth friend patiently waits his turn to speak and reasons with Job that God purifies and teaches through man's suffering. His counsel to Job is the best—that he should humble himself before God. Speaking longer than the others (chs. 32–37), Elihu provides the wisest insight for Job.

WHAT IS JOB'S STRUCTURE?

Seeing the overall structure of any book in the Bible is always important for any student of Scripture. This is most important with the Book of Job, a complex and intricately detailed book, one that involves intrigue, suspense, and a cast of many individuals, including God and Satan.

The Prologue (Job 1–2). After a brief introduction to Job, the scene abruptly shifts to heaven, where a conversation between God and Satan takes place. At God's initiation Job's name is entered into a direct challenge by God to Satan. Would Job worship God for nothing? God grants Satan permission to attack him, and he unleashes a perilous attack upon Job, resulting in the loss of his wealth and most of his family. But Job responds rightly by worshipping God (ch. 1). A second time God challenges Satan, leading to the loss of Job's health (ch. 2). Again Job exercises faith in God's sovereignty and does not sin. Shortly thereafter, three friends come to comfort Job.

The Dialogue (Job 3–26). Devastated by his losses, Job spirals down into a state of despondency and discouragement. Overcome with deep depression, Job laments his birth, wishing that he had never been born. Then he cries out, wishing he had died at birth. Finally he longs to die and escape his pain and agony. Job's three "friends" converge to console him but offer poor counsel (chs. 4–26). Eliphaz and Bildad address Job three times, and Zophar addresses him twice, each confronting Job with his sin. They conclude he must be suffering because of sin in his life. Each time Job defends himself, increasing in emotional intensity with each response. Through it all, a bitter spirit begins to fester in Job, leading him to want to appear before God in heaven to present his case and prove that God is wrongly punishing him.

The Monologues (Job 27–37). Having endured the onslaught of his three friends' attacks, Job responds in an extended monologue (chs. 27–31). He defends his innocence, extolls God's wisdom, contemplates his past happiness, considers his present pain, and maintains his personal purity. His personal holiness, he feels, does not deserve such a horrific punishment from God. At this point a fourth friend, Elihu, addresses Job, putting the matter in right perspective—divine perspective, to be specific (chs. 32–37). Offering the best counsel, Elihu tells Job that he needs to humble himself before God. Job, who had become filled with self-pity, needs to repent.

The Epilogue (Job 38–42). God himself suddenly bursts on the scene, speaking to Job from a whirlwind. Out of this storm God teaches Job some valuable lessons about his own sovereignty and the need to trust him completely (chs. 38–41). But first Job must humble himself in lowly repentance. Job does, and in the end God restores Job's losses twofold. God blesses him with seven sons and three daughters and grants him a long life (ch. 42). Through all this, God never gives Job any explanation for his suffering.

WHY DO THE RIGHTEOUS SUFFER?

Of particular interest in the Book of Job is the subject of theodicy—the vindication of the justice of God in light of man's suffering, especially the suffering of the righteous. The problem of the righteous undergoing divinely sent suffering is addressed head-on in this book. God is seen reigning sovereignly over man's suffering as he appoints it for his own glory. Further, God is seen using Satan in inflicting the pain of the righteous. In all of this, the Book of Job upholds the blameless character of God, affirming his sovereign right to do whatever he pleases (Job 38–41).

Yet deeper, the pressing question of Job is: Will the righteous praise God even in tough times? Will the righteous worship God in the midst of adversity? Consequently this inspired ancient book refutes the false view purported by many today that suffering is caused by one's sins. This was the prevalent view in Job's time, as well as in the time of Jesus (cp. John 9:2). Clearly this is the predominant thought expressed in the theology of Job's three friends.

So "*why* do the righteous suffer?" The answer is: The righteous suffer because God, according to his infinite wisdom, chooses for them to suffer. At first thought this may appear unfair or unjust. But in the Book of Job, the reader is allowed to go behind the scenes and see the higher purposes of God behind Job's suffering. Although Job lost a great deal through his soul-crushing experience, he gained far more than he lost (cp. 42:12–16). Through this fiery trial he perseveres and becomes an even stronger, more mature believer (cp. 42:5). More importantly the anguish he experiences is used by God to show the sovereign workings of God behind the veiled curtain of human circumstances for his own glory.

In the bigger picture the person who undergoes painful suffering must remember that his life is part of a much grander scheme than he could ever imagine. Pitted between the kingdoms of light and darkness stands the righteous person. He is the battlefield for the invisible war between the two unseen worlds. Satan is always pressing to destroy God's plans by attacking the human race, especially the righteous. At stake in this spiritual warfare is the glory of God. Honor is given to God when the righteous endure suffering patiently. Therefore, believers can face trials and tribulations triumphantly, knowing they are appointed for God's glory and their good.

Job 1

When All Hell Breaks Loose

Quote

"The grace of God exempts no one from trouble."

J. C. Ryle

I. INTRODUCTION

Tallest Tree in the Forest

The 1991 U.S. Open at Hazeltine National Golf Course, just outside of Minneapolis, Minnesota, proved to be memorable, but not just for the game of golf. On what began as a peaceful and calm day for the first round of the tournament, a bank of gray clouds gathered swiftly overhead. Turbulent skies blackened, and swirling banks of electricity collected. Lightning struck a few miles away. Forty thousand spectators scrambled for shelter.

Gathering under a bent willow tree near the eleventh tee, a group of spectators huddled together to keep from being drenched. An official asked them to find cover elsewhere. A few people dispersed and a few stayed, as lightning struck a tree behind the tenth green, splitting its trunk in half. Then a minute later a lightning bolt struck the tall willow tree. A dozen bodies toppled to the earth like bowling pins. Six men got up. Six lay dazed on the ground. One died with his hands in his pockets. The lightning had struck its target—the tallest tree in the area.

This certainly describes Job, a man who stood tallest in his day for God. Like this towering willow tree, Job was deeply rooted in his faith in God; and when the highly charged storm of adversity hit, Job was the lightning rod who drew the fire. Tragedy came not because there was anything wrong in his life but, to the contrary, because everything was right. He was the most righteous man on the earth, and thus he was marked to suffer.

The same is true for every believer who walks with God, whether they are towering sequoias or tender saplings. Every Christian will undergo divinely appointed times of suffering. No one escapes this world unscathed. Such suffering does not occur because there is anything wrong about a person's life. To the contrary, adversity often comes because everything is *right* about one's life. A believer may be marked to suffer because he or she stands tallest for God. One who is deeply rooted and grounded in Christ should never be surprised when such times of adversity come. Like Job, a person of great faith will suffer by divine appointment for the sake of righteousness.

In the first chapter of Job, we are introduced to the main character, Job. We are told who he was, where he lived, where his faith was, and how successful he was. But we also discover the origin of the storm that struck his life.

II. COMMENTARY

When All Hell Breaks Loose

MAIN IDEA: *Tragedy unexpectedly strikes the life of Job, the strongest believer, not in the form of chastening discipline but as an opportunity to worship God for who he is.*

A Job's Character (1:1–5)

SUPPORTING IDEA: *Job's strong faith in God is validated with a truly transformed life.*

1:1. Job lived **in the land of Uz**, a large territory east of the Jordan River, southeast of the Dead Sea, near modern-day Jordan. His faith in God grew strong, since he **was blameless and upright; he feared God and shunned evil**. The word "blameless" does not mean sinless but that he was beyond reproach in his personal character and conduct. No one could justly charge him with moral failure. Moreover, he was upright in his actions, literally, "straight," without deviating from God's holy standards. Job also feared God. He was filled with holy awe, reverence, and respect for God. He took God seriously, careful to live in a God-honoring manner. And Job shunned evil, resisting worldly temptation.

1:2. In addition, Job **had seven sons and three daughters**. Seven and three are ideal numbers, signifying completeness, signs of God's abundant favor. Job's sons and daughters loved one another. They met regularly to enjoy one another's company (Job 1:4,13,18–19). Job was greatly blessed as a father.

1:3. Further, Job was a very successful businessman, possessing much livestock and many servants. His vast herds and numerous servants were ancient measures of wealth. His **seven thousand sheep** provided him luxurious clothing and ample food; his **three thousand camels** gave him transportation; his **five hundred yoke of oxen** helped his servants plow the ground and provided more food; his **five hundred donkeys** kept him supplied with more offspring; and his **large numbers of servants** worked his sizable estate. Job was both godly *and* wealthy, a rare combination. Because of his wealth, Job's reputation was known far and wide. He was **the greatest man among all the people of the East**.

1:4. Job's seven **sons** would gather together at least seven times a year, probably on each son's birthday. Job was blessed with a close-knit family, the result of God's rich blessing. Surely Job's personal integrity earned him credibility with his children. His faith made an impact on their lives.

1:5. After these family gatherings, Job **would sacrifice a burnt offering for each of** his children. He was deeply concerned for the spiritual welfare of his children. So he offered burnt offerings to God, dedicating each child to God in recognition of God's ownership of their lives. Rather than holding his family with a clenched fist, Job offered them to God with an open hand.

B Job's Conspirators (1:6–12)

SUPPORTING IDEA: *By God's initiative, Satan requests and is granted permission by God to test Job's faith by taking all he owns.*

1:6. The scene suddenly shifts to heaven, providing a rare insight into the unseen world above. **One day the angels came to present themselves before the LORD**. This implies that this day was like any other day. The sons of God were the angelic hosts (Job 38:7; Gen. 6:2) who were reporting to the Lord by coming before the divine throne. These ministering spirits had been away, serving the Lord, and they returned for further orders. In the midst of this gathering, **Satan also came with them**. Once the highest archangel, Satan had been banished from heaven for his rebellion against God. Yet, mysteriously, he still could approach God's throne in heaven. So Satan joined them, once again, on this occasion.

1:7. **The LORD** asked **Satan, "Where have you come from?"** The omniscient God knew where Satan had been, as well as what he had been doing. This question was intended to elicit a confession from this fallen angel. **Satan answered the LORD, "From roaming through the earth and going back and**

forth in it." This was the devil's main activity, wreaking havoc on the earth as a "roaring lion looking for someone to devour" (1 Pet. 5:8). Never idle, Satan is always on the prowl as "the prince of this world" (John 12:31), blinding minds (2 Cor. 4:4), stealing God's Word (Matt. 13:19), opposing God's work (1 Thess. 2:18), sowing tares (Matt. 13:37–40), tempting God's people (1 Cor. 7:5), attacking God's Word (Gen. 3:1), spreading false doctrine (1 Tim. 1:3), persecuting God's church (Rev. 2:10), and deceiving the nations (Rev. 16:14).

1:8. The LORD said to Satan, "Have you considered my servant Job?" God knew the evil that Satan had been instigating on the earth. He praised the name of Job, his most trusted servant, knowing that Job would remain faithful to him if attacked by Satan. Job's involvement in this contest was certainly not due to any personal sin because God added, "**There is no one on earth like him.**" Job was the most righteous man on the earth. God's estimation of him was: "**He is blameless and upright, a man who fears God and shuns evil**" (cp. Job 1:1).

1:9. With shrewd cunning, "the accuser" replied, "**Does Job fear God for nothing?**" In this cunning response, Satan accused God of "buying" Job's worship. Job, Satan insisted, worshipped God for what prosperity he could gain from him, not for who God is.

1:10. Satan went on to say, "**Have you not put a hedge around him and his household and everything he has?**" Satan had already been trying to attack Job, but he could not touch him. This inability was due to a protective hedge of divine care built around him that prevented Satan's advances from harming him.

1:11. "But stretch out your hand," the devil challenged God, "**and strike everything he has, and he will surely curse you to your face.**" If God were to allow Satan to remove Job's many material blessings, the devil insisted, this so-called worshipper would withdraw his praise and curse the Lord.

1:12. Under the purview of his divine sovereignty, God granted Satan permission to attack Job's life. But Satan's attack could only go so far. God stipulated, **But on the man himself do not lay a finger**. The devil was given free access to remove Job's possessions and loved ones, but he could not touch his body to remove his health. Neither could he take his life. So **Satan went out from the presence of the LORD** and descended to the earth to unleash this attack upon Job. All hell was ready to break loose upon his life.

C Job's Catastrophies (1:13–19)

SUPPORTING IDEA: *At the hand of Satan, Job suffers the loss of his possessions, servants, and children.*

1:13–14. All in **one day** Job's prosperity was reduced to poverty as he lost all his livestock and servants, even his sons and daughters, in rapid-fire succession. It was on this day that **Job's sons and daughters were feasting and drinking wine at the oldest brother's house**. Job was abruptly notified of the first tragedy when **a messenger came to** him, **and said, "The oxen were plowing and the donkeys were grazing nearby."** It was just another normal day in Job's life.

1:15. But the disturbing report came that **the Sabeans attacked and carried them off**. The Sabeans were probably nomads from Sheba, the southern part of Arabia, and were descendants of Abraham and Keturah (Gen. 25:1–3). Later in Job the Sabeans are called "traveling merchants" (Job 6:19). References to Sheba and the Sabeans are found throughout the Old Testament (Ps. 72:10,15; Jer. 6:20; Joel 3:8). These merchant raiders stole Job's cattle and put **the sword** to his **servants**, slaughtering them. Only one traumatized helper escaped this catastrophic disaster to tell Job the tragic news.

1:16. While the sole surviving servant **was still speaking, another messenger** burst into the room, bearing more distressing news. His **sheep** and another group of **servants** had met an untimely death. These were **burned up** by a cataclysmic event described as **the fire of God** which **fell from the sky**, probably a lightning storm.

1:17. When it seemed that nothing worse could happen, still another disaster struck. **Three raiding parties** were formed by **the Chaldeans**, who stole Job's three thousand **camels**. The Chaldeans were a fierce, seminomadic group who eventually migrated into southern Mesopotamia, where they aided in the formation of the Babylonian Empire. These murderous savages spared none of the servants from the **sword** except one servant who **escaped** and brought Job the devastating news.

1:18–19. With tragedy upon tragedy mounting, yet another dagger was thrust into Job's heart. **Another messenger came** running, bearing the most tragic news of the day. Job's seven **sons** and three **daughters were feasting and drinking wine at the oldest brother's house**. They were together for an enjoyable family gathering, **when suddenly a mighty wind** struck the house where they were eating. This mighty wind was probably a tornado since it produced enough force to collapse **the four corners of the house** (cp. Isa. 21:1; Hos. 13:15) and brought about the death of all ten of Job's children.

D Job's Confidence (1:20–22)

SUPPORTING IDEA: *In response to these great calamities, Job praises God's sovereign rule over his life and possessions.*

1:20. Upon hearing of the loss of all his possessions and children, **Job got up and tore his robe** (Gen. 44:13; Judg. 11:35) **and shaved his head** (Isa. 15:2; Ezek. 7:18). These were outward expressions of his deep, inner sorrow, grief, and turmoil. Then Job **fell to the ground in worship**, prostrating himself before God in an act of humble submission and adoration. The worship continued as Job, unlike his wife (cp. Job 2:9), blessed the Lord.

1:21. Job declared, "**Naked I came from my mother's womb, and naked I will depart.**" He realized he would leave the world the same way he had entered it—naked. In all these losses he knew he would be eventually separated from them when it came time to leave this world. Job acknowledged God's unlimited sovereignty over all by saying, "**The LORD gave and the LORD has taken away.**" He realized all his possessions, servants, sons, and daughters were gifts from God (Jas. 1:17), who alone has the right to take them at his discretion. Therefore, he had no right to cling to them as if they were his. This lofty realization of God's sovereignty led Job to declare, "**May the name of the LORD be praised.**"

1:22. **In all this, Job did not sin by charging God with wrongdoing**. He responded with true faith in God, believing that he rules over all things according to his own perfect will. Irreverent accusations and bitter charges against God were not a part of Job's response. His high view of God's supremacy caused him to offer praise in the most tragic moment of his life.

MAIN IDEA REVIEW: *Tragedy unexpectedly strikes the life of Job, the strongest believer, not in the form of chastening discipline, but as an opportunity to worship God for who he is.*

III. CONCLUSION

God's Mysterious Ways

One of the greatest hymn writers the church has ever known, William Cowper, was a man who suffered greatly. The last hymn he wrote, composed in 1774, speaks of the mystery of God's design behind our adversity. Even when that divine purpose is not made known to the person who is afflicted, Cowper insisted that the ultimate act of worship is to bow humbly before God and rejoice in his goodness. Even when his ways are past our comprehension, God should be praised. Cowper wrote:

God moves in a mysterious way
His wonders to perform;
He plants His footsteps in the sea
And rides upon the storm.

Deep in unfathomable mines
Of never failing skill
He treasures up His bright designs
And works His sovereign will.

Blind unbelief is sure to err
And scan His work in vain;
God is His own interpreter,
And He will make it plain.

IV. LIFE APPLICATION

How to Handle Adversity

What can we learn from the response of Job as we face the trials of life? Job provides an outstanding case study in how to handle adversity. Consider the following truths.

1. *See the simplicity of knowing God.* In the absence of understanding *why* a particular tragedy has struck, the believer simply needs to know *who* is in control, God himself. God's thoughts are high above our thoughts, and his ways are far beyond our ways. Absolutely sovereign yet infinitely wise, God's ways are perfect. Thus, we can trust him. When tragedy strikes, there are no explanations sent from God explaining *why* such an ordeal has just been unleashed upon our lives. In the midst of life's tragedies, when we most want answers, so often there are none. In these difficult hours we must simply trust God.

2. *See the sincerity of knowing God.* Job's life revealed the marks of a true, vibrant faith. Such an authentic trust finds, at its core, a sincere fear of God. The emphasis here is that Job "feared God" (Job 1:1,8,9; 2:3), a reality rooted in knowing the Lord (Job 28:28). This is where the Christian life begins. Such a reverential awe is foundational to any personal knowledge of God. Fearing God is, quite simply, taking him seriously in our lives and giving him the unrivaled place of honor that belongs to him alone. This fear marked Job's life—a life recognized by God as stronger than any other on earth (Job 1:8). So it will be for believers today. At the core of a healthy, vital relationship with God is a trembling heart that stands in awe of his majesty.

3. *See the sufficiency of knowing God.* When answers are not forthcoming and trials overwhelm us, it is in these difficult times that the greatest worship is offered to God. Believers must respond as Job did in these dark hours by worshipping God. Though circumstances change, often from bad to worse, God remains the same, eternally unchanging, always worthy of our worship. As Job found an anchor for his soul in God, so may we as we put our trust in him.

V. PRAYER

God, our great Father, we praise you for your sovereignty over all your creation. We humbly bow and submit to you, asking that you grant us the ability to respond properly to the fiery trials you bring our way. May we, like your servant Job, acknowledge with praise your divine discretion to give and to take away possessions and people in our lives. We ask this in the name of your Son and our Savior, the Lord Jesus Christ. Amen.

VI. DEEPER DISCOVERIES

A. Uz (1:1)

Uz was a large territory in the area of northern Arabia, southeast of the Dead Sea. The territory was adjacent to Midian, where Moses lived for forty years before returning to Egypt. In Lamentations 4:21, Uz is equated with the territory of Edom. It was here that the city in which Job lived was located. Later in Job 29:7–8, the author notes that this city had a wall and gates. Thus, it was a city of considerable size with an organized defense.

B. Blameless (1:1)

The Hebrew adjective *tam,* translated as "blameless," means complete, whole, or upright and is always used in a moral sense of a person's integrity. It comes from the Hebrew verb *tamam,* which means to be complete, to be finished, or without blame. It does not mean that Job was sinless (cp. Job 6:24; 9:20) but morally upright (Job 1:8; Ps. 37:37).

C. Upright (1:1)

The word translated as "upright" (Heb. *yashar*) literally means straight. W. E. Vine, a great etymologist, said of this word, "The basic meaning is the root meaning to be straight in the sense of to be level. The Israelites designated an easy road for traveling as a level road. When *yashar* pertains to people, it is best translated just or upright."

D. Purified (1:5)

Job consecrated (purified) his children to God in what seems to have been a form of dedication. By this Job acted as an intercessor before God on behalf of his children. Since it is believed that he lived around the time of the patriarchs, their consecration occurred before the Aaronic priesthood and the sacrificial system of the old covenant. As to when or from what source Job derived instruction on consecration, we are not told. This account is given to show Job's reverence for God.

E. Satan (1:6)

The word *satan* is derived from the Hebrew verb meaning to accuse or to attack. The masculine noun form was used to speak of an adversary (1 Sam. 29:4; 1 Kgs. 5:4). When the definite article is attached, *satan* is correctly treated as a proper noun referring to the supernatural being of Satan. Scripture attests to the angelic nature of Satan (Jude 9), who rebelled against God (1 Tim. 3:6). This led to his losing his position as a preeminent cherub (Ezek. 28:12–16). This rebellion by Satan prompted one-third of the heavenly angelic host to rebel against God (Rev. 12:4). Satan's hostility and hatred of God were clearly demonstrated by his role in the fall (Gen. 3:15; Rom. 16:20) and his continual involvement in the affairs of heaven and men (Zech. 3:1). To the people of God, he is the accuser (Rev. 12:10). Satan's final destruction will be sealed in an eternal torment (Rev. 20:10).

F. Worship (1:20)

The Hebrew word for "worship" (*shaha*) means to prostrate oneself, especially before a superior (Gen. 18:2; 1 Sam. 24:8). Rarely is it before an equal (1 Kgs. 2:19). The word occurs over 170 times in the Hebrew Bible, most often of prayer (Gen. 22:5). As it refers more specifically to an attitude of the heart, it does not require a prostrated position (Gen. 47:31). It was most often used of worshipping God (1 Sam. 15:30; Isa. 27:13), yet sometimes, tragically, of idol worship (Deut. 8:19; Judg. 2:19). This word speaks of the total self-humiliation, submission, and adoration to be given to God.

VII. TEACHING OUTLINE

A. Job's Character (1:1–5)
   1. A strong believer (1:1)
   2. A satisfied father (1:2)
   3. A successful businessman (1:3)
   4. A spiritual leader (1:4–5)

B. Job's Conspirators (1:6–12)
   1. The distant gathering (1:6)
   2. The divine initiative (1:7–8)
   3. The devilish reply (1:9–11)
   4. The divine permission (1:12a)
C. Job's Catastrophies (1:13–19)
   1. Satan attacked with the Sabeans (1:13–15)
   2. Satan attacked with a great fire (1:16)
   3. Satan attacked with the Chaldeans (1:17)
   4. Satan attacked with a great wind (1:18–19)
D. Job's Confidence (1:20–22)
   1. Job humbled himself (1:20a,b,c)
   2. Job honored God (1:20d–21)
   3. Job constrained himself (1:22)

VIII. ISSUES FOR DISCUSSION

1. Am I blameless in both my actions and words?
2. Do I recognize and submit to God's sovereign rule over my life?
3. Do I own my possessions or do my possessions own me?
4. Do I immediately turn to God when tragedy strikes?
5. Do I praise God even in the fiery trials of life?

Job 2

The Invisible War

Quote

"I believe Satan to exist for two reasons: first, the Bible says so; and second, I've done business with him."

D. L. Moody

I. INTRODUCTION

Somebody Is Hitting Me!

An overmatched boxer was being badly beaten by his skilled opponent. Battered and bruised, he leaned over the ropes and said to his trainer, "Throw in the towel! This guy is killing me!"

The trainer replied, "Oh, no, he's not. That guy is not even hitting you. He hasn't laid a glove on you!"

At that point the whipped boxer spit blood from his bruised mouth and said, "Well, you had better watch the referee. *Somebody* is sure hitting me!"

Like the bloodied boxer in this story, all believers are sooner or later struck by the blows of life. We must understand that behind the knockout punches of life is a formidable foe, a real, personal adversary known as the devil—one who is able to send us reeling. Yet in spite of what the Bible so clearly teaches, some people live as if there is no devil. No matter what people think, the Bible teaches that Satan is alive and well on planet Earth. This adversary launches ferocious attacks against the souls of men and women.

Unfortunately, many well-meaning Christians live as if peacetime conditions exist. But in reality a bloody war is being fought all around them. Souls are being defeated. Lives are being attacked. None of us can afford to be uninformed about this invisible war. Satan, the evil emperor, is working behind the scenes, unleashing his diabolical power with fury and hatred. This sinister opponent is determined to attack every person's life, assaulting their faith, and conquering their souls.

Have you admitted that you face a real, spiritual foe, the devil? Are you on the alert for his advances? Have you recognized his destructive power? Or are you ignorant of his devices? If you are to remain strong in your faith, you must be vigilant in your spiritual life and remain firmly anchored to God.

As Job chapter 2 opens, the unfolding drama of Job brings us again into the throne room of heaven where God presides over the affairs of heaven and earth and where angels gather for further orders. Here in glory Satan appears before God to accuse and attack believers. But here it is also revealed how God sovereignly directs, limits, and even uses Satan to accomplish his purposes.

II. COMMENTARY

The Invisible War

MAIN IDEA: *God allows Job to be tested by Satan, who robs him of his physical health and vitality; yet Job remains faithful to God.*

Satan's Persistence (2:1–3)

SUPPORTING IDEA: *Satan is given permission by God to test the integrity of Job's faith, all under the boundaries of divine sovereignty.*

2:1. A second heavenly scene unfolds, one unseen and unknown by Job. It involves **another day** when **the angels came to present themselves before the LORD**. This repeated scene was, as before, yet another time of reporting by the angels, a day of reporting before God. As this time of briefing occurred, **Satan also came with them to present himself before him**. The appearance of Satan in this heavenly scene indicates a sustained access that he has into the presence of the Lord, before whom he continually accuses the righteous (Rev. 12:10).

2:2. By divine initiative the Lord asked the evil one, "**Where have you come from?**" This question was not asked out of ignorance as if God did not know. The Lord knows all things. Rather, it was meant to illicit a confession from this fallen angel. Satan answered the Lord, "**From roaming through the earth and going back and forth in it.**"

This world is the arena in which Satan is creating and wreaking havoc. Cast down to the earth with a third of the heavenly host (Rev. 12:10), Satan roams the earth like a condemned prisoner (Gen. 3:14), stalking prey, ambushing victims, until he will be finally placed into the bottomless pit of eternal destruction, a real place called hell (Rev. 20:10). But the devil is not yet in hell. Instead, he is actively roaming the earth, bent on destroying lives.

2:3. Knowing Satan had been wreaking destruction on the earth, the Lord said to Satan, **Have you considered my servant Job?** Knowing Satan's first round of attacks had failed to shake Job's faith, with sarcasm the Lord reminded Satan that Job was **blameless and upright, a man who fears God and shuns evil**. The Lord stated that Job **still maintained his integrity**, in spite of the devil's first assault upon his life. Job remained faithful and did not waver in his devotion to God. Although Satan had **incited** God **against** Job to **ruin him**, God maintained that Job's suffering was **without any reason**. Satan, not Job's sin, was to blame for Job's suffering. Although Job underwent severe trial and pain, it was not because of any sin he had committed.

B Satan's Persuasion (2:4–5)

SUPPORTING IDEA: *Cunningly, Satan reasons with God that Job in his selfishness would sacrifice the lives of his children, servants, and livestock in order to protect his own life.*

2:4. With audacious resolve, **Satan** indicted God by saying, "**Skin for skin!**" This was a bartering term that meant to trade one skin, such as that of an animal, for another skin. Satan, whose name means "the accuser," was charging Job with sacrificing the skin of his children, animals, and servants in order to preserve his own hide. Satan was convinced that Job would give all he had **for his own life**. If given the opportunity to choose between a loved one and his own personal health, Job, would protect his own hide and reamass his fortune in a future day, Satan accused.

2:5. Satan asked God to **stretch out** his hand and strike Job's **flesh and bones**. He believed this would lead Job to **curse** God to his **face**, his original conviction (Job 1:11). Since the mouth spoke from the heart (Matt. 12:34), Satan understood that cursing God would represent Job's refusal to submit to God's sovereign rule.

C Satan's Permission (2:6)

SUPPORTING IDEA: *Satan is granted permission by God to afflict Job's body with great harm, except he is prevented from taking Job's life.*

2:6. The Lord granted Satan permission to attack Job: "**Very well, then, he is in your hands.**" God removed the hedge of protection from around Job

(1:10) and allowed Satan even greater access to assail his life. This divine permission gave Satan virtually unrestrained power to harm Job's body. God's only restriction was, "**You must spare his life.**"

D Satan's Persecution (2:7–13)

SUPPORTING IDEA: *Struck by Satan, Job suffers the loss of his physical well-being, as he receives the foolish counsel of his wife and is approached by three friends who seek to comfort him.*

2:7. Immediately, Satan **went out from the presence of the LORD and** descended to the earth to unleash the full fury of his authority over Job's life. Without a moment's delay he **afflicted Job with painful sores**. These sores were like the ones the Lord sent upon Egypt (Exod. 9:8–11). Until Job's health was restored, these physical sores haunted Job and produced severe pain. Satan inflicted Job with these sores **from the soles of his feet to the top of his head**.

2:8. Perhaps to release infection from the boils or to stop the itching, **Job took a piece of broken pottery and scraped himself**. Further, Job went to the city garbage dump and **sat among the ashes** where the trash was burned. This was a humiliating experience for one of the leaders and elders of the city (Job 29:7).

2:9. An even greater attack came to Job's faith. **His wife** taunted him, "**Are you still holding on to your integrity?**" A negative answer was anticipated. Her faith buckled under this trauma as she was unable to cope with its suddenness and severity. In bitterness she called on Job to **curse God and die**. If he would curse God, it would surely lead to his death. She was insinuating that Job needed to forsake his spiritual integrity by cursing God, thus inviting divine discipline. This sin unto death (1 John 5:16–17) would end Job's present pain and suffering. In reality she had become the mouthpiece of the devil, parroting the exact words of Satan's challenge to God (Job 1:11).

2:10. His wife's bad counsel received a sharp rebuke from Job: "**You are talking like a foolish woman.**" This abrupt reproof was fully warranted since she had responded in unbelief (cp. Ps. 53:1). The unbelief of Job's wife led him to respond with one of the strongest statements of faith ever uttered about God and suffering. These words demonstrated Job's complete abandonment to God's sovereignty, one sure sign of true faith: "**Shall we accept good from God, and not trouble?**" Job's confidence in God remained unshakable, demonstrating that he had retained his integrity (cp. Job 2:3,9), whether receiving good or trouble from God. So, **in all this, Job did not sin in what he said**. Both good and trouble are brought into the lives of believers by God, Job acknowledged, and must be accepted in simple faith.

2:11. But next came the greatest assault Satan would hurl at Job—the counsel that came from his friends. What the devil spoke through Job's wife, he would speak even more convincingly through his three friends. Satan's lies can be spoken through another person, even from the lips of another believer (Matt. 16:22–23). So, having **heard about all the troubles that had come upon** Job, his **three friends** set out from their homes from various regions around Uz to support Job in his pain. His three friends **met together by agreement to go and sympathize with him**, all with the aim of bringing **comfort** to Job.

These friends were **Eliphaz the Temanite**, who came from the city of Teman, located in northern Edom; **Bildad the Shuhite**, a descendant of Abraham by Keturah (Gen. 25:2); and **Zophar the Naamathite**, an unknown area, perhaps in northwestern Arabia or Edom. Probably some time had elapsed before word of Job's troubles reached his three friends. Then some more time passed before they could travel to Uz.

2:12. As they approached Uz, Job's friends **saw him from a distance**, yet **they could hardly recognize him**. This marred appearance was due to Job's physical and emotional suffering. Their response to Job's pain was moving as they identified with him in his deep hurt. **They tore their robes and sprinkled dust on their heads** (2 Sam. 1:2; Mic. 1:10)—signs of great anguish—and **began to weep aloud**. To both Job and his friends, the end loomed near as he appeared to be tottering on the brink of death.

2:13. Then they sat on the ground with him for seven days and seven nights. This was a symbol of mourning and humility (Lam. 2:10). The seven days and seven nights are similar to other passages that convey a period of deep sorrow (Gen. 50:10; Ezek. 3:15). The suffering of Job was so great that **no one said a word to him**. The silence was deafening. Speaking to him would have been insensitive, unkind, and useless because of his suffering. As the rest of the book shows, their silence was the wisest thing they did.

MAIN IDEA REVIEW: *God allows Job to be tested by Satan, who robs him of his physical health and vitality; yet Job remains faithful to God.*

III. CONCLUSION

A Bulwark Never Failing

Worshipping God in the midst of great difficulty, much like Job, is a great challenge. It certainly was the soul-stretching experience of the great German reformer, Martin Luther. This man of God faced many difficulties and adversities throughout his life but none more painful than what he encountered in 1527. In that gruesome year the bubonic plague or Black Death swept through Germany, taking countless lives. Many of his students and fellow citizens abandoned Wittenberg, but Luther felt it was his obligation to stay. Further, his house was transformed into a hospital for others, his wife was pregnant and sick, and his own child almost died. The weight of responsibility from the Reformation that was thrust upon him grew heavier.

In this dreadful ordeal physical fatigue and illness gripped his body. In this most difficult hour of his life, Luther chose to worship God by writing his famous hymn, "A Mighty Fortress." Its words reveal the heart of a man who was a true worshipper, even in the face of great difficulties.

> A mighty fortress is our God,
> A bulwark never failing;
> Our helper He amid the flood
> Of mortal ills prevailing.
> For still our ancient foe
> Doth seek to work us woe.
> His craft and pow'r are great
> And armed with cruel hate
> On earth is not his equal.
>
> That word above all earthly pow'rs,
> No thanks to them abideth;
> The Spirit and the gifts are ours
> Thru Him who with us sideth.
> Let goods and kindred go,
> This mortal life also;
> The body they may kill;
> God's truth abideth still;
> His kingdom is forever.

IV. LIFE APPLICATION

How to Deal with Temptation

In our fight with Satan, we must recognize that he most often attacks us with temptation, or enticement to evil. God has chosen to allow such tests to prove our allegiance to him (Jas. 1:2,12). Every temptation is an opportunity to demonstrate our faith in God. How do we react to temptation?

1. *Expect it.* Each Christian should expect that Satan will launch his offensives against us. No believer is exempt from these hellish attacks. God's people may never face the full force of such a full-armed advance as Job did. But believers must brace themselves and be prepared to come under the fury of the devil's fire. By virtue of our faith in God, Christians are the avowed enemy of the devil. Thus, believers must be on the alert and realize that they live in a state of declared war between God and the devil.

2. *Detect it.* Every believer must sharpen his powers of discernment in spiritual warfare. Each Christian must detect the advances of the enemy. Satan wants to influence our minds. God's people must measure everything by the unfailing standard of truth, the Word of God. Only by the enlightenment of Scripture, aided by the Holy Spirit, can believers detect Satan's falsehoods and expose them for what they are. Satan's agenda to perpetrate his falsehoods must be recognized for what it is—an offensive against the Word of God (Matt. 16:23).

3. *Reject it.* Once the advance of the devil is detected, it must be firmly rejected. When "the flaming arrows of the evil one" (Eph. 6:16) are fired at Christians, they must extinguish them with the shield of faith. This requires a firm faith in God and his Word. Just as aggressively as Satan attacks us, so we must resist these assaults. No one can remain neutral, much less passive, in the evil day of Satan's attack. But with forceful resolve, aided by the Spirit's power, believers must reject the devil's hellish advances.

V. PRAYER

God, our Father, we know you are absolutely sovereign over our suffering. You use Satan to carry out your eternal purposes. We rest in your control over all. Teach us to accept whatever you bring into our lives. Teach us to accept both the good and the bad. May we be like your servant Job, who did not understand what was happening but he trusted you. In Jesus' name. Amen.

VI. DEEPER DISCOVERIES

A. God (2:3,9–10)

The Hebrew word *elohiym* is used throughout the Bible as a general name for the true God. Although it is sometimes used to refer to pagan gods or deities (Exod. 12:12; Judg. 17:5; 1 Kgs. 11:2; Ps. 86:8), angels (Ps. 8:5), men (Ps. 82:6), and judges (Exod. 21:6), it is used primarily to refer to the one true God who created all things out of nothing. In fact, *elohiym* is often used for

God in the early chapters of Genesis. The meaning of *elohiym* is debatable, but it seems to refer to the transcendence of God. The plural form indicates plentitude of power and majesty and also makes allowance for a plurality of persons in the one God. This would certainly allow for the Trinity of the Godhead which is more fully developed later in the Old Testament and especially the New Testament.

B. Integrity (2:3,9)

"Integrity" (Heb. *tumma)* appears several times in the Wisdom Literature of the Old Testament (Job 27:5; Prov. 11:3). *Tumma* is the feminine form of *tob,* which is used throughout the Bible for wholeness, completeness, and soundness. The English word *integrity* is used to speak of various aspects of one's life being integrated and coherent with the rest.

C. Sores (2:7)

"Sores" (Heb. *rah*) were inflamed ulcerous sores (Job 2:7) that produced itching (2:8), degenerative changes in facial skin (2:7,12), loss of appetite (3:24), depression (3:24–25), worms in the boils (7:5), hardened skin and running sores (7:5), difficulty in breathing (9:18), dark eyelids (16:16), foul breath (19:17), weight loss (19:20), continual pain (30:17), restlessness (30:27), blackened skin (30:30), and fever (30:30), all of which lasted for several months (29:2).

D. Sin (2:10)

The Hebrew word *hatta* reveals a different nuance of sin and means to miss the mark, to miss the way, to go wrong, or to go astray. This word was an archery term. It pictures a hunter with a bow and arrow, aiming at a target or an animal. He shoots the arrow, only to miss the mark and fall short (Rom. 3:23). This is what sin is—missing the mark of God's Word. It is one's life falling short of the standard by not measuring up. Here the standard is the glory of God, the sum total of all his divine perfections, most specifically his holiness.

VII. TEACHING OUTLINE

A. Satan's Persistence (2:1–3)
  1. Satan again appears before God (2:1)
  2. Satan again answers to God (2:2–3)

B. Satan's Persuasion (2:4–5)
  1. He indicts Job's motive (2:4)

2. He indicts God's majesty (2:5)

C. Satan's Permission (2:6)

1. God gives Job to the devil (2:6a)

2. God guards Job from death (2:6b)

D. Satan's Persecution (2:7–13)

1. Job is afflicted with physical pain (2:7–8)

2. Job is assaulted by his wife (2:9–10)

3. Job is approached by his friends (2:11–13)

VIII. ISSUES FOR DISCUSSION

1. Do I maintain my integrity through trials and suffering?
2. Do I fully trust God, although I may not understand why something is happening?
3. Do I surround myself with godly people who can offer me sound counsel?

Job 3

I Just Want to Die

Quote

"I am the subject of depression so fearful that I hope none of you ever get to such extremes of wretchedness as I go to."

Charles Haddon Spurgeon

I. INTRODUCTION

When Hell Had a Holiday

Martin Luther told a parable in which the devil was listening to his demons report their progress in destroying the souls of men. One evil spirit said, "There was a company of Christians crossing the desert, and I loosed the lions upon them. Soon the sands of the desert were strewn with their mangled corpses."

"But what good is that?" barked Satan. "The lions destroyed their bodies, but their souls were saved. It is their *souls* I am after."

Then another unclean spirit gave his evil report: "There was a company of Christian pilgrims sailing through the sea on a vessel. I sent a great wind which drove the ship on the rocks, and every Christian aboard was drowned."

But Satan retorted, "What good is that? Their bodies were drowned in the sea, but their *souls* were saved. It is their souls I am after."

Then a third fallen angel stepped forward to give his fiendish report: "For ten years I have been trying to cast one particular Christian into a deep despair and depression. At last, I have succeeded." And with that report, the corridors of hell rang with shouts of triumph. The sinister mission had been accomplished. The soul of a believer had been defeated.

This is only a fictitious story, but it does reveal the truth about Satan's evil intent to destroy the souls of men. This is what Job was facing. Under the vicious assaults of the devil, the pained patriarch had sunk into deep despair. Although initially responding with unflinching faith, he began to weaken under the relentless attack of the devil. In one devastating ambush, Job's family was stripped away, his possessions were reduced to rubble, and his fortune was decimated. But Job responded with unbending faith in a sovereign God (Job 1:20–21).

Then Satan reloaded his arsenal and unleashed his attack again, ravaging Job's skin from the crown of his head to the soles of his feet. Reeling under this assault, Job was devastated physically and emotionally. But again he responded with extraordinary faith (Job 2:10). Over the next seven days, Job sat in silence at the city garbage dump, with the crushing reality of these losses penetrating his soul. A heavy cloud of despondency settled over him. Despite his initial response of unshakable trust (Job 2:10), he began to weaken under this excruciating trial. He soon desired death itself over this painful experience. This is where we find Job in chapter 3 as he collapses under the weight of despair.

Every person has a breaking point. Even genuine believers have a point at which they can become severely discouraged, even depressed. Such despair can cause a person to want to give up on life. Maybe you can relate to this. Maybe you are tired of constant pain and suffering. Maybe you are worn down by the heaviness of your trials. Have you ever hurt so badly that you wished you could go to heaven? Or have you ever despaired to the point of longing for Christ to return? That is precisely where Job was. He was longing for relief, even the relief of death that would usher him into a state of perfect bliss in the presence of God. Job did not want to take his own life, but he wanted God to do so. He had lost his desire to live.

II. COMMENTARY

I Just Want to Die

MAIN IDEA: *Job wishes he had never been born and that he would die.*

A Job's Weeping (3:1–10)

SUPPORTING IDEA: *Job curses the day of his birth, wishing it had been blotted off the calendar.*

3:1. After this—that is, after losing his family, servants, possessions, and even his own health—**Job opened his mouth and cursed the day of his birth.** Job's grief and turmoil were so severe that he wished he had never been born. To curse means to reject, to spurn, or to hold someone or something in contempt. While Job did not curse God, he did regret his entrance into this world. All the joys and triumphs of life did not outweigh the trials and tribulations he was enduring.

3:2–3. He said, or more literally, Job answered and said, opening his burdened heart. **May the day of my birth** is a reference to his mother's delivery of him when he came into this world. He desired that that day **perish**, or be permanently removed from God's calendar, leaving him in a nonexistent state. Likewise, may **the night it was said, "A boy is born!"** also perish. This may refer to the time of Job's conception and his prebirth period of gestation. If so, he wished he could have avoided being conceived in his mother's womb (Job 10:10–11; Jer. 1:5).

3:4. Plummeting downward into an emotional spiral, Job lamented, "**That day—may it turn to darkness.**" Further, he longed that **God above not care about it** by abandoning all concern for it. He wished he had never seen the light of day. He desired that it had been covered over, never to be discovered or seen by anyone, especially God. He longed that **no light** would **shine upon it** and thus be forgotten.

3:5–6. Job hoped that it had been shrouded by **darkness** with a **deep shadow**, or a **cloud** of **blackness**. As thick darkness surrounded the **night** of his birth, he longed that it **not be included among the days of the year nor be entered in any of the months**. Job wanted that night in which he was delivered removed from human history, eliminated from the calendar, no longer numbered among the days of the months. He longed for the night of his birth to be erased from the annals of the past.

3:7–8. Instead of a **shout of joy** at his birth, he requested, **may that night be barren**, empty, and void as if he had never been conceived. The expression, **may those who curse days curse that day**, is probably a reference to professional prophets who, like Balaam (Num. 22–24), were compensated for cursing a client's enemies. Job hoped the curse had been powerful enough **to rouse Leviathan**, a mythological sea monster capable of devouring large objects.

3:9. This vivid, poetic language continued as Job cursed the day of his birth by stating, **May its morning stars become dark; may it wail for daylight is vain.** The phrase *morning stars* is a reference to the planets and stars which blanket the atmosphere before the rising of the sun. **The first rays of dawn**, literally "the eyelids of the morning," is a reference to the slow rising of the sun in the morning.

3:10. The reason Job cursed the day is that **it did not shut the doors of the womb on me**. The day of his birth, in fact, was allowed and did not stop his exit from his mother's womb. If it had interrupted his birth, it would have hid **trouble** from his eyes.

B Job's Wailing (3:11–19)

SUPPORTING IDEA: *Since the day of his birth did occur, Job wonders why he was not delivered stillborn.*

3:11. Job launched this next section by posing a rhetorical question for which he never received an answer. **Why did I not perish at birth, and die as I came from the womb?** Since the day of his birth did occur, Job wished he had entered the world stillborn, or born dead.

3:12–14. Further, he pleaded, "**Why were there knees to receive me and breasts that I might be nursed?**" Job wondered why his mother sustained his life at birth and did not abandon him to die if this tragedy was to be his lot. If she had abandoned him at birth, he **would be lying down in peace**. He reasoned that if he were now dead, he **would be asleep and at rest**. This would be far better than his present life of pain and misery. Then, in death, Job reasoned he would be in close association **with kings and counselors of the earth**. Death would be the great equalizer of the great and the small. He would be with royalty in the grave **who built for themselves places now lying in ruins**.

3:15. Job imagined his corpse being placed in magnificent tombs for **rulers who had gold, who filled their houses with silver**. Thus, in death, he would enjoy an association with the rich and mighty, a far better experience than he was going through.

3:16. Job's mind was again turned to the idea of being stillborn. He asked, **"Why was I not hidden in the ground like a stillborn child?"** Job yearned that he had been born as **an infant who never saw the light of day.** That is, if he had to be born, it would have been better to be born dead.

3:17–18. Job longed to die where even **the wicked cease from turmoil.** Even the ungodly enter the place where the **weary are at rest.** Job's trials motivated him to long for rest away from his present life of hardship. Beyond the grave, Job reasoned, captives also enjoyed **their ease.** In death, they are released from their imprisonment. Once in the tomb, **they no longer hear the slave driver's shout.** The slave driver is pictured as an oppressive task master (Exod. 3:7). Only in death is there relief from one's slavery to pain.

3:19. Death, being a place of rest, contains both **the small and the great.** Job was once great before tragedy struck, but now he saw himself as small because of his adversity. In this final resting place, he would be **freed from his master.**

C Job's Woe (3:20–26)

SUPPORTING IDEA: *Since Job was not stillborn, he longs to die now.*

3:20. Job rose to a crescendo by asking, **"Why is light given to those in misery, and life to the bitter of soul?"** Light is a poetic parallel of life, picturing the radiance, warmth, and energy that flow from human life. Job wondered why God continued to sustain his life through his present misery when he was so bitter of soul.

3:21–22. Like one in pursuit of **hidden treasure**, Job searched for it, knowing that once he found it, he would have discovered something valuable and priceless. But in spite of his search, **death** would **not come.** Death would fill him **with gladness** and cause him to **rejoice when** he reached **the grave.** Death had become desirable for Job, a cause for celebration.

3:23. Why is life given to a man whose way is hidden? Here is the fourth "why" in this chapter (cp. Job 3:11,16,20) that expresses the exasperation of Job's heart. Why did he have to continue to live when peace and prosperity were hidden from him, not to be seen and experienced? And why had God **hedged** him in? This is the same word that Satan used in describing Job's divine hedge of protection and blessing (Job 1:10). Satan could not enter, nor could Job exit.

3:24. Through this excruciating ordeal Job experienced a loss of appetite. Turning away from food, Job lamented, **"For sighing comes to me instead of food; my groans pour out like water."** The physical side effects caused by his depression would continue to haunt him until he recovered (cp. Job 6:7; 33:20).

3:25–26. Further, Job noted, "**What I feared has come upon me.**" This is not a reference to anything in particular but to suffering in general. Job also declared, "**What I dreaded has happened to me.**" This is a reference to the anxiety that had come upon him because of the loss of his beloved children, servants, possessions, and his own health. A growing panic had flooded his heart, replacing the peace he once knew. Job ended this sorrowful mourning by noting his loss of **peace**, **quietness**, and **rest**. Job was a devastated man.

MAIN IDEA REVIEW: *Job wishes he had never been born and that he would die.*

III. CONCLUSION

All Things for Him

John Henry Newman wrote these words on a memorial card for the father of a young man who died of cancer in 1877: "God has created me to do him some definite service. He has committed some work to me which He has not committed to another. I have a mission. I may never know it in this life, but I shall be told it in the next. Therefore, I will trust Him. Whatever I am, I can never be thrown away. If I am in sickness, my sickness may serve Him. If I am in sorrow, my sorrow may serve Him. He does nothing in vain. He knows what He is about. He may take away my friends. He may throw me among strangers. He may make me feel desolate, make my spirits sink, hide my future from me—still He knows what He is about."

This is the eternal perspective of faith that every believer must have in times of suffering. Trusting God like this is a matter of the will, not something that is driven by our feelings. When a person truly chooses to trust God, his feelings will eventually follow. But too often believers live by feelings rather than by faith. Believers must purpose to look to God, or they will be overwhelmed by feelings of despair. Faith must rise above our feelings rather than be pulled down by them.

Trusting God does not mean God's people do not experience pain. But it does mean they believe that God is at work through their adversity for their ultimate good. Thus, in the absence of understanding *why* certain calamities have befallen us, the heart that rests in God knows the Lord's peace. Resting in God who is sovereign, loving, and all wise brings the only rest and comfort the human soul can know. No matter how great the trial and how deep the pain, the peace of God is greater still.

IV. LIFE APPLICATION

How to Deal with Discouragement

What do we learn from this account in the life of Job? Discouragement is very real, even for the strongest believer. No one is exempt from low valleys of deep despair, regardless of how closely he walks with God. How do we deal with this discouragement?

1. *Remember that even the strongest believer can become discouraged.* Although he was the most righteous man on earth, Job bore all the marks of someone who is depressed. This spiritually mature man was filled with gloom, anger, anxiety, bitterness, confusion, fatigue, cynicism, fear, hopelessness, insomnia, dejection, sadness, and pessimism. Unquestionably, a true believer can be depressed to the point of great despair and heartache.

The apostle Paul experienced this when he wrote, "We were burdened excessively, beyond our strength, so that we despaired even of life; indeed, we had the sentence of death within [us]" (2 Cor. 1:8–9 NASB). The psalmist enjoyed the heights of worship, but he also knew the valleys of despair (Ps. 69:1–3). The great reformer Martin Luther experienced such deep depression. In writing of his grief, Luther said, "For more than a week I was close to the gates of death and hell. I trembled in all my members. Christ was wholly lost. I was shaken by desperation and blasphemy of God."

2. *Believers can suffer deeply on many levels at one time.* Job suffered on four different levels simultaneously. He suffered *physically,* so traumatized that he could not eat or sleep. He suffered *intellectually,* as his mind was flooded with questions he could not answer. He was confused and bewildered. He suffered *emotionally,* not being at ease or at rest within his own heart. Job also suffered *spiritually,* as he realized that God had hedged him in. This caused him to wish that God had never allowed him to be born. Similarly, there may be times in the lives of believers when they go through a dark night of adversity in which they also suffer, like Job, physically, intellectually, emotionally, and spiritually—all at the same time.

3. *Discouragement can cause God's people to lose perspective.* Job had lost a right perspective of God, and he overacted and made exaggerated statements. He jumped to wrong conclusions, losing sound judgment as a result. Depression affects a person's view of life, giving a twisted perception of reality. A distorted view of God leads to an unhealthy negative self-image. When believers

become discouraged, especially over an extended period of time, they can lose a right perspective on life and draw wrong conclusions, causing them to make exaggerated statements. Such dark nights of the soul can cause us to see life in a way that does not square with reality.

The antidote for such discouragement is deep trust and abiding hope in God.

V. PRAYER

Father, we acknowledge your sovereignty over the pain and suffering in our lives. You alone are in full control of the many trials and tribulations we face. We pray that you will continue to help us keep our focus on you, for you are our rock. We pray when we become distressed and downtrodden that you will give us hope and confidence in you alone. In Jesus' name. Amen.

VI. DEEPER DISCOVERIES

A. Perish (3:3)

"Perish" (Heb. *abad*) means to die or to undergo destruction. Among the various words that speak of destruction, *abad* is the most important. It is used to describe loss of strength and knowledge, the decline of nations (Num. 21:28–30), and is even applied to the destruction of pagan idols, images, and temples (Deut. 12:2–3). When used of people, the word is used mostly to refer to death, the cessation of life (Num. 16:33; Josh. 23:16). Yet *abad* was also used of the eternal destruction of the wicked beyond physical death (Ps. 83:17; Prov. 10:28). Clearly Job had the former and not the latter in mind.

B. Perish (3:11)

This word for "perish" (Heb. *mawet*) means to die, to expire, to kill, or to bring to death. *Mawet* usually refers to the demise of the body in death. Death and its symptoms, pain and suffering, have resulted from the fall (Gen. 3:3; Rom. 6:23) and will plague all of mankind (Heb. 9:27) until the return of Jesus Christ.

C. Vain (3:9)

"Vain" (Heb. *rig*) means emptiness, meaninglessness, or futility. In this case it refers to the utterly foolish plan of man to oppose God and to throw off his sovereign control. Such anarchy against God is foolish.

D. Turmoil (3:17,26)

"Turmoil" (*rogez*) is a Hebrew noun derived from a verb meaning to shake or quake. Here it is used to express agitation or restlessness. It was also used of a person who was deeply disturbed emotionally (cp. Job 14:1).

VII. TEACHING OUTLINE

A. Job's Weeping (3:1–10)
   1. Let my birth day be abolished (3:1–3)
   2. Let my birth day be darkened (3:4–6)
   3. Let my birth day be barren (3:7)
   4. Let my birth day be cursed (3:8)
   5. Let my birth day be removed (3:9–10)

B. Job's Wailing (3:11–19)
   1. I wish I had been miscarried (3:11–15)
   2. I wish I had been stillborn (3:16–19)

C. Job's Woe (3:20–26)
   1. Why is life given to the miserable? (3:20–22)
   2. Why is life governed by God? (3:23–26)

VIII. ISSUES FOR DISCUSSION

1. Do I ever find myself in a deep depression?
2. Do I ever lose sight of God in the midst of trouble?
3. Do I fully trust God alone to deliver me when trials come into my life?

Job 4
With Friends like These

Quote

"Satan is very clever; he knows exactly what bait to use for every place in which he fishes."

A. W. Pink

I. INTRODUCTION

Bad Company!

A flock of crows flew into a farmer's cornfield. His very sociable parrot flew over and joined the crows. The farmer loaded his shotgun, took careful aim, and fired at the unwanted birds. When he crawled under the fence to pick up the fallen crows, there was his parrot—barely alive. His children saw him carrying the parrot home and tearfully asked, "Papa, what happened?" Before the farmer could answer, the parrot spoke up: "Bad company."

This was to be Job's downfall. He would suffer from bad company in the form of his three friends, who would have a negative effect on his faith in God. What Satan could not do by taking away Job's wealth, destroying his family, and assaulting his health, he would accomplish through these so-called "counselors." While Job withstood the collapse of his business, the death of his children, and the infliction of disease, what came closest to defeating him was the adverse influence of his friends. These three associates—Eliphaz, Bildad, Zophar—were the devil's deadly instruments. They beat Job down and wore him out. Never underestimate the power of bad company.

A prolonged series of dialogues between Job and his three friends extends for the next twenty-three chapters (chs. 4–26). Each friend speaks in three consecutive cycles, the only exception being the third friend, Zophar, who remains silent in the third round. In response to each discourse, Job himself speaks in return. Throughout their speeches, these three counselors say the same thing—that all suffering is punishment for sin. They see a direct cause-and-effect relationship between sin and suffering. Each round becomes increasingly intense. In round one Eliphaz, Bildad, and Zophar hint at Job's sin. In round two they insinuate Job's sin. But in round three they cite Job's sin.

Through it all Job maintains his innocence and becomes demanding in his relationship with God. In the process Job's faith weakens, and his attitude soon sours. What follows now in Job 4 is the first speech by his first friend, Eliphaz.

II. COMMENTARY

With Friends like These

MAIN IDEA: *Eliphaz attributes Job's affliction to hidden sins, and he bases this on what he has heard and seen in life.*

A Eliphaz's Affirmation (4:1–6)

SUPPORTING IDEA: *Eliphaz begins his discourse with Job by making a positive, affirming statement in an attempt to connect with him.*

4:1–2. Then Eliphaz the Temanite—probably the eldest of these three friends, certainly the most sympathetic—**replied**. He was the first to speak to Job and break their weeklong silence. In sympathy with Job's miserable state, Eliphaz began by asking Job if he would become **impatient**. He asked that Job not blow up if he offered words of counsel. **But who can keep from speaking?** He could not prevent himself from offering help to Job, his hurting friend.

4:3. Eliphaz began with a positive commendation, **Think how you have instructed many**, but for a subtle reason. Now the roles had been reversed, and Job needed to be counseled with the words of Eliphaz. **You have strengthened feeble hands**. Job had helped many people throughout his life with his wise words. But now the tables were turned. He needed to receive counsel from Eliphaz.

4:4. Your words have supported those who stumbled. Eliphaz sounded so encouraging here, but it was to build Job up only to tear him down. **You have strengthened faltering knees**. Job had been a great encourager of many people. Those who staggered under the heavy blows of life were those whom Job had strengthened with his words.

4:5. **But now** Job was in need of instruction. He must now accept their counsel. Job, Eliphaz insisted, needed a dose of his own medicine. His diagnosis of Job was, **you are discouraged**. His countenance was crestfallen, and his heart was low. **Trouble**, Eliphaz noted, was devastating Job's life. Here is the same word Satan used to bait God to touch Job's life (Job 1:11; 2:5). "**And you are dismayed**," Eliphaz said, meaning Job was full of despair. All this resulted from the sudden, cataclysmic nature of his troubles and the bewilderment of unanswered questions about this tragedy.

4:6. **Should not your piety be your confidence?** Eliphaz was insisting that Job's own spirituality would count with God. If Job was living in personal integrity, then he could be sure a successful future awaited him. Further, Job's **blameless ways** would be his **hope**. In other words, Job had nothing to worry about if he were truly right with God.

B Eliphaz's Axiom (4:7–11)

SUPPORTING IDEA: *Eliphaz believes Job has sinned against God and should confess his sin if he is to be restored.*

4:7. **Consider now: Who, being innocent has ever perished?** The expected answer is *no one*. With this broad, sweeping statement, Eliphaz left no room for doubt about Job's guilt. The implication was that if Job were perishing, then he was surely not innocent. Eliphaz's theory was that Job must be suffering because he had sinned against God. **Where were the upright ever destroyed?** If Job was truly innocent, he would not be struck down like this.

4:8. Eliphaz's life philosophy was **as I have observed**. He had noticed that **those who plow evil and those who sow trouble reap it**. He had a direct cause-and-effect theory of life—that integrity always produces prosperity and sin inevitably produces adversity. Since Job was undergoing destruction, Eliphaz reasoned, he must be one of those who **sow trouble** and **reap it**. Eliphaz believed Job had sown his wild oats and was reaping a bitter harvest (cp. Prov. 22:8).

4:9. Eliphaz declared that those who lived in sinful rebellion would be **destroyed** and **perish** by **the breath of God** and **the blast of his anger**. He used strong imagery here to depict God's disciplinary judgment and wrathful vengeance against the stubborn who refused to repent. Eliphaz implied that Job was one such person.

4:10. Eliphaz believed Job was irresponsible and had not protected his children. The phrase **the lions may roar and growl** is an allusion to Job's loud wailing, **yet the teeth of the great lions are broken**. This devastation had come to Job, according to Eliphaz, because he had failed to care for his family.

4:11. **The lion**, no matter how strong he might be, **perishes for lack of prey**, eventually coming to an end. In this weakened state, **the cubs of the lioness are scattered**. This is a clear allusion to Job's failure to guard his children, who had been killed in these tragedies (Job 1:18–19). Because of Job's irresponsibility, his family had perished under God's judgment on his sin.

C Eliphaz's Authority (4:12–21)

SUPPORTING IDEA: *Eliphaz claims to have received his knowledge from a spirit in the middle of the night, one who argues that humans cannot be trusted because of their sin.*

4:12. Eliphaz asserted, **A word was secretly brought to me** in the middle of the night. This is an apparent claim to the reception of special revelation. His ears **caught a whisper of it** as words were spoken which no one else could hear. In other words, Elipaz had received a message that was delivered to him alone.

4:13–14. Amid many **disquieting dreams in the night**, Eliphaz claimed to have received a divine oracle or mysterious vision **when deep sleep falls on men** (i.e., at night). This was for Eliphaz a very disturbing event. As this eerie dream came, **fear and trembling** seized Eliphaz, making all his **bones shake** with fear. This strange encounter was unsettling! It was no ordinary dream or even a nightmare but a supernatural visit by an unidentified spirit.

4:15–16. **A spirit** with an indiscernible form glided past his face in spine-tingling fashion. The hair on his body **stood on end**. This hair-raising experience was mystical and supernatural, as it was mediated through an unknown mysterious messenger. **It stopped, but I could not tell what it was**, he declared. Appearing immediately before Eliphaz, this midnight messenger lingered in the air and remained unidentified by him. **A form stood before** Eliphaz's **eyes**, but it was not like that of a man. When it spoke, it sounded with **a hushed voice**.

4:17. The word that Eliphaz heard was: "**Can a mortal be more righteous than God? Can a man be more pure than his Maker?**" The anticipated answer was *no*. No man is morally good enough to stand before God with divine acceptance (Rom. 3:23). The message of this mysterious messenger was that man in his natural state is displeasing to God.

4:18–19. **If God places no trust in his servants** (i.e., his heavenly host, or angelic beings), then how can he trust sinful man? And **if he charges his angels with error**, how much more will he do the same with fallen humanity?

How much more will God charge **those who live in houses of clay** (i.e., earthly bodies with sin). Man's **foundations are in the dust**. He came from dust and will return to dust. Man is so fragile, **crushed more readily than a moth** (cp. Job 27:18). How then could fallen man ever stand before God in the judgment?

4:20. **Between dawn and dusk** (i.e., all day long) **they are broken to pieces** because of sin. **Unnoticed, they perish forever**. In his placated reasoning, Eliphaz proceeded to picture God as an uncaring, transcendent God.

4:21. **Are not the cords of their tent pulled up**? Their bodies are pictured as a temporary, tentlike home which folds up and collapses when it is time to move. So it is with sinful man in his death (2 Cor. 5:1,4). Because of their self-centered existence, **they die without wisdom**, having rejected God. An entire lifetime is insufficient to grasp God's wisdom.

MAIN IDEA REVIEW: *Eliphaz attributes Job's affliction to hidden sins, and he bases this on what he has heard and seen in life.*

III. CONCLUSION

For Better or for Worse

Our friends have an enormous influence on our lives, for either good or bad. Our peers may be used, by either God or Satan, to build us up or tear us down. As in Job's case, our companions may be precision tools used by the devil with ingenious skill to pry open our hearts for despair and despondency. This truth is taught throughout the Scripture. Solomon wrote, "A man of many companions may come to ruin, but there is a friend who sticks closer than a brother" (Prov. 18:24). One must choose his or her friends wisely because in the day of adversity, they will either lift us up or pull us down. A true friend will stand with us in times of trouble and will be used by the Lord for our good.

Scripture says, "A friend loves at all times, and a brother is born for adversity" (Prov. 17:17). When in the furnace of affliction, a genuine friend will provide much relief and strength. At the same time, "Bad company corrupts good character" (1 Cor. 15:33). Rather than having character, a bad friend is a character. May God surround us with true friends who, unlike Eliphaz, will genuinely love us and help us in our times of adversity.

IV. LIFE APPLICATION

How to Be a Friend

How can we be a good friend to someone who is hurting? Chapter 4 of Job provides the very antithesis of what we should be. In other words, Eliphaz shows us by negative example what a friend should *not* be. By looking at him, we can determine the very opposite of what we should be to others. Here are some of the characteristics believers should demonstrate when being a friend to someone who is suffering.

1. *Be sensitive.* Eliphaz was there for Job physically but not emotionally. His heart and sympathy remained far away. He was present to make theological points rather than to comfort Job. In order to be a friend to someone who is hurting, we must come alongside that person to comfort and console, not to correct and chastise. We must come alongside someone in need to help, encourage, and comfort. We need to be a friend who will put a gentle arm around another rather than shake an accusing finger in his face.

2. *Be sympathetic.* We should feel the pain of others, not inflict more. Eliphaz never did sympathize with Job. He failed to enter into his pain. His approach was intellectual, theological, and analytical—bottom-line oriented. Aren't we supposed to *bear* one another's burdens (Gal. 6:2)? This means to get under a brother's burden with him and help carry the weight of his hurt—not just sit across the room and explain what went wrong.

3. *Be supportive.* Eliphaz took an adversarial role. He lost sight of the original goal, which was to *comfort* Job. He spent his time trying to pin Job down rather than to lift him up. He tried to criticize and condemn Job and to document that Job was in sin. There was no comfort for Job from Eliphaz, only harassment.

V. PRAYER

God, our Father, thank you for your infinite love which carries us through the refining fires of affliction as you purify us and present us faultless to stand in your presence. Teach us to submit to you in quiet reverence, since you are working all things for good in the lives of your people. May we be those who are preserved and made faultless to stand before you. In Jesus' name. Amen.

VI. DEEPER DISCOVERIES

Spirit (4:15)

"Spirit" (Heb. *ruwach*) means air in motion, breath, or wind. In this instance it refers to a spirit being, one without form or physical body. Hence, this spirit being is like the wind, real and powerful, yet without physical form. This "spirit" was a supernatural being, a formless being. In some contexts, this word means air for breathing (Judg. 15:19), breath (Job 7:7), or air in motion (Job 41:16). Sometimes it refers to the element of life in a man (Gen. 7:22), a human soul (Prov. 16:2), the human spirit as breathed by God into man (Job 27:3). Other times it refers to a state of purposelessness and emptiness (Job 15:2) and even vain words (Job 16:3) and vain knowledge (Job 15:2). Also it refers to air in the nostrils (Job 27:3). When a person is sick, his spirit is consumed (Job 17:1). The *ruwach* of all mankind is in God's hands (Job 12:10). *Ruwach* may refer to a supernatural, angelic being from God (1 Sam. 16:23). Also Satan is the accusing spirit (1 Kgs. 22:22). Here it is a demonic spirit.

VII. TEACHING OUTLINE

- A. Eliphaz's Affirmation (4:1–6)
  - 1. Listen to me (4:1–2)
  - 2. Learn from me (4:3–6)
- B. Eliphaz's Axiom (4:7–11)
  - 1. The innocent do not suffer (4:7)
  - 2. The insolent do suffer (4:8–11)
- C. Eliphaz's Authority (4:12–21)
  - 1. A spirit came to me (4:12–16)
  - 2. A spirit counseled me (4:17–21)

VIII. ISSUES FOR DISCUSSION

1. Are there any sins in my life that warrant the discipline of God?
2. Do I seek godly counsel when suffering affliction?
3. What is God teaching me as I suffer affliction?
4. When offering counsel to someone, do I give counsel that is in line with Scripture?

Job 5

God Is Discipling You!

Quote

"Counterfeiting friendship is worse than counterfeiting money."

Thomas Watson

Job 5

I. INTRODUCTION

Definition of a Friend

An English publication once offered a prize for the best definition of a friend. Among the thousands of answers received were the following: "One who multiplies joys and divides grief." Another entry read, "One who understands our silence." One said, "A volume of sympathy bound in cloth." Yet another read, "A friend is like a watch which beats true for a time and never runs down." These were fine, but there was one definition that won the prize: "A friend is the one who comes in when the whole world has gone out."

Job certainly had three very good friends. His three companions were the ones who came in when the whole world went out. But *that* proved to be his problem. It was Job's three friends—Eliphaz, Bildad, and Zophar—who entered his life and actually pulled him down. Job's faith was doing fine until they arrived. As this "terrible trio" came in, they also brought with them their bad counsel and wrong advice. Job would have been better off without them. Eliphaz was the first to speak (Job 4–5), and he would later address Job two more times (Job 15; 22).

What Eliphaz said in confronting Job was correct. His emotional collapse (Job 3) did need to be addressed by his friends. But Eliphaz's challenge was misapplied to Job, and it was even dangerous to his spiritual health. Eliphaz was a dangerous man because he only spoke part of the truth. But he did not speak the whole truth, and knowing only part of the truth *is* dangerous. Further, what truth he did speak was spoken at the wrong time in the wrong spirit. In Job 5, we hear the rest of the counsel Eliphaz delivered to his hurting friend. This reminds us how careful we must be in counseling others.

II. COMMENTARY

God Is Discipling You!

MAIN IDEA: *Eliphaz claims that God is chastening Job for his sin and urges him to bring his case before God, believing that God will restore him once he has punished him.*

A Eliphaz's Appeal (5:1–16)

SUPPORTING IDEA: *Eliphaz says Job is suffering for his sin and should bring his case before God.*

5:1. Eliphaz's words became more direct and forthcoming. This counselor denied any possibility of intervention in Job's plight by asking, "**Call if you will, but who will answer you?**" The expected answer was that no one would be able to rescue Job from all this. **To which of the holy ones will you turn?** According to Eliphaz, not even the angels were able to deliver Job.

5:2. **Resentment kills a fool.** This is how Eliphaz interpreted Job's lament spoken irrationally earlier (Job 3). His bitterness would destroy his life. A fool is one who pays no attention to God. This is how Job had acted, like a person without God. **And envy slays the simple.** It is clear that Job was the being referred to here. All his emotional wailing would destroy him.

5:3–4. **I myself have seen a fool taking root.** Job was this foolish man who had been planted in the soil of prosperity and had begun growing. **But suddenly his house was cursed.** Now Job has suffered the loss of everything, proving himself to be a fool, according to Eliphaz. Job's unconfessed sins, Eliphaz believed, led to his ten **children** being **crushed in court without a defender.** This was a meritless indictment of Job, who was being charged as the responsible party for the death of his children.

5:5–6. Eliphaz said, "**The hungry consume his harvest,**" a reference to the raiding bands who depleted Job's wealth. The devastation of the barbarians was seen in the taking of his harvest (i.e., blessings by God) that was once protected by God. This great personal loss suffered by Job was seen as occurring because of unconfessed sin in his life. Eliphaz remarked, "**For hardship does not spring from the soil, nor does trouble sprout from the ground.**" Believing everything happens for a reason, Eliphaz asserted these afflictions did not appear from nowhere. They had been sown and cultivated by Job. He was reaping what he had sown.

5:7. As surely as sparks fly upward in a fire, so **man is born to trouble**. Man by his sin brings trouble on himself. Thus, it was inevitable that Job would suffer as he did, since trouble knows no exceptions.

5:8. Then in a sudden shift, Eliphaz advised Job to appeal to God. **But if it were I, I would appeal to God**. Here the seed is first planted into Job's mind that he should present his case to God. "**I would lay my cause before him,**" remarked Eliphaz, believing God would grant Job's desire for an appearance in court.

5:9–10. Job should understand that God **performs wonders** so great that they **cannot be fathomed**. His works are so awesome that they defy human comprehension. These divine miracles are so numerous they **cannot be counted**. Highlighting some of these works of God, Eliphaz noted that he **bestows rain**, which, in turn, **sends water upon the countryside**. This is all God's gracious doing, sending rain and good things to everyone (Matt. 5:45).

5:11–12. By this divine sovereignty, **the lowly he sets on high**. God is opposed to the proud, but he gives grace to the humble (1 Pet. 5:5). **Those who mourn are lifted to safety**. Like the sending of the rain, this is God's grace at work. He champions the cause of the helpless who cannot defend themselves. What is more, God **thwarts the plans of the crafty**, those who scheme evil plans, and brings them to ruin. Those who exalt themselves, God humbles (Luke 18:14). This God does **so that their hands achieve no success**, at least not in an ultimate sense.

5:13–14. Further, God **catches the wise in their craftiness** as they plot against the righteous. They will not get away with their sin. The evil **schemes of the wily** are designed to harm others. But they **are swept away** by God himself. Their sinister plans will not succeed; they are doomed to failure. **Darkness** (i.e., God's judgment) **comes upon them in the daytime**, frustrating the conniving. **At noon** the wicked **grope as in the night**. This divine intervention suddenly strikes them, leaving them blind in broad daylight, unable to cope with life.

5:15. On the other hand, God **saves the needy from the sword** in the mouth of the evil. Although they are armed to the teeth, they are unable to succeed in their plots against the righteous because God **saves them from the clutches of the powerful**. Deliverance of the godly comes from the Lord.

5:16. So the poor who trust in God **have hope**. They have confidence in the future, knowing that **injustice shuts its mouth**. God will deliver the humble who cannot save themselves. God will punish the strong and render justice to the poor and needy. Eliphaz assumed that Job was one of the mighty who had sinned and had been brought low by God. He must repent in order to make everything right.

B Eliphaz's Assurance (5:17–27)

SUPPORTING IDEA: *Eliphaz challenges Job to trust God to heal and defend him after he has punished him.*

5:17. The long discourse that follows was given by Eliphaz to remind Job that **blessed is the man whom God corrects**. The sinner should be happy when divine chastisement corrects him because it eventually puts him in right standing with God. So Job should rejoice in this tragedy; God will use it to restore their broken relationship. Thus, **do not despise the discipline of the Almighty**. Job should not resist it but receive it as corrective chastening which would bring him back to God (Heb. 12:5–10).

5:18. Job's happiness would be built on this principal, that God **wounds, but he also binds up; he injures, but his hands also heal**. Eliphaz declared that Job should cheer up because eventually God would relieve his pain and affliction. The problem with this advice is that it was based on the premise that Job's troubles had resulted from the disciplinary actions of God. Then Eliphaz proceeded to walk Job through a list of blessings he would receive if he would confess his sin.

5:19. From six calamities he will rescue you. This is to be taken poetically, not literally, for "many" troubles. **In seven** (the number of completeness) **no harm will befall you**. This restoration depended on Job's repentance. Eliphaz assumed that Job was in great sin.

5:20–21. In famine, God **will ransom you from death**. If Job would turn away from a life of secret sin, God would rescue him. **And in battle**, God would deliver him, **from the stroke of the sword**. All this divine blessing would come if Job would only repent. **You will be protected from the lash of the tongue**. That is, Job would escape the reproof of others, as well as their stern warnings, if he would only repent. Job **need not fear when destruction comes** because God would protect him from all harm. This divine deliverance would occur if Job would only confess his sin.

5:22. Job would **laugh at destruction and famine** because it would not harm him if he would become right with God. He **need not fear the beasts of the earth** because of God's supernatural defense, if only he would repent.

5:23. For you will have a covenant with the stones of the field. This was a figurative way of saying that the stones would be at peace with Job and not ruin his crops (cp. 2 Kgs. 3:19; Matt. 13:5). Further, even **the wild animals** would be at peace with Job, not causing him any harm. All these good things would happen if Job would only repent.

5:24. You will know that your tent is secure, that is, Job would have a great assurance of peace and safety. **You will take stock of your property and find nothing missing** through all these previously mentioned potential threats. None of these, Eliphaz claimed, would come against Job, if he were walking rightly before God.

5:25. In what had to be the most difficult statement of all for Job to hear, Eliphaz spouted off, "**You will know that your children will be many.**" This referred to Job's loss of his own children. Such a loss would not have occurred, Eliphaz contended, if he had been living in obedience to God. Job's descendants would be **like the grass of the earth**, if he were right with God. His children would have many children, and so on through future generations, if Job would only turn from his sin.

5:26. When it was time for Job to die at the end of life, Eliphaz said, he would **come to the grave in full vigor**, strong and healthy. He would be **like sheaves gathered in season**, a life in full harvest that would conclude in a state that was bountiful and fruitful. Such prosperity would happen to Job if he would only get right with God.

5:27. Eliphaz ended this long discourse by claiming its validity and truthfulness: **We have examined this, and it is true**. He conferred with Bildad and Zophar, and there was unanimous agreement among them about Job's plight and suffering. Eliphaz appealed for Job's response of obedience: **So hear it and apply it to yourself**. As this discourse concluded (Job 4–5), he called upon Job to turn from his sin against God and he would be restored.

MAIN IDEA REVIEW: *Eliphaz claims that God is chastening Job for his sin and urges him to bring his case before God, believing that God will restore him once he has punished him.*

III. CONCLUSION

A Tool of the Devil

It has been said that there are two kinds of people in the world—those who brighten the room when they *enter* it and those who brighten the room when they *leave* it. The converse is also true. There are those who darken a room when they walk into it. Eliphaz was this kind of man. He *darkened* the room in which Job was standing by entering his space. Although well meaning, Eliphaz was dangerous in what he spoke. In reality he was a tool of the devil, one sent to erode and weaken Job's faith in God. His arguments were well crafted, but they missed the mark with Job. All Eliphaz could think was, *What had Job done to bring such crisis upon himself?*

Yet, in reality, Eliphaz knew nothing about the battle between God and Satan recorded in the opening chapters. Rather than being a friend who brightened Job's world, Eliphaz darkened it. Although he could not have known about the cosmic contest transpiring in heaven, he should have been a source of encouragement to Job's broken heart, not an agent of discouragement. May each of us be a friend who is a "merchant of hope" to others in their sorrow, not a person who afflicts others with sorrow.

IV. LIFE APPLICATION

How to Help a Hurting Friend

1. *Be a listener.* In order to be a friend to one who is hurting, listen more than you talk. God gave us two ears and one mouth. We need to use them accordingly. Be quick to hear and slow to speak. People who are suffering do not need a lecture; they need love. They do not need a sermon; they need sympathy.

2. *Be humble.* Do not try to explain everything. Eliphaz did not know what he was talking about. He believed he had all the divine mysteries figured out. He presumed to know why everything was going wrong in Job's life. But in reality he did not have a clue. Do not pretend to know and explain everything.

3. *Be positive.* The flame of hope had been extinguished within Job's heart. He needed to have that fire rekindled. He needed to be told, "Job, there is a bright tomorrow out there. God is going to work through this. We're going to work through this together. God is going to work through this for *good.*" But Eliphaz was so focused on the negative that he had nothing positive to say. No wonder Job remained without hope. Eliphaz could only see what he *thought* were Job's faults. He attacked Job's shortcomings, but he never did see his strengths. To be a friend to someone who is hurting, we must look beyond that person's faults to his needs.

4. *Be balanced.* What was missing from all that Eliphaz said was God's love. All he saw was a God of strict justice, harsh judgment, swift discipline, and severe condemnation. He had a rigid view of God that allowed for no

mercy or grace. Let us never fall into such a hole. If we are to help others who are hurting, we need to emphasize God's love, tenderness, and mercy. God is *both* a God of judgment and a God of love. But one without the other is not God. Half the truth, when the whole truth is revealed, becomes no truth. There are people all around us who are going through difficult times. They need a friend just like you to help them through these days.

V. PRAYER

Father, help us to discern the truth through the many counselors who speak to us daily. We need your ability to sort through the advice that comes to us, even from well-meaning friends. Most of all, thank you for Christ, a friend who sticks closer than a brother. May we hear his guidance above all. In his name. Amen.

VI. DEEPER DISCOVERIES

A. Salvation (5:4,11)

"Salvation" (Heb. *yesha*) refers to deliverance, rescue, victory, help, or liberty. In its first usages, *yesha* referred to physical deliverance from one's enemies (Exod. 14:30; Ps. 18:3; Jer. 1:8,19), but later it came to connote a redemptive meaning (Ps. 51:14; Isa. 49:6; Ezek. 37:23). The former meaning is in mind here. These two instances are its only usages in Job.

B. Blessed (5:17)

"Blessed" (Heb. *esher*) means an overflowing joy and full contentment in God, a satisfaction and happiness in the Lord. This noun occurs forty-four times in the Old Testament, twenty-five times in the Psalms, eight times in Proverbs, and one time in Ecclesiastes. The word *happy* is a good synonym, although this word conveys far more than feelings of settled peace and contentment. This is its only usage in Job.

C. Fear (5:21–22)

"Fear" (Heb. *yare*) is found approximately 330 times throughout the Old Testament and is most often used to speak of reverential awe before God (Exod. 1:17; 2 Sam. 6:9; Ps. 102:15; Jon. 1:16). It is also used of those who honor God and take him seriously (Ps. 128:1; Neh. 7:2) or who fail to do so (Eccl. 8:13). In other instances, as in the present context of Psalm 23:4, *yare* is used as a fear produced by the anticipation of evil (Deut. 20:1,3,8; Judg. 7:3; Neh. 4:14; Ezek. 2:6).

VII. TEACHING OUTLINE

A. Eliphaz's Appeal (5:1–16)
   1. Plead your need for help (5:1)
   2. See the calamity of the fool (5:2–7)
   3. Appeal your case to God (5:8–16)

B. Eliphaz's Assurance (5:17–27)
   1. God disciplines sinners (5:17)
   2. God delivers sinners (5:18–27)

VIII. ISSUES FOR DISCUSSION

1. How does your understanding of who God is affect your faith as you go through a time of painful adversity?
2. What Eliphaz is there in your life who would wrongly represent God to you?
3. How can your faith be strengthened in your current situation as you press on in God's will?

Job 6
The Devil's Garage Sale

Quote

"Despair is Satan's masterpiece."

John Trapp

I. INTRODUCTION

The Most Worn Tool

One day the devil decided to have a garage sale. Taking his finest tools of destruction—hatred, envy, jealousy, deceit, lust, lying, pride—he priced each one according to its value and placed them on the driveway. But the most worn tool was set apart from the other instruments. A curious customer picked up this worn tool, looked it over, and noted that it carried the highest price. He asked, "Why is this tool higher than the others?"

The devil laughed, "That's the tool called 'discouragement.' It is more powerful than any other tool I have. When I use this tool on a person's heart, I can pry it open and then use all of my other tools. It is my most strategic tool and, therefore, comes at a higher price."

Although this is only a fictitious story, there is much truth in this parable. When Satan pries open a person's heart to sow discouragement, he becomes an easy prey for all the devil's other instruments. What exactly is discouragement? It is the emotional state of being deprived of hope. It is being dejected, disheartened, and deflated to such an extent that one wants to give up on life. It is being despondent, despairing, and so dismayed that one loses all sense of rational perspective and sinks into an emotional black hole. This is exactly the direction in which Job was moving.

Although Job initially responded well to his trials (Job 1:20–22; 2:8–10), his friends had become the devil's tool of discouragement to pry open Job's heart. He would become easy prey for the devil's other devices. What is most cunning by Satan is that this discouragement would stay under Job's spiritual radar, coming not from his enemies but from his friends.

II. COMMENTARY

The Devil's Garage Sale

MAIN IDEA: *Job admits his discouragement because he feels he is suffering unjustly.*

 Job's Defense (6:1–7)

SUPPORTING IDEA: *Job denies Eliphaz's charges of wrong-doing, contending that his pain gives him a right to moan as he does.*

6:1. **Then Job replied** to the unkind words that had been spoken to him by Eliphaz (Job 4–5). In reality he was speaking to all three friends, although Eliphaz had been the first to speak. This standard introduction will be repeated throughout the book (9:1; 12:1; 16:1; 19:1; 21:1; 23:1; 26:1).

6:2. Discouraged and in despair, Job lamented, **If only my anguish could be weighed and all my misery be placed on the scales!** His excruciating pain was incalculable, beyond measurement. He wanted his three friends to know how deeply he hurt. He appealed for a sympathetic hearing with these friends whom he wanted to understand the depths of his sorrow.

6:3–4. For Job, his misery **would surely outweigh the sand of the seas**. His grief was greater than could be told. It was beyond his ability to calculate. **No wonder my words have been impetuous**, he declared. That is, such extreme suffering would be expected to produce such emotion-packed **words** as he had stated earlier (cp. Job 3). Job agreed with Eliphaz in that he, too, believed it was **the Almighty** who had shot him with poisoned **arrows** and marshaled **terrors** against him. The arrows of the Lord are symbolic of his judgment (Deut. 32:23,42) or wrath (Ps. 38:1–2). All this, Job believed, was directed at him by God.

6:5. **Does a wild donkey bray when it has grass?** The answer to this rhetorical question is *no*. When this animal is well fed, it does not bray. Neither would Job when his needs were met by God. Would **an ox bellow when it has fodder?** The answer is *no*. Again, neither would Job if he had not endured such pain from God. As it was, he claimed the right to bray and bellow.

6:6–7. **Is tasteless food eaten without salt?** Again the answer is *no*. **Is there flavor in the white of an egg?** This rhetorical question begs a negative answer. Job believed he had been wounded by God (v. 4) and, in response, had been given unseasoned words by his friends that were not palatable. Job's counselors' words should have been seasoned with salt. For Job, tasteless food made him **ill**. He was also upset by the words of his friends. **I refuse to touch it**, he declared.

B Job's Despair (6:8–13)

SUPPORTING IDEA: *Job believes he has not denied God's Word.*

6:8–9. Oh, that I might have my request, that God would grant what I hope for. What was this desire? He had wanted to die in order to escape his suffering (Job 3:20–21). An early death would release him from this ordeal. Job longed **that God would be willing to crush** him so he could escape this pain. Only death, he believed, would lead to relief. He desired for God **to let loose his hand** and cut him off from life itself.

6:10–11. Job's one consolation was that he **had not denied the words of the Holy One**. Unlike his wife, he knew he had remained true to God. Job had not cursed God or rejected his **words**, which, in essence, would have been a denial of the Lord. So he preferred to die now, knowing he had kept the faith. Job defended his emotional response by citing that he was at a loss for **strength**. Being at the end of human resources, he was without **hope** and had lost all **prospects** to become **patient** in this painful and crushing ordeal.

6:12–13. Do I have the strength of stone? Job asked. The expected answer was *no*. He was greatly weakened by this trial. How could he continue in such a difficult state? **Is my flesh bronze?** Again the anticipated answer was *no*. His strength was not like stone or bronze. Job was now in a weakened condition. In desperation and misery, he declared that he was without **power** to help himself and **that success** had **been driven from** him. He saw himself as helpless to endure this trauma. This appears to be a reply to Eliphaz's opening words to him (Job 4:2–6).

C Job's Disappointment (6:14–23)

SUPPORTING IDEA: *Job accuses his friend of being undependable, unhelpful, undiscerning, and uncaring.*

6:14. Job addressed his disappointment with his friends by saying, **A despairing man should have the devotion of his friends**. Instead of encouraging Job, his friends were insensitive. Where was their support, **even though he forsakes the fear of the Almighty**. Even if Job had forsaken God, which he had not, they should have shown him love.

6:15. Job's **brothers** (i.e., his three friends), depicting their previous close relationship, were as **undependable as intermittent streams**. That is, these counselors were like rivers that **overflow** in the winter when water is not needed but are dry when water is needed (Jer. 15:18; Amos 5:24). Some help!

6:16–17. In the early spring the rivers overflow their banks **when darkened by thawing ice and swollen with melting snow**. In like manner the words of Job's friends were at flood stage. He was drowning in their verbosity. But in the **dry season**, when water is most needed, they **cease to flow**. In the heat of the summer nights, these streams dry up and **vanish from their channels**. So it was with his so-called friends. They spoke when he needed silence and were silent when he needed them to speak.

6:18–19. Caravans turn aside from their routes when the dry seasons come, looking for water. But they can find none. **They go up into the wasteland** in order to find water, but they **perish** for lack of it. So Job was unable to find comfort in their empty words. The **caravans of Tema** in the Arabian desert looked for **water** but it was scarce, and the **traveling merchants of Sheba** also searched for water in the south, but none was to be found. Although they looked in hope for water, they arrived at the riverbed "only to be disappointed" (Job 6:20). Likewise, these counselor's words were no help to Job.

6:20. These traveling caravans became **distressed** when they could find no water in the desolate desert. This dejection was multiplied **because they had been confident** of discovering water, only to lose hope and **be disappointed**. In similar fashion, Job was disappointed with his friends' poor counsel. They were only dry holes!

6:21. Like a dry river his friends had **proved to be of no help**. Job had hoped to receive help from them, but they offered nothing substantive. **You see something dreadful and are afraid**. This is a reference to Job's thin and emaciated frame. Their cowardice was shown in their failure to sympathize with Job in his suffering, perhaps because they feared to provoke God to bring the same discipline upon themselves.

6:22–23. Job then asked if he ever requested **something** of them on his **behalf**, such as a **ransom** from their **wealth**. The answer was *no*. He had only asked of them what cost no money and what should have been easy to give: their love and support. Had he ever asked them to **deliver** him **from the hand of the enemy** or **ransom** him from **the clutches of the ruthless**? No, he had not. All he wanted from them was their supportive friendship.

D Job's Demand (6:24–30)

SUPPORTING IDEA: *Job asks his friends to tell him specifically where he has gone wrong.*

6:24. Job then challenged his friends to **teach** him and **show** him where he had **been wrong**. Then he would **be quiet** and accept their correction. They had accused him of wrongdoing and had not been specific.

6:25. Job then retorted, **How painful are honest words!** Their words would be difficult to hear, but he wanted to hear them if they were true. But they had not been shown to be accurate. **But what do your arguments prove?** In other words, Job asked, which of your words actually indict me? Nothing said by the friends proved anything against Job.

6:26–27. **Do you mean to correct what I say?** Their words were meant to correct Job, yet they failed to do so. They treated his words **as wind**, or as if they were empty. How could they challenge what he said if they did not hear him out? Job accused them of demonstrating cruelty. They would **cast lots for the fatherless and barter away** their **friend**. No wonder they treated him so ruthlessly. They were heartless and indifferent toward his suffering.

6:28. Then Job changed his tone, appealing to his companions to reconsider him. **But now be so kind as to look at me**. He was pleading for their sympathy in his time of greatest need, not their further scourging. **Would I lie to your face?** No, he would not distort or misrepresent the truth to them. He longed for their support, not more lectures. He appealed for their help in his desperate hour.

6:29–30. **Relent** means change your words toward me. **Do not be unjust**, Job declared, by accusing him of wrongdoing when such had not been the case. Job's integrity was at stake. They had made him out to be a wicked man when he knew he was not. **Is there any wickedness on my lips?** Job did not see anything wrong in what he had said in defending himself. **Can my mouth not discern malice?** Contrary to their charges, he claimed to be an innocent man who did not deserve God's judgments and their accusations.

MAIN IDEA REVIEW: *Job admits his discouragement because he feels he is suffering unjustly.*

III. CONCLUSION

Sinister Seeds

Legend has it that a man found the barn where Satan kept his seed that were ready to be sown in human hearts. He discovered that the seeds marked "discouragement" were more numerous than all the others. When he questioned Satan, he learned that those seed could be made to grow almost anywhere. But in spite of their abundance, the devil admitted there was one place where he could never get them to grow—in the heart of a grateful person.

A thankful spirit is never overcome with despair. But Job had lost the virtue of thankfulness. Therefore, he was losing this war with Satan, at least at this point in his struggle. Discouragement was beginning to creep in.

C. S. Lewis quipped, "If Satan's arsenal of weapons were restricted to a single one, it would be discouragement." This sinister weapon had certainly been wielded against Job with devastating results. He was weakening under its force. He was beginning to abandon hope that he would ever be restored to his former favor with God. A discouraged person loses all sense of perspective, choosing to believe the worst rather than the best. At the center of a discouraged heart is always an ungrateful spirit—one that has lost sight of God's blessings and focuses instead on the burdens. So it was with Job. And so it often is with us. May we learn to keep our hearts filled with gratitude, even in difficult days.

IV. LIFE APPLICATION

How to Deal with Rejection

How does a person overcome being rejected? We are all subject to discouragement and despondency. How do we rise above such a low spirit?

1. *Rest in God's greatness.* No matter how great our trial or suffering may be, God remains greater still. As Jesus came walking on the waves to the disciples, so he comes to us as sovereign over our storms. Even in the midst of life's greatest struggles, God remains infinitely greater as Lord over all. Nothing is beyond his control.

2. *Rest in God's goodness.* Faith must remain confident in God, who is always working for the good of his people. Never will God deviate from his eternal purpose. Even when times are tough and difficulties are many, we must remain unwavering in the assurance that God is working all things after the counsel of his own will (Eph. 1:11). No matter how threatening the circumstances or how painful our losses, God remains enthroned in the heavens and is committed to working through our trials toward a positive end.

3. *Rest in God's grace.* In the midst of life's threatening storms, know and believe that God gives a greater grace. In our weakness his strength is made perfect. It is when discouragement threatens to overwhelm us that God's

grace is multiplied in lives that are yielded to him. No matter how great our disappointments, God's grace is greater still.

V. PRAYER

God, our Father, we praise you for your sovereign, providential watchcare over every detail of our lives. Thank you for your infinite love that carries us through the refining fires of affliction as you purify us and present us faultless to stand in your presence. In Jesus' name we pray. Amen.

VI. DEEPER DISCOVERIES

A. Holy (6:10)

"Holy" (Heb. *qodesh*) means, in a primary sense, that which is consecrated, sacred, set apart, dedicated, or hallowed. In Leviticus 10:10 and Ezekiel 22:26, *qodesh* is set over against that which is "common" (*chol*). Like the holy of holies (2 Chr. 3:8,10), the temple (Ps. 20:2), and the holy tabernacle (Exod. 35:19), the holy hill was holy because of God's intrinsic holiness (Isa. 6:3). The presence of God made the objects near him holy (Exod. 3:5). Because God is holy, his people must be holy (Lev. 19:2; 1 Pet. 1:16). In a secondary sense, holiness means that which is morally pure, sinless, and without moral or ethical blemish.

B. Hope (6:19)

"Hope" (Heb. *qawa*) means to wait. It does not refer to waiting to see if something will or will not occur but waiting with assurance that something will happen, to wait with expectation, to trust in the Lord (cp. Gen. 49:18; Ps. 130:5).

VII. TEACHING OUTLINE

A. Job's Defense (6:1–7)
   1. My words are rash (6:1–3)
   2. My wounds are deep (6:4)
   3. My words are justified (6:5)
   4. My woes are great (6:6–7)

B. Job's Despair (6:8–13)
   1. I desire death (6:8–10)
   2. I am weak (6:11–13)

C. Job's Disappointment (6:14–23)
  1. My friends are unkind (6:14–17)
  2. My friends are unhelpful (6:18–21)
  3. My friends are unsolicited (6:22–23)

D. Job's Demand (6:24–30)
  1. Show me where I am wrong (6:24–27)
  2. Look at me in the eyes (6:28–30)

VIII. ISSUES FOR DISCUSSION

1. Are there any sins in my life that warrant the discipline of God?
2. Do I seek godly counsel when suffering affliction?
3. What is God teaching me as I suffer affliction?

Job 7
An Emotional Meltdown

Quote

"Hopelessness and lifelessness go together."

William Gurnall

Job 7

I. INTRODUCTION

The Most Miserable Man

A young Midwestern lawyer suffered such deep depression that his friends actually thought it best to keep all knives and razors from him. At age 22, he failed in a business venture, suffered defeat for the state legislature, and then failed again in business. At age 26, his sweetheart died, crushing his heart. At age 27, he suffered a nervous breakdown from all the previously mentioned stress. At age 29, he was defeated for the office of speaker. At age 31, he was defeated for the office of elector. At age 34, he was defeated in his first attempt at Congress. At age 39, he was defeated again for Congress. At age 46, he was defeated in a bid for the Senate. At age 47, he was defeated for vice president. At age 49, he suffered another devastating loss for Senate. The man knew only loss after loss. During this time he broke down and wrote, "I am now the most miserable man living. Whether I shall ever be better, I cannot tell."

But he was wrong. He *did* recover from his bout with depression and went on to become one of America's most beloved presidents. His name was Abraham Lincoln. In the midst of his many losses, Lincoln suffered from heavy bouts of despair and defeat. Yet it was out of these awful depths that Lincoln rose to become a great American leader.

Although Job was a great man, he was not exempt from the heavy blows of life or from having a heart filled with bitter sorrow. From the heights of a prosperous career and a happy family, he came crashing down to the lows of depression. As Job began to pick up the broken pieces of his shattered life, he was left in the darkest gloom. He suffered an emotional meltdown.

In Job 7, we continue our investigation of his lament in which he bares his soul to God with soul-wrenching transparency. Here is an inner look at a devastated heart.

II. COMMENTARY

An Emotional Meltdown

MAIN IDEA: *Job laments the futility, misery, and emptiness of life in the midst of his pain and sorrow.*

A Job's Futility (7:1–5)

SUPPORTING IDEA: *Job talks to God about the futility of life.*

7:1. Having replied to Eliphaz (Job 6), Job then addressed his complaint toward God (Job 7). **Does not man have hard service** (i.e., literally, military service; Job 14:14) **on earth?** The anticipated answer is *yes*. Man's days are filled with forced labor in this world of woe, Job lamented. Likewise, **his days** are **like those of a hired man**, as if he were a weary slave under a grueling taskmaster.

7:2–3. Man longs for relief from the difficulty of life **like a slave longing for the evening shadows**. At the end of a long day, relief and rest are needed. So man is in need of relief in life, especially Job. He was like **a hired man waiting eagerly for his wages**, anticipating his hard-earned recompense. Likewise, **I have been allotted months of futility** (i.e., emptiness, worthlessness) and **nights of misery** (i.e., trouble, toil), Job declared. All this had **been assigned** to Job by the Lord.

7:4–5. At night, Job said, "**When I lie down I think, 'How long before I get up?'**" Tossing and turning in bed, sleepless and restless, Job endured the night, which seemed to drag by. At least hard-working hired men enjoyed the relief of sleep, but not Job. Describing his loathsome physical condition, he lamented, "**My body is clothed with worms and scabs.**" This was a reference to his skin disease. His skin was **broken and festering** (i.e., painful festering sores over his entire body; Job 2:7).

B Job's Brevity (7:6–10)

SUPPORTING IDEA: *Job saw his life passing quickly.*

7:6–7. Job saw his life on earth as lasting for a brief time and then gone forever. **My days are swifter than a weaver's shuttle**, tossed back and forth, moving rapidly with the thread running out. Then he would **come to an end without hope**, his life having been wasted and useless. Calling out to **God**, he pleaded that the Almighty would **remember his life**, which was **but a breath** that quickly came and went. He was convinced he would **never see** days of **happiness again**. There was no reason to continue living since he was robbed of the joys of living, specifically the presence of God.

7:8–9. Job declared, "**The eye that now sees me will see me no longer.**" He believed his death was imminent, and he even longed for it. Even God would see him no longer. His life would soon **be no more**. Job's days on earth were like **a cloud** that **vanishes** quickly when it is blown away, to be seen no more. He would soon go **down to the grave**, the place of the dead, never to **return**. Any trace of his existence would disappear.

7:10. Death meant that he would **never come to his house again**. Life's relationships and routines would be over. His place would **know him no more** because he would be gone forever. He had no sense of purpose in life.

C Job's Misery (7:11–16)

SUPPORTING IDEA: *Job cries out against God who would not leave him alone.*

7:11. Job could not withhold his complaining against God. "**I will not keep silent**," he declared. He would **speak out in the anguish** of his spirit to God, not hiding his disappointments with the injustices he felt he had suffered. He would **complain** against God.

7:12–14. God, Job felt, was treating him as a **monster of the deep**, a dangerous sea creature. He was convinced that God had put him **under guard**. He was a monster that had to be watched every minute. He longed for his **bed** to **comfort** him at night. He desired that his **couch** lessen his **complaint**. But such relief would not be forthcoming from God, he believed. Even in the night, God would **frighten** him **with dreams** (i.e., nightmares). God then would **terrify** him **with visions**. There was no rest for his weary soul, day or night.

7:15–16. In such a helpless, hopeless state, Job surmised, **I prefer strangling and death** to a life racked by such constant pain. Even the grave was to be preferred to living in **this body of mine**, he moaned. Spiraling down further in this emotional tailspin, Job complained, **I despise my life**. He despaired of life itself. Only death could ease his pain. So let death come early, even soon. "**Let me alone**," he cried to God. "**My days have no meaning**" (i.e., no purpose, significance, or fulfillment), only emptiness, he declared.

D Job's Perplexity (7:17–21)

SUPPORTING IDEA: *Job asks God why he should threaten him for no apparent reason.*

7:17. Job asked God a basic philosophical question: "**What is man that you make so much of him?**" Why would God bother to inflict so much pain on man? Is man really worth God's efforts? Why **give** man **so much attention** for no apparent reason?

7:18–19. Why would God **examine** man **every morning**? Why **test him every moment**? There seemed to be no purpose to these painful tests, only meaningless affliction. Job pleaded with God, "**Will you never look away from me?**" Will you not leave me alone? Or **let me alone even for an instant**? Job longed for a moment's rest from God and his affliction.

7:20. **If I have sinned, what have I done to you**? What despicable sin had Job committed that merited this kind of suffering? **Why have you made me your target?** Job believed that God was aiming his arrow of judgment at him (cp. Job 6:4). **Have I become a burden to you?** Was God trying to get rid of him?

7:21. Still perplexed with God, Job cried out, "**Why do you not pardon my offenses and forgive my sins?**" If God would only forgive him, this ordeal could be over. But he would not, **for I will soon lie down in the dust** of the grave, unforgiven and unrelieved. **You will search for me** on the earth, Job said, **but I will be no more** among the living.

MAIN IDEA REVIEW: *Job laments the futility, misery, and emptiness of life in the midst of his pain and sorrow.*

III. CONCLUSION

Empty or Exalting?

The world today is suffering from what Dr. Carl Jung calls "a neurosis of emptiness." He says, "When goal goes, meaning goes; when meaning goes, purpose goes; when purpose goes, life goes dead on our hands." Of course, we do not need a psychiatrist to tell us this. The Bible itself says the same. Such was the meltdown of Job's life because he lost sight of his true purpose for living—to glorify God in all that he said and did. In the midst of suffering, we must remain focused on our highest goal in life. We live for the glory of God; we suffer for the glory of God; we endure for the glory of God. As believers, one way we honor God is by the way we go through our trials. In order to do so successfully, we must keep before us our overarching ambition. What is the chief end of man? To glorify God and enjoy him forever.

IV. LIFE APPLICATION

How to Focus on God's Glory

How can we go through tough experiences without losing focus on the "big picture" of God's glory? If we ever lose sight of this fixed reference point, we are sure to wander away and dissolve into despair. Allow me to make a few practical suggestions.

1. *Read the Bible.* The Scripture is an anchor for the soul, a harbor and refuge for the storm-tossed life. There is no peace like the mind that is fixed on God through his Word. The soul is made strong when it is resting in God's truth. When your heart is troubled, read the Psalms. When your soul needs strength, read the Gospels. When your faith needs undergirding, read Revelation. Capture a high view of God.

2. *Read Christian biographies.* Read the biographies of great Christians who sacrificed their all for God. Read missionary biographies. Read about Christian martyrs. Learn about people who paid a great price for their faith in Christ. It will help put your life in proper perspective and help you endure your present suffering with patience.

3. *Read the Puritans.* The English Puritans of the sixteenth and seventeenth centuries had a strong faith and a way of communicating essential spiritual truths in a way that transcends time. They call for our singular devotion to Christ. Their message was soul stirring and heart fortifying. Their chief aim in life, to glorify God and enjoy him forever, comes through loud and clear in their writings.

V. PRAYER

Father, thank you for giving us a true purpose in living. Thank you that we may live for your glory and, in so doing, enjoy you forever. Thank you that true, abiding happiness comes through glorifying you. We ask that in the midst of life's many trials you keep our hearts burning with a passion for your glory. Amen.

VI. DEEPER DISCOVERIES

A. Remember (7:7)

"Remember" (Heb. *zakar*) is a verb meaning to contemplate, to recollect, or to bring to remembrance when used of past events; yet it does not mean that God has actually forgotten something and is now able to recall it. Rather, it is used to convey the idea that God calls himself into action based on his past promises. This word is used throughout the Old Testament to speak of God remembering, or executing, his covenant promises to his people (Exod. 2:24; Ps. 98:3; Jer. 31:34).

B. Offenses (7:21)

"Offenses" (Heb. *peshah*) literally means a going away from, departure, rebellion, or defiance. A transgression is a willful act of rebellion against God's sovereign authority and a refusal to acknowledge his right to rule the lives of his people. A transgression is not merely against other people whom a person may hurt by his sin, but it is always, ultimately, a treasonous act against God.

C. Sins (7:21)

The word "sins" is translated from the Hebrew word *awon*, which means corrupt, twisted, bent, perverse, or crooked. This word, which is often translated as "iniquity," focuses upon one's relationship to oneself. All sin is a self-defilement, a self-corrupting, a twisting of one's own character, and a bending of one's integrity. To the degree that a person sins, he becomes a twisted creature within his own soul.

VII. TEACHING OUTLINE

- A. Job's Futility (7:1–5)
  1. My suffering consumes me (7:1–4)
  2. My scabs cover me (7:5)
- B. Job's Brevity (7:6–10)
  1. My days are quickly ending (7:6–7)
  2. No one will see me (7:8–10)
- C. Job's Misery (7:11–16)
  1. God, you will hear from me (7:11)
  2. God, you set a guard over me (7:12)
  3. God, you frighten me at night (7:13–15)
  4. God, you must leave me alone (7:16)
- D. Job's Perplexity (7:17–21)
  1. God, what is man? (7:17–18)
  2. God, what have I done? (7:19–21)

VIII. ISSUES FOR DISCUSSION

1. What is your main purpose in life?
2. How can you give priority to this main purpose?
3. How can you encourage others to do the same?

Job 8

The Devil's Mouthpiece

Quote

"I think the devil has made it his business to monopolize on three elements: noise, hurry, crowds. Satan is quite aware of the power of silence."

Jim Elliot

Job 8

I. INTRODUCTION

Not a Word Spoken

In the days when the American West was being settled, a new commander was sent to a frontier army fort. There he soon found himself involved in negotiations with an important Indian chief. Working through a translator, the officer asked the chief a number of questions. But he received no reply to his various inquiries. After the meeting he asked the translator why he had obtained no answer to any of his questions. The translator replied, "That is what we call Indian time. He has enough respect for your questions to go away and think about them before answering."

That is precisely what Job needed from his three friends but did not receive. He needed friends who would listen to him and process carefully what he was saying. But no such care or consideration was given to him. Instead Job found himself embroiled in a rapid-fire series of exchanges. His three friends, while they may have listened to what he said, did not *hear* what he was saying. The entire time Job was speaking, his friends were thinking about their responses rather than processing what he was saying.

In the unfolding drama of Job, Bildad, the second of Job's three friends, now speaks in this chapter. Having listened to Eliphaz's presentation (Job 4–5) and Job's response (Job 6–7), Bildad was bursting at the seams to speak. But as he opened his mouth to speak, he did so without thinking through the issues carefully. Bildad misrepresented how God providentially cares for his people in this world. Bildad argued essentially as Eliphaz had done. Yet he did so from a slightly different angle. Where Eliphaz referred to a mystical experience as his authority, a midnight dream involving a spirit, Bildad appealed to the collective wisdom of past generations as his authority. He looked to history and traditions for insight.

II. COMMENTARY

The Devil's Mouthpiece

MAIN IDEA: *Bildad agrees with Eliphaz that Job has sinned against God and is suffering just punishment for his rebellion.*

A Bildad's Announcement (8:1–7)

SUPPORTING IDEA: *Bildad chides Job for resisting the discipline of God, but offers the hope of restoration if he will confess his sins.*

8:1–2. Bildad began by confronting Job: **"How long will you say such things? Your words are a blustering wind."** Job's words were like a forceful, continuous windstorm, filled with hot air. Apparently, Bildad harbored resentment about Job's refusal to accept Eliphaz's counsel. Bildad's words were like a destructive, uncontrolled wind (cp. Job 6:26).

8:3. Mounting his interrogation, Bildad asked, **"Does God pervert justice? Does the Almighty pervert what is right?"** Bildad assumed that since Job was suffering, he must have sinned because God would only exercise justice toward Job. Because God is just, Eliphaz surmised that Job had received what he deserved.

8:4. With a not-so-subtle allusion to the loss of his children, Bildad asserted, **"When your children sinned against him, he gave them over to the penalty of their sin."** He concluded that Job's sons and daughters died because of their sin. His children had surely provoked God to act in judgment. He certainly would not have punished them without cause.

8:5. The words **but if you look to God** is an allusion to Job humbling himself in true repentance. If this should happen, Job's life would be different.

Plead with the Almighty, insisted the forceful Bildad. This would signify a true change of mind in Job. His refusal to cry out to God would signify the opposite.

8:6. Yet, Bildad insisted, **if you are pure and upright**—a change brought about by his repentance—there would be a change. **Even now**, Bildad surmised, God would **rouse himself on your behalf and restore you to your rightful place**. If you would change your heart, he told Job, God would change his circumstances. Like Eliphaz (cp. Job 5:8,17–26), Bildad believed Job had sinned and needed to entreat God in repentance. If he would confess his sin, God would **restore** Job to his **rightful place**.

8:7. Job's **beginnings** would **seem humble** compared to his end if he would repent. Bildad's prophetic assertion would prove more true than he could have imagined (Job 42:10–17). If Job would humble himself, **prosperous** would his **future be**.

B Bildad's Appeal (8:8–10)

SUPPORTING IDEA: *Bildad tells Job to learn wisdom from former generations that will reinforce what he is saying.*

8:8–9. Bildad encouraged Job to **ask the former generations and find out what their fathers learned**. These godly ancestors taught this principle: where there is suffering, it is the result of sin. Such were the traditions of men, and such was the content of Bildad's counsel. Still Bildad rightly acknowledged that both he and Job knew nothing. The reason was that they **were born only yesterday** and thus did not have the acquired wisdom of the aged. **Our days on earth are but a shadow**, that is, short and fleeting (Ps. 144:4; Eccl. 6:12).

8:10. Assured that past generations can best impart knowledge, Bildad asked, "**Will they not instruct you and tell you?**" Surely sages from previous generations could teach Job a lot, Bildad reasoned. **Will they not bring forth words from their understanding?** The accumulated wisdom of the past must be heard and heeded, Bildad believed, if Job were to escape his present trial.

C Bildad's Assertion (8:11–19)

SUPPORTING IDEA: *Bildad admonishes Job that those who live without God die like a plant without water.*

8:11–12. **Can papyrus grow tall where there is no marsh?** No, and neither could Job without the wisdom of the past. **Can reeds thrive without water?** No, and neither could Job without consulting past generations. Bildad asserted that those who reject the wisdom and understanding accumulated by past generations will destroy their future destiny. **While still growing and uncut, they wither more quickly than grass.** Without man's wisdom, Job would waste away like grass during a drought. His life would perish without the insight of past authorities and godly ancestors.

8:13. Such is the destiny of all who forget God. From Bildad's viewpoint, this described Job. He was **godless** and his **hope** would perish because he had forgotten and forsaken God. But Job had not forgotten God, nor was he godless, as Bildad and the others asserted.

8:14–15. What he trusts in is fragile. This is a reference to man's strength and intelligence. But it will not hold him up. **What he relies on is a spider's web**, soon to be destroyed. Bildad wrongly asserted that Job now trusted in and relied on a spider's web. **He leans on his web, but it gives way.** This was a reference to Job's family, servants, and possessions. His entire support system had been taken away. But Job had not trusted in people or his possessions. Instead, his reliance had been on God (Job 1:21; 2:10).

8:16–17. Next Bildad compared Job to a **well-watered plant** that by all outward appearances was healthy. And under **the sunshine**, it grew, **spreading its shoots over the garden.** But it had placed its roots above the surface of the dirt, exposing it to the elements. Refusing to penetrate deep into the soil where it could be protected from the elements and receive nutrients, the plant chose to entwine **its roots around a pile of rocks.** Disowned and deserted by the good soil, the desperate plant looked for a place **among the stones.** So it was with Job's life. He was disowned and dying.

8:18–19. Then, unexpectedly, the plant was **torn from its spot**, and the place where it was firmly rooted now disowned it. So complete was this removal that one says, **I never saw you.** Job had been one of the most prominent and wealthy men of the Middle East, yet he was torn from his spot of prosperity. This, Bildad reasoned, was because of Job's sin. **Surely its life withers away** because of a lack of water needed to sustain the plant. Job's life was wasting away because of his sin. **From the soil other plants grow.** Other people prospered, but not Job.

D Bildad's Affirmation (8:20–22)

SUPPORTING IDEA: *Bildad calls Job to repent of his sin so he can be restored.*

8:20. Bildad closed his first address by reminding Job, "**Surely God does not reject a blameless man.**" If Job were really blameless, God would **not reject** him. This assertion demonstrated Bildad's blindness to the true character of Job, which God himself had assessed as blameless (cp. Job 1:1, 8; 2:3). Likewise God would not **strengthen the hands of evildoers.** With these words Bildad implied that Job's weakness was a result of God's judgment.

8:21–22. If Job accepted his counsel (cp. Job 8:5–6), Bildad asserted, God would bring him **laughter** and **shouts of joy**. The restoration of Job to the Lord would lead to a restoration of the happiness he once had. Further, Job's enemies would **be clothed in shame** if he would repent. "**The tents of the wicked will be no more**," Bildad declared. If Job would confess his sin to God and turn from it with godly sorrow, he would be restored.

MAIN IDEA REVIEW: *Bildad agrees with Eliphaz that Job has sinned against God and is suffering just punishment for his rebellion.*

III. CONCLUSION

A Loose Screw in the Speaker

The story is told of a speaker who was having difficulty with the sound system used to amplify his voice. No matter how well he spoke, there was constant feedback from the microphone. The static was nothing less than irritating. After much frustration the audio man walked to the podium and handed the speaker a note that read: "We've found what the trouble is. There's a screw loose in the speaker."

That was Bildad's problem. In the midst of his many words, it all sounded like static to Job's ears. The problem was that there was a loose screw in the speaker. Bildad's words were distorting the truth. His speech contained elements of truth. But what he said, the argument of his logic and the thrust of his application, had to be carefully interpreted in its context. And when they are carefully scrutinized, Eliphaz's words are found to be untrue. Half of the truth is no truth, and no truth is a lie. Thus Job had been listening to the devil's voice in the voice of Bildad, and it would poison Job's perspective on both God and himself.

This is a wise lesson for all of us. We need to be careful about who our friends are and what they say to us. In the trials of life, we are often weak and vulnerable, susceptible to the influence of others. May we surround ourselves with friends who will speak wisdom to our hearts.

IV. LIFE APPLICATION

How to Listen to Others

Listening to others should not be mere passive hearing, but an active experience in which we enter into the sorrow of others. Bildad shows us how *not* to listen to someone who is hurting. By negative example, he shows us how not to be a friend to someone who is hurting. Careful listening must be accompanied by astute thinking and a restrained mouth. There are certain principles that we should observe when listening.

1. *Do not dominate the conversation.* Listen more than you speak. Learn to be a good listener who listens not only to the words of others but to their heart as well. Do not formulate your next argument while the other person is speaking. Rather, hear what he is saying. Let him speak more than you talk.

2. *Validate the feelings of the other person.* Sympathize with his hurts. Verbally affirm him in the Lord. Express appreciation for him. This is something none of Job's "comforters" did. Say things like, "Yes, I see what you mean." Or, "I am so sorry to hear this." Or, "I know this must be painful."

3. *Do not interrupt the other person.* Allow him to finish his train of thought without breaking in on him. Allow him to complete his story enough to make his point. Interrupting him to make a point will only frustrate him further.

4. *Do not immediately correct the other person.* You should not correct the person to whom you are listening until you have the basic facts. To speak before you know the overall story from both sides is to speak inaccurately and to compound the problem.

5. *Ask insightful questions.* Rather than always making declarative statements, ask probing, revealing questions. Make inquiry like, "What happened then?" Or, "How did that make you feel?" This will probe deeper into the issue being discussed and help you get to the bottom of the matter.

V. PRAYER

Father, instruct us to be helpful friends to those around us who are hurting. May we be quick to listen and slow to speak so that we may be most effectively used by you. May we offer sound biblical counsel seasoned with love to those who are drowning in the storms of life. In Jesus' name we pray. Amen.

VI. DEEPER DISCOVERIES

A. Pervert (8:3)

"Pervert" (Heb. *awwata*) means to bend, falsify, subvert, or make crooked. Both Bildad (Job 8:3) and Elihu (Job 34:12) believed Job was guilty of wicked deeds and was receiving divine justice. So if Job argued his innocence, he was perverting justice by contending with God. Job believed God had "wronged" (Heb. *awwata*) him and failed to give him justice.

B. Pure (8:6)

"Pure" (Heb. *zak*) is an adjective that refers to that which is clean and transparent. *Zak* is used of olive oil (Lev. 24:2) and frankincense (Exod. 30:34). Outside of Exodus and Leviticus *zak* is found only in Job (Job 8:6; 11:4; 16:17; 33:9) and Proverbs (Prov. 16:2; 20:11; 21:8).

C. Earth (8:9)

"Earth" (Heb. *eres*) is the fourth most frequently used Hebrew noun in the Old Testament, occurring 2,504 times. *Eres* refers either to the entire physical planet (Gen. 18:18;), the land (Num. 13:20), the inhabitants of the land (1 Kgs. 2:2), soil (Lev. 25:19), or a designated territory (Deut. 34:2). Here it refers to the physical planet.

VII. TEACHING OUTLINE

- A. Bildad's Announcement (8:1–7)
  1. Job's words were wrongly spoken (8:1–3)
  2. Job's sons were rightly punished (8:4)
  3. Job's life will be rightly restored (8:5–7)
- B. Bildad's Appeal (8:8–10)
  1. Inquire of past generations (8:8)
  2. Ignore the present generation (8:9)
  3. Investigate past generations (8:10)
- C. Bildad's Assertion (8:11–19)
  1. Papyrus withers without water (8:11–12)
  2. People wither without God (8:13–19)
- D. Bildad's Affirmation (8:20–22)
  1. God will deliver you (8:20)
  2. God will delight you (8:21)
  3. God will defend you (8:22)

VIII. ISSUES FOR DISCUSSION

1. Am I truly innocent of any unconfessed sin?
2. Have I hidden or excused certain sins in my life?
3. Do I properly confess my sin, seeing it as God sees it?
4. When suffering, do I have a humble spirit that holds no bitterness toward God?

Job 9
I Want to Meet God in Court

Quote

"The fury of man never furthered the glory of God."

A. W. Tozer

I. INTRODUCTION

I Want to Sue God!

An Oakland, California, secretary recently took God to court. It seems that a lightning bolt struck near her home, creating a fire and destroying her four houses. The $100,000 damage suit charged God with "careless and negligent" operation of the universe. This scathing indictment included the mismanagement of the weather. Her attorney said he would try to collect the money by attaching a claim to some property that had been deeded to a Christian group. She claimed that the money should come to her if God failed to show up in court.

Job had a similar intention in mind, since he also wanted to take God to court. He believed that he could present his case of innocence and have the divine charges against him reversed. Job charged God with mismanagement of the universe, specifically his own life. He wanted his day in court to present his case before God and prove himself right. If the facts were brought out, Job reasoned, God would see the injustices in his life and reverse the charges against him.

Pain can distort even the best minds, causing them to draw exaggerated conclusions that are far removed from reality. Such was the case with Job. In the midst of his agony, he pressed for his day in court with God. He longed to have the opportunity to prove his own integrity. Perhaps God had mistaken him for someone else. Or maybe the wrong sentence had been assigned to him. Whatever the case, Job began to express his demand to appear in court before God and to plead his case with the Almighty.

In this chapter the language used by Job is that of a legal trial. A glance at some of his own language will reveal this, including: *dispute* (9:3,14), to enter into litigation; *answer* (9:3,15), to testify in court; *argue* (9:14), to present a case convincingly; *judge* (9:15), one who settles a dispute; *innocent* (9:15,20,28), to be cleared of charges; *summoned* (9:16,19), to be called to court; *hearing* (9:16), a court proceeding; *justice* (9:19), an impartial hearing; *condemn* (9:20), a guilty verdict; *guilty* (9:20,29), tried and condemned; *blameless* (9:21–22), found to be acquitted; *arbitrate* (9:33), to settle a dispute.

Job longed to appear in court and present his case before God in order to prove his innocence. Yet inwardly Job doubted that he could argue his case convincingly before heaven's Judge. He felt that he would only condemn himself, so he wanted a mediator to represent him before God.

II. COMMENTARY

I Want to Meet God in Court

MAIN IDEA: *Job seeks to defend himself against Bildad by proving himself right before God.*

A Job's Dilemma (9:1–24)

SUPPORTING IDEA: *Job feels he cannot prove his innocence to such an infinite, mighty God.*

9:1–2. Then Job answered Bildad, responding to what he had said in the previous answer (Job 8). This is Job's first speech to Bildad, a discourse that comprises two chapters (Job 9–10). Job began by acknowledging the truthfulness of some of Bildad's words. He agreed: "**Indeed, I know that this is true.**" He knew that the wicked do perish, just as Bildad had stated (Job 8:13). But the question was, Why was he suffering? He was not wicked. **How can a mortal be righteous before God?** This question does not deal with salvation but with vindication. That is, how can a man be cleared of charges brought against him by God?

9:3. Though one wished to dispute with him and prove his innocence with God, **he could not answer** God in court **one time out of a thousand**. Such a dispute with God, Job knew, would be useless.

9:4. As a finite man, Job could not argue his case before God, who is infinite. **His wisdom is profound**, beyond man's ability to understand, and **his**

power is vast, sufficient to do whatever he pleases. Job asked, "**Who has resisted him and come out unscathed?**" No one has been able to withstand the sovereign will of God.

9:5. To resist God would be spiritual insanity because God **moves mountains without their knowing it**. Who could resist such a God, who **overturns them in his anger**? The omnipotence of God is such that he can do unthinkable wonders with little effort.

9:6–8. This awesome God **shakes the earth from its place**. How could Job possibly resist him in court? He **makes** the earth's **pillars tremble**. So would man if he stood before God to argue his point. God's sovereignty is such that **he speaks to the sun and it does not shine**. How could Job hope to argue before God? One statement from God could silence Job indefinitely. He **seals off the light of the stars**. Then how could Job possibly instruct God? **He alone stretches out the heavens**, creating them out of nothing (Isa. 44:24) and then hanging them on nothing. God **treads on the waves of the sea**, assuming a position of superiority over them, controlling them for his own sovereign purposes.

9:9. He is the Maker of the Bear and Orion, the Pleiades (three constellations in the skies) **and the constellations of the south.** Pleiades is a group of seven stars, part of the constellation Taurus, always mentioned in connection with Orion. The Bear is also called the Big Dipper. By God's creative power, he created all these starry hosts and placed them in the sky.

9:10–11. Thus, God is incomprehensible. He **performs wonders that cannot be fathomed**. God is beyond man's capacity to figure out or understand. What is more, God's miracles **cannot be counted**. They are too numerous. Further, God is invisible, a spirit being without a corporeal body. Job pondered, "**When he passes me, I cannot see him.**" If Job could not see God, how could he understand him? **When he goes by, I cannot perceive him**. God is beyond man's finding out, and Job felt he was evading him.

9:12. God is irresistible in his power; his purposes cannot be thwarted. **If he snatches away, who can stop him?** *No one*. God is not restrained by a man-made system of right and wrong. He does not follow standards. He is the standard. **Who can say to him, "What are you doing?"** No one can call God into question. Such an attempt to query God is ludicrous. He is the law and, therefore, not under it. He remains unhindered and unthwarted in the execution of his sovereign will.

9:13. God does not restrain his anger. How then could lowly man restrain God? He cannot. **Even the cohorts of Rahab**, a mythological sea monster, **cowered at his feet**. How much more should mere men tremble before God? God does whatever he pleases, and no one can stop him. How could Job hope to contend with him?

9:14–15. Even if Job could meet God in court, he wondered, what would he say? **How then can I dispute with him? How can I find words to argue with him?** Job knew he could not answer God's cross-examination. Further, he realized he could not overturn God's decisions. Even if Job were innocent, he could not answer him. **I could only plead with my Judge for mercy.** God's perfect justice and equity would only result in further divine judgment upon him. Thus he must seek **mercy** from his Accuser.

9:16–17. Even if I summoned God to appear in court, Job calculated, **and he responded** to appear with me, **I do not believe he would give me a hearing.** God would not even listen to him, Job concluded. Certainly he could not plead his case and expect to win. Even if he did have his day in court with God, Job realized, **He would crush me with a storm and multiply my wounds for no reason.** Of course, Job was oblivious to the fact that God had allowed Satan to crush him for a higher purpose that had not been revealed to him. God did answer Job through a storm (cp. Job 38:1; 40:6) but to correct him, not to crush him.

9:18–19. Job believed that God was wearing him out, leaving him exhausted. He **would not let me regain my breath.** Job feared that God would overwhelm him with **misery.** He had no doubt that he would be devastated in a debate in court with God. In any direct confrontation with God, Job knew he had no hope of winning. **If it is a matter of strength, he is mighty!** Who could stronghold God? *No one.* **And if it is a matter of justice, who will summon him?** Who could call God into the courtroom? To whom is God accountable?

9:20. Even if I were innocent, with all the evidence in his favor, **my mouth would condemn me,** Job declared. Despite being innocent, Job knew he could never prove it before God. He believed he would become so disoriented and confused in court that he would actually testify against himself. Job would be too intimidated to respond clearly to heaven's inscrutable Judge.

9:21. Although I am blameless in whatever it is that is causing this punishment, **I have no concern for myself,** Job said. This was God's assessment of Job, having earlier declared him to be **blameless** (Job 1:1,8; 2:3). **I despise my own life.** Even though Job continued to believe he was right, his emotional state was such that he was losing the will to live.

9:22. It is all the same. That is, Job felt that it did not matter whether he was right or wrong. Either way, God would punish him: **He destroys both the blameless and the wicked.** Job was wrong, of course. Both the righteous and wicked do die by God's sovereign decree, but their destinies are different. In the end God rewards the righteous and punishes the wicked.

9:23–24. **When a scourge brings sudden death**, Job claimed, God **mocks the despair of the innocent**. This was not true, but Job's pain distorted his judgment and ability to think clearly. By this Job referred to himself as **the innocent** one. Job wondered if God had given the **land**, once belonging to the innocent, to **the wicked**. In so doing, God **blindfolds its judges** so they could not distinguish between right and wrong. With mounting self-confidence Job charged God with the injustices and inequities of this world. Surely these injustices must be behind Job's suffering.

B Job's Despair (9:25–31)

SUPPORTING IDEA: *Job believes even if he is innocent, God has attacked him without reason.*

9:25–26. The vanishing days of Job's life were slipping away **swifter than a runner** sprinting to the finish line. **They fly away without a glimpse of joy**, leaving him crushed and causing him to see the future outlook as void of good. His days **skim past like boats of papyrus**, speedily rushing downstream, and **like eagles swooping down on their prey**, descending rapidly. The time needed to prove his innocence was quickly passing.

9:27–28. Job's predicament was becoming more hopeless by the moment. If he said, **I will forget my complaint, I will change my expression, and smile**, it would not matter. Even if he tried to assume a joyful, positive attitude, it would not change his pain. Job surmised that his suffering was not an issue of mind over matter. **I still dread all my sufferings**, he declared. He believed they would not go away but that they would continue and perhaps even intensify. **I know you will not hold me innocent**, no matter what the evidence may show.

9:29–31. **Since I am already found guilty, why should I struggle in vain?** It didn't matter, Job reasoned. He was **guilty**, regardless of what the record showed. Why bother to question his plight? **Even if I washed myself with soap and my hand with washing soda**, Job lamented, God would still **plunge** him back **into a slime pit**. Even if he cleaned up his life and repented of his sin, God would still condemn him. Job was convinced that God was against him, so it did not matter what he did.

C Job's Defense (9:32–35)

SUPPORTING IDEA: *Job realizes that it will be impossible to approach God and prevail. Thus, he needs a mediator.*

9:32–33. God **is not a man like me that I might answer him, that we might confront each other in court**, Job said. Even if Job should appear in court before God, the Almighty would ask only one question, and he would be rendered speechless, unable to **answer**. All Job's loud talk would then dissipate. Therefore, he could not approach God to plead his case. **If only there were someone to arbitrate between us**, a court official, one who could bring them together and resolve this issue. Job needed someone **to lay his hand upon us both**, an advocate to bring resolution, an umpire or referee between them. It would be wrong to assume that Job had a glimpse of Christ here. He was not looking for someone to forgive him but for one to speak about his innocence.

9:34. Such a mediator would surely remove **God's rod** of discipline from him and, thus, win the case for Job. The rod is a symbol of God's judgment (2 Sam. 7:14; Isa. 10:5). Then God's **terror** would no longer **frighten** him.

9:35. Only **then** would Job be able to speak up to God **without fear** of divine repercussion. If God were a man, then Job could approach him and plead his case. But God is not a man. Thus, without an arbitrator, someone to mediate for him, Job could not possibly approach Almighty God in order to plead his case and set this matter right.

MAIN IDEA REVIEW: *Job seeks to defend himself against Bildad by proving himself right before God.*

III. CONCLUSION

A Vicious Spiraling Down

As this chapter shows, Job had been caught in a vicious downward spiral. His life had plunged deeper and deeper into despair. The more he pondered his devastating situation, the more his reasoning became distorted. What is worse, Job was jumping to wrong conclusions about God, making assumptions that were injurious to the reputation and honor of God. The truth is that God was *not* against Job, as he so loudly declared. Neither had Job committed any sin that had brought on this suffering. Yet Job had concluded both to be true.

Prolonged suffering can have an adverse effect on us by creating vain imaginations. A long-term hurt can create negative thoughts within us about

God and ourselves. When our understanding of God becomes distorted, our own self-perception becomes altered. Wrong thoughts about God inevitably lead to wrong thoughts about ourselves. What Job needed was to return to a right view of God, one in which God was seen as holy, just, and good. Only then could Job see his own life in right perspective. May the Lord help each of us to preserve a right understanding of himself. Only then can we make sense of our lives.

IV. LIFE APPLICATION

How to Find Comfort

When hurting deeply, what are some practical steps believers can take to find comfort for their aching hearts?

1. *Memorize and meditate on Scripture.* The Word of God is always a soothing balm to a sorrowful heart. Scripture in the heart is the greatest healer of a troubled life.

2. *Stay plugged in to Christian fellowship.* Believers need the strength that other Christians can provide. Isolation is never the answer when trying to weather the storms of life. God's people need to allow others to affirm them in the Lord. All Christians need to be around others as they laugh and enjoy life. Look for that kind of contagious fellowship.

3. *Have a prayer partner.* Find a soul mate with whom you can pour your heart out and with whom you can share your hurts and disappointments. Find someone who will pray for you and with you—someone who is truly trustworthy. There is something powerful about hearing another person's voice pray for you and offer requests for you at a time when you are weak.

4. *Minister to someone else.* Take your focus off yourself and place it on others. Begin to serve others who are in need, and it will heal your hurting heart.

5. *Listen to good Christian music.* The psalmist says that God inhabits the praises of his people. Praise has the effect of lifting our hearts to God and enabling us to sense his presence. One of the most soul-strengthening exercises a person can do is to listen to Christian music that elevates God. David played his harp for Saul. It softened Saul's bitter soul, if only for a time. David also played his harp for himself for soothing comfort.

6. *Maintain physical exercise.* Walk, jog, ride a bike, plant a garden, or take up a new hobby. Physical exercise is critical to the well-being of the soul.

V. PRAYER

God, our Father, truly your ways are not our ways, neither are your thoughts our thoughts. As the heavens are higher than the earth, so are your ways higher than our ways and your thoughts higher than our thoughts. Remind us often, O Lord, that you are the Potter and we are the clay. Teach us to patiently accept all that you bring our way and to trust in you alone. In Jesus' name. Amen.

VI. DEEPER DISCOVERIES

A. The Heavens (9:8)

The heavens (Heb. *shamayim*) is a plural noun form that literally means the heights or that which is raised up or lofty. It refers to the realms of outer space in which the stars, the moon, and the planets exist (Gen. 1:14–17).

B. Someone to Arbitrate (9:33)

The phrase "someone to arbitrate" (Heb. *yakach*) refers to a daysman, court official, umpire, mediator, referee, judge, or one to settle a dispute between two parties. Used in the context of a lawsuit, a daysman was one with authority to set the day when competing parties came together to settle their dispute. In the East the arbitrator put his hands on the heads of the two disputing parties to remind them that he was the one with the authority to settle the question. Job longed for someone who could do this for him with God. Job was not directly predicting the mediatorship of Christ here, although the New Testament speaks of such a Mediator who stands in the gap between God and man and brings forgiveness and salvation (1 Tim. 2:5–6).

VII. TEACHING OUTLINE

A. Job's Dilemma (9:1–24)
   1. How can a man answer God? (9:1–13)
   2. How can a man argue with God? (9:14–20)
   3. How can a man avoid God? (9:21–24)

B. Job's Despair (9:25–31)
   1. My days are fleeing (9:25–26)
   2. My dread is great (9:27–31)

C. Job's Defense (9:32–35)
   1. I cannot go to court with God (9:32)

2. I need a mediator in court with God (9:33–35a)
3. I fear to speak in court to God (9:35b)

VIII. ISSUES FOR DISCUSSION

1. Do I accuse God of injustice?
2. When trials arise, do I examine my life to see if I am concealing sin?
3. Am I incurring the discipline of God for unconfessed sin?

Job 10
Why Live?

Quote

"Is life a living death or a dying life?"

Augustine

Job 10

I. INTRODUCTION

Waiting to Die

William Moulton Marston, the noted psychologist, surveyed three thousand people and asked this question: "What do you have to live for?" Ninety-five percent of those polled said they were just enduring the present while they waited for the future. They were simply waiting for "something" to happen. Some were waiting for their children to grow up and leave home. Others were waiting for next year. Still others were waiting for another time to take a long-desired trip. Many were waiting to die. All these people were waiting for tomorrow without realizing that all they have is today. Yesterday is gone, and for many people tomorrow never comes.

Marston's discovery speaks to the painful place where Job had arrived in his life. Having abandoned all hope for any restoration in the present, he was waiting to die in the future. He was waiting for tomorrow to come to rescue him from the pain of today. His aching body and agonizing soul caused him to long to depart this world for the welcome relief of death. In the bitter thralls of a life wracked with pain, Job questioned why God had created him. Was it only to suffer destruction?

Maybe you feel like Job. Perhaps there is a deep cry in your heart. You wonder why God made you if it is only to live a life filled with so much agony. Life only has meaning as it is lived for the glory of God. Only in such a transcendent life pursuit is divine purpose found that causes a person to rise above the bitter disappointments of life. Whenever a person loses sight of this divine purpose, he is ready to give up on life. May God use suffering to encourage endurance in each of us as we press on through our present disappointments.

II. COMMENTARY

Why Live?

MAIN IDEA: *Job wonders why God allows him to live, when his days are filled with nothing but pain and agony.*

A Job's Disturbance (10:1–7)

SUPPORTING IDEA: *Job becomes so bitter that he assumes God will not reveal the charges against him.*

10:1–2. Because no arbitrator for Job was found (Job 9:32–35), he collapsed into deeper despair and spoke out of **the bitterness** of his soul to God. He loathed his life, hating the turn it had taken. **Therefore, I will give free rein to my complaint** against God, he declared. Job pleaded that God would tell him **what charges** were being made **against** him. How could God hold him guilty when he would not read him the charges?

10:3. Like a courtroom lawyer, Job interrogated God with a series of searching questions. **Does it please you to oppress me**? What enjoyment could God possibly gain from tormenting and oppressing him? To Job, God had spurned him, **the work of** God's **hands**, though he was righteous, while God apparently smiled **on the schemes of the wicked**.

10:4–5. **Do you have eyes of flesh?** Job hoped that God would look beyond the outward to the inward and see Job's true inward state. **Do you see as a mortal sees?** Job asked if God was as limited in his perceptions as his friends were. "**Are your days like those of a mortal or your years like those of a man?**" he queried God sarcastically, wondering if God were as limited as his friends to discover his true spiritual condition. The implication is that God was acting like a finite human who was limited by time.

10:6–7. Surely God had searched out Job's faults and probed his sins. God had investigated Job and had searched and sifted every area of his life. Job was confident that God would find nothing in his life that would deserve the suffering he had endured. "**Though you know that I am not guilty,**" Job said, why do you still punish me? Obviously, God had no good reason for this punishment, Job concluded. Yet he had no higher court of appeal to plead his case and seek a reversal. Thus, no one could rescue him from God's hand.

B Job's Difficulty (10:8–17)

SUPPORTING IDEA: *Job asks if God had created him only to destroy him.*

10:8–9. Job continued to cross-examine God as if he were a legal opponent in court. Job admitted, "**Your hands shaped me and made me.**" But in frustration he complained, "**Will you now turn and destroy me?**" How could God, who had so skillfully created him, also punish him to the point of destruction? Why would God make him, only to destroy him? **Remember that you molded me like clay**. Wonderfully wrought was Job with great precision. "**Will you now turn me to dust again?**" Job asked. Why did you make me, only to return me to dust (cp. Gen. 3:19)?

10:10. Having introduced the subject of his birth (vv. 8–9), Job proceeded to give a poetic description of God forming a baby in the womb (cp. Ps. 139:13–16). Clearly Job saw life beginning at conception. **Did you not pour me out like milk and curdle me like cheese**? Here his own embryonic development is pictured like the curdling of milk into cheese, from a liquid to a solid.

10:11–12. In this mysterious maturation process, Job stated, God did **clothe me with skin and flesh and knit me together with bones and sinews**. Job pictured the placing of his veins and muscles in their appropriate places as a person would knit clothes. In this creative process, Job noted, "**You gave me life and showed me kindness.**" God chose to shower Job with his covenant love. But why had God suddenly turned against him? **In your providence**, Job noted, you **watched over my spirit**. It was incongruent for God, he reasoned, to destroy what he had labored to make.

10:13. But this is what you concealed in your heart. Why would God conceal a plan to destroy him? **I know that this was in your mind**. God knew all along that this was his purpose. How could God have been so kind to him for so long, all the while concealing his plan to destroy him?

10:14–15. Job was confident that if he had **sinned**, God would have been **watching** him and **not let** his **offense go unpunished**. Job had no problem with this. He would deserve to be punished if he had sinned. **If I am guilty—woe to me!** Punishment would be due, he reasoned, if the charges were true. But here was the rub. **Even if I am innocent, I cannot lift my head, for I am full of shame and drowned in my affliction**. Though innocent, Job's condition caused him to be full of shame and to drown in his own affliction, making him unable to lift his own head.

10:16. If I hold my head high (a reference to living in the confidence of his innocence before God in spite of this inner assurance) **you stalk me like a lion**. Holding one's head high was an indicator of arrogant pride (Gen. 40:20; Ps. 27:6). God, having displayed his power to create Job, appeared to be displaying his **awesome power** against him to harm him.

10:17. Job claimed that God brought his friends to him to accuse him of the sin he had not committed. **You bring new witnesses against me** (his so-called counselors), who testified about his wrongdoing.

C Job's Desire (10:18–22)

SUPPORTING IDEA: *Job says he was created only to be destroyed; it would have been better if he had died at birth.*

10:18–19. Job returned to his original soul-searching question: **Why then did you bring me out of the womb?** For what purpose did God create him? To destroy him? If so, Job noted, **I wish I had died before any eye saw me**, never to have experienced such pain and misery. If only he had **never come into being**, then Job would have escaped all this torment. He surmised that it would have been better if he had been stillborn. He should have **been carried straight from the womb to the grave**, never to have lived to feel such hurt.

10:20–21. Job desired to live what little time remained free from God's presence. **Are not my few days almost over?** This being the case, Job requested that God would **turn away from** him. Give me some breathing room, he said, **so I can have a moment's joy**. If only God would leave him alone, Job could enjoy some peace before he died. He longed for some relief before he went **to the place of no return**, or death. Such a final, ultimate destination in the grave Job described as **the land of gloom and deep shadow**. Death was envisioned by Job as better than life with its miseries.

10:22. Job concluded this chapter with further references to death, which he preferred over life. Death was depicted as a journey **to the land of deepest night, of deep shadow and disorder**. Death, he foresaw, was a place of blackest darkness **where even the light is like darkness**. Once again Job's speech ended on the note of death (Job 3:20–22; 7:21). Death was preferred to living in such misery in this present life.

MAIN IDEA REVIEW: *Job wonders why God allows him to live, when his days are filled with nothing but pain and agony.*

III. CONCLUSION

Sorrow and Sighing

Joseph Parker, a nineteenth-century English pastor (1830–1902), once commented on the closing words of Isaiah 35:10, "Sorrow and sighing shall flee away." He said, "Looking through the dictionary, you will occasionally come across a word marked 'obsolete.' The time is coming when these two words *sorrow* and *sighing* shall be obsolete. The things which mar life here and now will then belong to the past." Every person's life in varying degrees is marked by sorrow and sighing. But how comforting it is for believers to know that the time is coming when all trials and tears will pass away. In that day God will wipe all tears from our eyes. But until then God's people must learn to live with the pains of life.

This is certainly where Job was. He had sunk to a deeper level of despair and discouragement. He was ready to give up on life, preferring the grave to such groaning. Can you relate to such low feelings? If so, you are not alone. The key to overcoming these times of despondency is to keep your eyes fixed on the Lord and to trust his love and mercy.

IV. LIFE APPLICATION

How to Deal with Despair

Several important life lessons on how to deal with despair emerge from this chapter.

1. *Do not keep your deep pain to yourself.* One of the things that drained Job's spirit of strength was his silence as he and his friends sat in the garbage dump. During this excruciating time Job could have been sharing his burdens with them. Instead, he internalized his pain, keeping it on the inside. The mounting pressure built up within him so that when it was finally released, it came spewing out. These outbursts could have been diverted by unburdening his heart with his companions. Our friends can be a great help to us in bearing our heavy loads. Galatians says, "Bear one another's burdens" (Gal. 6:2 NASB). Romans says, "Weep with those who weep" (Rom. 12:15 NASB). Job should have freely shared what he was going through. So should we.

2. *Remember that God always has a purpose behind suffering.* As long as you are alive, God has a purpose for your being here on earth. And until the moment we die, we are still in the process of fulfilling that purpose.

Therefore, we need to stay focused here until God determines our time is over. God will not take us home until we have fulfilled our purpose. Jesus said, "We must work the works of Him who sent Me, as long as it is day; night is coming when no man can work" (John 9:4 NASB). While we have life and opportunity, we need to do what God has called us to do.

V. PRAYER

God, our Father, teach us to count our blessings and to ponder afresh your goodness. You truly are good to your people and demonstrate that goodness through gifts and blessings. We know that every good and perfect thing comes down from you, and we ask that you continue to shower your people with your loving blessings. In Jesus' name. Amen.

VI. DEEPER DISCOVERIES

A. Rescue (10:7)

"Rescue" (Heb. *nasal*) means to snatch away, draw out of, save, or pull away. The word was used countless times by David when he petitioned God to rescue him from his enemies who were seeking to take his life. In other psalms the word is used of deliverance from one's transgressions (Ps. 39:8) and the grave (Ps. 86:13). Asaph wrote, "Help us, O God our Savior, for the glory of your name; deliver (*nasal*) us and forgive our sins for your name's sake" (Ps. 79:9). The word was also used in requesting God for the power to resist sin (Ps. 120:2). The theme of deliverance is one of the dominant themes of the Psalms.

B. Kindness (10:12)

"Kindness" (Heb. *hesed*) means mercy, favor, or steadfast love and is found about 250 times in the Hebrew Bible (cp. Exod. 34:6; Num. 14:18; Mic. 7:18). *Hesed* is derived from *hasad*, which means to bend or bow oneself or to incline oneself. It denotes a condescending love of God to his chosen people. Sometimes *hesed* is called God's covenant love because of its occurrence in Deuteronomy 7:12 and 2 Samuel 7:15.

C. Watched Over (10:12)

"Watched over" (Heb. *shamar*) means to put a hedge around something, to set a watch, or to guard for safekeeping. It is used over four hundred times in the Old Testament in many different contexts, some of which are to refer to someone acting as an overseer over a garden (Gen. 2:15), flocks (Gen. 30:31), or a gate (Isa. 21:11). In the Psalms it speaks of physical protection (Ps. 34:20), the guarding of life (Ps. 86:2), and the Lord's watchcare of his people (Ps. 121:3–4,7). In Job, it is used of God taking note of Job (cp. Job 10:14), Job keeping God's way (cp. Job 23:11), and of the adulterer awaiting the twilight (cp. Job 24:15).

VII. TEACHING OUTLINE

A. Job's Disturbance (10:1–7)
 1. I loathe my life (10:1)
 2. I will say to God (10:2–7)

B. Job's Difficulty (10:8–17)
 1. God has made me (10:8–11)
 2. God has blessed me (10:12)
 3. God has punished me (10:13–14)
 4. God has misjudged me (10:15–16)
 5. God has opposed me (10:17)

C. Job's Desire (10:18–22)
 1. Why was I born? (10:18–19)
 2. Are not my days few? (10:20–22)

VIII. ISSUES FOR DISCUSSION

1. Do I internalize my pain and frustrations when I am suffering?
2. Do I surround myself with people who listen and attempt to understand my suffering?
3. Do I pray openly and honestly to God, humbly sharing my pain and frustrations?

Job 11

Caught in the Critic's Crosshairs

Quote

"It is much easier to be critical than to be correct."

Benjamin Disraeli

I. INTRODUCTION

Your Tongue Is Too Long

John Wesley, founder of Methodism in the eighteenth century, was once preaching when he noticed a lady in the audience known for her critical attitude. Through the entire service she sat and stared at his new tie. When the meeting ended, she came up to him and said, "Mr. Wesley, the strings on your bow tie are much too long. They are an offense to me!" Wesley asked if any of the ladies present might have a pair of scissors in their purse. One woman did. When the scissors were handed to him, Wesley gave them to his critic and asked her to trim the strings to her liking. After she clipped them off near the collar, he asked, "Are you sure they're all right now?" "Yes, that's much better," she admitted.

"Now, let me have those shears a moment, if I may," said Wesley. "I'm sure you would not mind if I also gave *you* a bit of correction. I do not want to be cruel, but I must tell you, madam, that tongue of yours is offensive to me. It is quite too long! Please stick it out. I'd like to take some off!" This woman got the point.

Job was facing much the same problem in his life. The tongues of his critics had become much too long. The cutting words of his three friends had become like a pair of scissors, slicing Job to pieces. Their words were sharp and penetrating. All this was supposedly done in the name of love.

In chapter 11 of Job, we find the first words of Zophar, a Naamathite. He was probably the youngest of Job's three friends—a reasonable assumption because he spoke last. He undoubtedly waited his turn in deference to his elders, in accordance with the custom of the day. Yet, as he spoke, he did so with the angriest tone of all. The least sympathetic of the three friends, Zophar spoke with bitter animosity as he launched his scorching rebuke. He was rude, blunt, insensitive, and impatient. His message was essentially the same as the other two: Job was suffering because he had sinned.

II. COMMENTARY

Caught in the Critic's Crosshairs

MAIN IDEA: *The third friend, Zophar, attacks Job, accusing him of unconfessed sin.*

A Zophar's Confrontation (11:1–6)

SUPPORTING IDEA: *Zophar rashly attacks Job, accusing him of suffering the judgment of God for unconfessed sin.*

11:1–2. Then Zophar the Naamathite replied. What Zophar said was in response to the feeble words that had been offered by Job. This begins his insensitive interrogation of Job. **Are all these words to go unanswered?** The implied answer is *no*. Job's words must be answered, and he, Zophar, was confident that he was the one to do it. **Is this talker to be vindicated?** Again, *no* is the implied answer. Job would not be vindicated of the charges.

11:3. Zophar believed that Job had been too quick to speak as he attempted to **silence** his friend's counsel with **idle talk** (i.e., false words, empty words). Job's hasty words to Eliphaz made him appear to Zophar to **mock** God because Eliphaz believed he was speaking for God.

11:4–5. So, Zophar spoke, **"You say to God, 'My beliefs are flawless and I am pure in your sight.'"** Although Job had admitted that he was not **flawless** (Job 7:21; 10:7), he maintained his innocence of committing a terrible sin (cp. 1:1,8; 2:3). Zophar desired that **God would speak** and **open his lips**, believing God's words would be **against** Job. Zophar wanted God to silence Job.

11:6. Zophar wished that God would show Job the **secrets of wisdom**, yet Zophar did not realize that both he and Job were in need of wisdom. Both needed to see into the heavenly scenes. This perspective would have clarified the reasons for Job's suffering (cp. Job 1:6–12; 2:1–7). A proper understanding of the secrets of wisdom would have ended Zophar's unwarranted accusations and Job's complaints against God. Job never received a direct answer about his plight. Yet it was the secrets of wisdom (Job 38–41) that God would use later to remind Job of his limited understanding. With confidence Zophar asserted, "**Know this: God has even forgotten some of your sin.**" Job should be satisfied in not receiving punishment for all of his sins.

B Zophar's Challenge (11:7–12)

SUPPORTING IDEA: *Zophar interrogates Job about the greatness of God with the aim of reminding him of his limited capacity for understanding God.*

11:7. Zophar questioned Job about his understanding of God's infinity. Job had never denied the infinity of God (cp. Job 9:3–12). **Can you fathom the mysteries of God?** Job's expected answer is *no*. **Can you probe the limits of the Almighty?** Again the assumed answer is negative. Job was finite and limited in his ability to grasp the magnitude of God. But of course, so were his three friends.

11:8. The mysteries of God are **higher than the heavens** and **deeper than the depths of the grave** (Sheol), Zophar declared. But he used these great truths in a sinister way to attack Job and to accuse him of speaking beyond what he understood. Zophar had no mercy for the suffering Job.

11:9. **Their measure is longer than the earth and wider than the sea.** There is nothing that Job could do to rise above this. What could he do? Nothing. What could he know? Nothing. Zophar understood the infinitude of God, yet the implication was that Job remained ignorant of God's infinity. Just as Eliphaz and Bildad had done, Zophar accused Job of sins that he had not committed and perverse thoughts that had never entered his mind.

11:10. Elaborating upon the justice of God, Zophar asked, "**If he comes along and confines you in prison and convenes a court, who can oppose him?**" God is the standard of justice, accountable to no one. Who can protest his actions?

11:11–12. To Job's apparent disadvantage, Zophar believed that God **recognizes deceitful men; and when he sees evil, does he not take note?** Believing Job was refusing to repent because of stubborn arrogance, Zophar sought to humble Job by reminding him that God would take every sin into account. With cutting sarcasm Zophar used a proverb in which he stated that Job was a **witless man** with as much likelihood of becoming more wise as **a wild donkey's colt can be born a man.**

C Zophar's Call (11:13–20)

SUPPORTING IDEA: *Zophar calls Job to take the necessary steps to demonstrate true repentance while assuring Job that doing so will bring the blessings of God back into his life.*

11:13. Zophar gave specific steps of repentance that he believed Job must take if he was to know forgiveness from God. Job must **devote** his **heart**, meaning Job needed to conduct his life in a righteous way. Further, Job must **stretch out** his **hands to him**, undoubtedly a reference to prayer.

11:14. What is more, Job must **put away the sin** that was in his **hand.** This was a reference to hidden sin in his life. Also, Job must **allow no evil to dwell** in his tent, probably a reference to tolerating sin within his family. Zophar presented a simple solution to the complex affliction Job was enduring. This false solution, repentance, was based upon the false assumption that Job was under the discipline of God for his sin.

11:15–16. Zophar proceeded to guarantee the blessings which would be Job's if he repented: **Then you will lift up your face without shame.** In contrast to his present condition, Job would **stand firm and without fear.** Acknowledging his sin would enable Job to **forget** his **trouble**. The word *trouble* is used in Job to speak of the dreadful consequences of sin (Job 3:10; 4:8; 5:6–7). Then, Job would be **recalling it only as waters gone by**—that is, water under the bridge, long since past.

11:17–18. Life would **be brighter than noonday**, shining with happiness and hope. The **darkness** of sorrow would **become like morning**—gone. Job would **be secure** because there would then be hope of a bright future. He would look about him and see his troubles gone. He would take his rest **in safety** then, following his repentance and God's restoration.

11:19. Job would **lie down** in sleep and be confident that **no one** would make him **afraid**. All men would be at peace with him, unlike what Job had experienced at the hands of the Sabeans (Job 1:14–15) and Chaldeans (Job 1:17). To the contrary, **many** would court his **favor**, admiring him rather than attacking him. If Job had repented, it would have demonstrated that his obedience was truly based on God's blessings (cp. Job 1:9) rather than his unwavering trust in God in spite of the circumstances (cp. Job 13:15).

11:20. Zophar ended his discourse by warning Job, "**But the eyes of the wicked will fail, and escape will elude them; their hope will become a dying gasp.**" These biting words implied, much like Bildad's closing words had done earlier (Job 8:22), that if Job failed to repent, God would end his wicked life.

MAIN IDEA REVIEW: *The third friend, Zophar, attacks Job, accusing him of unconfessed sin.*

III. CONCLUSION

Who Has the Right to Criticize?

Abraham Lincoln once said, "He has the right to criticize who has the heart to help." In other words, it is not enough just to point out where another person has erred. Instead, one must be committed to help such a person work through his limitations or failures in order to help him. It has been said that it takes no size to criticize. Anyone can point out the faults of others. The mark of a great person is helping people overcome their failure.

Unfortunately, Zophar had not come to such a place in his life. He did not have the heart to help Job. Therefore, he forfeited the right to criticize him. "People do not care how much you know until they know how much you care" is an old adage. Zophar should have heeded this advice in his dealings with Job. Zophar was a noisy gong and a clanging cymbal (cp. 1 Cor. 13:1).

IV. LIFE APPLICATION

How to Speak in Love

Zophar's problem was not so much in what he said, but in what he did *not* say. Further, Zophar fell short in *how* he said it. From this we learn about how to speak to a friend who is going through a difficult time.

1. *Speak of God's love.* Zophar was all justice and no mercy. He represented a high view of God, but he failed to emphasize that God is patient and tender toward his people. This is a truth that we must bring out to others. We who love the sovereignty of God, as Zophar did, must be equally quick to point out the sympathy of God. When people are hurting, they need to hear about the unconditional love of God for them. We must remind troubled souls of the love that God extends to those who suffer.

2. *Speak of God's justice.* God can be trusted to do what is right. This was also missing from Zophar's message. God can *only* do what is right. And he will *always* do what is right. This is what we need to emphasize to those who are going through difficulty.

3. *Speak of God's peace.* In the midst of every fiery trial, God provides a supernatural peace that surpasses all understanding. This must be spoken to hurting hearts. But Zophar said nothing of this inner tranquility to Job. As we minister to those who are undergoing life's adversity, we should be quick to speak to them of the divine serenity that only he can provide. Be an encourager of discouraged souls, offering God's peace.

V. PRAYER

Father, you are infinite and all wise in all your ways. You see all things as everything is open and laid bare before you. Iniquity cannot be hidden from you, for you see into the inner recesses of human hearts. Teach us to confess our sins to you and teach us to remember the supreme sacrifice of Jesus Christ, whose blood covers and cleanses our sin. In his name we pray. Amen.

VI. DEEPER DISCOVERIES

A. Pure (11:4)

"Pure" *(bar)* is a rare Hebrew adjective that is used just a few times in the Old Testament (cp. Job 11:4; Ps. 73:1; Prov. 14:4). *Bar* is a derivative of *barar* and refers to that which is pure (Ps. 18:26; Zeph. 3:9), cleansed (Jer. 4:11), polished (Isa. 49:2), clear (Eccl. 3:18), clean (Isa. 52:11), or chosen (1 Chr. 16:41).

B. Fail (11:20)

"Fail" (Heb. *kala*) is found 237 times in the Old Testament in various forms. It means to be completed, finished, destroyed, or at an end. The meaning derived from the root is to bring a process to completion. The best corresponding English word is "finished." This completion or ending may have negative or positive connotations. Obviously the connotation here is negative and points to the complete destruction of the wicked. In this sense this word was used to describe the judgment of God that will fall upon the wicked (Pss. 18:37; 78:33; Isa. 29:20; Ezek. 5:13). At times God threatened to consume or finish off the rebellious Israelites (Exod. 32:10; Lam. 3:22). The word is also used to describe the devastating effects of war (1 Sam 15:18).

VII. TEACHING OUTLINE

A. Zophar's Confrontation (11:1–6)
   1. He rebuts Job's words (11:1–3)

2. He references Job's words (11:4)
3. He refutes Job's words (11:5–6)

B. Zophar's Challenge (11:7–12)
1. God is infinite and unfathomable (11:7–9)
2. God is independent and irresistible (11:10)
3. God is all knowing and all seeing (11:11–12)

C. Zophar's Call (11:13–20)
1. The requirements of Job's repentance (11:13–14)
2. The results of Job's repentance (11:15–20)

VIII. ISSUES FOR DISCUSSION

1. Do I patiently listen to a hurting friend before offering counsel?
2. Do I lovingly correct an erring brother or sister when he or she questions God?
3. Do I seek to understand the physical, mental, and spiritual pressure people feel when they are under great trauma?

Job 12
Get Off My Back!

Quote

"If you were not strangers here, the dogs of the world would not bark at you."

Samuel Rutherford

I. INTRODUCTION

You Cannot Please Your Critics

An old man was traveling with his young grandson, riding his donkey. When they passed through a country village, the onlookers grumbled, "Look at that old man walking while that strong young boy is capable of walking." The criticism cut deeply into the heart of the grandfather, so he changed positions and started riding the donkey while the boy walked. But within minutes other people started mumbling, "Look at that! A healthy man riding the donkey and making that poor little boy walk!"

So the old man changed positions again. This time both he and the boy rode on the donkey. But the critics howled, "Look at those heavy brutes making that poor donkey suffer." So the old man and his grandson jumped down and started walking. *No one will criticize us for this,* the old man thought to himself. But he underestimated the critical nature of people. Soon he heard the people say, "Would you look at that. A perfectly good donkey not being used." So to stop all criticism, the old man carried both the donkey and the boy.

No matter what we do, someone is likely to criticize us. Regardless of how carefully we conduct ourselves, we cannot please all the people all the time. The key to enduring unwarranted criticism is how we respond to it. Like the old man in this story, if we listen to our critics without discernment, we will surely end up carrying a heavy load. A person must know how to deal with criticism when it comes his way. That's where Job was. No matter what he did, his friends rode him hard. It was not easy for him to know how to respond to their criticism.

As the unfolding story of Job comes to chapter 12, the protagonist remains in the hot seat. He is a lightning rod in the storm, an easy-to-hit target for the devil's fire. Having lost his fortune, family, health, and his wife's support, Job became the object of his friends' unjust criticism. His rebuttal to Zophar's harsh words appears in Job 12.

II. COMMENTARY

Get Off My Back!

MAIN IDEA: *Job responds to Zophar's attacks, asserting his innocence and affirming God's mysterious and sovereign ways with mankind, while verbally attacking his friends and building his case to present to God in court.*

A Job's Rebuke (12:1–6)

SUPPORTING IDEA: *Job rebuts Zophar's accusations by reaffirming his innocence and the mysterious dealings of God with mankind.*

12:1–2. Then Job replied with a lengthy response, one that spans three chapters (Job 12–14). **Doubtless you are the people, and wisdom will die with you!** When Job's friends died, he chided them, all wisdom would go with them. These were cutting and sarcastic words for his "expert" counselors. He castigated them for acting as if they had all wisdom and insight.

12:3. Job retorted, "**But I have a mind as well as you.**" He claimed that his thoughts and perspective should be heard as well. **I am not inferior to you.** His accusers held no monopoly on truth! Job repudiated their counsel by asking, "**Who does not know all these things?**" Their wisdom was commonly held by most people of that time. Job needed more than just advice. He needed insightful counsel, not empty words.

12:4–5. Exasperated and frustrated, Job poured out his anger toward them. Although he had become a **laughingstock** of men, he believed that he was **righteous and blameless**. This was also God's conclusion (Job 1:8; 2:3).

Yet Job missed the times when he **called upon God and he answered** (cp. Job 13:22; 31:35). His close counselors were **men at ease** who had **contempt** for those who fell into **misfortune** and whose feet were slipping. Instead of helping Job endure his affliction, his smug friends seized the opportunity to criticize him.

12:6. He argued his case, stating, "The tents of marauders are undisturbed." Even wicked, idolatrous robbers prosper. So how could his suffering mean that he was unrighteous? **Those who provoke God are secure—those who carry their god in their hands**. Prosperity does not mean a person is righteous, just as affliction does not mean a person is unrighteous. Thus, Job concluded that his friends must be wrong.

B Job's Ridicule (12:7–12)

SUPPORTING IDEA: *Job chides his friends that even the animals know that evil sometimes overcomes good.*

12:7. Job sarcastically instructed Zophar by saying, "**Ask the animals, and they will teach you.**" Since Zophar compared Job to a wild donkey (cp. Job 11:12), Job struck back by telling Zophar that he had much knowledge and instruction to gain from **the animals** and **the birds**. Specifically, Job's friends would learn that the righteous often do suffer and the wicked do succeed, contrary to what they had said. Even they knew God's sovereign reign and providential control over his creation.

12:8. Still chiding his friends, Job responded that they could learn from **the earth**. It would teach them the very same lesson. Often the righteous suffer and the wicked succeed in this world. **Let the fish of the sea inform you** of these basic life truths, he declared. They needed to be retaught.

12:9–10. Rhetorically, Job asked, "**Which of all these does not know that the hand of the LORD has done this?**" The implied answer is *none*. Everyone knew this, or should. And if everyone knew this, then what did that say about the three friends who did not know it? Job declared, "**In his hand is the life of every creature and the breath of all mankind.**" All things are in the hand of God (cp. Job 10:12). Job reminded his friends that his present afflictions were under the control of God's sovereignty, even though he was righteous and blameless. Job's strong, God-centered theology gave him a perspective which accepted from God both good and bad (Job 2:10).

12:11–12. Just as the **ear tests words** and **the tongue tastes food**, so Job had tasted the counsel of his friends and found it lacking. Nearly the exact phrase is quoted by Elihu in Job 34:3, meaning this may have been a proverb or an oft-repeated phrase of their day. The misleading advice of his peers provoked Job to ask, "**Is not wisdom found among the aged? Does not long life bring understanding?**" Both wisdom and understanding are presumed to be found in those who have lived a long life (cp. Job 8:8).

C Job's Reverence (12:13–25)

SUPPORTING IDEA: *Job acknowledges God's supreme rule over both rulers and nations.*

12:13. Despite the supposed wisdom of Job's know-it-all friends, gained through unreliable means such as personal experience and subjective mysticism, Job knew otherwise. He understood that **to God belong wisdom and power**. The man-centered reasoning of Job's counselors rendered their advice empty of godly **wisdom and power**. God alone has true **counsel and understanding**, Job emphasized. This was a strong indictment against the three friends who offered unsound **counsel** and had a distorted **understanding** of God, man, and suffering.

12:14. In an attempt to answer Zophar's questions about God's mysterious ways (cp. Job 11:7–8), Job affirmed that God's ways are past human understanding. **What he tears down cannot be rebuilt; the man he imprisons cannot be released.** God's power is irresistible and irreversible. What God chooses to do cannot be altered (cp. Jer. 1:10).

12:15–16. Job knew that whether God brings **drought** or flood, his sovereign will remains unhindered. To God alone belong **strength and victory** as the sovereign Lord over all the affairs of men. God's power cannot be resisted, and it leads to his own triumph no matter how great the opposition. Thus, both **deceived and deceiver** are under God's control. Captives and captors alike serve divine purposes.

12:17. As a further display of his divine sovereignty, God **leads counselors away stripped**. Even those who advise and direct others are proven to be helpless under God's all-controlling providence. In addition, God **makes fools of judges**, reversing their verdicts in order to carry out his eternal purposes. Not even judges, the strongest of men, can resist God.

12:18. Reversing the actions of the mightiest men, God **takes off the shackles put on by kings**. He liberates the captives, overturning the seemingly irreversible decrees of royalty. God **ties a loincloth around their waist** and leads them out to freedom.

12:19. Answering to no human being regardless of the position they hold in society, God **leads priests away stripped** of what power they possess if he so chooses. God has overthrown men **long established**, both kings and priests. The sovereign reign of God orders and directs all mankind, even those who hold the most honorable positions in the land.

12:20–21. God **silences the lips of trusted advisers**, confounding their limited insight, depriving them of good sense. He **takes away the discernment of elders**, showing his own discerning wisdom to be infallible and the wisest of men to be fools. Further, **he pours contempt on nobles** as he removes their honor. He **disarms the mighty** by overpowering them with weakness. Thus, counselors, judges, kings, priests, advisors, elders, nobles, and all the mighty (vv. 17–20) are unable to provide true understanding and sound counsel apart from God.

12:22. Yet God, all knowing and all wise, **reveals the deep things of darkness**. What appears as **deep shadows** to the most ingenious of men appears to God as **light**. What is incomprehensible confusion from earth's perspective is comprehensible order from heaven's perspective. This statement was, surely, a response to Zophar's earlier question, "Can you fathom the mysteries of God?" (Job 11:7a).

12:23. Not only does God determine the rising and falling of individual kings and emperors; he sovereignly decrees the destruction of their collective kingdoms and empires. God **makes nations great, and destroys them**. The future of any nation is in the hands of God; he reserves the right to cause them to flourish or fall.

12:24–25. Removing all restraints, God **deprives the leaders of the earth of their reason**, allowing them to suffer the penalty of their depravity (Dan. 4:28–37). He leaves them to wander through the **trackless waste** (cp. Job 6:18; Ps. 107:40) as kings without kingdoms. Like blind, drunken men, these rulers **grope in darkness with no light**. All discernment and ability to reason have been removed. They have been made by God to **stagger** without the ability to determine the way of God's will (cp. 1 Cor. 2:14).

MAIN IDEA REVIEW: *Job responds to Zophar's attacks, asserting his innocence and affirming God's mysterious and sovereign ways with mankind, while verbally attacking his friends and building his case to present to God in court.*

III. CONCLUSION

It's Not the Critic Who Counts

The following quote is attributed to Theodore Roosevelt, a man who knew what it was to face his critics: "It's not the critic who counts. Not the one who points out how the strong man stumbles, or how the doer of deeds might have done it better. The credit belongs to the man who is actually in the arena whose face is marred with sweat and dust and blood. Who strives valiantly. Who errs and comes up short again and again and again. Who knows the great enthusiasms, the great devotions, and spends himself in a worthy cause. Who, if he fails, at least he fails while daring greatly, so that his place shall never be with those cold and timid souls who know neither victory nor defeat."

Keep this perspective in mind the next time you are facing criticism. Most critics are sideline quarterbacks who have never known victory or defeat. Most have never been in the arena of faith, making an eternal difference. When your face is beaten and bloody from life's devastating blows, it is probably because you have been in the game, serving God and living for his glory, making a difference.

IV. LIFE APPLICATION

How to Deal with Criticism

1. *Examine your critics' counsel.* When you are suffering strikes, many people will offer counsel. You must receive criticism with a teachable spirit. Listen with an open heart, examining what is said. Evaluate it and consider carefully what has been spoken. Then determine whether it is true. Sometimes the criticism will be right on target. If so, God will use it for your correction and maturity. But at other times the criticism will not be true. It will miss the mark. In such cases it will actually steer you off course and bring you harm. Do not buy criticism just because someone is selling it. Every criticism must square with God's Word, his character, and his will.

2. *Examine your heart condition.* Look within your own heart and see if what your critics speak applies to you. Search your own heart by asking, "God, is there really sin in my life? Show me if I am wrong." The Bible states, "The heart is more deceitful than all else and is desperately sick; who can understand it?" (Jer. 17:9 NASB). It is hard to know your own heart. Only the Spirit of God can convict your heart and reveal your sin. The psalmist cried, "Search me, O God, and know my heart; try me and know my anxious thoughts; and see if there be any hurtful way in me, and lead me in the everlasting way" (Ps. 139:23–24 NASB). The natural tendency is to resist what our critics say. But we must open our hearts to the Lord and ask, "God, is it true in my life?"

V. PRAYER

Father, we praise you for your guidance in our lives. We thank you for watching over us as our lives are few in days and full of trouble. We ask you to give us patience with all those who seek to harm us. Lord, teach us to respond to them as you would respond. May we endure all persecution brought against us so that you will be glorified in all that we say and do. In Jesus' name. Amen.

VI. DEEPER DISCOVERIES

A. The Righteous (12:4)

"The righteous" (*saddiq*) is the person who has put his trust exclusively in God for salvation. The word itself means conformity to a standard, namely, the perfect holiness of God. It refers, first, to a positional righteousness, or the forensic right standing of man before God that only God can declare (Gen. 15:6). Likewise, it speaks of a practical righteousness before God, which is a progressive conformity to the character of God. Regarding this latter usage, this word means that a person's life is being lived in increasing conformity to the unchanging standard of God's own holy character.

B. Marauders (12:6)

"Marauders" (Heb. *shadad*) is found fifty-seven times in the Old Testament and is used of destruction (Prov. 11:3), the ruin of a country or city (Ps. 137:8; Jer. 51:55–56), and the destroyers of the city of Jerusalem (i.e., Babylon; Jer. 12:12). Here it refers to the wicked who, though they plundered the goods of others, were seemingly prosperous.

C. LORD (12:9)

"LORD" (Heb. *Yehovah*) is the personal proper name of God given to Israel, who knew it to be the "glorious and awesome name" (Deut. 28:58). This occurrence is the only one in the book of Job. Derived from the tetragrammaton (YHWH), *Yehovah* occurs 5,321 times in the Hebrew Bible and is the most frequently used name of God in Scripture. God was considered so holy that the name *Yehovah* was never to be said aloud. Instead, the vowel markings for *Adonai* were inserted to direct the reader of Scripture to say *Adonai* instead of *Yehovah*.

The meaning of *Yehovah* has been debated, but it is safe to infer that it refers to God's underived self-existence. The ancient Hebrews connected the word with *hava*, which meant "to be," as when God instructed Moses from the burning bush, "God said to Moses, 'I AM WHO I AM'" (Exod. 3:14). In this instance the divine name implies God's eternality, autonomy, independence, and immutability.

This divine name was often used in reference to God's covenants to Israel (Gen. 15:18; Deut. 7:9; Isa. 26:4). The name also signified God's personal relationship and nearness to his people: "I will take you as my own people, and I will be your God" (Exod. 6:7). It was to this name that the worship of Israel was to be directed (Amos 3:2).

D. Counsel (12:13)

"Counsel" (Heb. *esa*) means consultation, deliberation, or advice and was used to speak of aides who advised a leader or king. Moses was given counsel by Jethro (Exod. 18:19), Absalom was given counsel by Abithophel (2 Sam. 16:20,23) and Hushai (2 Sam. 17:4). More importantly God gives counsel (Isa. 19:17; Jer. 50:45) and frustrates the counsel of the wicked (Neh. 4:15). The word is found eight times in Job (5:13; 10:3; 18:7; 21:16; 22:18; 29:21; 38:2; 42:3).

VII. TEACHING OUTLINE

- A. Job's Rebuke (12:1–6)
  1. I am unimpressed with my friends (12:1–2)
  2. I am equal to my friends (12:3)
  3. I am mocked by my friends and by others (12:4–5)
  4. I am surpassed by my friends (12:6)
- B. Job's Ridicule (12:7–12)
  1. Inquire of the animal kingdom (12:7–8)
  2. Learn of the heavenly kingdom (12:9–10)
  3. Inquire of the aged men (12:11–12)
- C. Job's Reverence (12:13–25)
  1. God is over all things (12:13–15)
  2. God is over all people (12:16–25)

VIII. ISSUES FOR DISCUSSION

1. How have I recently been downcast or depressed by my circumstances?
2. How do I respond to criticism?
3. Do I examine my life objectively to see if the criticism I receive is warranted?
4. When criticizing others, do I exercise self-control and loving patience?

Job 13
Hanging On to Hope

Quote

"Hope can see heaven through thickest clouds."

Thomas Brooks

Job 13

I. INTRODUCTION

All the Hope of God

Alexander Solzhenitsyn was a man who knew how to hang on to hope. As a political prisoner in Russia for many years, he became an icon of perseverance through suffering for the cause of freedom. Forced to work twelve hours a day at hard labor while existing on a starvation diet, he became gravely ill. The doctors predicted his imminent death. One afternoon he stopped working, even though he knew the guards would beat him severely. He just could not go on any longer.

At that precise moment another prisoner, a fellow Christian, approached him. With his cane the man drew a cross in the sand and erased it. Instantly, Solzhenitsyn felt all the hope of God flood his soul. In the midst of his despair, that emblem of hope where Christ fought to win the victory over sin gave Solzehenitsyn the courage to endure that difficult day and the grueling months of imprisonment that lay before him. When we hang on to hope, we can go through anything.

Job, much like Alexander Solzhenitsyn, was also a man who underwent an excruciating trial in a hopeless situation. His spirits were sinking lower and lower. Death seemed to be the only way out. But in the midst of his despair, his soul was suddenly strengthened with hope—a renewed hope in God. Job said, "Though he slay me, yet will I hope in him" (Job 13:15). Despite his agony he found new hope in God and restored confidence in a positive future. Hanging on to this hope kept him going when he wanted to give up.

II. COMMENTARY

Hanging On to Hope

MAIN IDEA: *Job challenges Zophar to hear his defense, accusing him of using lies, and he expresses his desire to speak to God in order to prove his innocence.*

A Job's Defense (13:1–12)

SUPPORTING IDEA: *Job demeans his friends and prepares to present his case before God in court.*

13:1–2. As a witness to his own testimony, Job noted, "**My eyes have seen all this, my ears have heard.**" Although his friends treated him like a fool, Job had **understood** God's intervention in the lives of people and nations. "**What you know, I also know,**" claimed Job. He believed that he was not **inferior** to them in wisdom or insight (cp. Job 12:3; 15:17). Thus, what this terrible trio had spoken to him had provided no real help. Their grueling dialogue had been pointless.

13:3–4. Realizing the futility of continuing to debate with his friends, Job resolved, "**I desire to speak to the Almighty.**" Rather than face the counsel of his critics who deemed him guilty as charged, Job longed to **argue** his **case** with God. With God he would receive a fair hearing. Before God, Job would be fairly judged, unlike the three friends who smeared him **with lies**. In fury, Job lashed out at them, "**you are worthless physicians, all of you.**" Unlike physicians who diagnose and treat ailments, Job's friends were worthless, not able to diagnose his problem or render an effective treatment.

13:5–6. His friends had been **silent** during their first week with Job (2:13). He noted that it **would be wisdom** for them to be quiet again. The less they said, the better. Pleading for his friends to **hear** and **listen** to him, Job prepared to ask six rhetorical questions in which he challenged the competency of his friends to offer counsel as though they were speaking for God.

13:7. The first question Job asked was, "**Will you speak wickedly on God's behalf?**" Then he asked, "**Will you speak deceitfully for him?**" It is a serious claim to say that you speak for God. Yet it is far more serious to misrepresent God with wickedness and deceit by attributing to him actions and words that are misrepresentations. This was the charge Job brought against his friends.

13:8. Further, they viewed themselves as God's prosecuting attorneys, showing **partiality** as they attempted to **argue the case for God**. What proud presumption they had, believing God had appointed them for this and was using them to destroy Job. In reality, these questions revealed Job's desire for them to remain neutral.

13:9. Job asked his friends, "**Would it turn out well if he examined you?**" Job wondered if his counselors could withstand the same examination by God if they were the defendants. In reality, Job knew that no one can **deceive** God. Thus, these three friends would be exposed just like anyone else.

13:10–11. With confidence Job asserted, "**He would surely rebuke you if you secretly showed partiality.**" This charge was shown to be true when God's verdict was rendered (cp. Job 42:8). Each friend seemingly attempted to side with God and thus opposed Job. Continuing with the thought of his friends being placed under examination, Job wondered, "**Would not his splendor terrify you? Would not the dread of him fall on you?**" Even though they were filled with prideful arrogance as they looked down on Job, he reasoned that even they would experience terror and **dread** when no one could defend them (cp. Job 31:23).

13:12. Job concluded that their **maxims**—sayings worthy of memorization—were only **proverbs of ashes**. Their arguments should be burned and thrown into the ashes of the city dump. Their self-styled **defenses** of God's justice were **defenses of clay**. Job was probably still on the ash heap of the city dump as he spoke these words, and he may have held a broken piece of pottery as he said the second line (cp. Job 2:8).

B Job's Declaration (13:13–19)

SUPPORTING IDEA: *Job prepares himself to present his case of self-vindication before God's court.*

13:13–14. Having expressed a desire to present his case to God (Job 13:3), Job now prepared himself for such a heavenly court appearance. Again, Job asked his friends to **keep silent** so he could **speak** (cp. 13:5–6). He was willing to take the consequences for his words: **let come to me what may**. Job asked his friends, "**Why do I put myself in jeopardy and take my life in my hands?**" The risk of placing himself **in jeopardy** was one Job would take if he could authenticate his innocence. Why would he go to all this trouble to maintain his blameless character?

13:15. With unwavering trust in God, Job declared, "**Though he slay me, yet will I hope in him.**" Even if God were to kill Job for approaching him inappropriately, he would still trust in God to vindicate him of all charges. If God did not kill Job, this would demonstrate proof, he believed, of his own blamelessness. This stay of judgment would give him ample opportunity to **defend** his **ways** to God's **face**. But even if God did destroy him, he would still have a strong confidence in him and his vindication. Even the fear of death would not deter Job from claiming his innocence before God.

13:16. Job believed an appearance before God would **turn out** for his **deliverance** because he knew that **no godless man would dare come before him**. Unlike his friends, Job demonstrated a proper understanding of God. He knew that to enter into God's presence with unconfessed sin would mean certain death for the person standing on holy ground. Further, Job's willingness to plead his case before God was an indication that he was innocent. No one argues a case he does not believe he can win.

13:17. For the third time in this chapter, Job begged for the ears of his friends (vv. 6,13,17). He asked them to **listen carefully** so they could take in what he had to say since he had prepared his case. Obviously, as Job spoke, they were not listening but were preparing their next argument.

13:18–19. In confidence Job stated, "**I know I will be vindicated.**" Job was convinced that if he were given the opportunity, he would win his case before God. Boldly, Job asked, "**Can anyone bring charges against me?**" If someone could prove his guilt, he would **be silent and die**. In other words, if Job was guilty as charged, he was ready to pass away in silent shame. But he believed such an indictment could not be served against him.

C Job's Desire (13:20–27)

SUPPORTING IDEA: *Job pleaded with God to stop afflicting and terrifying him.*

13:20–21. Seeking vindication by presenting his case before God, Job prayed, "**Only grant me these two things, O God, and then I will not hide from you.**" Job sought to present his case before God if the Lord would follow through with two requests. The first request was that God would **withdraw** his **hand**. The second request was that God would **stop** the **terrors** which were **frightening** Job. If these conditions were met, then Job would meet with God by no longer hiding from him.

13:22. Growing in his desire for a court appearance before God, Job requested, "**Then summon me and I will answer.**" He longed for God to convene his heavenly court so the Almighty would make his case either for or against him. If God would not respond, then Job requested, "**Let me speak, and you reply.**" He would conduct his own hearing if God did not act soon. Either God would convene his court, or Job would convene his own.

13:23. Frustrated, Job asked, "**How many wrongs and sins have I committed?**" He wanted to know if his suffering outweighed the number of his sins. If Job only knew the number of sins that had caused his pain and grief, then he could possibly accept his suffering, or repent and change his life accordingly. This statement shows that Job, weary and worn down, was beginning to believe his friends' accusations against him. Accordingly, he asked God, "**Show me my offense and my sin.**" Job asked God to list the sins he had committed which had provoked the intensity of God's affliction.

13:24–25. Why do you hide your face? God appeared to Job to be hiding his face from him. Earlier he had stated that he was the one hiding (cp. 13:20). Why would God treat him like his **enemy**, he wondered. Like a **leaf** being blown around in the wind, or a piece of **chaff**, Job felt he was helpless and worthless before God, leaving him perplexed about why God even noticed him.

13:26. Growing in his exasperation, Job charged God, "**You write down bitter things against me and make me inherit the sins of my youth.**" He accused God of keeping a written record of his sins (cp. Ps. 25:7), like the records containing the crimes of a criminal. Job believed he must have received a delayed sentence for crimes he had committed earlier, perhaps long ago in his youth.

13:27. Job felt like a prisoner under maximum security confinement and strict surveillance. It was as if God had fastened his **feet in shackles** while keeping a **close watch** over all his paths. He could not escape God's imprisonment and all-seeing eye.

D Job's Despair (13:28)

SUPPORTING IDEA: *Job once more emotionally collapses, concluding that man's final destiny is death and deterioration.*

13:28. Job despaired, "**Man wastes away like something rotten.**" Through his many pains and hurts, he had learned that man is slowly decaying to nothing. Job believed he was disintegrating **like a garment eaten by moths**, a useless garment that would soon be thrown away.

MAIN IDEA REVIEW: *Job challenges Zophar to hear his defense, accusing him of using lies, and he expresses his desire to speak to God in order to prove his innocence.*

III. CONCLUSION

Hope for the Future

Some time ago the powers-that-be decided to build a hydroelectric dam across a valley in Maine where a small town had been situated for many years. The people were to be relocated and the town submerged under water. During the time between the initial decision to begin the project and the completion of the dam, this well-kept town began to fall into disrepair. One resident explained, "Where there is no hope for the future, there is no work in the present." When hope leaves, so does the inner drive to work and endure. But when there is hope, life flourishes.

This was the same battle that raged within Job's soul. The upward pull of hope makes us confident in God's eternal purposes, especially when our circumstances reveal nothing but disorder and confusion. It is in these difficult hours that we must remain convinced that God is in control, that he is ruling supremely, and that he is causing all things to work together for his glory and our good. This is the supreme hope of all believers even through the darkest nights.

IV. LIFE APPLICATION

How to Kindle Hope

How can we have hope, even in the darkest trials of life? How can we find the hope that enables us to remain strong amid the many difficulties of life? We can find hope by remembering several truths about trials.

1. *God sends trials.* This was certainly the case in Job's life. His painful trial originated before the throne of God. Its source was the will of God. So it is with us. We must remember that the supreme ruler of the universe sends trials our way according to his perfect plan for our lives.

2. *God uses trials.* God has a divine purpose for our trials. "God causes all things to work together for good" (Rom. 8:28 NASB). Knowing this theological truth inspires hope when we are enduring tough times. God is always working for his glory and our good, even in the most dire circumstances. No suffering is without its purpose.

3. *God controls trials.* No storm of life is ever out of control. God always defines the limits to which a trial may go. Though it may seem otherwise, even our most tempestuous ordeals remain under God's all-controlling hand. He is never any more in charge than in our trials.

4. *God removes trials.* No trial is without its end, at least for the believer. Weeping may last for the night, but joy comes in the morning. There will eventually come a break in the storm. According to God's perfect timing, this present trial will pass. It may be soon, or it may be later. It may be in this life, or it may be in the life to come. But this trial will pass. So we should have hope in God. He will eventually clear out this turbulence in our lives.

V. PRAYER

God, strengthen and increase our hope in you. Through every trial and difficult storm, may our faith remain focused and fixed on you. Cause our confidence in you to deepen and our assurance of your wisdom and grace to be unwavering. Our lives are in your sovereign hands. Work in us that which is pleasing in your sight. In Jesus' name. Amen.

VI. DEEPER DISCOVERIES

INIQUITY OR SIN (13:23,26)

"Iniquity" or "sin" (Heb. *awon*) means corrupt, twisted, bent, perverse, or crooked. Iniquity focuses upon our relationship to God. All sin is a self-defilement, a self-corrupting, a twisting of one's character, and a bending of one's integrity. To the degree that a person sins, he becomes a twisted creature within his own soul. When David sinned, he became unclean and dirty. Psalm 51:2 says, "Wash me thoroughly . . . cleanse me" (NASB). Psalm 51:10 pleads, "Create in me a clean heart" (NASB). David felt dirty because his sin had defiled and perverted him.

VII. TEACHING OUTLINE

A. Job's Defense (13:1–12)
   1. You say nothing new about God (13:1–2)
   2. You say nothing true about God (13:3–9)
   3. You will be reproved by God (13:10–12)

B. Job's Declaration (13:13–19)
   1. I will argue before God (13:13–17)
   2. I will be acquitted by God (13:18–19)

C. Job's Desire (13:20–27)
   1. God, grant my requests (13:20–23)
   2. God, answer my questions (13:24–25)

3. God, hear my heart (13:26–27)

D. Job's Despair (13:28)

1. Man decays like a rotten thing (13:28a)
2. Man decays like a moth-eaten garment (13:28b)

VIII. ISSUES FOR DISCUSSION

1. How can our hope remain strong in the Lord?
2. What forces would cause our hope to erode?
3. What factors would cause our hope to grow strong?

Job 14
Drowning in Deep Despair

Quote

"Despair is Satan's masterpiece; it carries men headlong to hell as the devils did the herd of swine into the deep."

Thomas Brooks

I. INTRODUCTION

Who Died?

Martin Luther, the reformer who began the Protestant Reformation, often suffered severe periods of depression. Not even the spiritual success of translating the Bible into the German language could cause these attacks to subside. Describing the extremity of his emotional state, Luther said, "For more than a week I was close to the gates of death and hell. I trembled in all my members. Christ was wholly lost. I was shaken by desperation and blasphemy of God." On another occasion Luther was experiencing deep despair. His wife came to breakfast one morning wearing a black armband. "Who died?" Luther asked. She answered, "With the way you have been carrying on around here, I thought God had."

At this point in the unfolding drama of Job, we see a man who was beginning to act as if God had died. As a result, he was showing signs of a depressed mental state. His once-resilient, resolute faith (Job 1:21) was weakening and wavering, and the emotional state of his soul was buckling as well. A severe period of depression had settled into his heart, leading to bouts of despair. Deep darkness was his close companion. It was in this time that Job turned to God in prayer.

This chapter contains Job's prayer offered at the end of the first round of the debates with his friends. Eliphaz, Bildad, and Zophar had addressed Job with their barbed counsel, and the suffering patriarch responded to all three with his claim of innocence. At the end of this first round of speeches, Job offered a soul-searching prayer to God (Job 13:20–14:22). This is the right response for any traumatized life.

II. COMMENTARY

Drowning in Deep Despair

MAIN IDEA: *Job sinks into the depths of despair as he ponders death, the finality of death, and the devastating aftermath as man's existence is permanently erased from the minds of both God and men.*

A Job's Anguish (14:1–6)

SUPPORTING IDEA: *Job suddenly descends into a desperate state as he questions life itself while remembering the certainty of death.*

14:1. Speaking from a depressed state, Job uttered, "**Man born of woman is of few days and full of trouble.**" Man—a reference to all mankind who is born of a sinful woman—is a sinner and experiences all the consequences thereof: a life of a few days in devastation and filled with trouble. Contrary to the advice of Job's friends, he declared that everyone experiences trouble, not just the wicked.

14:2. To illustrate his point, Job noted that **like a flower**, man's life **springs up** bursting forth with life, yet it quickly **withers away** as its life juices drain away with time (cp. Ps. 37:2; Isa. 40:6–7). **Like a fleeting shadow** that soon disappears with the rising and setting of the sun, man **does not endure**. David understood that life is like a shadow (1 Chr. 29:15; Pss. 102:11; 144:4).

14:3. Seeing the brevity and difficulties faced in this life, Job asked, "**Do you fix your eye on such a one?**" Job wondered if God would continue to watch over him, never allowing him out of his providential care. Further, Job wondered, "**Will you bring him before you for judgment?**" In his battered condition, Job asked if he would be leaving his earthly judgment for a heavenly judgment.

14:4. With a proper understanding of man's fallen condition, Job asked, **"Who can bring what is pure from the impure?"** Faced with his inability to be sinless, he acknowledged his corrupt condition yet was confused about why he was reaping such severe affliction. **No one**, Job exclaimed, is able to keep himself in a sustained state of sinlessness.

14:5–6. Job reminded himself that **man's days are determined**, fixed in the unchanging, eternal plan of God. Submitting to the sovereignty of God, he acknowledged that God had **decreed the number** of man's months, having **set limits** which man **cannot exceed** (cp. Eccl. 3:1–2). Then Job pleaded for God to **look away from him and let him alone** (cp. Job 10:20). He longed for relief from God's afflicting gaze and piercing presence **till he has put in his time like a hired man**. He requested a break from his pain before his short life ended.

B Job's Analogy (14:7–12)

SUPPORTING IDEA: *Job laments that the future of a tree is better than that of a man because a tree can sprout again after it dies.*

14:7–9. Job compared himself to a tree, and the tree came out better. **At least there is hope for a tree** because after it dies, it will sprout anew and live again. **If it is cut down, it will sprout again**. But not Job. Such future **hope** evaded him. **Its roots may grow old in the ground** and eventually die. **And its stump die in the soil**. Yet such appearances are deceitful: the tree awaits spring, so it can burst forth with new life. **At the scent of water it will bud**. The tree will detect **water** nearby and **will bud** like a new plant. Though the tree or plant may appear dead, life is still present, awaiting the proper time to rejuvenate.

4:10. By contrast, **man dies and is laid low** in the grave. He **breathes his last and is no more**. Job sensed no hope that he would live after death and see himself vindicated before God. Thus, a tree had more hope than he did after death. To Job, a person's death was final and irrevocable.

4:11. Job shifted the metaphor from a tree to water. He compared man to water that evaporates and is no more. **Water disappears** through evaporation into the sky, or **a riverbed becomes parched and dry** because no more water is flowing into it.

14:12. By comparison, **so man lies down** in death **and does not rise**. He has no hope of living again beyond the grave. This extinction is permanent. It lasts **till the heavens are no more**. Using still another metaphor, Job compared death to sleep from which man will not awaken. As those lying down to sleep in the grave, **men will not awake** but will remain unconscious in death. Men will not **be roused from their sleep**.

C Job's Advantage (14:13–17)

SUPPORTING IDEA: *Job contemplates the benefits that would be his if he were to die.*

14:13. Job longed for death as the only way to escape God's wrath that had been poured out on him in this ordeal. **If only you would hide me in the grave**. At least in the grave, Job would find relief. There, he asked God, **conceal me till your anger has passed**. Only the grave could provide escape from the divine fury Job felt. **If only you would set me a time** (i.e., a limitation for his time in death) **and then remember me**! Then surely God would call Job back to life, and this fiery trial would be over.

14:14. **If a man dies, will he live again?** This was the longing of Job's heart, a universal desire—the possibility of life after death (1 Cor. 15:51–58). **All the days of my hard service** (literally, warfare; his life is pictured as hard military service) **I will wait** upon God to raise me. Then change would come, Job believed.

14:15. After a period in the grave, Job believed, God would call him back to life, and he would **answer** him. God would long for the **creature** his **hands** had made to be restored to life. Job was confident he would be restored even if he died. He believed that God would not forsake him completely.

14:16–17. **Surely then**, after Job was raised, God would count his **steps**, but with a great difference when compared with his present life. Then God would not keep track of Job's sin and continue to punish him as God was now doing. When Job was raised, his offenses would be **sealed up in a bag**. God would cover his sin and then he would have a new start in life.

D Job's Agony (14:18–22)

SUPPORTING IDEA: *Job ponders his current state of suffering, cataloging his loss of any future earthly hope.*

14:18–19. Communicating with more metaphors from nature, Job referred to a mountain crumbling and washing away as picturing man's hope being eroded by God. **But as a mountain erodes and crumbles** by the powerful hand of God, **and as a rock is moved from its place**, so man's hope will be drastically removed by God. **As water wears away stones**, causing them to disappear, **and torrents wash away the soil** in a flash flood, **so you destroy**

man's hope, Job declared. His expectation of a positive future and even life itself had been worn out and washed away.

14:20–21. **You overpower him once for all** in death, **and he is gone** to the grave, Job said. **You change his countenance** as the flush of life leaves his face in death. You **send him away** to the grave. **If his sons are honored, he does not know it.** Death prevents a man from knowing his family's successes on earth. **If they are brought low, he does not see it.** Neither can a dead man know his family's losses and suffering.

14:22. **He feels but the pain of his own body** in the grave, unable to feel the pains of others. He **mourns only for himself** in death, unable to weep with his family when they weep.

MAIN IDEA REVIEW: *Job sinks into the depths of despair as he ponders death, the finality of death, and the devastating aftermath as man's existence is permanently erased from the minds of both God and men.*

III. CONCLUSION

Walking Around Half Dead

Park Tucker, former chaplain at the federal penitentiary in Atlanta, Georgia, told of walking down the street in a certain city feeling depressed and worried about circumstances in his life. As he walked along, he saw these words posted on the window of a funeral home: "Why walk around half dead? We can bury you for $69.50. P.S. We give green stamps."

Tucker said the sign struck him as humorous and helped put everything in right perspective. Why should *he* be walking around as he was, half dead, when he could be living life to the fullest? Many people are doing just that—walking around as if they are devoid of life. Such people are limping along with one foot in the grave. Only as a person keeps his focus on the glory and grace of God can he overcome such despondency and live victoriously.

IV. LIFE APPLICATION

How to Overcome Despair

How do we overcome despair and despondency? How do we rise above the many discouragements of life? A few points are worth noting.

1. *All suffering is temporal.* No matter how painful the ordeal we are undergoing, it will eventually pass. Even if it is lifelong, it will one day pass

away in death. So no matter what pain we are experiencing, there is relief ahead. The storm will subside. The night will turn to morning. A new day will eventually come.

2. *All suffering is useful.* God uses our trials to advance his kingdom. In Job's case, it was to shame the devil. So it is with all believers today. Suffering is never needless but always with divine design. God uses our tribulations to conform us to the image of Christ. They wean us off the world and cause us to live for eternity. Our trials teach us humility and dependence on God. They also prepare us to minister to other people in their sorrow.

3. *All suffering is Christlike.* The Lord Jesus Christ was a man of sorrows who was acquainted with grief. If we are to truly know him, we must enter into the fellowship of his suffering. Human pain identifies us with Christ, who knew adversity in this world. He lived with the cross before him and suffered under the most grueling death imaginable. As we undergo trials, we are actually being drawn closer to Christ, our suffering Savior.

V. PRAYER

Father, life is filled with turmoil, yet you reign in and over the lives of your people, constructing the circumstances in which we find ourselves. Remind us of the beauty of life. Teach us to number our days. Help us to use our lives for your glory as we rescue the perishing and care for the dying. In Jesus' name. Amen.

VI. DEEPER DISCOVERIES

A. Trouble (14:1)

"Trouble" (Heb. *rogez*) is a term used of both outer commotion and inner agitation. It is used only seven times in the Old Testament. Job used it in reference to the wicked (Job 3:17), his restless condition (Job 3:26), of all humanity born of woman (Job 14:1), of the raging of a horse in battle (Job 39:24), and thunder that proceeds from the mouth of God (Job 37:2). Isaiah used *rogez* of Israel's future enslavement (Isa. 14:3), and Habakkuk used it to express the wrath of God (Hab. 3:2).

B. Clean (14:4)

"Clean" (Heb. *tahor*) is an adjective that occurs ninety-four times in the Old Testament. It is a derivative of the verb *taher*. The word is used either in the material, ceremonial, or ethical sense. The pollution or spiritual contamination that enters the heart of man is impossible for him to clean in his own strength. Job asked, "Who can bring what is pure from the impure?" (Job 14:4). In contrast to the sinful pollution within man, God's words are absolutely pure (Ps. 12:6) and his eyes are "too pure to look on evil" (Hab. 1:13). The Lord alone can make sinful man clean (cp. Jer. 33:8; Ezek. 37:23).

C. Hard Service (14:14)

"Hard service" (Heb. *saba*) refers to a mass of persons and is often used of fighting and warring. It is also used to refer to a designated length of time given in service, especially warfare. Job used *saba* to refer to his time of heavy hardship and calamity (cp. Job 7:1; 14:14). Both Isaiah and Daniel used *saba* in the same sense (Isa. 40:2; Dan. 10:1). Job was serving his time of suffering upon the earth.

VII. TEACHING OUTLINE

- A. Job's Anguish (14:1–6)
  1. Man's days are few (14:1)
  2. Man's days are fleeting (14:2)
  3. Man's days are filthy (14:3–4)
  4. Man's days are fixed (14:5–6)
- B. Job's Analogy (14:7–12)
  1. A tree dies but sprouts again (14:7–9)
  2. A man dies and stays dead (14:10–12)
- C. Job's Advantage (14:13–17)
  1. God, hide my life in death (14:13)
  2. God, raise my life from death (14:14–15)
  3. God, cover my sin in death (14:16–17)
- D. Job's Agony (14:18–22)
  1. God, you destroy man's hope (14:18–19)
  2. God, you overpower man's life (14:20–22)

VIII. ISSUES FOR DISCUSSION

1. Do I properly understand the brevity of life?
2. Do I use all of my resources and time to further the glory of God?
3. Do I acknowledge the sovereignty of God in both the giving and taking of life?

Job 15

The Devil's Dirty Work

Quote

"It is a sad fact that the tongues of professing Christians are often all too busy doing the devil's work."

Donald Grey Barnhouse

Job 15

I. INTRODUCTION

A Double Fee

A young man once came to Socrates, the noted philosopher, to be instructed in oratory. The moment the young man was introduced, he began to talk in an incessant stream. This went on for some time until the great philosopher could stand it no longer. Putting his hand over the young man's mouth, Socrates said, "Young man, I will have to charge you a double fee."

"Why?" the young pupil asked.

"Because I will have to teach you two sciences," Socrates replied. "First, the science of holding your tongue; and then the science of using it correctly."

Job's three friends needed to learn this lesson. They needed to acquire the skill of holding their tongue and then to use it correctly. Less is more when it comes to the use of the tongue. Generally, the less said the better. But rather than limiting their words, Job's comforters only added to their many words. They were silent only long enough to reload their guns and fire their arguments back at Job with greater force.

This unfolding drama now comes to the second round of Job's dialogues with his three friends (Job 15–21). The entire time Job had been answering his friends, they were busy reformulating their same arguments. Instead of listening to Job, they appeared to be waiting for him to stop talking so they could relaunch their scathing attack. The only thing on their minds was correcting him. Eliphaz, Bildad, and Zophar were like selfish lawyers seeking to win their case. They should have been trying to restore and help a brother.

Round one of cross-examination was over, and now Eliphaz, who spoke first in round one, was the first to speak in round two. To this point Eliphaz had been the most sympathetic of the three counselors. But now even he became impatient with Job. What was initially a discussion turned into a full-blown dispute.

II. COMMENTARY

The Devil's Dirty Work

MAIN IDEA: *Eliphaz launches his second round of strong words against Job, maintaining that Job is suffering because of sin in his life.*

A Eliphaz's Denunciation (15:1–6)

SUPPORTING IDEA: *Eliphaz tells Job that he is acting foolishly.*

15:1–2. **Eliphaz the Temanite replied** in what was his second speech to Job. Unlike the first dialogue (Job 4–5) where Eliphaz patiently confronted Job, this time Eliphaz struck abrasively, asking, "**Would a wise man answer with empty notions or fill his belly with the hot east wind?**" This was no doubt a reference to earlier comments by Job to Eliphaz (Job 6:26). He accused Job of being a windbag who spoke **empty notions** from his **belly**.

15:3–4. Eliphaz believed that Job sought to **argue with useless words** and **speeches** that had **no value**. To him Job was all talk, no substance, all profitless platitudes. Later Job would admit that he had spoken words without knowledge (cp. Job 42:3). **But you even undermine piety and hinder devotion to God.** Eliphaz clearly saw Job's assertions as being the by-product of inward iniquities, secret though they were. Job's challenging words to God were hindering Job's relationship with God.

15:5–6. **Sin**, Eliphaz believed, was prompting Job's **mouth**. Surmising Job to be in a constant state of sin, Eliphaz believed sin had prompted Job's irreverent mouth and had given him **the tongue of the crafty**. Defending himself against Job's charges of speaking false accusations, Eliphaz pronounced, "**Your own mouth condemns you, not mine.**" He was convinced that Job's **own lips** were testifying against himself rather than against his friends.

B Eliphaz's Defamation (15:7–13)

SUPPORTING IDEA: *Eliphaz attacks Job's line of reasoning and his approach to life.*

15:7. Seeking to refute what he saw as weak wisdom from an arrogant source, Eliphaz sought to humble Job with a barrage of rhetorical questions, all assuming that Job believed he was more wise than his counselors and even God himself. Eliphaz asked, "**Are you the first man ever born? Were you brought forth before the hills?**"

15:8. Eliphaz asked, "**Do you listen in on God's council?**" This insinuated that Job believed himself to know the secret things of God, a counsel hidden from Job's friends. Then with biting sarcasm, Eliphaz interrogated Job by asking, "**Do you limit wisdom to yourself?**" Job's arrogance was so severe that Job, Eliphaz felt, believed no one else had wisdom—a charge that included God.

15:9. With belittling mockery, Eliphaz asked, "**What do you know that we do not know? What insights do you have that we do not have?**" These questions were accusations that Job believed himself to have more wisdom and insight than his friends. This was an illegitimate charge to be leveled against Job, who had only claimed a wisdom of the kind that his friends had (Job 12:3b; 13:2a). Never had he stated that he had a monopoly on true wisdom, as Eliphaz claimed.

15:10. Eliphaz noted that **the gray-haired and the aged are on our side, men even older than your father**. This argument reminded Job that he was relatively new on the scene and thus without wisdom. Eliphaz did not understand that age alone does not guarantee wisdom (Ps. 119:97–104).

15:11. Assuming that the aged acted as God's mouthpieces, Eliphaz asked the afflicted Job, "**Are God's consolations not enough for you, words spoken gently to you?**" To his friends Job had no right to question the counsel of his elders. Yet Eliphaz had assumed that the aged possessed God's wisdom, just as he had assumed that they had **spoken gently**.

15:12. Placing all the blame on Job, Eliphaz asked, "**Why has your heart carried you away, and why do your eyes flash?**" Eliphaz accused Job of losing his grip on reality, being carried away by his emotions. The fact is that Eliphaz, not Job, was the one not in control of his emotions.

15:13. Continuing his interrogation, Eliphaz wondered why Job vented his **rage against God** and poured out such words from his mouth. In reality, it was the irrational emotions of Eliphaz and his friends that had led them to assume that Job was suffering from the just retribution of God. Although at times Job was angry with God, it is clear that at this point he was frustrated and angry at his friends as well.

 Eliphaz's Declaration (15:14–16)

SUPPORTING IDEA: *Eliphaz accuses Job of being unholy and morally corrupt.*

15:14. The doctrine of human depravity was understood and taught by Eliphaz, although never applied to himself. He asked, "**What is man that he could be pure, or one born of woman, that he could be righteous?**" This depravity is found throughout the Book of Job (4:17; 5:7; 9:2; 14:4; 25:4) and will reappear as the dialogue continues. Job understood this truth that recognizes that all men are impure and unrighteous.

15:15–16. Repeating an earlier message (Job 14:17–19), Eliphaz noted that God **places no trust in his holy ones** (angels), nor **the heavens**, which are **not pure**. This being true, **how much less** trust does God place in **man, who is vile and corrupt**. Man is vile and corrupt, or filthy (cp. Ps. 53:3). So vile is man that he **drinks up evil like water**. As a person drinks water without any effort, so man imbibes evil without thought of God or his own well-being.

D Eliphaz's Description (15:17–29)

SUPPORTING IDEA: *Eliphaz assumes Job is wicked because he is suffering greatly.*

15:17. Drawing from his own experience, Eliphaz appealed to past tradition, forgetting that truth is superior to tradition. **Listen to me and I will explain to you; let me tell you what I have seen**. In other words, Eliphaz hoped to motivate Job to repent by ordering him to listen as he attempted to explain the reason for Job's suffering.

15:18–19. Job should know **what wise men have declared**. Appealing to past wisdom, Eliphaz declared that their counsel could be trusted since they were **hiding nothing received from their fathers**. This wisdom from of old, according to Eliphaz, was infallible and not open to revision or correction. To emphasize the superior wisdom of these ancestors, Eliphaz noted, these wise sages were those **to whom the land was given when no alien passed among them**, possessing pure traditions untouched by the philosophies and foreign traditions of alien peoples.

15:20. Eliphaz described the destruction of the wicked, attempting to move Job to repentance. Eliphaz noted, **All his days the wicked man suffers torment, the ruthless through all the years stored up for him**. This was conveyed to Job to cause him to consider the reason for his present torment. Again, the flawed theology of Eliphaz is evident—the false belief that if a person suffers, it must be because of sin. The judgment of God upon the wicked is so sure to happen that **the years** of suffering are **stored up**, or reserved for them (cp. Job 14:5).

15:21. Haunted by their own guilty conscience, **terrifying sounds fill** the wicked's **ears** as they fear suffering the terrors they have inflicted upon others. Then, **when all seems well, marauders attack** the wicked man without warning. These words were like an arrow in the heart of Job, since Eliphaz knew this very thing had happened to Job (1:13–19).

15:22. The wicked man **despairs of escaping the darkness**, which means there is no escape for the ungodly from suffering. In his godless madness, the wicked man believes he is **marked** out **for the sword**. Thus, the wicked man spends his days awaiting God's inevitable judgment.

15:23. Like a nomad, the ungodly man **wanders about** searching for **food** while he has time, because **he knows the day of darkness is at hand**. Hoarding food while he can, the unrighteous man knows a day will come when he will be unable to gather food because of his sin.

15:24–25. As he lives out his days, **distress and anguish fill** the wicked man **with terror**, as he awaits the judgment he deserves. Those who seek restitution for his malicious ways **overwhelm him, like a king poised to attack**. This terrible judgment awaits the wicked **because he shakes his fist at God** in defiance. Like a soldier poised for battle, the wicked in his contempt of God **vaunts himself against the Almighty**. What a foolish position Job had chosen!

15:26–27. Further, according to Eliphaz, Job was defiantly charging against God with a **thick strong shield**. Job, however, did not feel that he was battling God but instead that God was battling him (Job 7:20; 13:24). Continuing to paint a picture of the wicked man and to build his case against Job, Eliphaz noted the wicked's **face is covered with fat and his waist bulges with flesh**. In the Ancient Middle East, **fat** was a symbol of wealth and abundance and was often used to describe the wicked (Jer. 5:28) and the arrogant (Ps. 119:70).

15:28–29. Having robbed others of their possessions, the wicked man would find himself in **ruined towns**, living in **houses where no one lives**. Once the wicked man enjoyed the luxuries of affluence, but now he will **no longer be rich and his wealth will not endure**. No person can take his wealth with him, and his wealth would not be **spread over the land**.

E Eliphaz's Devastation (15:30–35)

SUPPORTING IDEA: *Eliphaz accuses Job of pride, which has brought on his troubles.*

15:30. The wicked person's deeds will bring him down to the grave where **he will not escape the darkness** (cp. Job 10:21–22). The **shoots** of his crops **will wither**, destroying his food supply, and **the breath of God's mouth will carry him away**.

15:31. Seeking to destroy any glimmer of hope Job had (cp. Job 13:15), Eliphaz warned, "**Let him not deceive himself by trusting what is worthless.**" Eliphaz refused to believe that Job had done nothing to warrant his suffering. He believed Job was trusting in his own vanity. For this, Eliphaz knew, the wicked would **get nothing in return**.

15:32–33. Having sown the seeds of sin in this life, the wicked **before his time . . . will be paid in full**. He will reap a bitter harvest. **Like a vine stripped of its unripe grapes**, or the **olive tree shedding its blossoms**, the unrighteous person will not flourish.

15:34. Mercilessly, Eliphaz indicted Job by saying, **the company of the godless will be barren**. Undoubtedly, this is a reference to Job's tragic loss of his children, as well as his wife, who was now **barren**. Corrupt people **love bribes** and, therefore, will find their **tents** consumed by **fire**. This is an allusion to the fiery destruction of Job's sheep and servants (cp. Job 1:16).

15:35. Eliphaz ended his scathing discourse with an illustration drawn from an unborn child. The wicked **conceive trouble** and give **birth to evil**. Between the conception and birth, **their womb fashions deceit**. Eliphaz ended his discourse the way he began it—by implying that Job was wicked and was suffering God's judgment against his godless lifestyle.

MAIN IDEA REVIEW: *Eliphaz launches his second round of strong words for Job, still maintaining that Job is suffering because of sin in his life.*

III. CONCLUSION

It Is Well with My Soul

Horatio Spafford was successful by all appearances. But in April 1871, tragedy struck as Spafford's business holdings were destroyed by the great Chicago fire. As Spafford struggled to recover from his financial losses, there was a brief period of joy in 1873 as the family welcomed their first son to their family of six. Yet tragedy struck again when the young child died.

D. L. Moody, the world-renown evangelist and close friend of the Spaffords, invited the family to join him in Europe on an evangelistic campaign. Horatio placed his wife and four daughters on the *Ville du Havre*, planning to follow a few days later. In the mid-Atlantic, the *Ville du Havre* was struck and sank. Only able to get information from newspaper headlines, Horatio was unaware if his family had survived. Finally, a terse telegram arrived which read, "Saved. Alone."

In great pain and agony, Spafford sailed for Europe to join his grieving wife. Then as the ship crossed the area where his four daughter's bodies rested in the water below, Spafford's mind was focused on a poem. Grieving yet confident in the sovereign plan of God, Spafford penned the venerable hymn, "It Is Well with My Soul." The Spaffords eventually settled in Jerusalem and started a new family. In the holy city they were greatly used by God as they spread the gospel.

If Horatio Spafford had been alive during the time of Job, the friends of Job would have concluded that his suffering was due to hidden sins. Yet Spafford's life, like Job's, illustrates the truth that suffering does not indicate unrighteousness in the life of the sufferer.

IV. LIFE APPLICATION

How to Comfort Others

Here are a few insights on how to be used in the life of a person who is hurting.

1. *Shorten your words.* Eliphaz erred because of his many words. He overwhelmed Job with his long-windedness. Ironically, Eliphaz charged Job with wordiness (Job 15:2), yet he himself was the most guilty of this offense. We should limit our words with people who are hurting. The more Eliphaz talked, the more harm he did. We must not be afraid of silence in consoling others.

2. *Season your words.* Eliphaz was too abrupt and abrasive. Some tact and diplomacy would have served him well. From this we should learn the need for kind words, which, according to Proverbs, are like apples of gold. At times we can be insensitive to the feelings of others. Let us be kind and tenderhearted in the words we express to others in their pain. Jesus knew not only *what* to say but *how* to say it (John 12:49–50). So must we.

3. *Scrutinize your words.* Part of the problem with what Eliphaz said was that he spoke incorrectly. The problem with his statement about the judgment of the wicked is that it is not always true. Many wicked people *do* go

through life apparently happy and successful. To the contrary, many godly people experience suffering and failure. Let us learn from this that we must know biblical truth if we are to be used as counselors to others. We must have a strategic grasp of Scripture if we are to be used by God. Let us measure our words by the truth of the Bible.

V. PRAYER

God, Lord of heaven and earth, teach us to restrain our lips from making hasty assertions about you and the events of life. How unsearchable are your judgments and how unfathomable are your ways! Teach us to trust and obey even when we do not understand what you are doing. In Jesus' name. Amen.

VI. DEEPER DISCOVERIES

A. Crafty (15:5)

"Crafty" (Heb. *arum*) is used in the negative sense by Eliphaz. *Arum* is an adjective describing one who is crafty or sly. Job used it earlier to describe those whose evil plotting God interrupts (Job 5:12). The most infamous usage of *arum* occurs in Genesis 3:1: "Now the serpent was more *crafty* than any beast of the field which the LORD God had made" (NASB, emphasis added). Here it is used by Eliphaz to describe the language with which Job chose to defend himself.

B. Wither (15:30)

"Wither" (Heb. *yabesh*) means to dry up and to be parched. It is used of vegetation that has lost the fluids needed to sustain life. *Yabesh* is at times used to describe the fragile state of human beings as they are compared to grass (cp. Ps. 90:6; Isa. 40:7–8). Job used it in the previous chapter to describe death (Job 14:11), and Eliphaz used the same term to describe God's judgment upon the wicked.

VII. TEACHING OUTLINE

A. Eliphaz's Denunciation (15:1–6)
  1. Your words are empty (15:1–2)
  2. Your words are useless (15:3)
  3. Your words are irreverent (15:4)
  4. Your words are deceptive (15:5)
  5. Your words are self-incriminating (15:6)

B. Eliphaz's Defamation (15:7–13)
   1. Wisdom did not begin with you (15:7–8)
   2. Wisdom is not limited to you (15:9–10)
   3. Wisdom comes from God to you (15:11–13)

C. Eliphaz's Declaration (15:14–16)
   1. Man is not pure at birth (15:14)
   2. Angels are not pure in heaven (15:15)
   3. Man is not pure in life (15:16)

D. Eliphaz's Description (15:17–29)
   1. I will tell you the source of wisdom (15:17–19)
   2. I will tell you the substance of wisdom (15:20–29)

E. Eliphaz's Devastation (15:30–35)
   1. The wicked trust vainly (15:30–31)
   2. The wicked die prematurely (15:32–34)
   3. The wicked live sinfully (15:35)

VIII. ISSUES FOR DISCUSSION

1. Do I speak God's wisdom or the world's wisdom?
2. Do I test my words before I speak?
3. Do I guard my mouth from slandering others?

Job 16

I Need Some New Friends

Quote

"If you really want to know who your friends are, just make a mistake."

Anonymous

Job 16

I. INTRODUCTION

Go Buy Another Dog

A few years back, Pepper Rogers, then head football coach at UCLA, was going through a terrible losing season. The media was attacking him. The alumni of the school were calling for his job. His friends were becoming more scarce by the day. Nothing seemed to be going his way. Week after week he was handed setbacks and defeats. Rogers did not think even his wife was encouraging him enough. He told her, "My dog is my best friend. But a man needs at least two friends."

"Go buy another dog," she replied.

Job could certainly relate to this. His friends and wife had turned on him, becoming his worse critics. Without any emotional support or encouragement, Job was left with only faultfinding and accusations. As his losses accumulated, he sank deeper and deeper into despair. But it was the harsh treatment he suffered at the hands of his so-called "friends" that most devastated him. Job was in need of some *new* friends. He needed someone to stand with him, not against him. He needed someone to build him up, not tear him down.

This is the focus of Job 16. He spoke out of a growing frustration with his friends and then with God. In this chapter we hear Job's second reply to Eliphaz—a lengthy retort that fills two chapters (Job 16–17).

II. COMMENTARY

I Need Some New Friends

MAIN IDEA: *As he spirals down emotionally, Job reaches deeper levels of frustration with his friends and God, and he longs for a mediator between himself and God.*

 Job's Frustration (16:1–5)

SUPPORTING IDEA: *Job charges his friends with speaking many empty words yet claims he would help them if their situation were reversed.*

16:1–2. **Then Job replied**, answering his critical friends. Specifically, he responded to the words of Eliphaz, who has just spoken in the previous chapter. **I have heard many things like these**. They had said nothing new in their many words. "**Miserable counselors are you all**," Job declared, referring to all three of them. They were no help to Job. In fact, they increased his misery with their misguided counsel.

16:3. Growing weary of their accusations, Job asked, "**Will your long-winded speeches never end?**" They were full of hot air. Their speeches would seemingly never end. Wondering what compelled them to question him unceasingly, Job asked, "**What ails you that you keep on arguing?**" At this point their absence rather than their presence would have been comforting. What was wrong with them that they continued haranguing him?

16:4. In an effort to change their perspective, Job called for his friends to put themselves in his place. With emotion-laden words he attacked their method of counseling. **I also could speak like you, if you were in my place**. If Job's friends were walking in his shoes, they would change their approach and soften their words. If he were in their position, he could just as easily **make fine speeches against** them as they had against him.

16:5. If the tables were turned, Job's **mouth** would **encourage** them. If he were a counselor, instead of shaking his head, an art of mocking and derision (cp. 2 Kgs. 19:21; Ps. 22:7; Lam. 2:15), he would seek to **comfort** and bring **relief**. Why would they not do the same for him?

B Job's Devastation (16:6–17)

SUPPORTING IDEA: *Job laments that God, like his friends, has turned against him.*

16:6–7. Not only was Job growing increasingly agitated with his friends (vv. 1–5), but his frustration with God was growing (vv. 6–17). In this miserable state of affliction, Job knew, whether he spoke or remained silent, his pain would **not** be **relieved**. Feeling tormented by God, Job addressed him, saying, "**Surely, O God, you have worn me out.**" Job felt that God had preyed upon him, like a hunter stalking an animal, devastating his **entire household**.

16:8–9. Like a fleeing fugitive who could not escape, Job could not alleviate his pain. God had **bound** Job with endless affliction that seemed to testify as a **witness** against him. To make matters worse, God, according to Job, was like a fierce enemy who assailed and tore at him. He believed that God had appeared to him as a blood-thirsty **opponent**, seeking his harm. In divine rage, he was gnashing his teeth and fastening on Job **his piercing eyes**. God, according to Job, had planned his destruction.

16:10–11. Adding to Job's growing frustration, men were opening their mouths to jeer at him. They were striking his **cheek in scorn**. His frustration was compounded as Job saw those around him, especially his friends, seeking to **unite together against** him. In his limited perspective, Job analyzed his current dilemma. Hopelessly, he concluded, God had turned him over to evil men and thrown him **into the clutches of the wicked**. This may be a reference to the invading Sabeans (Job 1:13–15) and the raiding Chaldeans (Job 1:17). Or it may refer to the verbal attacks of his friends.

16:12. Either way, Job remembered better days from his past when **all was well**. Against that backdrop, he lamented that God had **shattered** him, **seized** him **by the neck**, and **crushed** him. His happy days were over. Instead, God had brought painful days into his life. Believing himself to be divinely marked out for destruction, Job used graphic word pictures to describe God's assault on him. He said that God had **made** him his personal **target**.

16:13. His archers, a reference to his three friends, **surrounded** Job. There was no escaping their verbal attacks, as they came from every side. Job felt that he was specifically targeted by God to suffer. Remarkably, he was unaware of how true this proved to be (cp. Job 1:8). **Without pity**, God used these friends, like highly trained archers, to pierce Job's **kidneys** (i.e., his inner soul) with their pointed words and spill his **gall on the ground**.

16:14–15. Relentless in his attack, **again and again**, God burst upon Job as he rushed at him **like a warrior**. God, Job insisted, was enraged with a vicious desire to take his life. The effects of Job's affliction at the hand of God were clearly seen as he devolved into lower levels of despair. Nevertheless, he maintained his personal innocence. In humiliation, Job responded, **I have sewed sackcloth over my skin**. This outward act symbolized Job's inner grief and pain (cp. Gen. 37:29; Josh. 7:6; 2 Sam. 13:19; Ezra 9:5). Giving expression to his defeated state, Job **buried** his **brow** in the **dust**. He was a devastated and destroyed man.

16:16. Overwhelmed with waves of emotion, Job's **face** was **red with weeping** as **deep shadows** formed around his **eyes**. This physical appearance was due to his prolonged crying and sleeplessness.

16:17. Yet, through it all, Job contended that his **hands** were **free of violence**. This means that he was innocent of a major sin, like shedding the blood of others. Furthermore, his **prayer** was **pure**, meaning he was blameless and totally committed to God. This was the answer given by David about who could enter the Lord's sanctuary for worship (cp. Ps. 24:4).

C Job's Vindication (16:18–22)

SUPPORTING IDEA: *Job desires that a man would act as an arbitrator in heaven and present his case before God.*

16:18. There was a sudden shift in Job's tone as he longed for God to vindicate him. He cried out, "**O earth, do not cover my blood.**" To cover a victim's blood was an attempt to hide the evidence of a murderous crime (cp. Isa. 26:21). **May my cry never be laid to rest!** Although Job's body might be placed in the ground, he hoped his cry would not stop until he was cleared of all charges.

16:19. Although his outlook was bleak, Job remained hopeful that he would be vindicated before God. He stated, "**Even now my witness is in heaven; my advocate is on high.**" Apparently, Job was not referring to God as his advocate. Rather, this was a desire for someone to stand in heaven and plead his case before God. This person, Job believed, could defend him as a witness and argue his case as an advocate. If Job could not appear before God, as he hoped (cp. Job 9:1–4; 13:6–8,19), then perhaps a third party could.

16:20. Job longed for an **intercessor**, one who would appear on his behalf and represent him before God. Although Job was condemned by his earthly friends, this intercessor would be Job's heavenly **friend**. In representing Job before God, this mediator could cry **tears to God**, seeking Job's acquittal. With limited revelation Job could only hope for such an intercessor. Believers today know such a heavenly advocate and high priest represents them—the

Lord Jesus Christ (cp. Heb. 4:14–16). But Job did not know of such a perfect mediator.

16:21. Job argued that this intercessor should plead **with God as a man pleads for his friends**. Before the divine throne, this advocate-intercessor should intercede on his behalf and prove his innocence before God. This neutral third party would argue Job's case before the divine bench.

16:22. This part of the discourse concluded with Job slipping back into hopeless despair. He lamented, "**Only a few years will pass before I go on the journey of no return.**" He fully expected to die, although not until he had lived a few years. Then he would come, finally, to the point of death.

MAIN IDEA REVIEW: *As he spirals down emotionally, Job reaches deeper levels of frustration with his friends and God, and he longs for a mediator between himself and God.*

III. CONCLUSION

A Perfect Advocate in Heaven

Robert Murray McCheyne once stated, "If I could hear Christ praying for me in the next room, I would not fear a million enemies. Yet the distance makes no difference. He is praying for me." The fact is, Christ *is* interceding for his people, representing them before the Father in heaven. Christ is pleading our case before God, seeking our good according to his perfect will.

Job yearned for such a mediator to represent him before God and to plead his case. Such an advocate has now been revealed to us through the pages of the New Testament. God has provided the perfect advocate to represent us before himself in the person of the Lord Jesus Christ. The Bible says, "There is one God and one mediator between God and men, the man Christ Jesus" (1 Tim. 2:5).

A mediator is someone who intervenes between two parties to resolve a conflict. In man's fractured relationship with God, Jesus Christ is the only mediator who can restore peace between these two. This he did through his substitutionary death upon the cross. Accordingly, John wrote, "We have an Advocate with the Father, Jesus Christ the righteous; and He Himself is the propitiation for our sins" (1 John 2:1–2 NASB).

Even when family and friends desert us, we have an advocate with the Father, to intercede on our behalf—"a man, Jesus Christ" (1 Tim. 2:5). Even when others misjudge us and condemn us, we have a perfect mediator who knows us and loves us unconditionally.

IV. LIFE APPLICATION

How to Persevere

How easy it is for people to get caught up in the spiral of an emotional collapse. This is certainly where Job was, and it is where we can head if we are not careful. Frustration with our friends soon leads to frustration with God. How can we overcome such tough times when it seems like the bottom has fallen out and we are in danger of crashing?

1. *Stop listening to bad counsel.* Job was right in his assessment that his friends were "miserable comforters" (Job 16:1). He needed to turn a deaf ear to them because they were pulling him down. We also should refuse to listen to well-meaning friends who offer flawed counsel. If someone is giving you bad advice, stop taking in the devil's poison before it kills you.

2. *Start listening to good counsel.* Seek out people who know God and his Word, and can give you the mind of God in your particular situation. To seek the advice of any friend or counselor who is not rooted and grounded in God's Word is foolish. Seek direction only from someone who has been enlightened by God's Word and his Spirit.

3. *Stay anchored to God.* Rather than questioning God, we must trust him implicitly. We must accept whatever he brings our way as ultimately in God's plan for our lives. God is an immovable rock and refuge. As long as we remain fixed on him, we will rise above the storms. Believers must remain resolute in their dependence on God. We must always be in God's Word, riveted upon his glorious person and holy character. When we focus on God, we find the strength to persevere in his name.

V. PRAYER

God our Father, as we encounter the storms of life, show us the lessons you want us to learn. Break our pride and remove any arrogance that dwells within us. Give us clean hands and strengthen us so we may be a light in the darkness. Teach us to hope in you alone. In Jesus' name. Amen.

VI. DEEPER DISCOVERIES

A. Miserable (16:1)

"Miserable" (Heb. *amal*) means heavy labor (Eccl. 2:11) and toil, or the trouble and distress produced by such labor (Ps. 105:44). It represents sorrow, suffering, oppression, travail, or weariness (Gen. 41:51; Isa. 53:11). This is the kind of counselor Job's three friends proved to be to him. They caused him to look on the dark side of life.

B. Reproach (16:10)

"Reproach" (Heb. *herpa*) is a Hebrew noun that occurs seventy times in the Old Testament. It means to disgrace, scorn, shame, contempt, or rebuke. In some instances, *herpa* carries the idea of an accusation or blame that is cast upon someone (Jer. 31:19). In addition, *herpa* is used of a person who is despised (Gen. 30:23; Joel 2:17,19). It is used to describe the taunting of one's enemies (Ps. 119:42) and of the defamation of a person's character (Neh. 6:13).

VII. TEACHING OUTLINE

A. Job's Frustration (16:1–5)
   1. I have sorry comforters (16:1–3)
   2. I have sound advice (16:4–5)

B. Job's Devastation (16:6–17)
   1. God has inflicted me with pain (16:6–14)
   2. God has left me in ruin (16:15–17)

C. Job's Vindication (16:18–22)
   1. My innocence is clear (16:18)
   2. My acquittal is coming (16:19–21)
   3. My life is passing away (16:22)

VIII. ISSUES FOR DISCUSSION

1. Do I confront those who are undergoing severe trials?
2. Do I humble myself before God with a broken spirit as I am burdened with trials?
3. Do I surround myself with friends who offer sound counsel?

Job 17
When Hope Is Gone

Quote

"*Hope* can see heaven through the thickest clouds."

Thomas Brooks

I. INTRODUCTION

Hope Is the Medicine

A famous American cardiologist noted, "Hope is the medicine I use more than any other. Hope can cure nearly everything." Quoting another doctor, he commented, "If you lead a person to believe there is no hope, you drive another nail in his coffin." Hope is what keeps the human heart alive when all else has failed. Hope in a positive future can propel the weakest soul through any trial. When a person loses his confident expectation of a positive tomorrow, the inner drive to live and move forward is extinguished. It has been said that a person can live three minutes without air, three days without water, three weeks without food, but not one second without hope.

Job was at this point in his life. He had lost all hope that he could ever escape the pain of his suffering except through death. He had lost confidence that he would ever be vindicated by God. He was resolved that he would die in pain as a condemned man, suffering under God's hand of judgment. In fact, he felt so hopeless that he believed there was absolutely nothing he could do to change his situation. He had lost the will to live and was ready to die.

Job had taken his eyes off the Lord. He no longer believed that God was working for his good. To the contrary, Job believed that God was working against him. Is it any wonder that he had lost all hope? In order to turn around his dreadful despair, Job had to see God in a totally different light. This would not happen until later.

Chapter 17 of Job completes his second response to Eliphaz. This chapter makes a unique contribution to what seems to be an endless barrage of words. Here, at the end of this chapter, we discover that Job's hope is in God and that his confidence in a positive outcome is all but extinguished. This is what trust in the Lord looks like in a person's life when hope is gone.

II. COMMENTARY

When Hope Is Gone

MAIN IDEA: *Job loses all hope that God will deliver or vindicate him, and he sinks deeper into despair.*

A Job's Regression (17:1–2)

SUPPORTING IDEA: *Job slips into further emotional decline as he considers his hopeless situation.*

17:1. Exasperated and losing the fight for his life, Job felt that he could not continue in his present state. He lamented, "**My spirit is broken.**" Believing himself to be dying before his time, he agonized, "**My days are cut short.**" He was convinced that he was dying at an early age. The physical affliction by itself would have been enough to kill anyone. But his pain was compounded by the harsh words of his wife and friends.

17:2. These so-called friends—Eliphaz, Bildad and Zophar—were **mockers** who sought to **surround** Job and drain him of all hope with their depressing counsel. **Their hostility**, or rebellion, demonstrated to the discerning eyes of Job an unbridled spirit that refused to live in submission to God.

B Job's Request (17:3–5)

SUPPORTING IDEA: *Job asks God to vindicate him.*

17:3. Job requested, "**Give me, O God, the pledge you demand.**" Job was asking God for some authentication to verify his innocence. **Who else will put up security for me?** Job was asking, "Who else but you, God, can prove me to be right?" Thus, Job was asking God for a guarantee that he was right and not guilty of the sins for which he was apparently being punished.

17:4. In Job's reasoning, only God's testimony could change the minds of his three friends. God, it seemed to Job, had **closed their minds to understanding**. Their assumptions about Job's spiritual state and their unwise counsel proceeded from ignorance, he believed. Because God had blinded the eyes of his friends, Job believed that God would **not let them triumph**.

17:5. Seeking to prove his case to his friends, Job quoted this proverb: **If a man denounces his friends for reward, the eyes of his children will fail**. In other words, if Job's friends were denouncing him so they might receive a reward, they had better be careful. The children of that judgmental man would become blind. If he was indeed innocent, their charges could result in great harm to their families. Job was becoming increasingly frustrated with his friends, who, he believed, were selfishly seeking his reward, or possessions.

 Job's Reproach (17:6–9)

SUPPORTING IDEA: *Job laments his becoming an object of derision, and he blames God for his situation.*

17:6. The frustration of Job again shifted from his friends to God, as in the previous chapter. Job indicted the Lord, saying, "**God has made me a byword to everyone.**" To his peers Job had become a "proverb," or an object lesson of shame to his countrymen. He was the object of taunting and derision, one **in whose face people spit**. His friends despised him in his sad state, kicking him while he was down.

17:7–8. Deteriorating under his affliction, Job lamented that his eyesight had **grown dim** and his loss of weight made his bodily **frame** look like a **shadow** (cp. Job 16:8; 19:20). Physically, Job was deteriorating. His vision was blurred; his body was bent over. **Upright men are appalled at this**, meaning the righteous were stunned to see the physical problems suffered by Job. This suffering was so severe that the **innocent** observers were **aroused against the ungodly**. This is probably a reference to Job's friends.

17:9. **Nevertheless**, Job would not surrender to his friends. In a brief moment Job rallied his heart before crashing back down again. He reasoned, "**The righteous will hold to their ways.**" Believing himself to have **clean hands**, Job desired to **grow stronger**.

D Job's Resignation (17:10–16)

SUPPORTING IDEA: *Job resigns himself to death as he considers the hopeless circumstances of his suffering.*

17:10. Job proceeded to castigate his unhelpful counselors. He attacked his friends by saying, "**But come on, all of you, try again! I will not find a wise man among you.**" Job invited his friends to continue in their assaults, knowing that not one of them had proven himself to be a wise man.

17:11. Job saw his death as inevitably approaching and observed that his **days**, **plans**, and **desires** would never come to pass. He would die prematurely with unfulfilled plans and desires. All hope was dashed without any possibility of restoration.

17:12. Accusing these self-appointed experts of having no discernment between right and wrong, Job noted, "**These men turn night into day.**" That is, they called black, white and white, black. They called wrong, right and right, wrong. They inverted reality. These friends predicted **in the face of darkness** that **light** was **near**, meaning they promised all would turn out well for Job if he would only repent.

17:13–14. Job believed the darkness of sheol (i.e., death) was imminent and that he would soon make his **bed in the darkness**. He was convinced he would die before he was vindicated. Job moaned that there was no real hope for him. Having lost his entire family with the exception of his wife, he noted that his closest family relations were now to be the **corruption** and the **worm** of the grave.

17:15–16. In his despair, Job asked, "**Where then is my hope? Who can see any hope for me?**" He had no hope left. He was a helpless man who was overwhelmed with the hopelessness of his situation. Hope, in Job's mind, would **go down to the gates of death** and **descend together** with him **into the dust**. Hope, he believed, would die with him and be buried with him. This discourse ended with no confidence in Job's mind that he would be rescued from his pain and despair.

MAIN IDEA REVIEW: *Job loses all hope that God will deliver or vindicate him, and he sinks deeper into despair.*

III. CONCLUSION

Cape of Good Hope

Years ago the southern tip of Africa was called the Cape of Tempests. Its choppy waters, swirling seas, and adverse weather conditions caused sailors great anxiety, and it took many lives to a watery grave. But a certain Portuguese sailor, determined to find a safer route through those seas, discovered a calmer passage around this promontory. This new route was named the Cape of Good Hope.

This is what Job needed to discover in his life. He found himself in the swirling waters of his stormy trial, overwhelmed and hopeless. He thought he would be taken to his grave. Job needed a new route to travel through these unchartered waters, one that would give him a good hope. This present storm might not immediately subside, but the turbulence within his heart certainly could. He could know peace if he recaptured hope. But in order for this to happen, Job had to shift his focus to God. If Job could see God working positively through this trial, then he would have hope for the future.

Maybe that is what you need today. Maybe your greatest need is to see God working in your present crisis. Maybe you need to see him working for your eternal good. Take your eyes off your circumstances. Do not look at God as if he were indifferent toward you. See God as he is. See God working in your trial, behind the scenes, for his glory and for your good. If you will see God this way, great will be your hope. A restored hope will reroute you from the "Cape of Tempests" to the "Cape of Good Hope."

IV. LIFE APPLICATION

How to Strengthen Hope

How can your hope be strengthened? The key is to focus your gaze on God, not on your circumstances. As you look to God, see him as working for your good. Meditate on the following three important aspects about God. These will inspire and replenish hope.

1. *Focus on God's sovereignty.* God remains in control over all of life. He has never relinquished his government over the earth. As Lord over all, God controls the storms of life, just as he directs the peaceful seasons. Lift up the eyes of your heart and behold your God. "The LORD has established His throne in the heavens, and His sovereignty rules over all" (Ps. 103:19 NASB). "Our God is in the heavens; He does whatever He pleases" (Ps. 115:3 NASB). Even in the midst of your trial, God remains in charge, ruling and reigning.

2. *Focus on God's wisdom.* God executes his sovereignty with perfect wisdom. He knows what is best for your life. He does not make mistakes. He knows exactly what you need. He knows precisely what you can endure. He knows how to use this trial for your greatest good. Nothing can catch him unaware. He has perfect plans to take you safely through your difficulty.

3. *Focus on God's love.* This God who controls your storm also loves you with a perfect love. He has your best interests in mind. He would do nothing to harm you. Like a surgeon who makes an incision only to heal, so God allows us to undergo his scalpel, but only for our good. God's love is unchanging and is never stronger than when we are experiencing disappointment and pain.

V. PRAYER

God, strengthen our hearts when hope runs thin. Replenish our confidence in your sovereign providence. Teach us to accept what you choose to bring into our lives. May we sense your hand upon us, always working in our lives for your glory and our good. Undergird us with your grace. In Jesus' name. Amen.

VI. DEEPER DISCOVERIES

Grave (17:13)

"Grave" (Heb. *sheol*) occurs sixty-six times in the Old Testament and is a reference to the realm of the dead, the grave, and the underworld. Both the righteous (Gen. 37:35) and the unrighteous (Num. 16:30) will go to sheol. People enter sheol because it is God who brings them there (1 Sam. 2:6). It is a place of man's conscious existence (Ps. 16:10) from which no one will return (Job 17:14–16). The New Testament equivalent is not the Greek word *gehena* but *hades* (cp. Matt. 11:23, where Jesus quotes Isa. 14:13–15). The body of every person will go to sheol, although all souls will not enter into the same final destiny.

VII. TEACHING OUTLINE

A. Job's Regression (17:1–2)
  1. My life is over (17:1)
  2. My friends are overwhelming (17:2)

B. Job's Request (17:3–5)
  1. God, show me to be right (17:3)
  2. God, show them to be wrong (17:4–5)

C. Job's Reproach (17:6–9)
  1. God has made me suffer scorn (17:6)
  2. God has made me suffer sickness (17:7)
  3. God has made me suffer stigma (17:8–9)

D. Job's Resignation (17:10–16)
  1. He was resigned to defeat (17:10–12)
  2. He was resigned to death (17:13–16)

VIII. ISSUES FOR DISCUSSION

1. How have you found yourself discouraged in the past? Did you find yourself losing hope? Give a specific example.

2. How can your hope be renewed when it becomes weak? What steps can you take to have your hope restored?
3. Do you have friends who encourage you when you are down? How do they lift your spirits?
4. How can you inspire hope in others?

Job 18
Death: A Very Grave Subject

Quote

"Just as the tree cut down, that falls
To north or southward, there it lies;
So man departs to heav'n or hell,
Fix'd in the state wherein he dies."

Isaac Watts

Job 18

I. INTRODUCTION

Abandoned in Death

Voltaire, the French philosopher of the eighteenth century, was lying on his deathbed. Addressing his doctor, the bitter author said, "I am abandoned by God and man. I will give you half of what I am worth if you will give me six months' life." The doctor replied, "Sir, you cannot live six weeks." To which Voltaire responded, "Then I shall go to hell, and you will go with me." Soon thereafter, he died in a Christless state and entered hell. The death of the wicked is never a pretty sight.

Such a tragic way to die. Yet this is precisely how countless souls pass from this life to the next. The wicked perish without hope because they die without God. Know God, know hope. No God, no hope. Sinners without God have nothing to hang on to when encompassed by death. Far worse, they have no one to hang on to them—no Savior, no Redeemer, no Conqueror of death.

This is how Bildad believed Job would face death—alone. He was convinced that Job, as one of the wicked, would die in empty despair. Bildad saw that Job was suffering, and he concluded that Job had lived a life of hidden sin that was now being exposed by God. Unless he repented, Job was sure to die the death of the wicked. He was certain to perish without hope and without help from God. So, in order to arouse a confession of sin from Job, Bildad described for his friend the awful death of sinners. Such would be Job's ending in this world, he concluded, if he did not repent of the sin that had brought such severe treatment from God.

The truth is that the wicked *do* die a horrible death. Bildad was correct in this description. But Job had not sinned grossly against God. He would not face such a terrible fate in the end. Job 18 records Bildad's second speech to Job, a discourse in which he describes the death of the wicked.

II. COMMENTARY

Death: A Very Grave Subject

MAIN IDEA: *Bildad surmises that the wicked will die without hope and they will not escape God's judgment.*

A Bildad's Denunciation (18:1–4)

SUPPORTING IDEA: *Bildad further rebukes Job for reacting unreasonably to his counsel.*

18:1. Growing more perturbed by the moment, **Bildad the Shuhite** replied to the self-defense excuses offered by Job. This was Bildad's second time to address Job, and he became even more pointed and abrupt in this address.

18:2. Bildad asked, "**When will you end these speeches?**" He was agitated that Job would not stop talking. Of course, the same could be said of Bildad. **Be sensible, and then we can talk.** If only Job would become reasonable and listen to Bildad's counsel, they could have a forum to talk. But as long as Job persisted in his lengthy defenses, they could not dialogue. Job needed to listen and not talk.

18:3. Bildad queried, "**Why are we regarded as cattle and considered stupid in your sight?**" Apparently, he resented the implication made by Job earlier (Job 12:7–9) and rebutted this previous insinuation. Sarcastically, Bildad rebuked Job for his arrogant self-righteousness. Bildad could certainly dish it out, but he had difficulty taking it.

18:4. Pointing to Job's outbursts of rage, Bildad asked, "**You who tear yourself to pieces in your anger, is the earth to be abandoned for your sake?**" Earlier Job had stated that God had torn Job in his anger (Job 16:13). But Bildad could not let that statement go unchallenged. It was actually Job who was destroying his own life; this was not God's doing. **Or must the rocks be moved from their place?** This question implied, Would God move everything just for Job? *No* is the implied answer. Job, not God, would have to change his tune.

B Bildad's Description (18:5–21)

SUPPORTING IDEA: *Bildad details the awful death of the wicked because he believes that Job is suffering for his sin.*

18:5. Bildad launched into a long discourse on the terrible death of the wicked, a description that will extend through the end of the chapter. Like a candle suddenly extinguished, **the lamp of the wicked is snuffed out** in death, Bildad claimed. Job's flickering life, symbolized by a lamp, would blow out (Job 21:17). Such an end would result in complete darkness (i.e., uncertainty, confusion, and despair). With obvious allusion to Job, Bildad said, **the flame of his fire stops burning**. His life would soon end if he did not repent.

18:6. **The light in his tent becomes dark** when death comes for the wicked, leaving him disoriented and lost. **The lamp beside him**, representing his life, **goes out**, resulting in total darkness and disorientation when his life is snuffed out.

18:7. **The vigor of his step is weakened**, leaving the wicked without any strength. He loses all strength and energy with which to press on in life. Surely, this sudden and shameful end awaited Job. **His own schemes throw him down**, or he would become trapped by his own conniving plans. He could not escape a terrible death, no matter how smart he pretended to be.

18:8–9. **His feet thrust him into a net**, like one used to catch birds (Prov. 1:17). Surely the wicked are in great danger before God, certain to be caught in their wickedness. **He wanders into its mesh** (i.e., the covering over a pit) and is ensnared in divine judgment. **A trap seizes him by the heel** so that he cannot escape. Such an awful death was inevitable and unavoidable for the wicked. **A snare holds him fast**, making death inescapable for the ungodly.

18:10–11. **A noose is hidden for him on the ground.** Although the wicked cannot see their own end, it is near. No matter what Job did, he would be ensnared, Bildad warned. A trap was in Job's **path**, a pitfall into which he would fall and from which he could not escape. With such a horrible fate awaiting Job, Bildad cautioned, **terrors startle him on every side**. How could he live with such a terrible death that dogs **his every step**. It was as if Job were hunted prey waiting to become a victim.

18:12. Calamity was Job's stalking pursuer and was **hungry** for him, waiting to spring on him without warning. **Disaster** was ready for him when he fell, poised to pounce upon him to devour him and take him down to the grave.

18:13. When the wicked goes down to death, **it eats away parts of his skin** as his corpse rots in the earth. This alluded to Job's skin problem. **Death's firstborn devours his limbs**. This is a figurative expression indicating that a deadly disease would consume Job's body in death.

18:14. When death comes for the wicked person, **he is torn from the security of his tent**. He is removed suddenly, forcibly, from his home. He is **marched off to the king of terrors**, consigned to the place of the dead. Death is personified as a reigning king, full of terrors, who cannot be resisted or evaded.

18:15. As with God's judgment on the wicked at Sodom and Gomorrah, so it is with the end of all the wicked. **Fire resides in his tent**, destroying his home and everything in it. **Burning sulphur is scattered over his dwelling**, raining down divine wrath upon the ungodly. The implications were clear: Job was suffering because of sin in his life, and such a terrible fate surely awaited him.

18:16–17. As if a once-flourishing tree, the **roots** of the wicked **dry up below**. His much-deserved death is pictured as the death of a tree. **His branches wither above**, signifying the death of his descendants who would follow (Isa. 11:1,10). In the death of the wicked, the memory of him perishes from the earth. He leaves no good influence behind. Thus, all remembrance of him fades because he has no heirs or a lasting legacy. He has no name in the land that is thought of positively—only shame.

18:18–19. He is driven from light into darkness. No one remembers a wicked person, like Job, who was already in the darkness of death (Job 12:25; 18:5–6), Bildad reasoned. In such a state, the ungodly were **banished from the world** by being sentenced to the grave. In his death, the wicked **has no offspring or descendants among his people**. This loss is because his heirs are removed from him even before his death. There is probably an allusion here to the loss of Job's ten children, further indicting him as being wicked. For the ungodly man, there was **no survivor where once he lived**. He dies alone without any family.

18:20. The only good influence the wicked will leave behind is the warning that those who follow him along these same evil paths should expect a similar fate. **Men of the west are appalled at his fate**, so much so that they would be jolted to pursue a different course of action. Likewise, **men of the east are seized with horror** at the sight of the death of the wicked. Surely they would follow a path of righteousness, having witnessed his horrible death.

18:21. Surely such is the dwelling of an evil man, a horrific ending to such a wasted and useless life. **Such is the place of one who knows not God.** It is a place of an ignominious death and a forgotten life. This is because the wicked have no intimate knowledge of God.

MAIN IDEA REVIEW: *Bildad surmises that the wicked will die without hope, and they will not escape God's judgment.*

III. CONCLUSION

A Difference in Death

Just before he died, F. B. Meyer, the great British preacher of the nineteenth century, wrote a perceptive note to his wife. "Dear, I have just learned to my surprise that I have only a few days to live. It may be that before this reaches you, I will have entered the Palace. We shall meet in the morning."

London had seldom witnessed such a funeral. As the service began, the people in the audience rose to their feet with bowed heads. To their surprise, the organ sounded the triumphant notes of Handel's "Hallelujah Chorus." In the death of a believer, could there be any other response than such a note of celebration? A faithful soldier of the cross had fought valiantly and victoriously and had entered into the king's presence.

This is the difference between the death of the godly and the wicked. One death is triumphant, the other tragic. One life ends in victory, the other in defeat. Bildad's words in this chapter should cause everyone to pursue God and his Son, Jesus Christ, who alone has conquered death.

IV. LIFE APPLICATION

How to Be Gentle and Discerning

In considering these words from Bildad, several words of application should be made. How can we live out this chapter? We learn from the negative example of Bildad two important lessons.

1. *Be gentle.* When counseling those who are undergoing suffering, believers must be gentle. Bildad had lost his patience with Job, becoming

increasingly insensitive with each discourse. The tone of his rhetoric was wrong. *What* Bildad said was wrong, and *how* he said it was wrong. His voice, especially in these opening verses, was too stern and condescending. Rather than extending sympathy, Bildad spoke harshly to his hurting friend. As we speak to others, remember, it is not only *what* we say but *how* we say it that matters.

2. *Be discerning.* God's people must also be discerning when counseling those who are enduring trials and tribulations. Bildad concluded that Job was suffering because of his sin. While Bildad's description of the wicked in their death is correct, it was delivered to the wrong person. Bildad should have been more discerning in his remarks. So must all believers be. As believers, we must not jump to conclusions about others in our counseling. We must show caution in what we say, not automatically assuming the worst.

V. PRAYER

Father, thank you for the difference that you make in our lives, not only in life, but also in death. Thank you that Christ has conquered death and that in him, we have his victory over the grave. Teach us to number our days that we may present to you a heart of wisdom. May we always live with an eternal perspective, ready to meet death at any moment. In Jesus' name. Amen.

VI. DEEPER DISCOVERIES

A. Calamity (18:12)

"Calamity" (Heb. *eyd*) means destruction, ruin, or disaster. Of the twenty-four times this word is used in the Old Testament, each instance is in a poetical section. This word expresses the devastation and eternal ruin that awaits the wicked when they die.

B. Horror (18:20)

"Horror" (Heb. *sa'ar*) means a terror or a tempest. The word is used only three other times in the Old Testament, twice for horror (Ezek. 27:35; 32:10) and once for a storm (Isa. 28:2). This speaks of the stormy consternation, disruptive charge, and unrest that accompany the death of the wicked.

C. Wicked or Evil (18:21)

"Wicked" or "evil" (Heb. *'avval*) means an unrighteous person, a wrongdoer, or an unjust person. It refers here to one who does not know God and does not pursue God's holiness. Such a person is marked by ungodliness, or failure to be conformed to the character of God.

VII. TEACHING OUTLINE

- A. Bildad's Denunciation (18:1–4)
  1. Be silent (18:1–3)
  2. Be still (18:4)
- B. Bildad's Description (18:5–21)
  1. The wicked are like a light extinguished (18:5–6)
  2. The wicked are like an animal ensnared (18:7–10)
  3. The wicked are like a criminal entrapped (18:11–14)
  4. The wicked are like a tree uprooted (18:15–21)

VIII. ISSUES FOR DISCUSSION

1. Are you gentle and discerning with those who disagree with you?
2. Do you need to respond to others in a more Christlike manner?
3. What kind of hope do you have as you think about the certainty of death?

Job 19

A Faith That Will Not Break

Quote

"Faith does the same against the devil as unbelief does against God."

John Bunyan

Job 19

I. INTRODUCTION

A Lesson in Faith

A man was attempting to cross Canada's St. Lawrence River in the dead of winter. Unsure if the ice would hold him up, he first tested it by cautiously placing one hand on it. The ice held firm. Then he got down on his knees and began crawling across it, fearful that the ice might crack and drop him into the icy waters. Again, the ice held firm. When he got to the middle of the frozen river, he was trembling with fear as he knew it could break at any moment and he would be pulled below the frozen surface. Then, suddenly, he heard a loud noise that sounded like the ice breaking.

A team of horses bolted onto the ice, pulling a wagon loaded with firewood. While he sat there on all fours, the wagon passed him. He realized that if the ice were solid enough to hold a team of horses with a loaded wagon, it was more than sufficient to hold him until he was safely on the other side.

This is the place where Job found himself. He was at the breaking point, a place where his faith appeared to be ready to collapse under the weight of his trials. His debate with his three friends had reached fever pitch, as he felt their fiery condemnation. But what is worse, he felt abandoned by God. If ever there were a time when his faith was faltering on the brink of failure, this was the time. Satan had wagered God that this breaking point would come. But God had declared that Job would not deny him. His saving faith might bend, but it would not break.

This nineteenth chapter records the strength of Job's faith while under severe pressure. Under the assault of the words of his friends and suffering the pain of his adversity, his faith held strong, just as God had said it would. In the midst of his despair, his personal confidence in God was renewed. At this moment in his ordeal, Job refocused on God. It was his deep conviction about God, whom he believed he would see on the last day, that pulled him through the storm.

II. COMMENTARY

A Faith That Will Not Break

MAIN IDEA: *In spite of Job's despair, he remains strong in his faith in the living God.*

Job's Ridicule (19:1–6)

SUPPORTING IDEA: *Job moans that his three friends have rejected him with an endless barrage of empty words.*

19:1–2. Then Job replied. What follows is Job's response to the words of Bildad in the previous chapter. He asked, "**How long will you torment me and crush me with words?**" Such was the effect of their words upon Job. They caused him painful torment that was worse than the trial itself.

19:3. The three friends had relentlessly insulted Job. **Ten times**—a round number meaning over and over again—**now you have reproached me**. To Job, there seemed to be no end to their barrage of words. **Shamelessly you attack me**. Rather than help, comfort, or console him, their dialogue harmed him, leaving him in despair.

19:4. If it is true that I have gone astray. Job was not confessing that he had sinned but was making a hypothetical statement that even if he had, his error remained **my concern alone**. That is, it was his business, not the business of his friends. This was a personal, private matter between him and God and had nothing to do with them.

19:5. If indeed you would exalt yourselves above me is not a hypothetical statement because they had **indeed** done so. They had, in fact, elevated themselves to a position of moral superiority above Job. Job claimed they were using **humiliation** against him. In essence, they had been kicking a good man when he was down, preying on him at a vulnerable time in his life.

19:6. If this was true, **then know that God has wronged me**. This argument, Job insisted, was not that his sin had been the cause of his suffering but rather that God had mistreated him. This was not a new charge of injustice voiced by Job but one that had already surfaced (Job 8:3; 9:23–24; 10:6–7; 16:11–13) and would surface again by Elihu (34:12). The word *wronged* carries the idea of "perverted." Thus, the charge was that God had perverted justice against him. What is more, Job claimed, God had **drawn his net around me**, as if he had been caught like an animal by his stalker. This mistreatment by God, Job felt, was why his friends had rejected him.

B Job's Ruin (19:7–12)

SUPPORTING IDEA: *Job believes that his suffering is the result of being rejected by God.*

19:7. Continuing this thought of being rejected by God, Job expanded it by noting, **Though I cry, "I've been wronged!" I get no response**. He felt that he was suffering injustice at the hands of God. Interestingly, his three friends as well as Job recognized that his suffering was from God, but for different reasons. They claimed Job was receiving from God what he deserved, while Job felt he was receiving from God what he did not deserve. Although Job called for help from God, there was **no justice**, only the injustice of suffering what he did not deserve. What was worse, God was ignoring Job's pleas for help.

19:8–9. God **has blocked my way so I cannot pass**, Job declared. He perceived that God had obstructed his path so he could not escape this ordeal. God had shrouded his paths **in darkness**, making it impossible for him to see his way through this trial. He had **stripped** Job of his **honor**, leaving him devoid of honor and in disgrace before his peers. Further, God had **removed the crown** from his head, signifying the removal of respectability and esteem that Job had received from others. Humiliated, Job felt that he had been stripped of his former position.

19:10–11. In this same vein, Job continued, God **tears me down on every side till I am gone**, as if he were a house or building being demolished. He had uprooted his hope **like a tree**, leaving him devoid of any confidence about a bright future or positive outlook. "**His anger burns against me**," Job moaned, imagining God's displeasure with him. "**He counts me among his enemies**," noted Job, as he felt rejected and believed himself to be at war with God. Job was jumping to conclusions about God—conclusions that assumed that God was mad at him. Perhaps the counsel of the friends was getting to him.

19:12. Referring to himself as an attacked city, Job lamented, "**His troops advance in force.**" He pictured his troubles as enemy soldiers assaulting him. They were building **a siege ramp against** him, mounting a ramp on every side to lay siege to his life by allowing his trials to enter his life unmitigated. These afflictions encamped around Job's **tent**, not leaving his side but staying close by.

C Job's Rejection (19:13–22)

SUPPORTING IDEA: *Job claims that his family and friends have turned against him.*

19:13. Further, under this rejection by God, Job testified, "**He has alienated my brothers from me.**" He believed that God, as a part of his punishment, had isolated him from those who were closest to him. "**My acquaintances are completely estranged from me,**" he declared, withdrawn and removed as Job had become an outcast even to his closest friends.

19:14–16. My kinsmen have gone away. They were no longer a part of Job's inner circle. **My friends have forgotten me.** Job felt they had abandoned him, leaving him to die alone. **My guests and my maidservants count me a stranger.** They acted as if they did not even know him. They turned an indifferent shoulder toward him. **They look upon me as an alien.** They treated him as a foreigner and avoided him. **I summon my servant, but he does not answer.** No matter how much Job pleaded for assistance, those who once served him no longer did so.

19:17. Moving to his innermost circle, that of his wife, Job wailed, "**My breath is offensive to my wife.**" She refused his attempts to get close to her, probably because of his many diseases. **I am loathsome to my own brothers.** Those who were closest to Job and who were expected to stand with him were most repulsed by him.

19:18–19. Even the little boys scorn me. Instead of showing Job honor and respect reserved for prominent elders, they mocked Job because of his foul condition. **When I appear, they ridicule me.** They belittled him with degrading taunts. **All my intimate friends detest me.** This was certainly true of Job's three counselors, as well as all others who had forsaken him. **Those I love have turned against me.** No matter how kind Job was to them, they rejected him.

19:20. I am nothing but skin and bones. Job was physically emaciated and withered away. His skin was clinging to his bones. **I have escaped with only the skin of my teeth.** This expression meant that he had just barely escaped with his life.

19:21–22. Turning to address his friends, Job appealed, "**Have pity on me, my friends, have pity.**" He asked for their compassion and comfort, not their cutting remarks. They should offer such kindness to him, for the **hand of God** had **struck** Job. They should provide what God had not—pity. **Why do you pursue me as God does?** Job felt like a hunted animal with nowhere to hide.

D Job's Resolution (19:23–29)

SUPPORTING IDEA: *With renewed hope, Job resolves to hope in a future redeemer who will vindicate him of all accusations.*

19:23. From the depths of despair, Job cried out, **Oh, that my words were recorded** permanently for all future generations to read. Unknown to him, this would happen—and you are now reading those words from the Bible. He desired **that they were written on a scroll** so his innocence might be proven to all who would read the evidence.

19:24. Job longed for his words to be **inscribed with an iron tool on lead,** permanently transcribed so everyone would know that he had not sinned to the extent of his suffering. He wanted his life's record to be **engraved in rock forever.**

19:25. With a burst of renewed faith in God, Job asserted, "**I know that my Redeemer lives.**" In the face of his own approaching death, Job believed that God, his Redeemer, would eventually vindicate him. After his death, God would **stand upon the earth** and show him to be in the right in this matter. Despite the deep despair of his heart, this was a strong statement of faith in God. Job believed that no matter how others saw his life presently, God would have the last word and finally vindicate him.

19:26. Job confessed, "**And after my skin has been destroyed, yet in my flesh I will see God.**" In the future, when death would take Job's life and his skin would decompose, he believed that he would live again and see God. This reveals a confident trust in God, who would vindicate and reward him on the last day.

19:27. Job confided, "**I myself will see him with my own eyes—I, and not another.**" To gaze upon God in all his glory throughout all eternity was the only joy Job desired. He would see God face-to-face, and such an all-consuming vision was all he wanted. **How my heart yearns within me!** His entire inner being was ready to burst with a holy passion to look upon God. This was the spiritual heartbeat of one who was consumed with the experience of a direct vision of God.

19:28. Turning to address his three friends again, Job said, "**If you say, 'How we will hound him, since the root of the trouble lies in him.**'" He acknowledged that they wanted to accept their major premise—that his sin was the cause of his suffering. They believed the problem lay within Job, which was hidden sin in his life.

19:29. In response to this, Job rebutted, **you should fear the sword yourselves**. The divine judgment they said would come to him, he concluded, would actually come to them. This devastation would eventually come to them because **wrath will bring punishment by the sword**. Once this divine wrath came to the three counselors, Job warned, **then you will know that there is judgment**.

MAIN IDEA REVIEW: *In spite of Job's despair, he remains strong in his faith in the living God.*

III. CONCLUSION

Fight to the Finish

William Booth, the founder of the Salvation Army in London, persevered faithfully to the end of his life. At age eighty-two and almost blind, Booth stood before an audience of ten thousand at Royal Albert Hall in London and gave his last public address. His final words reveal an unbreakable faith that remained steadfast to the Lord, firm to the finish.

> While women weep as they do, I will fight.
>
> While children go hungry as they do, I will fight.
>
> While there is a drunkard left, I will fight.
>
> While there is a poor girl left on the streets, I will fight.
>
> While there remains one dark soul without the light of God, I will fight.
>
> I will fight—I will fight to the very end.

True faith presses on to the end. Such was William Booth's faith. Such was Job's faith. And such must be our faith as well. If it is real, we will fight to the end. May we know that our faith *in* God is, first and foremost, a faith *from* God and, therefore, is resilient and relentless. It may be shaken, but it will not fail.

IV. LIFE APPLICATION

How to Defeat Death

The Lord Jesus Christ is the ultimate Redeemer who will abolish the "last enemy"—death (1 Cor. 15:26). As the resurrected Savior, Jesus has overcome death and has demonstrated his power over death. He is the prince of life because "he has put everything under his feet" (1 Cor. 15:27), especially death. Christ himself will render death powerless by the resurrection at his second coming. This will make the bodies of believers imperishable and immortal (1 Cor. 15:53).

Christ is the Conqueror of death. He will "swallow up death for all time, and the Lord GOD will wipe away tears from all faces, and He will remove the reproach of His people from all the earth" (Isa. 25:8 NASB). Therefore, when facing death, the believer may remain confident that this foe will be defeated and we will see God. The victory is sure because God himself has secured the victory in the Lord Jesus Christ. Jesus said, "He who believes in me will live, even though he dies; and whoever lives and believes in me will never die" (cp. John 11:25–26).

V. PRAYER

God, our Father, we praise you for being the God of life who gives eternal life to those who call upon the Lord Jesus. Thank you that you have secured victory over death for your people through the resurrection of your Son and our Savior. Thank you for the future resurrection hope that will make our bodies imperishable and immortal. In Jesus' name. Amen.

VI. DEEPER DISCOVERIES

A. Shame (19:3)

"Shame" (Heb. *bosh*) means to be confounded, disappointed, ashamed, disgraced, or perplexed. The root occurs 155 times in the Old Testament, mostly in Psalms and Isaiah. This word conveys the idea of the public embarrassment one feels after a plot to sin has failed and ended in disgrace. It means to become pale or to blush when one's sin is exposed and judged by God. It conveys the total defeat and utter humiliation of evildoers. Disenchantment and despair follow those who are put to shame (Isa. 1:29; Dan. 9:7). This is the only usage of the word in Job.

B. Redeemer (19:25)

"Redeemer" (Heb. *goel*), used forty-four times in the Old Testament, comes from a verb meaning to lay claim to a person or thing, to free, or deliver. A redeemer in the Old Testament was a person who provided protection or legal preservation for a close relative who could not do so for himself. He could redeem the relative's property that had passed into other hands (cp. Lev. 25:23–25); he could avenge a slain relative (2 Sam. 14:11); he could marry his brother's childless widow (Ruth 4:10); he could buy a close relative out of slavery (Lev. 25:47–55); and he could defend his cause in a lawsuit (Prov. 23:11).

VII. TEACHING OUTLINE

A. Job's Ridicule (19:1–6)
   1. How long will you oppose me? (19:1–3)
   2. How you have harmed me! (19:4–6)

B. Job's Ruin (19:7–12)
   1. God does not answer me (19:7)
   2. God has assaulted me (19:8–12)

C. Job's Rejection (19:13–22)
   1. Job described their rejection (19:13–20)
   2. Job appealed for their help (19:21–22)

D. Job's Resolution (19:23–29)
   1. My words will be recorded (19:23–24)
   2. My eyes will see God (19:25–27)
   3. My life will be vindicated (19:28–29)

VIII. ISSUES FOR DISCUSSION

1. Do I look to the future Redeemer for future salvation?
2. Do I anticipate the future resurrection from the dead?
3. Do I long to see God?

Job 20

Then Go to Hell!

Quote

"The fury of man never furthered the glory of God."

A. W. Tozer

Job 20

I. INTRODUCTION

Gloating over Hell

A church that needed a pastor invited several candidates to come and preach. One minister spoke on Psalm 9:17, "The wicked shall be turned into hell" (KJV). The chairman of the board was not in favor of him. A few weeks later another preacher came and used the exact same verse for his sermon. This time the chairman said, "Let's call him." The other board members were surprised and asked, "Why did you like him? He used the very same text as the other minister." "True," he replied, "but when the second man emphasized that the lost will be turned into hell, he said it with tears in his eyes and concern in his voice. The first preacher almost seemed to gloat over the sinner's death."

This is where Zophar was. He was so angry with Job that he did not seem to care he was dying the death of the wicked. The wicked die a painful death, Zophar had contended in his first response to Job, because they have lived a life of unbridled sin. Zophar tried to frighten Job into confessing his sins and "getting right with God" by describing the awful end of the wicked. Rather than showing compassion for Job's suffering, he condemned him for his assumed sins.

This twentieth chapter of Job contains Zophar's second and final speech to Job. He was the most blunt of Job's three friends. Rather than encouraging Job, Zophar lambasted him, leaving him all the more devastated. Here is another discourse on the fate of the wicked as held by the strict "sin brings suffering" theology of Job's three friends (Job 8:11–19; 15:20–35; 18:5–21). Zophar expressed that the death of the wicked was an awful end, leading to devastation and disaster. This is where Zophar believed Job was headed if he did not repent and come back to God. His anger caused him to threaten Job all the more with the merciless end of the ungodly.

II. COMMENTARY

Then Go to Hell!

MAIN IDEA: *Zophar attacks Job by stating that he will face the fate of the wicked because he desires the ways of the wicked.*

Zophar's Attack (20:1–3)

SUPPORTING IDEA: *Offended by Job's rebuke, Zophar feels he must respond to his words.*

20:1–2. **Then Zophar the Naamathite replied** with his second discourse, once again attacking Job. He reminded him that God would punish the wicked man, robbing him of his wealth if he did not repent. He implied that Job was such a sinful man who needed to repent. Job's previous response to Bildad (cp. Job 19) gave Zophar **troubled thoughts** which prompted him to **answer** with further scathing indictments. He was **greatly disturbed** that Job had not yet confessed his sin. Job insisted instead upon his innocence, and this infuriated Zophar.

20:3. Zophar stated, **I hear a rebuke that dishonors me**. This was a reference to Job's warning (cp. Job 19:28–29). Or it may have been in response to Job's earlier challenge, "Will your long-winded speeches never end?" (Job 16:3). Zophar felt compelled by his faulty understanding to reply to Job. His answer demonstrated that the three friends remained locked into their position that Job had sinned against God and was suffering as a result.

B Zophar's Argument (20:4–11)

SUPPORTING IDEA: *Zophar returns to the attack, reiterating his theme of the painful fate of the wicked.*

20:4. Appealing to the past, Zophar stated, "**Surely you know how it has been from of old.**" He mocked Job for claiming to be a know-it-all. He belittled Job for acting as if he knew all the natural order and unbreakable laws of the universe that had been in place **ever since man was placed on the earth**.

20:5. Specifically, Zophar reminded Job **that the mirth of the wicked is brief**, meaning the celebration of the wicked at the expense of the godly is only for a short season. Zophar also knew that **the joy of the godless lasts but a moment**, meaning their present happiness was short-lived. Implied by Zophar is the age-old principle of God's retribution against the **wicked** and **godless**. He believed this principle was the cause of Job's troubles. Zophar understood that the wicked would not prosper (Job 9:22; 12:5–6), a truth reaffirmed by both Bildad (Job 8:13–19) and Eliphaz (Job 15:29–35).

20:6. The root sins beneath the unrighteous actions of the wicked are pride and a haughty head. **His pride reaches to the heavens**, towering and puffed up above the clouds. **His head touches the clouds**, as if his own arrogance exalts him above others. Job was growing more and more frustrated and bewildered by his friend's refusal to see that he was not the wicked man he believed him to be.

20:7–8. The godless, Zophar surmised, will **perish forever, like his own dung**. Such an end is repulsive and loathsome. The unrighteous man will disappear, being swept away into destruction. His ruin will be so swift and total, Zophar noted, that **those who have seen him will say, "Where is he?"** Suddenly, without warning, he will be carried away into God's judgment. Zophar noted, **Like a dream** the wicked person **flies away, no more to be found**. This means there is no trace of his existence after death since he is **banished like a vision of the night**.

20:9. Further, **the eye that saw him will not see him again**. Although the wicked person once enjoyed a prominent position in society, now in death **his place will look on him no more**. He will be removed without a trace of his former existence.

20:10. Then, in an unexpected shift, Zophar looked forward to the consequences of the wicked person's sins and concluded that **his children** would be responsible to **make amends** for his illegal and immoral business dealings with **the poor**. Zophar implied that the wicked person's children would pay for the sins of their father and possibly even forfeit their own inheritance to do so.

20:11. The wicked person lived with **youthful vigor** as he carried out his devious deeds, full of energy to pursue his sin. But no more. Now in his death, it **will lie with him in the dust**. His own strength, great as it was, will not enable him to escape his inevitable fate—death.

C Zophar's Appeal (20:12–19)

SUPPORTING IDEA: *Zophar in colorful words describes the wicked's love and desire for his evil deeds.*

20:12–13. Zophar described in vivid terms the joy it gives the wicked person to take from others and the wrath of God that abides on him as a result of his selfish actions. **Evil**, Zophar asserted, **is sweet in his mouth**. With a sick pleasure the wicked person savors the instant satisfaction of his evil that he hides **under his tongue**. His addiction to evil is so consuming that **he cannot bear to let it go and keeps it in his mouth**. Thus, his slavery to sin is all absorbing (cp. Rom. 6:6).

20:14. The wicked person's addiction to the sweet **food** of evil practices will lead to his destruction. Suddenly, sin will **turn sour in his stomach**—a reference to his own death. To make matters worse, the consequences of his actions **will become the venom of serpents within him**, deadly and damning, and lead to his certain destruction (cp. Jas. 1:15).

20:15–16. The bitter consequences of the wicked person's evil practices will cause him to **spit out the riches** he had received through his immoral business practices. Neither will the wicked person's exploitation of the poor go unnoticed by God, who will make his **stomach vomit them up** (his riches received by robbery). His own death will cause him to give up all these things. Deceived and drunk with his own success, the wicked person will **suck the poison of serpents**, a deadly drink. He will be struck by **the fangs of an adder** that will **kill him.**

20:17. The satisfaction of the wicked person's ill-gained riches will be short-lived, argued Zophar. His enjoyment of prosperity, symbolized by **streams** and **rivers flowing with honey and cream**, will end when he suffers his just penalty in death.

20:18–19. What the wicked **toiled for** by plundering the little of the poor, he will **give back uneaten**. Of what was gained through **trading, he will not enjoy the profit** as he lies dead, rotting in the grave. Having accumulated great wealth, he will lose it all in eternity. The wicked's heartless and greedy business transactions **oppressed the poor and left them destitute**. In his self-centered greed, no act proved to be too evil as he stooped to seize **houses he did not build**. Zophar wanted Job to understand that the wicked man is driven by his desire to feed his appetite for evil.

D Zophar's Admonition (20:20–29)

SUPPORTING IDEA: *Zophar asserts that the wicked will be overtaken by the burning anger of God both in this life and the life to come.*

20:20–21. The wicked person cannot satiate **his craving** for worldly gains though he believes he can **save himself** with his **treasure**. The Scripture is clear that a person cannot avoid judgment because of wealth (cp. Ps. 49; Prov. 18:11). Having obliterated the wealth of others, **nothing is left** for the wicked **to devour**. Zophar asserted with confidence that **his prosperity will not endure**. Wealth gathered by unrighteous means will not be carried into eternity.

20:22. Confident in amassing **his plenty**, the wicked are suddenly and unexpectedly overtaken by the **distress** that **will overtake him**, and **the full force of misery will come upon him**. God's wrath will burst forth in great force and overtake the wicked at the most unexpected time, even when they believe themselves to be secure because of their wealth.

20:23. This painful end will come **when he has filled his belly** to the point of gluttony with his ill-gained treasure. Then **God**, in unstoppable fury, **will vent his burning anger against** the wicked. His righteous vengeance will be demonstrated by the **blows** that will **rain down** on the wicked in merciless judgment.

20:24–25. God, like a fighting warrior, will hunt down the wicked man as **he flees**, striking him with **an iron weapon**. Zophar described the violent death that awaited the wicked. The death blow is given by **a bronze-tipped arrow** that **pierces** through **his back** with the **gleaming point** sticking through his front side and **out of his liver**. Zophar believed that the wicked would suffer a disastrous end in divine judgment. After death, Zophar reasoned, **terrors will come over him** as he faces the eternal judgment assigned to the wicked. This may be a reference taken from an earlier defense by Job (cp. Job 16:13).

20:26. Zophar calculated that **total darkness** will overtake the wicked's **treasures**, and **fire unfanned will consume him**. He then made a heartless application to Job's life as he stated that **fire** would **devour what is left in his tent**. This is a reference to the untimely deaths of Job's children (Job 1:18–19).

20:27. Job had stated that he believed an advocate in heaven would defend his innocence and vindicate him of all charges (cp. Job 16:19–21). Zophar denied that Job had an advocate in heaven as he claimed. Seeking to rob Job of all hope, Zophar argued that **the heavens will expose** the **guilt** of the wicked. And just as Job looked to the earth to not cover his blood (i.e., innocence; cp. 16:18), Zophar asserted that the earth would **rise up against him** as a testimony to his guilt.

20:28–29. God would pour out his **wrath** like a **flood** of rushing waters, overwhelming the wicked. This divine judgment would surely carry **off his house**. Like Job who had pronounced a curse on his friends (Job 19:28–29), so Zophar pronounced a curse on the wicked. Ending his second speech with no mention of repentance, Zophar surmised that the **fate** and **heritage** of the **wicked** are appointed by God. Divine justice was surely appointed for Job. On this grim note Zophar ended his final speech.

MAIN IDEA REVIEW: *Zophar attacks Job by stating that he will face the fate of the wicked because he desires the ways of the wicked.*

III. CONCLUSION

The Anger of Man

An old Englishman known by his fellow villagers as Father Graham was greatly loved because of his positive influence. One day an angry young man who had just been badly insulted came to see him. As the offended man explained the situation to Father Graham, he said he was on his way to demand an apology from the person who had wronged him. "My dear boy," Father Graham said, "take a word of advice from an old man. One insult is like mud; it will brush off much better when it is dry. Wait a little, until he and you are both cool, and the problem will be easily solved. If you go now, you will only quarrel." The young man heeded the wise advice, and soon he was able to go to the other person and resolve the issue.

Unfortunately, Zophar was filled with anger and tried to intimidate Job into confessing his sins with high-pressure tactics, but it did not work. Zophar's anger did not produce the desired effect upon Job. It only drove the wedge between Job and his friends deeper. The fear of the Lord is a legitimate motive for obedience, as presented by Zophar, but it must be balanced and tempered with expressions of divine love. Zophar was all wrath and woe but no grace and mercy.

The Bible says that we must speak the truth, but we are to do so in love (Eph. 4:15). If we speak eloquently, as with the tongues of angels, but do not have love, we are a noisy gong and a clanging cymbal (1 Cor. 13:1). This kind of tender love was missing with Zophar. He was so right that he was wrong. He was like a porcupine; he had a lot of good points, but he was hard to get close to. Had Zophar controlled his anger, he might have been more sensitive in his counsel for Job.

IV. LIFE APPLICATION

Justice for the Wicked

1. *Judgment is sure.* Let there be no doubt, the fate of the wicked will end in eternal perdition. God will judge the wicked in perfect righteousness. Zophar was right when he noted of the wicked's destiny that "they perish forever." Eternal destruction awaits the unrighteous who rebel against God (cp. Job 4:20). This eternal state of ruin is designed by God, for "upon the wicked He will rain snares; fire and brimstone and burning wind will be the portion of their cup" (Ps. 11:6 NASB). This is the eternal state of perishing that awaits the wicked.

2. *Hell is real.* Scripture describes hell as a place of fire (Matt. 5:22; 18:9) and torment (Luke 16:23). For the wicked God has reserved the wine of his fury, which will be poured out in full strength. There the wicked will experience unceasing torment (Rev. 14:10–11). The agonizing pain will cause them to gnaw their tongues in agony and to curse the God of heaven because of their pain (Rev. 16:11). Believers should never "play down" the fate of the wicked who reject God and his Son, the Lord Jesus Christ.

V. PRAYER

God, our Father, you are Creator and you reign in the heavens over your creation. You will judge the wicked in holy righteousness. You will reward the unrighteous according to their evil works. You will bring down the wicked with terror. In your anger you will right the wrong and establish your justice upon the earth. Usher in that great day when you will reward the righteous and judge the wicked. In Jesus' name. Amen.

VI. DEEPER DISCOVERIES

Rebuke (20:3)

"Rebuke" (Heb. *musar*) is a term conveying oral instruction with the purpose of giving correction, learning, and education. *Musar* is found once in the Torah (Deut. 11:2) and four times in Job (5:17; 12:18; 20:3; 36:10). Most instances occur in the Book of Proverbs, the most prominent being: "My son, do not reject the discipline [*musar*] of the LORD, or loathe His reproof, for whom the LORD loves He reproves, even as a father corrects the son in whom he delights" (Prov. 3:11–12 NASB). Sometimes this correction involves the "rod of discipline [*musar*]" (Prov. 22:15). This was the indication of Eliphaz as he reminded Job to "not despise the discipline of the Almighty" (Job 5:17b). Here Zophar accuses Job of correcting God.

VII. TEACHING OUTLINE

- A. Zophar's Attack (20:1–3)
  1. You have caused my anxiety (20:1–2)
  2. You have reproached me (20:3)
- B. Zophar's Argument (20:4–11)
  1. The wicked temporarily succeed (20:4–5)
  2. The wicked arrogantly sin (20:6)
  3. The wicked eternally perish (20:7–9)
  4. The wicked abruptly end (20:10–11)
- C. Zophar's Appeal (20:12–19)
  1. Evil is initially sweet (20:12–13)
  2. Evil is inevitably sour (20:14–16)
  3. Evil is ultimately sorrowful (20:17–19)
- D. Zophar's Admonition (20:20–29)
  1. The wicked will suffer loss (20:20–22)
  2. The wicked will suffer judgment (20:23–26)
  3. The wicked will suffer wrath (20:27–29)

VIII. ISSUES FOR DISCUSSION

1. Do I understand the judgment of God that awaits the wicked?
2. Do I warn others of God's wrath that will consume the wicked?
3. Do I seek to understand a person's standing with God before giving counsel?

Job 21

When Good Things Happen to Bad People

Quote

"The goodness of God is as curious as His disappointments."

J. A. Motyer

Job 21

I. INTRODUCTION

Do We Have Good News?

A pastor and a deacon were calling on people who had visited their church, hoping to present the gospel and draw them into their fellowship. As they drove to one man's house, the address brought them to an affluent neighborhood. Block after block was filled with beautiful, luxurious mansions. As they drove up to this man's house, they were awed by what they saw. The house was a virtual castle. Tall columns rose up across the front of the house. The large number of rooms gave it the appearance of a hotel. The lawn was perfectly manicured. Several expensive cars were parked in the driveway. A brick wall surrounded the house.

As they approached the front door, the pastor and deacon peered through the front window. The man of the house was seated in his luxurious living room in a beautiful chair, surrounded by antique furniture. As they approached the front door, the deacon turned to the pastor and asked, "Are you *sure* we have good news for him?"

The wicked often *do* prosper in this world. Temporal blessings *do* accompany their lives, sometimes more than the righteous. But this is certainly contrary to what Job's counselors had told him. Sinners, they insisted, always suffer in this life and never succeed. They never get ahead. While this is sometimes true, it is not always the case. This tight, cause-and-effect formula by which the righteous *always* prosper and the wicked *always* suffer is not applicable to all cases. In fact, as Job argued from his personal observation, good things often happen to bad people. The wicked do become wealthy by wicked means. Sinners do succeed, if only for a season. This is the thrust of what Job says in this rebuttal in chapter 21.

Job's remarks in this chapter are direct refutations of Zophar's words in Job 20. However, Job is also addressing Eliphaz and Bildad as well. "You" is plural (vv. 2,27–29,34), and the verbs are also plural (vv. 2–3a,5,29,34). Job countered their arguments and contended that the wicked often *do* prosper. Rather than dying early, unbelievers sometimes live full, long lives. In essence, what Job said here to refute Zophar is that good things *do* sometimes happen to bad people. Thus, by implication, the reverse must be true as well. Bad things sometimes happen to good people.

II. COMMENTARY

When Good Things Happen to Bad People

MAIN IDEA: *Job surmises that the wicked do prosper in life, but death will find even the wicked though they are buried with great honor.*

A Job's Complaint (21:1–6)

SUPPORTING IDEA: *Job appeals to his friends to listen carefully to his words.*

21:1–2. **Then Job replied** to Zophar, once more demanding the ear of his friend. Job's frustration is increasingly evident. What they have said must have his response. He must be heard. **Listen carefully to my words**. This implies that Job's friends were not truly listening to what he had been saying. **Let this be the consolation you give me**. The best way they could give him comfort was for them to hear him while they remained silent.

21:3. Having listened to their endless criticism, Job requested, "**Bear with me while I speak.**" Then in biting sarcasm, Job noted that **after** he had spoken, they could continue to **mock on**. These words demonstrated Job's estimation of their empty advice. He saw it as nothing more than destructive criticism.

21:4–5. **Is my complaint directed to man?** The implied answer was *no*. Instead, Job's harsh words were directed to God. Having received no response from heaven, he became **impatient**, demanding that he receive a response. Job declared, "**Look at me and be astonished.**" His friends should have been so overwhelmed by Job's gruesome condition that they would **clap** their hand **over** their **mouth** in silence (cp. Job 13:5). One look at his oozing sores should have quietened them.

21:6. Considering what he was about to say about the earthly lot of the wicked, Job was **terrified** as trembling seized his body. Unlike his friends, he did not presume to understand what God was doing, but he did reflect on the prosperity of the wicked.

B Job's Correction (21:7–16)

SUPPORTING IDEA: *Job rejects the theory offered by his friends that the wicked do not prosper.*

21:7. Rejecting the skewed belief that the wicked do not prosper, the view propounded by his friends (Job 15:20–35; 18:5–21; 20:5–11,15–28), Job wondered why the **wicked** seemingly **live on** in their unrighteousness while he was dying in his righteousness. He argued against Zophar's false assertions. Job pondered, How is it that I should die at a relatively young age, having lost all authority, while the wicked are seemingly **growing old and unceasing in power**?

21:8–9. Although Bildad and Zophar believed the wicked had no offspring to survive them (Job 18:19; 20:26), Job countered that the wicked **see their children established around them, their offspring before their eyes**. On the other hand, he had lost all his children in one swift act (Job 1:19). Domestically, the wicked's **homes are safe** (cp. Job 20:21,23,28) making them **free from fear**. Job credited the peaceful prosperity and domestic tranquility of the wicked to the fact that the **rod of God** was **not upon them** (cp. Job 9:34), yet Zophar believed God's wrath haunted the wicked (Job 20:23,28).

21:10–11. Continuing to catalogue the blessings of the wicked, Job noted that their investments in livestock were abundant. Seemingly, their bulls never failed **to breed**, and their cows calved and did not miscarry. Reverting back to the wicked's offspring, Job noted that he had **a flock** of **children**, an outward sign of blessing (Ps. 127:4–5). Furthermore, the **little ones** appeared happy as they danced about, unlike the children of the wicked whom Zophar had described (cp. Job 20:10).

21:12–13. Job noted that the wicked **sing** and **make merry to the sound of the flute**. Outwardly, they were delirious with merriment, apparently never suffering for the sins of their fathers. **Their years**, like their fathers', they spend **in prosperity**, an observation that contradicted Zophar's earlier observation, which asserted a quick judgment bringing an unexpected end (cp. Job 20:15,17–18).

21:14. Having chronicled the outward appearance of the wicked, Job looked inward to the rebellious attitude of the godless wicked. **Leave us alone** was the thought of the wicked. They wished God would leave them alone as they attempted to live life outside of his watchful presence. As they ignored both natural and special revelation, they resisted God because they had **no desire to know** God's **ways**.

21:15. In arrogant disdain, they asked, **Who is the Almighty** that they should humble themselves before him and **serve him?** Even when difficult times arose, the defiant wicked asked themselves, "**What would we gain by praying to him?**" Unlike Zophar's estimation that the wicked would have their sins unveiled (cp. Job 20:27), Job believed the wicked would never suffer retribution for their rebellion.

21:16. Then in a sudden shift, Job implied that **their prosperity** was under the divine sovereignty of God and was **not in their own hands**. Having presented the wicked in such prosperous terms, he then stated, "**I stand aloof from the counsel of the wicked.**" This meant he had no longing to follow the wicked, although they were prosperous.

C Job's Confession (21:17–26)

SUPPORTING IDEA: *Job acknowledges that death awaits both the good and the bad, the rich and the poor.*

21:17. Questioning Bildad's logic that the wicked would suffer a fate befitting their lives (cp. Job 18:5,12), Job asked, "**Yet how often is the lamp of the wicked snuffed out?**" He believed that not very often did **calamity** rain down on the wicked. To Job it was not often that God alloted **in his anger** a just fate for such a rebellious lifestyle.

21:18. Although Zophar had indicated the wicked's life is short-lived (Job 20:8–9), Job asked how **often** the wicked were **like straw before the wind** or **like chaff swept away by a gale**. This indicates he had rarely witnessed such a sight.

21:19. Perhaps quoting a proverb of the day that stated, "**God stores up a man's punishment for his sons,**" Job planned to attack the assertion that a wicked man's children suffer his fate. Job reasoned that God would **repay the man himself**, so that the wicked would know that God was judging him.

21:20. If the **Almighty** made him **drink of** his **wrath** (cp. Ps. 11:6; Matt. 26:39), then **his own eyes** would witness his own **destruction**. The implication is that God's punishment of the wicked's children would not be an effective deterrent against sin because they would not witness their own demise.

21:21. If a man's punishment is reserved for his sons, Job argued, how effective can this deterrent be if the wicked does not **care about the family he leaves behind when his allotted months come to an end.** Job reasoned that future punishment of one's prosperity was no deterrent to sin.

21:22. Believing his friends' sudden judgment of his case to be presumptuous, Job questioned, "**Can anyone teach knowledge to God, since he judges even the highest?**" In other words, did they have more knowledge than God? The clear answer was *no.* They needed to admit that God blesses and curses both the righteous and the wicked.

21:23–24. The fate of both groups varies, for **one man dies in full vigor,** being **secure and at ease.** Job's point was that there are no set rules that govern the earthly plot of the unrighteous. Even with the wicked, Job argued, he dies with his **body well nourished,** fat and happy, and **bones rich with marrow,** or healthy. So a person's physical condition is not an indicator of his standing before God.

21:25–26. For the sake of comparison, Job continued to give the description of a man like himself. **Another man dies in bitterness of soul, never having enjoyed anything good.** Deprived of earthly benefits, this man had never tasted **good.** Yet, **side by side** they both lie in the dust while the **worms** consume their flesh. Death is the great equalizer, bringing down to the grave both the righteous and the ungodly. Death is a fate that awaits all humanity.

D Job's Conclusion (21:27–34)

SUPPORTING IDEA: *Job concludes that the wicked often prevail in life and are buried with great honor.*

21:27. Expecting his friends' response to be exactly the same as before, Job declared, "**I know full well what you are thinking.**" He knew his discourse had not changed their minds, and he anticipated that their **schemes** to **wrong** him would continue. Quoting Bildad, Job demonstrated that he had a grasp of their erroneous position (cp. Job 8:22; 18:21).

21:28. Job refuted their assertion that God destroys the house and tents of the wicked. **You say, "Where now is the great man's house, the tents where wicked men lived?"** It does not always end in destruction in this life.

21:29. Job asked, "**Have you never questioned those who travel?**" Having known these three friends well and having heard their misguided assertions, Job wondered if they had paid no regard to the **accounts** of those who travel. Surely they would not challenge the observation of men who had traveled far and wide, those who had a broader spectrum of practical knowledge.

21:30. Job said that if his "comforters" had paid attention to those who traveled widely, they would know **that the evil man is spared from the day of calamity**. Yet Scripture is replete with passages that the wicked will not be **delivered from the day of wrath**. The wicked will surely perish and suffer the consequence of their evil lifestyles (Jer. 23:12).

21:31–32. Job questioned, **who denounces** the **conduct** of the wicked or **who repays him for what he has done**? To Job, the wicked were accountable to no one, especially God (Job 21:14–15), and were confronted by no one. Even in death, the wicked man is honored as **he is carried to the grave**, his funeral procession filled with ornate pomp and splendor. Then after his body is entombed, he receives special treatment as **watch is kept over his tomb**.

21:33. Even the soil that covers his corpse **is sweet to him**, meaning even death is good to the wicked. Job surmised that the wicked are followed by **all men** and are preceded by a **countless throng** that **goes before him**.

21:34. Job ended the second round of discussions by noting that his friends' attempt to **console** him consisted of **nonsense**. Furthermore, Job reckoned their **answers** as **falsehood**, meaning their explanations were filled with treacherous ideas which lacked divine enlightenment.

MAIN IDEA REVIEW: *Job surmises that the wicked do prosper in life, but death will find even the wicked though they are buried with great honor.*

III. CONCLUSION

Taking the Long Look

One day, a young law student came to William Gladstone to talk about his future. "What are you going to do when you graduate?" Gladstone asked.

"Put out a shingle and practice law," the young man replied.

"Then what?" Gladstone inquired.

"Get rich," came the confident reply.

"Then what?" Gladstone probed further.

"Retire," the student replied.

"Then what?" Gladstone pressed.

"Die."

"Then what?" Gladstone asked.

And the trembling words came, "I don't know."

"Young man," Gladstone stated, "you had better take the long look. You had better look beyond this world to the world to come. Only then will you be ready to live in the present."

Job failed to take the long look in life, choosing only to focus upon the temporal life before him. It was this shortsightedness which caused him to see only a person's life here and now. Because of this limitation, Job was looking at what was seen, not what was unseen. He was gazing on the physical, not the spiritual. He was fixed on the earthly, not the heavenly. Job needed to take the long look and by faith see what was eternal.

As Job considered the wicked, he needed to take the long look and see their end in the judgment. He was fixed upon their present prosperity rather than their future destruction. Likewise, he was riveted upon his present pain rather than his future reward. When we walk by sight rather than by faith, our assessments of life are always skewed.

IV. LIFE APPLICATION

Minimize and Maximize

1. *Minimize the temporal perspective.* In the midst of trying circumstances, we may lose all hope in God and despair of life itself. Often when tragedy strikes, we can lose the heavenly perspective and fall into depression. Never is this depression more exacerbated than when it is coupled with excruciating physical pain and suffering. Having experienced excessive physical turmoil (2 Cor. 11:23–29), Paul noted that he and his companions did "not lose heart" (2 Cor. 4:16). Their stamina remained strong because "though outwardly we are wasting away, yet inwardly we are being renewed day by day." Paul knew that though his body was wasting away, this pain had the effect of setting his mind on things above. This inward transformation so revolutionized Paul that he called the sufferings he experienced at the hands of his persecutors "light and momentary troubles" (2 Cor. 4:17a).

2. *Maximize the eternal perspective.* Paul remained strong through his suffering because he knew God was storing up for him "an eternal glory" (2 Cor. 4:17b) that far outweighed his present sufferings. Maintaining this eternal perspective was achieved by not fixing his eyes on "what is seen, but on what is unseen. For what is seen is temporary, but what is unseen is eternal" (2 Cor. 4:18). Paul chose to take the long look. He remembered that the heavenly realities are what count. This is the perspective that Job had lost and needed to regain. When believers maintain the upward look, they can endure life's trials with joy.

V. PRAYER

God, our Father, often it appears that the wicked perish while the righteous suffer. You have never promised your people ease and comfort because all who live godly for Christ Jesus will suffer persecution in this life. We praise you for the future hope that is ours in Christ Jesus alone, the reward that awaits those who eagerly anticipate the Son's appearing. Prepare us for that day. In Jesus' name. Amen.

VI. DEEPER DISCOVERIES

A. Repay (21:19)

"Repay" (Heb. *shalam*) has various connotations, but here it means to recompense. In this context it is God rendering divine retribution for accumulated sins. *Shalam* is used in the same way in other contexts (Judg. 1:7; Ps. 62:12; Jer. 50:29) and in Job (21:31; 34:11,33)

B. Man (21:19)

"Man" (Heb. *adam*) is used more than five hundred times throughout the Hebrew Bible to speak of mankind, but it is also used of individuals.

C. Wrath (21:20)

"Wrath" (Heb. *hema*) means heat and figuratively speaks of poison, fire, and the sun, all of which produce heat and sometimes fever. Generally, *hema* connotes inner emotional rage, anger, indignation, and displeasure. As in this passage, *hema* is often used in reference to God's wrath. It is demonstrated to unfaithful Israel (Jer. 42:18) and on other disobedient peoples (Nah. 1:2,6).

VII. TEACHING OUTLINE

A. Job's Complaint (21:1–6)
   1. He desired a hearing (21:1–3)
   2. He defended his cause (21:4–6)

B. Job's Correction (21:7–16)
   1. The wicked often succeed (21:7–13)
   2. The wicked always sin (21:14–15)
   3. The wicked often survive (21:16)

C. Job's Confession (21:17–26)
   1. The wicked rarely suffer (21:17–21)
   2. The wicked inevitably die (21:22–26)

D. Job's Conclusion (21:27–34)
   1. Listen to your own reasoning (21:27–28)
   2. Listen to the traveler abroad (21:29–33)
   3. Listen to my aching cry (21:34)

VIII. ISSUES FOR DISCUSSION

1. Do I question God about the prosperity of the wicked?
2. Do I question God about the persecution of the righteous?
3. When I suffer persecution, what is God trying to teach me?

Job 22

Sinner in the Hand of an Angry Counselor

Quote

"The worst of slaves is he whom passion rules."

Phillips Brooks

Job 22

I. INTRODUCTION

A Scathing Letter

Edwin Stanton, secretary of war under President Abraham Lincoln, was well-known for his highly inflammable temper. The pressure of war kept his nerves frayed and his tongue sharp. Once when he complained to Lincoln about a certain general, Lincoln told him to write the man a letter. "Tell him off," Lincoln advised. Stanton, blustered by the president's support, promptly wrote a scathing letter in which he tore the man to shreds. He showed the letter to the president.

"Good," said Lincoln. "First rate. You certainly gave it to him." As Stanton started to leave, Lincoln asked, "What are you going to do with it now?" "Mail it, of course," said Stanton. "Nonsense," snorted the president. "You do not want to mail that letter. Put it in the stove! That's what I do when I have written a letter while I am angry. You had a good time writing that letter. Now write another."

The problem with Job at this point in the book is that his three counselors were furious with him and kept directing their scathing accusations his way. Rather than withholding their anger, they had unloaded it on Job. He was reeling under the onslaught of their outbursts of temper. Their anger had raised Job's anger against them and God. This had been the undoing of Job's once-strong confidence in God.

In this chapter, Job 22, the third cycle of speeches between Job and his three friends begins. Their speeches become shorter and shorter while Job's grow longer and longer. In fact, Zophar, the angriest of the three, will abstain from speaking. This is the final round of this painful dialogue, as Eliphaz (Job 22) and Bildad (Job 25) will finish their say. As Eliphaz speaks for the last time, his message is the same: Job is suffering because of sin. But what is different now is the tone of the rhetoric as Eliphaz becomes vindictive.

II. COMMENTARY

Sinner in the Hand of an Angry Counselor

MAIN IDEA: *Eliphaz hammers Job again with accusations of living in hidden sin, calling him to repent, offering hope that he will be restored if he returns to God.*

A Eliphaz's Assumption (22:1–4)

SUPPORTING IDEA: *Eliphaz accuses Job of being a sinner without limits.*

22:1–2. **Then Eliphaz the Temanite replied**, responding once again to the many words that Job had already spoken. Eliphaz would now try harder than ever to prove that Job was a great sinner. Eliphaz began his last speech by asking, "**Can a man be of benefit to God?**" Eliphaz repeated his emphasis on the holy, transcendent nature of God. He claimed that God is so high and lofty that he is indifferent toward sinners like Job. Man cannot draw God to himself by his goodness.

22:3–4. In fact, Job brought God no **pleasure**, even if he were **righteous** and **blameless**. Eliphaz was implying that man was so insignificant before God that it didn't matter whether man was righteous. Eliphaz reasoned that it would certainly not be for Job's **piety** that God was bringing **charges against** him. Eliphaz's words dripped with sarcasm as he expressed his conviction that Job harbored unconfessed sin.

B Eliphaz's Accusation (22:5–11)

SUPPORTING IDEA: *Eliphaz accuses Job of specific sins committed against the needy and helpless as the reason for his troubles.*

22:5. The reason for God's indictment, according to Eliphaz, was the magnitude of Job's sin. **Is not your wickedness great?** This, in fact, was a direct indictment of Job, a charge of multiple sins in his life. **Are not your**

sins endless? This rhetorical question implied a positive answer. To Eliphaz there was no end to the list of sinful deeds that Job had committed.

22:6. In his first speech (Job 4:2–4) Eliphaz acknowledged that Job had reached out to help the weak. But not being able to point to specific sins in Job's life, Eliphaz now began to speculate on what Job's sin must have been. **You demanded security from your brothers for no reason.** Common decency dictated that if a man were forced to give his outer garment to a creditor as a pledge of payment, the garment should be returned to him for the cold night. Yet, according to Eliphaz, Job had not even done this but instead **stripped men of their clothing, leaving them naked**, even in the cold.

22:7–8. Eliphaz charged Job with further social sins against the needy. He claimed, **You gave no water to the weary**, nor **food** to **the hungry**. Job left them thirsty and hungry, without the bare necessities of life, Eliphaz claimed. He also accused Job of coldness of heart toward weary travelers. When Job had been wealthy, **a powerful man** with much **land**, he could have easily met these needs, but he had not. Or, at least, this is what Eliphaz claimed.

22:9–10. What is more, Eliphaz accused Job of abusing **widows** and **fatherless** orphans. He charged Job with sending them away **empty-handed** without any food. To refuse a widow or orphan was the lowest crime of all as one chose to remain insensitive about the plight of the destitute. The result of these atrocious sins was that Job deserved **snares** to trap him. These traps would bring **sudden peril** to terrify him, much as he was already experiencing.

22:11. Likewise, said Eliphaz, this was **why** it was **so dark** around Job, emotionally, and **why** a **flood** of troubles covered him. This was a direct reference to the tragedies that Job had suffered, surely the result of his sin, Eliphaz assumed. Darkness was the time when desert pirates roamed the land, and torrential floods could overcome the unsuspecting.

C Eliphaz's Argument (22:12–20)

SUPPORTING IDEA: *Eliphaz charges Job with thinking that God does not see or care about his sin.*

22:12–13. Behind these acts of sin (vv. 6–9), Eliphaz believed, Job had an attitude of arrogance and defiance against God. **Is not God in the heights of heaven?** But Eliphaz was putting words in Job's mouth, words he had not spoken. He charged Job with asking, "**What does God know?**" But this was a trumped-up charge. Job had not said this. **Does he judge through such darkness?** The assumption was that Job must think he could get away with anything, as if thinking God was in the dark about his sin. But Job had not said or thought these things. Eliphaz had conjured up these statements and attributed them to Job.

22:14–15. Thick clouds veil him, so he does not see us. This is what Eliphaz accused Job of thinking. But such a charge was a fabrication. It must have been difficult for Job to listen to this. Eliphaz then asked if Job would continue in the **old path that evil men have trod**, that is, in the wrong direction. The path of the wicked was a well-worn path. Would he persist in his sin? If so, he could expect more suffering.

22:16–17. If Job would not repent, Eliphaz warned, he would die an early death. Eliphaz said it was common knowledge that those who are evil will be **carried off before their time**. In their sin of pride, the wicked said, "**Leave us alone!**" They did not want God running their lives. So, they said, "**What can the Almighty do to us?**" The implication was clear. Eliphaz believed Job had been following a path of arrogant defiance against God.

22:18–20 Yet it was he who filled their houses with good things. Despite Job's many sins, he claimed God had blessed him. While this first line seems to align Eliphaz with Job at this point, Eliphaz quickly blurted, "**I stand aloof from the counsel of the wicked.**" This was a repetition of what Job had just said (Job 21:16). **The righteous see their ruin**, the judgment that is coming to these audacious sinners, and **rejoice**, knowing how deserved it is. They say, "**Surely our foes are destroyed, and fire devours their wealth.**" This was what good people were saying about Job and his losses.

D Eliphaz's Appeal (22:21–30)

SUPPORTING IDEA: *Eliphaz calls Job to repent so God's blessings can be restored to him.*

22:21–22. Eliphaz concluded his third and final discourse by challenging Job to repent. **Submit to God** in complete surrender of your life to him, he declared. **Be at peace with him**. The result would be **prosperity**. **Accept instruction from** God's **mouth** with a yielded, teachable spirit that is eager to learn and receive instruction, Eliphaz directed. **Lay up his words in your heart** in order to obey them.

22:23–24. "**If you return to the Almighty,**" Eliphaz exhorted Job, "**you will be restored.**" Your family and fortune will be given back to you. **Remove wickedness** far from you. These are the marks of true repentance. Further, Job should **assign** his gold **nuggets to the dust**, meaning he should assign a lesser importance to pursuing his gold and focus instead on seeking God. He should assign his **gold of Ophir**, which was the finest gold of the day (1 Kgs.

9:28; Ps. 45:9), **to the rocks in the ravines**. That is, Job should assign them to others so he could pursue God.

22:25–27. If Job would repent, an act demonstrated by giving up his wealth, then he could be confident that God would be his **gold** and **choicest silver** (i.e., his priceless treasure). Surely then he would **find delight** in God, enjoying him more than anything else. The giving up of earthly pursuits would bring him happiness. Repentance would restore Job's love for God, so Eliphaz claimed. God would hear Job's prayer, but only if he repented. Then Job would know prosperity and success which are not measured in gold but in the blessings of God.

22:28–29. What you decide on will be done. That is, God enables those who pray and repent to do his will. **And light** (i.e., God's favor) would **shine** on Job's **ways**, lighting his way through his present darkness. God would bless Job if he would only humble himself and turn from his sin. Likewise, he would know influence because he would say, "**Lift them up**!" and he would be lifted from his humiliating position. God would **save the downcast** (i.e., the one thrown down by God's discipline).

22:30. God would **deliver even one who is not innocent**, if only Job would repent. **The cleanness** of Job's **hands** would lead to his full restoration, as well as to the deliverance of others. With these words Eliphaz concluded his third and final speech. Ironically, Eliphaz's prediction would be fulfilled eventually through Job's prayers for his three friends.

MAIN IDEA REVIEW: *Eliphaz hammers Job again with accusations of living in hidden sin, calling him to repent, offering hope that he will be restored if he returns to God.*

III. CONCLUSION

The Devil's Deadly Poison

Some of the deadliest snakes in the world include the Indian cobra, the Russell's viper, the Indian krait, the Ceylon krait, the tiger snake and the African mamba. In South America alone, about forty-five hundred people die each year from contact with deadly reptiles such as these. The fangs of these venomous snakes consist of grooved or hollowed teeth that are connected with sacs of poison in the snake's cheeks. When it strikes, the snake uses a squeeze-bottle technique that squirts a stream of venom into its victim. In less than half a second, the reptile can strike, inject its venom, and return to normal stance. So poisonous is the venom of some species, such as the inland taipan of Australia, that people have died in less than a minute after being bitten.

Unknown to Job, he had been bitten repeatedly by the worst serpent of all. The devil's deadly poison had been injected into his soul. Through the untruths told to him by Eliphaz and the other two counselors, he had been harmed by the devil's lies. As Eliphaz finished his final speech, he sank his fangs deep into Job's heart. He indicted Job with a long litany of sins that Job had not committed. With each accusation Eliphaz's anger escalated until it reached a climax.

The charges were not true, and they confused the issue. Eliphaz could not convince Job of his guilt, although he made every effort to do so. Under this heated attack, Job was beaten down, and this caused his focus to shift. Satan used Eliphaz in his relentless attempt to subvert Job's faith. The devil's poison had been injected into Job's soul by his angry counselor. This poison would almost destroy Job's confidence in God.

IV. LIFE APPLICATION

Double Nevers

1. *Never play the Holy Spirit.* A friend should never play the Holy Spirit. Eliphaz had tried to bring conviction to Job's heart by accusing him of sin. But he crossed the line with Job and went too far. As Martin Luther once said, "I can only bring God's Word to the ear but can go no further. The Holy Spirit must take the Word from the ear to the heart." Eliphaz tried to do the latter, a work that only the Holy Spirit can do. It is the Holy Spirit who has come into the world to convict of sin, righteousness, and judgment—not Eliphaz. He presumed to know Job's heart and assumed to know what Job was thinking in the secret counsels of his mind. Worse, he speculated about what Job was thinking about God. Eliphaz attempted to put words into Job's mouth about his understanding of God.

2. *Never judge by outward appearance.* Man looks on the outward appearance; only God looks on the heart (1 Sam. 16:7). The apostle Paul refused to let others judge his heart. Standing up to the Corinthians' judgmental spirit about his life and ministry, he wrote, "I care very little if I am judged by you or by any human court; indeed, I do not even judge myself" (1 Cor. 4:3). In like manner believers must be careful not to judge the motives of others. This is a task reserved only for God. Let us *not* attempt to be "experts" on what others are thinking or feeling. Only God can see behind the veil of the flesh and discern the thoughts and intentions of the heart.

V. PRAYER

God, help us to be a good friend to others, not beating them down but lifting them up. Prevent us from being harsh and judgmental. Restrain us from being cold and callous. Use us to help a brother or sister in Christ who has become embroiled in a fiery trial not to add to their burden but to strengthen and encourage them in your name. Through Christ our Lord. Amen.

VI. DEEPER DISCOVERIES

A. Good (22:18)

"Good" (*tob*) is a broad Hebrew adjective used to describe something or someone who is excellent, favorable, pleasant, lovely, or sound. It is used in a wide variety of ways to describe the abstract. Here, as in other passages (cp. Gen. 2:18; Deut. 6:24; 2 Sam. 16:12), good denotes a person's well-being.

B. Instruction (22:22)

"Instruction" (Heb. *tora*) comes from a root meaning to project or to teach and refers to any direction or instruction flowing from the Word of God that points out or indicates God's will. It refers not only to the moral, civil, or ceremonial law but to the whole teaching, instruction, or doctrine of Scripture.

VII. TEACHING OUTLINE

A. Eliphaz's Assumption (22:1–4)
   1. God is indifferent to man's goodness (22:1–2)
   2. God is aroused by man's guilt (22:3–4)

B. Eliphaz's Accusation (22:5–11)
   1. He declared Job's sins (22:5)
   2. He detailed Job's sins (22:6–10)
   3. He denounced Job's sins (22:11)

C. Eliphaz's Argument (22:12–20)
   1. You continue with wrong assumptions (22:12–14)
   2. You continue down old paths (22:15–17)
   3. You continue with old arguments (22:18–20)

D. Eliphaz's Appeal (22:21–30)
   1. He called for Job's repentance (22:21–24)
   2. He promised Job's restoration (22:25–30)

VIII. ISSUES FOR DISCUSSION

1. How have I wrongly judged the character of others?
2. Do I prayerfully seek the face of God before reproving others?
3. Do I point suffering people to God for comfort and strength?

Job 23
Where Is God?

Quote

"The injuries men do to us should drive us to God, for to him we may commit our cause."

Matthew Henry

I. INTRODUCTION

Tell Me Where God Is Not

An agnostic college professor decided to have some fun with a small boy who was reading a Bible lesson. Trying to trip up the faith of the young lad, he said to him, "Tell me where God is, and I will give you an apple." The boy replied, "I will give you a whole barrel of apples if you tell me where he is not."

The omnipresence of God is one of the most basic truths of theology. The Bible clearly teaches that there is no place where God is not present. This is a foundational truth which Job seems to have forgotten. He claimed not to be able to find God in order to present his case before him. But the truth is that God, a spirit being, is present everywhere. Job could have presented his case at any time to God, who was readily available and always accessible. What Job desired was already a reality to him. The problem was not with God but with Job.

Job 23 records Job's desperate desire to find God and to plead his case of innocence. But he could not find God. The long speeches of his friends had worn him down. Job was a devastated man as he spoke from the depths of a broken heart. This pained patriarch felt that he was suffering injustice with

God for sins he had not committed. So he desired to take the Almighty to court. He wanted to appear before God and argue his case in an attempt to have the charges against him reversed. His desire to take God to court is the theme of Job 23.

II. COMMENTARY

Where Is God?

MAIN IDEA: *Job complains because he cannot find God in order to present his case before him.*

 Job's Despair (23:1–9)

SUPPORTING IDEA: *Job longs to find God in order to present his case before him.*

23:1–2. In response to Eliphaz's third speech (Job 22), Job replied with more words of empty despair (Job 23–24). "**Even today my complaint is bitter,**" Job lamented. The injustices he had received had caused him to be filled with festering bitterness toward God. He believed that God's **hand** was heavy upon him, pressing him down. He could no longer suppress his **complaint** against God or relieve his inward **groaning** for answers.

23:3–4. Job longed to appear before God in order to present his case before him. Thus, he lamented, "**If only I knew where to find him.**" If Job could only **go to his dwelling** place in heaven, he would plead his case. With mounting confidence, Job boasted, "**I would state my case against him.**" He would present the evidence of his life and prove both his innocence and God's injustice. Job would demonstrate to God that his suffering did not match the sin he had allegedly committed. Whatever his alleged breach of divine law was, the punishment did not fit the crime. Given the opportunity to appear before heaven's bar, Job would **fill** his **mouth with arguments** in presenting his case. He felt that God was being elusive, avoiding him, making it impossible to have the divine charges against him reversed.

23:5–6. With mounting self-assertion and growing arrogance, Job convinced himself, **I would find out what he would answer me.** He would **consider** what would be God's answers to his arguments and skillfully refute them. Job pondered, **Would he oppose me with great power** and resist my charges? **No, he would not press charges against me.** Job honestly believed he could vindicate himself before God's judgment seat, showing God to be wrong and himself to be right.

23:7. Pointing to a much desired court appearance before God, Job surmised, "**There an upright man could present his case before him.**" By this third-person reference, Job alluded to being this upright man. If he could only secure such a divine hearing, he **would be delivered forever** from his judge—acquitted.

23:8. But Job's dilemma was that he could not find God. If the judge did not appear in court, the court could not be called into session, and his case could not be presented. **But if I go to the east, he is not there; if I go to the west, I do not find him.** No matter where Job looked, God could not be found.

23:9. Referring to God, Job said, "**When he is at work in the north, I do not see him; when he turns to the south, I catch no glimpse of him.**" No matter where Job looked, north or south, east or west (v. 8), he could not find God to plead his case. Thus, he could not find the relief he wanted. His search for God seemed to be in vain.

B Job's Dependence (23:10–12)

SUPPORTING IDEA: *Job affirms his obedience to God, whom he thinks is testing him in order to purify him.*

23:10. Job felt that God was avoiding him. He stated, the Almighty **knows the way that I take**. If God actually appeared in court with Job, he would surely have to reverse his charges and declare him not guilty. Nevertheless, he affirmed his confidence that there was a divine purpose in this ordeal. **When he has tested me** in this trial, he declared, **I will come forth** purified **as gold**. Job saw his trial as a testing that would make him a stronger, better person (cp. Jas. 1:2–4; 1 Pet. 1:7).

23:11. With a deepening resolve to remain committed to God, Job pledged, "**My feet have closely followed his steps.**" He wanted to walk closely with God in humble obedience. With firm confidence, he asserted, "**I have kept to his way without turning aside.**" Job claimed that he had not fallen away in disobedience. This claim was in contrast to Eliphaz's accusation that he had followed the path of evil men (Job 22:15).

23:12. Job claimed personal obedience to the commands of God. "**I have not departed from the commands of his lips,**" he declared. He felt he had remained true to the words of God. Moreover, he had **treasured the words** of God's **mouth more than** his **daily bread**. God's Word was his nourishment, more important than his regular meals. Job found in divine revelation the only food that strengthened and satisfied his inner person (Isa. 1:2; Jer. 15:16; John 4:31–34).

C Job's Determination (23:13–17)

SUPPORTING IDEA: *Job testifies that God's sovereign will in this trial is unalterable, a truth that creates fear.*

23:13. Returning to his earlier expressed desire to appear before God, Job realized that even if he did find God, it would be impossible to overturn God's will and reverse his divine verdict. God **stands alone**, meaning he is unique and one-of-a-kind, unlike humans. Thus, no one could oppose him successfully, certainly not Job.

23:14. As a result, Job realized that God executed **his decree** against him without changing his will. God's eternal decree was unconditionally fixed and absolutely unalterable and would come to pass. "**Many such plans he still has in store**," he declared. This fact terrified Job. What else could God have in store for him?

23:15–16. This truth of God's immutable sovereignty is why Job was **terrified before him**. "**When I think of all this, I fear him**," he said. Such lofty theology was sobering for Job. It caused him to fear God. These grand thoughts about God's supremacy made Job's **heart faint** within him, nearly to the point of collapsing. "**The Almighty has terrified me**," he declared. This was the right response to the knowledge of God.

23:17. Despite all his assertions, Job could not overcome **the thick darkness** of trouble that covered him in despair. He felt trapped by his trials and troubles.

MAIN IDEA REVIEW: *Job complains because he cannot find God in order to present his case before him.*

III. CONCLUSION

Litigation Wars

As Job considered taking God to court, it would be much different from modern court proceedings. Today high-profile court trials are covered heavily by the media. From well-known professional athletes to movie stars, famous defendants in the courtroom are much in the news. In addition, the trials of mafia grandfathers and politicians dot the landscape. These well-reported trials have become media events in which famous defendants seek to be acquitted through trumped-up popular support. Public sentiment often shapes the thinking of the jury as the trial is played out before the watching eyes of the world. In these courtroom dramas, justice is rarely achieved. Highly paid, media-savvy lawyers are skilled in swaying the jury through polls and public opinions. Sometimes even picking an impartial jury is impossible.

But in Job's case, he just wanted to have a private court appearance before God. Without any legal representation he wanted to present his own case before God and secure an acquittal. Like an adept lawyer, Job sought to present his arguments in what he believed to be an airtight case. Before the judge's bench, he would listen to God and give irrefutable answers. Then, Job believed, God would drop all charges against him.

But such was a vain hope. It was based on the supposition that God had made a mistake in handling Job's life. This was impossible. God, who is perfect, does all things well. In reality there was nothing Job could have presented that would prove God to be in the wrong. He never mishandles a case.

IV. LIFE APPLICATION

How to Find God

Job was anguished over not being able to find God in order to plead his case. Where *can* we find God? Several spiritual truths need to be kept in mind.

1. *God is found in his Word.* God primarily makes himself known in the pages of Scripture. The written Word of God is the chief place in which he has chosen to reveal himself to man. It is in his inerrant, infallible Word that God clearly speaks to us. It does not matter where we may be geographically if we are trying to meet with God. All that really matters is that we have his Word. This conveys to us the mind and presence of God.

2. *God is represented by his Son.* There is only one way to come before God, who is revealed in his Word, and that is through his Son, the Lord Jesus Christ. Jesus said, "No one comes to the Father except through me" (John 14:6). No one may come to God except through his Son, the only mediator between God and man—Jesus Christ (1 Tim. 2:5–6). If we are to come before God's throne of grace and find acceptance with him, it necessitates coming by the one divinely prescribed way, and that is exclusively through Christ (Heb. 4:14–16). "We have one who speaks to the Father in our defense—Jesus Christ the Righteous One" (1 John 2:1).

3. *God is revealed by his Spirit.* All spiritual truth about God must be revealed by his Spirit. Spiritual darkness veils all people from the ministry of God's Spirit. But by the Spirit there is spiritual enlightenment and illumination that opens the eyes of our hearts to the reality and presence of God. It is possible to read the Scripture and merely know about God yet still not know God. The ministry of the Holy Spirit makes God known to us and leads us to

him. Only the Spirit can bring us to be connected with the Lord in a living relationship.

V. PRAYER

God, we long for you to hear our humble cry and restore us to yourself. You alone have ordained for us to enter fiery trials, and we know you alone can remove us from the fire. We thank you that you walk through the fires of life with your people and we are never alone. Thank you for the privilege of walking in the paths that our Lord walked. For if we suffer like him, we will also be glorified like him. In Jesus' name. Amen.

VI. DEEPER DISCOVERIES

A. Commands (23:12)

"Commands" (Heb. *miswa*) signifies a definite, authoritative command or anything ordained by the Lord. It designates the general body of imperative commands contained in God's law.

B. Terrified (23:15–16)

"Terrified" (Heb. *bahal*) occurs fifty times in the Old Testament, including the eleven times its equivalent is found in the Aramaic sections of the Old Testament (Daniel). The word means to be terrified, frightened, perplexed, or confounded. It is used to refer to the distressing reaction God provokes in the nations (Exod. 15:15; Isa. 13:8) and in Israel (Ezek. 26:18). Likewise, people become distressed or terrified at the thought of God (Ps. 104:29). This word is also used to demonstrate the dread that people may bring upon others (2 Sam. 4:1). Here it connotes the same meaning—a terror that produces reverential fear of the Lord.

VII. TEACHING OUTLINE

A. Job's Despair (23:1–9)
   1. My heart is pained (23:1–2)
   2. My presentation is prepared (23:3–7)
   3. My pursuit is futile (23:8–9)

B. Job's Dependence (23:10–12)
   1. God knows the path I take (23:10a)
   2. God tests the person I am (23:10b)
   3. God develops the purity I have (23:10c–12)

C. Job's Determination (23:13–17)
1. God is absolutely sovereign (23:13–14)
2. Job is absolutely terrified (23:15–16)
3. Job is absolutely determined (23:17)

VIII. ISSUES FOR DISCUSSION

1. Do I feel that God does not hear me when I cry out to him?
2. Do I ever contend with God because I am unhappy with my circumstances?
3. Do I treasure the words from God's mouth more than food?

Job 24

Why Doesn't God Do Something?

Quote

"He who does not punish evil commands it to be done."

Leonardo da Vinci

Job 24

I. INTRODUCTION

When God Settles His Accounts

An arrogant, irreligious farmer had developed a strong disdain for the religious faith of many people in his community. Most of the farmers there were godly men who gathered to worship the Lord on Sunday instead of working the fields. But this farmer chose to plow on Sundays, often saying, "Hands that work are better than hands that pray." Part of his land bordered the church, and he would make a point of driving his tractor by during worship services. Weary of hearing how God had "blessed" so many of the other farmers, he decided to make a statement about his own abilities without God. He plowed, fertilized, and cultivated his field, all without God's help—or so he believed.

When October's harvest came, this farmer had the finest crop in the county. When the bumper harvest was complete, he submitted a lengthy letter to the editor of the local paper, attempting to belittle the farmers who believed their harvests resulted from God's blessings: "Sir, I have been trying an experiment with a field of mine. I plowed it on Sunday, planted it on Sunday, cultivated it on Sunday, harvested it on Sunday, even carted the crop home to the barn on Sunday. Now, Mr. Editor, what was the result? Well, this

October I got more bushels to the acre from that field than any of my Sabbath-keeping neighbors got from theirs. Where is their God?"

He expected enthusiastic support from the editor, a man also not known for his religious beliefs. But when his letter appeared in the local paper, the editor added this pithy comment: "God does not settle all his accounts in October."

This was the problem Job had with the limited perspective his three counselors were touting. They assumed that God settles all his accounts in October. His friends presumed that God closes out all his books in this lifetime. But God does not always execute his justice immediately. Sinners often succeed in this life, and saints often suffer. This was just the opposite of what Job had been hearing from his friends. Eliphaz, Bildad, and Zophar had been telling him that all sinners suffer and they pay for their sins *now*.

Unfortunately, Job had begun buying into this warped perspective. He began to question God's justice. He could not understand why God was silent and indifferent in the face of human misery. The fact that God *waits* to punish the wicked was contrary to the statement his three friends had been making. What Job says in chapter 24 is that God judges the wicked, but he does so in his own good time.

II. COMMENTARY

Why Doesn't God Do Something?

MAIN IDEA: *Job struggles with understanding why God allows the unrighteous to go unpunished, only to reaffirm that God will eventually bring judgment.*

Job's Frustration (24:1)

SUPPORTING IDEA: *Job questions why God does not set certain appointed days to judge the wicked.*

24:1. Job lamented, "**Why does the Almighty not set times for judgment?**" That is, why did God not set aside specific times for judging the injustices in this world? If God would do so, the righteous could live in peace under divine protection. **Why must those who know him look in vain for such days?** Job bemoaned the reality that God does not communicate such regular days of judgment to man. If God would appoint such specified days for judging, then the righteous would be less frustrated over sin. But the righteous were left to wrestle with God's apparent indifference toward sin and sinners.

B Job's Observations (24:2–12)

SUPPORTING IDEA: *Job catalogues the unjust practices of the wicked who take advantage of others.*

24:2. The first injustices that Job cited were those committed in the country. The phrase **Men move boundary stones** refers to the ancient practice by which corrupt landowners often increased their holdings by expanding the landmarks that marked off property lines. This was a serious crime in ancient times (Deut. 19:14). By moving the landmarks, they were able to steal **the pasture flocks** of the annexed land.

24:3. Often such a corrupt practice involved stealing the land and flocks of orphans and widows. In so doing, Job declared, they drove away **the orphan's donkey** and took **the widow's ox in pledge**. Those who moved landmarks were those who stole the donkey and ox of the needy.

24:4–5. **They thrust the needy from the path and force all the poor of the land into hiding.** The poor among them were forced to hide in order to escape further injustices and oppression at the hand of the wicked. Why did God not judge these crimes on a regular basis, Job wondered. These mistreated poor were **like wild donkeys in the desert**, destitute and without a permanent home. They were left to eke out a meager existence in the wilderness **wasteland** by **foraging food**.

24:6–8. What is worse, the poor were left to work for **the wicked**. They gathered fodder in the fields of the wicked and gleaned in the vineyards of the wicked. Such cruelty resulted when God did not judge the ungodly. The oppressed, **lacking clothes**, were forced to sleep without anything **to cover themselves in the cold**. Job was denying the accusation made by Eliphaz that he withheld the outer garment from the poor (Job 22:6). Living and sleeping in these open fields, the needy were **drenched by mountain rains**, left to **hug the rocks** for **shelter** from the elements. Again, why did not God judge such wicked actions?

24:9–10. Job continued to catalogue injustices that he observed in the world that seemed to go unpunished. The fatherless child was **snatched from the breast** by ruthless men, even while these babies were being fed. Similarly, **the infant of the poor was** taken as collateral for a **debt**. So destitute were these poor and oppressed that they went about **naked** and **hungry**. Such abject poverty left them at the mercy of disease and death.

24:11. **They crush olives among the terraces** for their oppressive masters, Job declared. **They tread the winepresses, yet suffer thirst**. Their needs went unmet. If human courts punished the wicked, why did God not do the same?

24:12. Their **groans** under this mistreatment rose as they cried out for help. But in spite of such obvious injustice, God charged no one with **wrongdoing**. Why did God not do something, Job lamented. He protested against God for ignoring those who cried for help.

C Job's Description (24:13–17)

SUPPORTING IDEA: *Job describes the character of the wicked who go unpunished by God.*

24:13. Job detailed the ungodly whom God did not judge and who had caused so much harm. **There are those who rebel against the light**. They were oppressors and criminals who operated under the cover of darkness and sinned secretly in the night. They operated under the dark cloak in order to remain undetected and unnoticed by the watching eyes of others. Secretly, they strayed from the **paths** of honesty and decency.

24:14–15. Committing their offenses when daylight was gone, they robbed and killed **the poor and needy**. Thus, **the murderer** rose up to perform his evil, undetected by others. **The adulterer**, waiting for **dusk**, brazenly thought, **No eye will see me** and unashamedly launched into the night to commit unrestrained sins. Yet God sees all (cp. Heb. 4:13).

24:16–17. Likewise, **in the dark**, other evil men broke into **houses**, confident they would not be detected. Ancient houses were often built with mud bricks and, thus, thieves would dig through them. But **by day**, these thieves sat idly by so they would not be caught by their unsuspecting victims. While most people arose early to work hard in the **morning**, the opposite was true for these thieves. **Deep darkness is their morning**, the time when they worked hardest in carrying out their sin.

D Job's Clarification (24:18–24)

SUPPORTING IDEA: *Job quotes his friends' words to refute them, declaring that if their view is correct, the wicked would already be punished.*

24:18. Job quoted the words of his friends spoken earlier. His logic was if they were correct, that God always punishes the wicked, then all the wicked should be presently suffering punishment. But they were not. The wicked were **foam on the surface of the water**, unstable in all their ways, accumulating filth. Their portion of the land was **cursed**, unproductive in spite of all their labors. Thus, no one went to their **vineyards** to buy their produce.

24:19. As a result, as the **snow** was **melted** by the **heat** of the sun, **so the grave snatches away those who have sinned**, causing the wicked to perish eternally. The ungodly would melt under the fierce fury of God's future, final judgment that follows death. But not until the grave.

24:20. **The womb** that bore the wicked **forgets them** and when they die, **the worm feasts on** their decaying body. Thus, they are **no longer remembered**, cut off and severed like a fallen **tree** as their bodies waste away.

24:21. These evil men **prey on the barren and childless woman** and **the widow**, showing **no kindness**. Such is the depraved character of the wicked that is not moved even by the most pitiful plight.

24:22. **But**, Job now confessed, **God drags away the mighty by his power** in judgment. No matter how **established** they are in this world, **they have no assurance of life** before God. They will not escape his divine judgment. It will sweep them away into eternal judgment. God will do this in his own time.

24:23. God may allow the wicked to have **a feeling of security** for now. But be assured, his all-seeing eyes are **on their ways**. God sees their sins, takes notice, and will take it up in the final judgment.

24:24. For a while the wicked are **exalted** in this world, wealthy and powerful. But they will be soon **gone** from the scene in death and judgment. They will be **brought low** by the Lord, **gathered up like all others**, and **cut off like heads of grain**, harvested into judgment.

E Job's Conclusion (24:25)

SUPPORTING IDEA: *Job challenges his friends to correct his statements, something he believes they cannot do.*

24:25. Job concluded this response by challenging his three friends to disagree with him and prove him wrong. "**If this is not so**," he declared, "**who can prove me false and reduce my words to nothing?**" This was a clear challenge that Job issued to his friends, inviting them to overpower his arguments.

MAIN IDEA REVIEW: *Job struggles with understanding why God allows the unrighteous to go unpunished, only to reaffirm that God will eventually bring judgment.*

III. CONCLUSION

The Final Judgment *Is* Coming!

Thomas Brooks, the noted Puritan, once wrote, "All men's secret sins are printed in heaven, and God will at last read them aloud in the ears of all the world." There is a final hour of reckoning for the human race. This day is fixed and sure, indelibly etched upon God's calendar. Sin will be judged, sinners will be condemned, righteous deeds will be revealed, and saints will be rewarded.

God has set a day of judgment in which he will judge the world in righteousness. That day is surely coming. The justice of God will be executed on the wicked in that hour. All of the unrighteous and the wicked, both the "great and small," will be there. The divine books contain the record of every sin ever committed in the long history of mankind. In the end the unrighteous wicked will be "thrown into the lake of fire." This eternal punishment will forever be inflicted upon the wicked by the vengeful hand of God, rendering justice for their evil deeds. To be sure, the Almighty has set a time of judgment against the wicked.

There is only one way to escape this final judgment before the Judge of heaven and earth. That is to settle out of court. Come to Christ and believe on him, the sinner's perfect sacrifice for sin and the penalty of sin. Upon the cross Jesus bore our sins, dying in our place, and in so doing, suffered the eternal wrath of God on behalf of sinners. If you would escape this final judgment of the wicked, you must believe upon the Lord Jesus Christ. Come to him to escape the fury of God's wrath in the last day.

IV. LIFE APPLICATION

Some Truths About Life

1. *Life is uncertain.* The only certainty in life is that there are no certainties except God. There are no guarantees in life except what God has promised. Job noted, "They have no assurance of life" (Job 24:22). The continuity of life itself is uncertain and unknowable. Tragedy can strike suddenly and unexpectedly.

2. *Life is short.* Every person is just one heartbeat away from death and eternity. James asked, "What is your life? You are a mist that appears for a little while and then vanishes" (Jas. 4:14). Life appears for a short time, only to end with no trace of its existence.

3. *Life is passing.* David understood this when he prayed, "We are aliens and strangers in your sight. . . . Our days on earth are like a shadow, without hope" (1 Chr. 29:15). The future is never guaranteed because life itself is fragile and easily ended. Solomon asked in Ecclesiastes, "No one knows what is coming—who can tell him what will happen after him?" (Eccl. 10:14). Although God may let the wicked "rest in a feeling of security" (Job 24:23),

he is sure to bring their appointed death. Death is the great equalizer. When it comes, it robs people of their ability to control what they once controlled. Believers must live in light of eternity, knowing that tomorrow may never come. Today God's people must give their all, living to their fullest while God gives life.

V. PRAYER

God, we acknowledge your sovereign right to punish the wicked in judgment. You have promised to reward the wicked according to their works, and you will keep your word. May we as your people rescue the wicked from the fire because we ourselves were lost until you sought us out. In Jesus' name. Amen.

VI. DEEPER DISCOVERIES

A. Sinned (24:19)

"Sinned" (Heb. *hata*) is an adjective meaning that which is bad, evil, wicked, or corrupt. It is used of evil words (Prov. 15:26), evil thoughts (Gen. 6:5; 8:21), and evil actions (Deut. 17:5; Prov. 2:14; 2 Kgs. 3:2).

B. Broken (24:20)

"Broken" (Heb. *shabar*) occurs 147 times in the Old Testament and means to bring destruction, to break, shatter, or ruin. It was used of the breaking of nations and peoples in divine judgment (Jer. 28:2; Amos 6:6) and destroying or dashing to pieces certain objects or idols (Exod. 32:19; Jer. 43:13). Here it is used metaphorically to describe a condition of the heart in which a person is shattered within by sin or by the scorn of others (Ps. 69:20).

VII. TEACHING OUTLINE

A. Job's Frustration (24:1)
   1. God does not set times for judgment (24:1a)
   2. Man does not see times for judgment (24:1b)

B. Job's Observations (24:2–12)
   1. He observed that the wicked go unpunished (24:2–4)
   2. He observed that the needy go unprotected (24:5–8)
   3. He observed that the wicked go unrestrained (24:9–12)

C. Job's Description (24:13–17)
   1. The wicked sin against light (24:13)
   2. The wicked sin in the dark (24:14–17)

D. Job's Clarification (24:18–24)
   1. Sinners will face their sin (24:18–21)
   2. Sinners will face their God (24:22–24)

E. Job's Conclusion (24:25)
   1. Who can prove me wrong? (24:25a)
   2. Who can make me nothing? (24:25b)

VIII. ISSUES FOR DISCUSSION

1. Do I focus on the prosperity of the wicked?
2. Am I envious of the wicked?
3. Do I remind myself of the horrible fate that awaits the wicked?

Job 25

You Maggot!

Quote

"A tongue that is set on fire from hell shall be set on fire in hell."

Thomas Manton

Job 25

I. INTRODUCTION

A Tongue Set on Fire

Billy Sunday, the noted evangelist of the early twentieth century, was once approached by a talkative woman who tried to justify the quickness of her own tongue by saying, "It soon passes. It is over with quickly." To which Sunday replied, "So is a shotgun blast." Yes, the devastation of a quick tongue may pass quickly, but it also harms quickly.

John Wesley was once approached by a young lady who said, "I think I know what my talent is." Wesley said, "Tell me." Without hesitation she replied, "I think it is to speak my mind." Wesley said, "I do not think God would mind if you bury that talent." Anyone who speaks his mind, running roughshod over others, should bury his tongue before others are buried by it.

This is what Job had been facing. He was subject to attack by the quick tongue of friends who had not hesitated to speak their mind. Rather than speaking with sensitivity to Job, they spoke with the subtlety of a shotgun blast. The result of these tongue-lashings was soul-jarring for Job, leaving him reeling under its force. Rather than helping Job, they reloaded and fired their verbal ammunition with renewed intensity.

This twenty-fifth chapter contains Bildad's final speech. It was brief, but he held nothing back. This short, pithy lecture may indicate that Job's three friends were running out of arguments and accusations. Also, the absence of a third speech by Zophar indicates that their one-sided arguments were finally running out. What is remarkable about Bildad's final speech is that everything stated here is true. Job could not disagree with a word that Bildad spoke. Neither would we. He stated the sovereignty of God and the sinfulness of man in clearest terms.

The problem with Bildad's speech was not so much with what he said but in what he did not say. Bildad spoke of man's depravity, but he forgot to offer God's grace. When the Bible speaks of human depravity, it also offers a way of salvation, something Bildad failed to do. He brought bad news but neglected to bring good news. His words also lacked love.

II. COMMENTARY

You Maggot!

MAIN IDEA: *Bildad argues that an infinite chasm separates the majesty of God and the depravity of man.*

A God's Sovereignty (25:1–3)

SUPPORTING IDEA: *Bildad declares that God is absolutely sovereign and cannot be resisted.*

25:1–2. Rather than responding to Job's concern for God's apparent apathy toward injustice (24:1–17), **Bildad** spoke to a higher subject—God's sovereignty. He declared, "**Dominion and awe belong to God.**" God's sovereignty over all heaven and earth should evoke awe in the hearts of all people. The fact that dominion belongs exclusively to God means that he reigns unrestricted in the heavens. He governs over all, controlling all and using everything for his glory. When this truth is understood, awe should fill the hearts of all mankind, including Job. In addition, Bildad declared, God **establishes order in the heights of heaven**. What may appear to be disorder and confusion to man is perfect order in heaven; he causes all things to work together with divine purpose and design.

25:3. Bildad asked, "**Can his forces be numbered?**" The unspoken but clearly implied answer was *no*. No one can number God's forces in the heavens. They are too many to be numbered. These forces refer to the angelic armies who are always at God's command, ready at a moment's notice to do his will. Thus, the execution of his sovereign purposes cannot be resisted by Satan, demons, man, creation, nature, or events. Furthermore, Bildad asked,

"**Upon whom does his light not rise?**" Again the implied answer is so obvious that it need not be expressed. No one escapes the reach of his all-seeing gaze and perfect knowledge. His light penetrates to all persons and places.

B Man's Depravity (25:4–6)

SUPPORTING IDEA: *Bildad rebukes Job by declaring that no mortal person can stand before a holy God and claim to be righteous.*

25:4. In the light of such a holy God, Bildad reasoned, "**How then can a man be righteous before God?**" Once again this rhetorical question, like those raised in the previous verse, begs for a negative answer. No person in his own righteousness **can be righteous before God**. All have sinned and fallen short of his glory (Rom. 3:23). All people have been weighed in God's balances and have been found unrighteous, and this includes Job. Bildad asked further, "**How can one born of woman be pure?**" The implied answer was *no one*. The entire human race is spiritually unclean in the eyes of God, corrupted by sin (Rom. 3:10–18).

25:5. Driving home his final argument, Bildad made a comparison. Beginning with the luminaries above, he stated, "**If even the moon is not bright and the stars are not pure in his eyes.**" His point was that the moon and stars are bright in the heavens above, but compared to the brightness of the sun, they are nothing. The moon only reflects the greater light of the sun. Neither are the stars bright in comparison to the luminous sun.

25:6. In the same way, neither is man clean when compared to God. **How much less man, who is but a maggot**. "Maggot" is a translation of the Hebrew word for putrefying worms. This was quite a slam for Job, whose flesh was covered with worms (Job 7:5). Likewise, how much less is **a son of man, who is only a worm**. This word for "worm" speaks of weakness. With this comparison, Bildad pushed for Job to face up to his own weakness and worthlessness.

MAIN IDEA REVIEW: *Bildad argues that an infinite chasm separates the majesty of God and the depravity of man.*

III. CONCLUSION

A Fly Across the Canvas

MacNeile Dixon, writing in his *Gifford Lectures*, depicts a fly crawling across Raphael's masterpiece in the Vatican. How much can it know about the picture? It knows something, of course. It knows there are smooth places and rough places and that some pigments are brighter than others. But it has no overall view of the painting. This restriction is not because there is something wrong with the mural but because of the fly's limited vision.

This was essentially the message that Bildad brought to Job. He told Job that God is infinite and man is finite. Thus, man will always be limited in his relationship with God. Bildad announced the sovereignty of God and the depravity of man. Both of these truths are theologically accurate. Nevertheless, what Job needed to hear was the compassion of God for sinners. Man is limited in grasping the supremacy of God, but he *is* the object of God's tender care. May all of us be encouraged with the knowledge of his love for us.

IV. LIFE APPLICATION

Bildad's Bad Theology

Bildad's theology was all wrong. Humans are not maggots. Man is not a worm. He is God's creation, and he bears the image of God. Sin has caused man's fall, resulting in depravity and the ruin of God's image in him (see Rom. 3:10–18). Salvation is a renewal of the image of God in believers (Col. 3:10). God's image in humans has not been altogether blotted out, only marred by sin. Consequently, fallen man is not a maggot, lower than the lowest of animals. Humans are God's special creation, corrupted by iniquity but bearing God's image nevertheless. Job was not worthless, as Bildad charged. He was of great value to his Maker.

Bildad forgot that this same argument applied to himself. The same gulf existed between God and Bildad. He, too, did not have God figured out. Whenever you point an accusing finger at someone else, there are always several fingers pointing back at you. Like a Pharisee, Bildad failed to practice what he preached. He refused to take a dose of his own medicine. There's a lesson here for God's people. When accepting counsel and advice from others, consider the life of the persons giving counsel. Is there a consistency of life and advice about them? Any humility? Do they model the message? Do they admit their own shortcomings? If not, then they are probably wrong.

V. PRAYER

God, our Father, dominion and awe belong to you. Only you bring order to the heavens. Only you control the armies of heaven. Nothing and no one is out-

side your sovereign gaze, so how can we be righteous before you? We trust in Christ alone. He is our righteousness. He alone can make the unclean clean. In the name that is above every name we pray. Amen.

VI. DEEPER DISCOVERIES

A. Maggot (25:6a)

"Maggot" (Heb. *rimma*) in all seven usages in the Old Testament describes a worm that is always associated with decay. In Exodus 16:24 it is used of maggot not getting into manna because it did not ruin. In Job, *rimma* is used by Job as he stated, "My body is clothed with worms and scabs, my skin is broken and festering" (Job 7:5). The implication is that Bildad probably saw the maggots on Job when he made this statement. The root form of the word is found in three different places in Job (17:14; 21:26; 24:20).

B. Worm (25:6b)

"Worm" (Heb. *tolea*) is a reference to a larva or grub. The worm is the larva of certain types of insects. *Tolea* is an insect that feeds on plants (Jon. 4:7) and even corpses (Isa. 14:11). As in this passage, *worm* is used in other passages to communicate the insignificance of man (Ps. 22:6).

VII. TEACHING OUTLINE

A. God's Sovereignty (25:1–3)
1. His dominion is exalted (25:1–2a)
2. His order is established (25:2b)
3. His forces are empowered (25:3a)
4. His light is extended (25:3b)

B. Man's Depravity (25:4–6)
1. He is unjust before God (25:4a)
2. He is unclean before God (25:4b)
3. He is unworthy of God (25:5–6)

VIII. ISSUES FOR DISCUSSION

1. Do I meditate upon the dominion and awe of God?
2. Do I understand that nothing escapes the all-seeing eye of God?
3. How does my life demonstrate unrighteousness and impurity?

Job 26

God Incomprehensible

Quote

"Bring me a worm that can comprehend a man, and then I will show you a man that can comprehend the triune God!"

John Wesley

Job 26

I. INTRODUCTION

It Just Will Not Fit

Augustine, the great thinker and theologian, was once walking along a beach, perplexed by the incomprehensible truth of the Trinity. Trying as he might, he simply could not grasp the vast truth of the triune nature of one God who exists eternally in three persons. Because he could not fully understand it, he was tempted to reject it. Augustine continued to walk along the shoreline until he came upon a little boy playing on the beach. As he watched, he saw the child run to the ocean with a seashell, fill it with water, and then return to pour it into a small hole he had dug in the sand. "What are you doing, my little man?" asked Augustine. "Oh," replied the boy, "I am trying to put the ocean into this hole."

Augustine smiled at the little boy's faith. Such a task was impossible even for the greatest of men. Then it suddenly struck him. He was guilty of exactly the same futile act. "That is what I am trying to do with God," he later confessed. "Standing on the shores of time, I am trying to get the infinite things of God into this little finite mind. It just will not fit."

This was the deepening realization to which Job had arrived. With new awareness he understood that he was attempting to reduce the infinite, eternal God into the limited confines of his finite mind, and such a reduction is not possible. God, the Alpha and Omega, the beginning and the end, is too vast, too immense, and too expansive to fit into the confined space between our ears.

Job 26 contains Job's fiery response to Bildad's final speech in the previous chapter. It is a marvelous extolling of the greatness of God's power in creation and providence as he rules over life and death, heaven and earth. God exceeds our limited capacity to grasp who he is. Job chided Bildad and his friends for their shallow counsel that was grounded in a restricted view of God.

II. COMMENTARY

God Incomprehensible

MAIN IDEA: *Job rebukes Bildad and magnifies God's great power in the universe that is beyond human comprehension.*

A Job's Mocking (26:1–4)

SUPPORTING IDEA: *Job rebukes Bildad and his friends by asking whom they have helped by their counsel.*

26:1–2. Job began by ridiculing the "comfort" of his friends, saying, in effect, they had been no help whatsoever: "**How you have helped the powerless!**" These words drip with sarcasm and contain biting irony. In essence, Job said, "Thanks for absolutely nothing." Bildad had viewed Job as one with no power, but his counsel had not helped him any. **How you have saved the arm that is feeble!** This is to say, you have not saved me whom you consider to be feeble. Instead of helping Job up when he was down, they had kicked him.

26:3. Job continued with sarcasm by saying, "**What advice you have offered to one without wisdom.**" The implication was that they had contributed no wise counsel to Job, in spite of their many words. Further mocking Bildad, Job taunted, "**And what great insight you have displayed!**" Of course, he meant the opposite. Bildad had given no helpful insight into Job's suffering.

26:4. Finally, Job blasted Bildad: "**Who has helped you utter these words?**" The obvious response was no one with any clear thinking. Pressing further, Job queried, "**And whose spirit spoke from your mouth?**" The inference was clear. Bildad spoke by way of a spirit, an evil spirit from the kingdom of darkness that had corrupted his counsel. This was precisely the supernatural source that Eliphaz had claimed earlier as his informant (Job 4:15).

B Job's Magnification (26:5–13)

SUPPORTING IDEA: *Job reminds his critics that the vast universe is only a small microcosm of God's mighty power.*

26:5. In response to Bildad's declaration of God's greatness, Job responded with his own discourse on divine supremacy, specifically as it pertains to God's greatness over death and the grave. Job proclaimed, "**The dead are in deep anguish, those beneath the waters and all that live in them.**" The word for *dead* referred to giants, or the elite among the dead. Even the leaders who have departed this life tremble under the greatness of God's sovereignty.

26:6. Death is naked before God, that is, clearly in view of his all-seeing gaze. No one can escape God, not even in death. **Destruction lies uncovered**, fully exposed to God's penetrating sight and sovereign authority.

26:7–8. He spreads out the northern skies over empty space. God stretched out the heavens like a tent on a pole, the northern skies being the uppermost, highest point of the universe. **He suspends the earth over nothing**, upheld by God's command in outer space, not resting on anything. Describing the skies with clouds, Job elaborated, "**He wraps up the waters in his clouds.**" Amazingly, the heavy weight of the water is suspended in midair by nothing material. **Yet the clouds do not burst under their weight** but float in thin air.

26:9–10. God, Job contended, **covers the face of the full moon, spreading his clouds over it.** In so doing, God obscures the celestial bodies from man's vision. What is more, God **marks out the horizon on the face of the waters.** The word for *horizon* means a circle, or a circular, globe-shaped sphere. Here is an amazingly accurate, scientific statement about the earth's round shape recorded long before such a discovery was made by modern man.

26:11. The pillars of heaven is a figurative expression for towering mountains, those peaks that appear to be holding up the skies (Job 9:6). These majestic mountain ranges **quake** and, metaphorically speaking, are **aghast** whenever God's voice is lifted to **rebuke** them. Even the strongest of God's creation, these impregnable mountains, tremble when the divine word is spoken.

26:12. By God's **power**, even the expansive **sea** is churned up. **By his wisdom he cut Rahab to pieces.** *Rahab* is a term describing natural forces that bring devastation to the earth. Job said that even those powers which overpower creation are overpowered by God.

26:13. By his breath, referring to either the wind, God's spoken word, or, possibly even to his Spirit (Job 33:4), **the skies became fair**. Probably the latter is true, but any of these possibilities could be correct because God himself controls the weather. The Lord Almighty clears out the clouds after a storm. **His hand pierced the gliding serpent**. This is a reference to God's dispelling of the clouds. They move away in what appears to be a snakelike form.

C Job's Marveling (26:14)

SUPPORTING IDEA: *Job realizes that the greatness of God is beyond man's capacity to fully understand.*

26:14a-b. Job declared, "**And these are but the outer fringe of his works.**" In other words, these extraordinary truths which he had previously stated about the supremacy of God were only a fraction of the total magnitude of his divine greatness. All that Job had cited about God's unrivaled power over the grave and nature were a fragmentary outline of the infinite, incomprehensible sovereignty of God. Job stated, "**How faint the whisper we hear of him!**" What truth man has heard about God is only a soft whisper compared to the loud shout of his fuller revelation. Only a small part of the whole truth about God had been made known in his friends' many words.

26:14c. Finally, **who then can understand the thunder of his power?** The implied answer to this question is *no one*. Not one person can grasp the profundity of God's limitless power that is displayed in creation and providence. If God were to speak in the thunder of his power, as opposed to a mere whisper as he has done, man could not understand him. The full range of his power defies human comprehension. God is infinitely greater than what any person can imagine.

MAIN IDEA REVIEW: *Job rebukes Bildad and magnifies God's great power in the universe that is beyond human comprehension.*

III. CONCLUSION

God Incomprehensible

Augustine was right. Trying to fit the infinite truth of God into the finite limitations of man's mind is like attempting to fit the Atlantic Ocean into a small seashell. The infinite simply will not fit into the finite. Richard Rolle once said, "He truly knows God perfectly who finds him incomprehensible and unable to be known." That is, the more we learn about God, the more we realize how little we know about him.

The Almighty exceeds our greatest thoughts of him, no matter how lofty they may be. Our minds simply cannot conceive it. May we, like Job, stand in absolute awe and utter amazement of this infinite God. May we lower ourselves before him with humility. May we adore and magnify the one who alone is worthy. May we give him the glory due his name.

IV. LIFE APPLICATION

True Worship

In the context of realizing the true greatness of God with all its attendant mysteries, true worship occurs. You cannot worship a God whom you entirely understand. If we could, he would be reduced to peer status—an equal of the worshipper. But such a low thought of God is blasphemy. God is beyond our comprehension of him. It is in the face of this sobering realization that our hearts become filled with awe and reverence toward God. The Almighty exceeds our highest, loftiest thoughts of him.

True worship of God is fueled by a deepened knowledge of God. Head knowledge that does not lead to heart worship is worthless and leads only to pride. But when our knowledge of God is growing in depth and fervor, our worship will also grow in depth and fervor. When we have a fresh understanding of the attributes of God, there is a great admiration of the majesty of God that occurs when worshipping. This appreciation is experienced by those who have an encompassing view of God's greatness. Do you have a deepening knowledge of God? Do you convert head knowledge into fervent heart knowledge? Is your worship fueled by your knowledge of God?

V. PRAYER

God, open our eyes that we may behold deeper measures of your greatness. Forgive us when we attempt to limit you by our understanding. Forgive us for our self-imposed restrictions in which we determine to worship you only to the extent of what we understand about you. May we welcome the divine tension of mysteries within our hearts as we seek to worship you. In Jesus' name. Amen.

VI. DEEPER DISCOVERIES

Rebuke (26:11)

"Rebuke" (*geara*) is a feminine Hebrew noun that occurs fourteen times in the Old Testament. It means to chide, scold, or reprove. The word sometimes refers to God's power in overthrowing a warrior (Ps. 76:6) and to drying up the sea (Isa. 50:2), and of God's commands that created the channels of the sea and laid bare the foundations of the earth (2 Sam. 22:16). In a similar way, rebuke is used here to convey God's powerful reproving commands, which can make the pillars of heaven tremble.

VII. TEACHING OUTLINE

A. Job's Mocking (26:1–4)
   1. He mocked the substance of Bildad's words (26:1–3)
   2. He mocked the source of Bildad's words (26:4)

B. Job's Magnification (26:5–13)
   1. God is sovereign over life and death (26:5–6)
   2. God is sovereign over heaven and earth (26:7–13)

C. Job's Marveling (26:14)
   1. This truth is only the outer fringe (26:14a)
   2. This truth is only a faint whisper (26:14b)
   3. This truth is beyond our understanding (26:14c)

VIII. ISSUES FOR DISCUSSION

1. Do I confront the unbiblical counsel of others?
2. Do I testify of the greatness of God to others?
3. Do I regularly testify to God's greatness over heaven and earth?

Job 27

God, I Demand Justice!

Quote

"We may see non-justice in God, which is mercy, but we never see injustice in God."

R. C. Sproul

Job 27

I. INTRODUCTION

Justice Instructing the Judges

Paul Robert, internationally acclaimed artist, was commissioned to paint a mural that would hang in the stairway leading up to the supreme court in Switzerland. After much careful thought, Robert chose to express on canvas what Samuel Rutherford had spoken earlier in provocative words, the title of the painting being "Justice Instructing the Judges." In the foreground of this masterpiece are various litigants—the wife against her husband, the architect against the builder, and the like. Above them stand the Swiss judges with their distinctive white shawls. The searching question is: How are these judges going to judge the people?

Robert's answer is simple but profound. Justice, usually portrayed as blindfolded with a vertical sword, is pictured in this mural without a blindfold. The drawn sword of justice is pointing downward to a book. A closer look reveals that on this book is written "the Word of God." Divine justice is portrayed as instructing human judges.

Job wanted this virtue to be made real in his life. He longed for divine justice to rule on his behalf in the midst of his seeming injustice. He yearned for God to set the record straight about his life and show him to be innocent of all charges against him. The suffering he was going through led Job to one conclusion—that he had been charged guilty by God of an unknown crime. If he could plead his case before God, surely divine justice would render a favorable verdict on his behalf.

Job 27 contains Job's plea to God about his own innocence. He still wanted to take God to court and get the verdict reversed. He swore that he was guiltless of all charges that had been brought against him by the Lord. He maintained that he would go to his grave believing that he was right in this matter. But bitterness had crept into Job's heart because God would not act as he believed he should. Trials, it has been said, will either make you bitter or better. In Job's case they had made him bitter.

II. COMMENTARY

God, I Demand Justice!

MAIN IDEA: *Job reaffirms his innocence, calls for God's wrath to be unleashed on his enemies, and announces his confidence in the judgment of God in rewarding the wicked according to their deeds.*

A Job's Defense (27:1–6)

SUPPORTING IDEA: *Job protests his innocence and vows to continue his pursuit of holiness and integrity.*

27:1. The opening line of this chapter, **And Job continued his discourse**, signals that this section stands separate from the preceding chapter. In fact, Job 27–31 forms one enlarged section that brings this heated debate to a conclusion. No longer will his three miserable friends speak—only Job, a fourth friend, and God.

27:2. Job began his response, **As surely as God lives**. He was taking a solemn oath by invoking God's name. What Job said, he claimed, was as certain as God's existence. In this bold assertion Job protested that God had denied him justice. He held to his innocence with unwavering tenacity, even at the risk of saying that God had erred in the handling of his case. Assigning blame to God, Job spoke of God as **the Almighty, who has made me taste bitterness of soul**. It was God, Job concluded, who had provoked his soul with this unjustified punishment and his resulting sorrow.

27:3–4. Job pledged that as long as he lived, his **lips** would **not speak wickedness** by admitting his own guilt and he would **utter no deceit** by confessing uncommitted sins. This would be an admission of personal guilt and would not be truthful on his part, Job felt.

27:5. He vowed not to change his conviction of personal innocence in this matter, not **till I die**. He would take this conviction of being right to his grave. "**I will never admit you are in the right**," he protested to God. "**I will not deny my integrity.**" He would not agree with his friends' false diagnosis that he was suffering under God's heavy hand because of his own sin.

27:6. Job concluded this opening part of his speech by declaring, "**I will maintain my righteousness.**" That is, he was holding fast to his claim of personal innocence. He purposed that he would **never let go** of this deep-seated, inner conviction, no matter what. Unknown to Job, God himself had spoken the same of him (Job 1:1,8; 2:3). Refusing to live with a guilty **conscience**, he maintained that his conscience **will not reproach me as long as I live**. In this bold assertion Job claimed that he had lived in a God-honoring way, and he would continue to do so all his days.

B Job's Denunciation (27:7–12)

SUPPORTING IDEA: *Job calls for God's judgment to be unleashed on his foes.*

27:7. Job desired that his **enemies be like the wicked**. That is, he called upon God to judge his three friends like foes. He referred to his three self-appointed counselors as his enemies because of the destruction they had wrought in his life. They were like **adversaries** who had assumed an adversarial role. Thus, Job called for his friends to be treated by God as opponents, not companions.

27:8. The **godless** man, Job noted, has no **hope** when he is **cut off**. This is a reference to his three friends who were conducting themselves like **the godless**, not like the righteous. God **takes away his life** and judges him, Job declared. So it will be for his three counselors if they continued in their personal attack against him.

27:9–10. **Does God listen to his cry?** Job was referring to the prayers of the godless for divine assistance. The answer is *no*. His friends' petitions would go unanswered by God. Though **distress comes upon him**, Job knew God would refuse to hear their cry. **Will he find delight in the Almighty?** Again, the assumed answer is *no*. **Will he call upon God at all times?** No, the godless man will not delight in or call upon God. The implication is that his three friends were acting like unsaved men whom God must deal with.

27:11–12. Speaking directly to Eliphaz, Job stated, "**I will teach you about the power of God.**" Earlier, Eliphaz had told Job that he would instruct him about God. Now, the tables were reversed. Job claimed he would teach Eliphaz and his friends about God. Job said, "**You have all seen this you-selves.**" Thus, Job's words would only restate what they already knew to be true. But Job believed this most basic dialogue between them should not even be stated. **Why then this meaningless talk?** In other words, his friends should know better than to pour forth their empty rhetoric.

C Job's Declaration (27:13–23)

SUPPORTING IDEA: *Job notes that the wicked are headed for certain destruction.*

27:13. Taking the long look at the wicked, Job stated emphatically, "**Here is the fate God allots to the wicked.**" There is a deserved judgment that **a ruthless man receives from the Almighty**. This statement repeated the words of Zophar spoken earlier (Job 20:29). In this sense, Job agreed with his three friends that the ungodly do suffer greatly.

27:14–15. Job argued that the wicked will suffer the loss of their own **children**, often by **the sword**. Although Job himself had suffered this tragedy, he affirmed that this fate also awaited the ungodly. In other cases, **the plague will bury** the sons and daughters of the ungodly man. They suffer in their mortal bodies the wrath of God's just retribution. What is more, **their widows will not weep for them**. This is because they will see the deaths of their husbands as acts of divine justice. Even those closest to the wicked, their own spouses, will not mourn their passing.

27:16–17. What is more, the ungodly will lose their wealth. **He heaps up silver like dust and clothes like piles of clay**. These images portray the wealth of the wicked like a common commodity. But the monetary means and possessions of the wealthy will be taken away. Nevertheless, what the rich man **lays up, the righteous**, who are **innocent, will wear**. The items stolen and plundered by the ungodly man will eventually be passed down to and divided up by the innocent when God issues justice.

27:18–19. **The house** of the ungodly **is like a moth's cocoon**—a flimsy, temporary **hut made by a watchman**. This means that the evil person's most valuable possessions will collapse because they are made for temporary and not eternal use. The wicked man **lies down** to sleep, surrounded by his wealth, but when he awakens, **all is gone**. His vast holdings will be taken away by God while he rests in comfort, not thinking about the future.

27:20. The **terrors** of losing family and wealth will **overtake him like a flood**. Such loss is inescapable and irreversible when God's justice is unleashed. A **tempest** (i.e., windstorm) will **snatch him away in the night** when he least suspects it, rendering the sinner defenseless and helpless.

27:21. The east wind is a Palestinian sirocco that blows in from the desert in late spring and early fall (Hos. 13:15). It is a strong, dry wind that **carries him off** into judgment. So great are its destructive effects that **it sweeps him out of his place**, meaning he is removed permanently from where he has lived.

27:22–23. This windstorm **hurls itself against him** with vicious force. **He flees headlong**, trying to avoid its effect, but the wicked is unable to escape its mighty **power**. The ungodly cannot hide from God. This whirlwind **claps its hands in derision**, mocking the ungodly. It **hisses him out of his place**, another gesture of contemptuous treatment by God. This will be the end of the wicked—ridicule and rejection by God.

MAIN IDEA REVIEW: *Job reaffirms his innocence, calls for God's wrath to be unleashed on his enemies, and announces his confidence in the judgment of God in rewarding the wicked according to their deeds.*

III. CONCLUSION

When Wrong Is Right

In life, right often appears to be wrong and wrong right. Such was the strange case recently when Judge Leon R. Yankwich, a federal judge in Los Angeles, was presented a civil case that made him want to scream. Two men, Luther Wright and Hermann Rongg, were assigned to appear before his court, each claiming ownership of a patent. Attempting to moderate the dispute, Judge Yankwich declared, "One of you must be wrong." "That's right," replied Rongg, "I'm Rongg, and I'm right." Then Wright interrupted, "He's wrong, your honor. I'm right and Rongg is wrong."

So *who* is wrong? And *who* is right? Largely upon the strength of a letter that Wright wrote Rongg, Judge Yankwich terminated the Wright-Rongg dispute by ruling, "Paradoxical though it may appear in this case, Wright is wrong and Rongg is right, and I so enter my judgment."

This is the confusion that Job felt as he pled his case before God. He felt that he was suffering in this life as if right were wrong and wrong were right. He knew that he was right. But he felt he had been suffering as if he were wrong. Right and wrong seemed to be confused. Injustice seemed to be prevailing.

IV. LIFE APPLICATION

How to Stay Focused on God

When suffering the bitter trials of life, our vision of God can become obscured, and gross distortions of reality can result. Prolonged pain can lead us to make wrong assumptions about God. When this occurs, all of life gets out of focus. How can this be avoided?

1. *Stay in God's Word.* In the Scripture the truth about God's character is clearly revealed. In the pages of the inspired Word, we discover the reality that God is incapable of any injustice. He can do only what is right. Therefore, let us anchor ourselves in God's Word when the storms of life howl against us. The Scripture reveals that God can always be trusted to do what is right. Listen to the Word, not your worries.

2. *Stay on your knees.* The only perspective from which to see God clearly is from a position of humility. Only as we lower ourselves in God's presence can we have a proper view of the Lord, as well as our lot in life. But whenever we elevate ourselves before God, seeking to complain against him, we lose all sense of reality. We must stay humble and yielded before God. Only in a low posture of the soul can we see who God is and what he is doing in our lives.

3. *Stay in the right spirit.* Attitude is everything, especially when we experience the bitter disappointments of life. In every trial, let us set a watch over our hearts and never allow negative thoughts to enter. We must always remain bright in our outlook, even through the darkest night. We must remain positive, in spite of the negatives all around us. Our thought life must remain strong in its trust and reliance on God.

V. PRAYER

God, we have no rights before you, since our life is your life and your life is now our life. May we never speak evil of or defame your name in any way. For your ways are just and righteous. May we never contend with you, our Maker. In Jesus' name. Amen.

VI. DEEPER DISCOVERIES

A. Embittered (27:2)

"Embittered" (Heb. *marar*) occurs fifteen times in the Old Testament and means to be bitter, grieved, provoked, or vexated. It is used of events or experiences which are devastating in their effects (Gen. 49:23; 2 Kgs. 4:27; Ruth 1:13). *Embittered* is used in Ruth (Ruth 1:20) as it is used in Job.

B. Meditates (27:4)

"Meditates" (Heb. *haga*) denotes a low sound such as to mutter, murmur, or moan. Most usages of the word are found in the poetry literature of the Old Testament, particularly in Psalms and Isaiah. The term was used to refer to righteous ponderings (Prov. 15:28) and reflective meditation (Josh. 1:8; Ps. 143:5). Here in its only usage in Job, he notes that he will speak no deceit.

VII. TEACHING OUTLINE

- A. Job's Defense (27:1–6)
  1. He swore by God's existence (27:1–4)
  2. He swore to his integrity (27:5–6)
- B. Job's Denunciation (27:7–12)
  1. May my friends be like the wicked (27:7–10)
  2. May my friends be taught about God (27:11–12)
- C. Job's Declaration (27:13–23)
  1. The wicked lose their children (27:13–15)
  2. The wicked lose their wealth (27:16–17)
  3. The wicked lose their house (27:18–19)
  4. The wicked lose their life (27:20–23)

VIII. ISSUES FOR DISCUSSION

1. Do I acknowledge God's right to do whatever he chooses with my life?
2. When trials and tribulations come, do I continue to live in integrity and righteousness?
3. Do I delight in the Almighty?
4. Do I call upon God at all times?

Job 28
In Search of Wisdom

Quote

"If God would concede me his omnipotence for twenty-four hours, you would see how many changes I would make in the world. But if he gave me his wisdom, too, I would leave things as they are."

J. M. L. Mousabre

I. INTRODUCTION

Wisdom for the Oval Office

When William McKinley took the oath of office as president of the United States, he placed his hand upon these words: "Give me now wisdom and knowledge, that I may go out and come in before this people" (2 Chr. 1:10 NASB). Although he had advanced to the highest office in the land, he was aware of his need for divine wisdom.

This is true for every believer. All Christians need God-given wisdom if they are to face their duties in a way that honors the Lord. Wisdom is the spiritual insight from God that provides discernment, or insight, into a life situation, seeing it for what it is, and the proper application of biblical truth to that situation. It is one thing to know truth but something else entirely to know how it applies to our lives. Knowledge is the understanding of truth, and wisdom is the proper application of the understood truth. Wisdom is seeing ourselves for who we are and any situation for what it is and applying

God's truth accordingly. Wisdom is essential if we are to take spiritual inventory of our lives.

This is precisely where Job found himself at this point in this unfolding saga. He was a man in dire need of divine wisdom. If he was to face his suffering successfully, he needed wisdom from above. What is more, if he was to be rightly instructed by his three friends, they also needed wisdom. This soliloquy in Job 28 is a declaration of what is so desperately needed—heavenly wisdom from God, not worldly wisdom from man.

II. COMMENTARY

In Search of Wisdom

MAIN IDEA: *Job extols the virtue of wisdom, desiring that his three friends might have spoken to him with such divine wisdom.*

A God's Wisdom Cannot Be Sought (28:1–11)

SUPPORTING IDEA: *Job describes the various ways man mines for gold in the earth but is unable to find wisdom.*

28:1. Job began with an illustration of metal ore being mined by man. **There is a mine for silver**, dug deep into the earth, and the ore is excavated by men by back-breaking labor. And there is **a place where gold is refined**, meaning smeltered and refined as it is heated and separated from the rock.

28:2–3. **Iron is taken from the earth** by considerable effort as the material is lifted to the surface. And **copper is smelted from ore** by intense heat and fire, separating the copper and rock. Digging deep below the surface of the earth, man penetrates into **the farthest recesses**, into the **blackest darkness**, in his search for precious metals. By digging deep into the earth, man goes where no man has gone before.

28:4–5. **He cuts a shaft** into the earth and **dangles and sways** by a rope, being lowered into the mining shaft. He swings back and forth, probably in a basket as he is suspended by the rope, in pursuit of precious gems and metals. **The earth**, referring to this shaft, **is transformed below as by fire**. It was an ancient practice to ignite the walls of the tunnel and then pour water on it, causing the heated rock to crack, revealing precious stones and valuable metals.

28:6–7. **Sapphires come from its rocks** but only after it is dug out by the use of manpower. **And its dust contains nuggets of gold**, well worth the sweat and effort expanded to mine it. So secret and secluded is this deep mining that **no bird of prey knows that hidden path, no falcon's eye has seen it**. It remains unseen and undetected even by the trained eye.

28:8–9. **Proud beasts do not set foot on it** since such riches are inaccessible. **No lion prowls there.** These precious metals are imbedded within the inaccessible caverns of the earth. This mining operation is hidden from view, deep within the recesses of the earth. In his ingenuity and industrious efforts, **man's hand assaults the flinty rock**. So great is his ambition that he excavates deep into **the roots of the mountains**.

28:10–11. In so doing, man **tunnels through the rock** until he can **see all its treasures**. Then the miner **brings hidden things to light**, as he brings to the surface the treasures that were hidden beneath the earth's surface. God **searches the sources of the rivers**, discovering what no person can find out. God knows and reveals what man could never discern on his own. What is true of God's physical world (i.e., with rivers) is also true spiritually. Only God can make his wisdom known to man. No human can discover divine wisdom unless God chooses to make it known.

B God's Wisdom Cannot Be Bought (28:12–22)

SUPPORTING IDEA: *Job declares that wisdom, far more valuable than precious metals and stones, cannot be bought at any price.*

28:12. Job raised the question, **But where can wisdom be found?** That is, what steps must man take in order to find it? Job's words imply that wisdom exists and can only be discovered and not created. **Where does understanding dwell?** No amount of effort by man searching the world will yield such divine insight.

28:13–15. **Man does not comprehend its worth**. It is so great, its value cannot be ascertained. **It cannot be found in the land of the living**. Nowhere on earth reveals its true value. **The deep** of the ocean says, "**It is not in me.**" Wisdom is not to be found there. **The sea says, "It is not with me.**" Nor is wisdom there. Divine wisdom is invaluable. **It cannot be bought with the finest gold**, not with the greatest of all metals. **Nor can its price be weighed in silver**. Wisdom is costly and inaccessible to man.

28:16–19. Wisdom **cannot be bought with the gold of Ophir**, the finest gold to be found (1 Kgs. 9:28; Ps. 45:9). Neither can it be purchased **with precious onyx or sapphires** or **coral and jasper**. The value of divine wisdom surpasses all of these. **The price of wisdom is beyond rubies**. It is so far beyond the best rubies that it is not even worth the negotiation. **The topaz of Cush cannot compare with it**. Wisdom is incomparable in worth. **It cannot be bought with pure gold**. The best gold cannot purchase God's wisdom.

28:20. Job then raised the question again, **Where then does wisdom come from?** This is virtually identical to verse 12, and the answer that follows in verses 21–22 is virtually the same as verses 13 and 14. **Where does understanding dwell?** Where is it to be found?

28:21–22. Wisdom **is hidden from the eyes of every living thing,** not to be found even by **the birds** above. Even from their lofty perspective, they cannot discern the location of wisdom. **Destruction and Death** claimed to have heard **a rumor** about wisdom, but they are unable to grasp its reality. Even the dead are not privy to such wisdom.

C God's Wisdom Comes Only from Above (28:23–28)

SUPPORTING IDEA: *Job states that only God knows where to find wisdom and that true wisdom consists of fearing the Lord.*

28:23–24. The source of wisdom is found in **God** alone who **understands the way to it.** Only God **knows where it dwells.** It is by divine design that he alone has wisdom. Being all knowing, he **views the ends of the earth.** Nothing is hidden from his all-seeing, all-knowing gaze. All wisdom is with God himself.

28:25–26. God **established the force of the wind** at the time of creation, as well as matters dealing with measuring **waters.** All this was done with wisdom that God alone possesses. When God **made a decree for the rain and a path for the thunderstorm,** he consulted wisdom to do so, meaning he consulted himself. Both the rain and thunderstorm are controlled by God.

28:27. **Then he looked at wisdom and appraised it,** perfectly and accurately. **He confirmed it and tested it** to be true. This verse and the two that precede it closely resemble the wisdom hymn of Proverbs 8:22–31.

28:28. Thus, God said to man, "**The fear of the Lord—that is wisdom.**" That is, wisdom is the result of fearing God and reverencing him. Reverence toward God is the primary quality that makes us wise. Not until we stand in awe of the greatness of God and his limitless attributes can we become truly wise. Likewise, wisdom involves shunning **evil.** Wisdom and evil cannot exist in the same heart; one displaces the other. This is the quality that characterized Job from the beginning (Job 1:1,8; 2:3)

MAIN IDEA REVIEW: *Job extols the virtue of wisdom, desiring that his three friends might have spoken to him with such divine wisdom.*

III. CONCLUSION

Wisdom from Above

A student attending Columbia University believed he had been assured by the university that he would be taught wisdom. Feeling that the university had failed him in the matter, he filed suit against it for eight thousand dollars. The superior court dismissed the case. The presiding judge declared, "These charges were set in a frame of intemperate, if not scurrilous, accusations. . . . Wisdom is not a subject that can be taught and . . . no rational person would accept such a claim made by any man or institution."

No human institution can teach wisdom. Such God-given insight into life comes only from God and his Word. Wisdom comes from above, not from here on the earth. Thus, people must seek God if they are to find wisdom. Only those who fear him will find this treasure that is more valuable than gold and silver.

IV. LIFE APPLICATION

How to Fear God

According to this chapter, "The fear of the Lord—that is wisdom" (Job 28:28). What is the fear of the Lord? How can we fear him?

1. *Reverence God.* To fear God means to be filled with reverence, awe, and respect for him. It means to honor God with highest esteem and to take him seriously. Fearing God means to realize that God is our Creator and we are accountable to him alone. It means to remember that we are on his earth, breathing his air, and able to live only the number of days he has allotted us. It is to know that he controls our eternal destiny. Thus, we must hold him in highest regard as the one, true sovereign over our lives. This is the fear of God.

2. *Submit to God.* Fearing God means to humble ourselves before him and give him control of our lives. It means to bow before him with loving trust, yielding to him in all things. Thus, we must live before God in a state of continual surrender to him

There are many benefits to fearing the Lord. True fear of God leads to service (cp. Deut. 6:13; 1 Sam. 12:14). Fear of God also leads to wisdom (Prov. 1:7; 9:10). Furthermore, those who fear the Lord receive life (cp. Prov. 19:23) and blessing (Ps. 128:1) as God delights in them (cp. Ps. 147:11). Do you fear

God? When was the last time you were in awe of God? If you are to have God-given wisdom to see your life with spiritual insight, you must fear God.

V. PRAYER

Father, teach us to fear you so that we may present to you a heart of wisdom. Open our eyes that we may behold your sovereign glory and awesome majesty. In seeing you for who you truly are, cause our hearts to reverence you more fully and hold you with greatest awe. May our lives be saturated with and dominated by a lofty view of you, mighty and lifted up. Fill our hearts with your divine wisdom so we may walk in a manner worthy of our calling. In Jesus' name. Amen.

VI. DEEPER DISCOVERIES

A. Shadow of Death (28:3)

"Shadow of death" (*salmawet*) is a Hebrew compound word that joins together the two Hebrew words for *shadow* and *death*. Therefore, *salmawet* refers to the shade of death, terror, or calamity. In Psalm 23:4, the meaning is that God will lead his sheep through dark places, even the experience of death. Used numerous times in Job (3:5; 12:22; 16:16; 28:3; 38:17), it carries the idea of a thick fog or deep shadow. The Lord is depicted as a God who can extinguish the darkness (Amos 5:8) and even bring the darkness into judgment (Jer. 13:16). The word is also translated as "the shadow of death" (Isa. 9:2). The Messiah would be a light to those who lived in such darkness (Isa. 9:2).

B. Lord (28:28)

"Lord" (*adonay*) means master or lord, and this is its only usage in Job. *Adonay* signifies majesty or intensification and is always used of God. Found throughout the Hebrew Bible, in the Pentateuch it is used as a reverent way of addressing God (Exod. 4:10,13). *Adonay* is prominent in the prophets and is used fifty-five times in the Psalms. Its use in certain passages, "Lord of all the earth" (Josh. 3:13; Mic. 4:13), "Lord of lords" (Deut. 10:17), "the Sovereign LORD, the God of Israel" (Exod. 34:23), and the contexts of other passages alludes to the meaning of *adonay* as the sovereign Lord who has ultimate authority, power, and rule. It is used of the Messiah in Psalm 110:1.

VII. TEACHING OUTLINE

A. God's Wisdom Cannot Be Sought (28:1–11)
   1. Man mines for precious metals (28:1–2,6)

2. Man mines with ingenious methods (28:3–5,9–11)
3. Man mines in unseen places (28:7–8)

B. God's Wisdom Cannot Be Bought (28:12–22)
1. Man cannot find wisdom (28:12–14,20–22)
2. Man cannot buy wisdom (28:15–19)

C. God's Wisdom Comes Only from Above (28:23–28)
1. God knows where wisdom is (28:23–27)
2. God defines what wisdom is (28:28)

VIII. ISSUES FOR DISCUSSION

1. Do I search for wisdom?
2. Do I understand the superiority of God's wisdom over man's wisdom?
3. Do I understand that God alone is the true source of wisdom?
4. Do I fear God?

Job 29

Remembering the Past

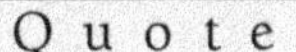

"The past must be a rudder to guide us and not an anchor to hold us back."

Warren Wiersbe

Job 29

I. INTRODUCTION

A Good Memory

Seneca, one of the most notable ancient teachers of rhetoric (about 55 B.C.–A.D. 37), had extraordinary powers of memory. He was able to repeat long passages of speeches he had heard many years earlier. He would impress his students by asking each member of a class of two hundred to recite a line of poetry, and he would then repeat the lines they had quoted. More than that, he would recite them in reverse order. The mind is a powerful tool when properly used.

Job was a man with a good memory. As he closed his defense, he reflected on the blessings he had enjoyed before his life-changing crisis. All of Job's memories were empty reflections of a bygone past. Job had enjoyed a rich and rewarding life. But now all that was gone. Thus, he wished he were back in the prime of life. It is not uncommon in times of trial to think back on how good the past was. When believers are undergoing a painful ordeal, it is only natural to long for previous days when God's blessings were abundant. For Job, remembering the past caused him to be more discontent with the present.

Job 29 is the record of Job's remembrance of his blessed past. He looks back on the joys from previous days. He remembers the blessings that he and his family enjoyed before the soul-numbing crisis. His mind reflects on past times when the sun beamed down on his life and everything seemed to be wonderful. This chapter begins the final summing up of Job's case that will conclude in Job 31.

II. COMMENTARY

Remembering the Past

MAIN IDEA: *Job reflects on the blessings he enjoyed before his great suffering began.*

Job's Faith (29:1–6)

SUPPORTING IDEA: *Job remembers the intimacy he enjoyed as he walked in close fellowship with God.*

29:1–2. **Job continued his discourse**, following his words on wisdom in the previous chapter (Job 28). This begins Job's final summation, a look to the past, to times when his life was prosperous and free of pain. He recalled how God's presence had permeated his life before his painful ordeal began. How he longed **for the months gone by** when God's favor was upon his life. Here is a small hint that, by this point, these sufferings had been going on for several months. He longed for the days when God watched over him with devoted care, shielding his life from harm.

29:3. In previous days, the **lamp** and **light** of God's presence and guidance were clearly experienced, even through his uncertain times. Though times of **darkness** arose, Job **walked through** them. He came through them unscathed.

29:4–5. "**Oh, for the days when I was in my prime**," Job declared. He longed for the days prior to his troubles when God seemed so close to him. It was then **when God's intimate fellowship** blessed his house. Literally, this reads, "When God's counsel was by my tent," picturing close, uninterrupted companionship. Job enjoyed personal companionship and fellowship with the Lord back **when the Almighty was still with** him. By contrast, Job now felt that God had deserted him.

29:6. In former days Job remembered his **path was drenched with cream** (i.e., the richest milk) and **streams of olive oil** (i.e., the best in abundance). This hyperbolic expression suggested God's overflowing blessing and prosperity in Job's life.

B Job's Fame (29:7–17)

SUPPORTING IDEA: *Job remembers the time before his suffering when great men respected him, listening to his wise counsel.*

29:7–8. Job reflected on the days before his ordeal began when great men treated him with respect. **The gate of the city** was the place where the leaders of the community gathered to conduct their business **in the public square**. Both **young men** and **old men** showed him the great honor enjoyed by an elder of his stature. They **stepped aside**, yielding to him, and **rose to their feet**, showing him great respect. Job enjoyed the honor given to a king or judges.

29:9–10. **Chief men refrained from speaking** in order for Job's counsel to be heard. When the counsel of city leaders gathered, all waited with **covered mouths** for Job's pearls of wisdom. Even **nobles were hushed**, men who were accustomed to issuing decrees. **Their tongues stuck to the roof of their mouths** in silence, yielding to Job's wisdom. They deferred to Job as they waited for him to render his verdicts and issue his opinions.

29:11. All men **spoke well** of him, Job remembered, and **commended** him for his insight and counsel. Following his discourse came the affirming accolades of his colleagues that applauded Job's counsel.

29:12. Such respect in the community was due Job because of the integrity of his life. He **rescued the poor** and assisted **the fatherless**. These were marks of a virtuous life. The fact that he stooped to help those who could give nothing in return placed him head and shoulders above the rest of his companions. By this, he denied the charges that he had oppressed the poor (Job 20:19; 22:6–9).

29:13–14. Job helped the **dying** and **made the widow's heart sing**. He was a source of blessing to people who were helplessly desperate. He administered impartial **righteousness** and **justice** in cases over which he presided. As an arbitrator of disputes, he was unsurpassed as he judged by using a righteous judgment.

29:15–16. He assisted people who were handicapped whether they were **blind** or **lame**. Illustrating his generosity, he said that he was **eyes to the blind** and **feet to the lame**. Job volunteered to guard and transport the handicapped of society. He championed the cause of **the needy** and **the stranger**, being like **a father** to them. His gracious hospitality was experienced by even the most desperate outcast.

29:17. Job also rescued the **victims** of oppression. The imagery is of the wicked sinking their **fangs** and **teeth** into the flesh of the innocent. If a man's true greatness was measured by his support of the weak, then Job stood tall in his day—the opposite of what his three friends had concluded about him (Job 22:1–11).

C Job's Future (29:18–20)

SUPPORTING IDEA: *Job remembers earlier days when he lived with a confident outlook about the future.*

29:18–19. Job recalled how he once thought, **I will die in my own house**, prosperous to the end. He had believed that his days would be **as numerous as the grains of sand**, living a long, full life. "**My roots will reach to the water**," he declared. He pictured himself as a healthy tree that had tapped into a source of life-giving sustenance. This metaphor represented the abundant life he once anticipated would be his to enjoy.

29:20. "**My glory will remain fresh in me**," Job said. He believed he would be vibrant and strong to the end of his life. **The bow**, a symbol of his strength, was **ever new** in his hand. At one time Job rested comfortably in his position and power.

D Job's Favor (29:21–25)

SUPPORTING IDEA: *Job reflects on the respect he was once shown by others.*

29:21. In previous days, Job recalled, men listened to him **expectantly**. This was in contrast to the disrespect shown by his three friends. There was a time when the leaders hung on Job's every word. Others waited **in silence** for Job to speak, giving proper homage to the successful patriarch.

29:22–23. And when Job spoke, **they spoke no more**. Job's counsel was so brilliant that there was no need for anyone else to speak. His **words fell gently on their ears**, well remembered and received. They drank in his words of counsel, like the parched ground receives the **showers** of a **spring rain**. In addition, his insight yielded a great harvest in their lives. They hung on every word of wisdom that proceeded from his mouth.

29:24. Even Job's smile was an encouragement to them. He loomed so large in their eyes that they could scarcely believe he would smile at them. Everyone longed for his approval. **The light** of his countenance **was precious to them** as they saw him as a source of stability. He was a rock of security and strength to those around him.

29:25. Job gave his counsel to others, acting as their **chief**, and they followed his direction explicitly. In reality, Job spoke with the authority of **a**

king among his troops, giving orders and instructions. Yet, he was also able to lower himself and comfort those who mourned.

> **MAIN IDEA REVIEW:** *Job reflects on the blessings he enjoyed before his great suffering began.*

III. CONCLUSION

Buying Memories

Three men in Canada invented the popular game Trivial Pursuit in which participants are called upon to remember facts, events, and people from the past. When one of them was interviewed about why the game was successful, he answered, "People are buying memories."

There were many memories that Job was buying up in his own life, reflections of better days gone by. Job longed for the days when he was experiencing the blessings of God. Yet, unfortunately, his happiness was tied directly to his prosperity in the present. Martin Luther was right when he wrote in his famous hymn, "A Mighty Fortress Is Our God," "Let goods and kindred go, this mortal life also." The righteous must have an indomitable trust in God that is not dependent on people, prosperity, or circumstances. Like a diamond that is strengthened by heat and pressure, the believer must be strengthened by the heat and pressure of trials and tribulations.

Rather than looking to the past, believers must look to the future and a bright tomorrow in which God will work for our good. The past must be released if the present is to be experienced triumphantly. "Forgetting what is behind and straining toward what is ahead, I press on toward the goal to win the prize for which God has called me heavenward in Christ Jesus" (Phil. 3:13–14).

IV. LIFE APPLICATION

A Skewed View of God

The problem that had crept into Job's life was his skewed view of God which looked upon the blessings of the Lord as indicators of his lovingkindness. Job interpreted the loss of blessings as an indication of the displeasure of God. True, God sometimes chooses to remove showers of blessing from his people—but not always. Jesus reminded his disciples, "He [God] causes his sun to rise on the evil and the good, and sends rain on the righteous and the unrighteous" (Matt. 5:45). In other words, neither the absence nor presence of blessings is a sign of the favor or disfavor of God. Many times believers view tragic events or circumstances in the lives of others as consequences of hidden sin. But absence of the blessings of God is not proof of his displeasure.

This truth is seen in the account of Jesus and the blind man. When the disciples saw the blind man, they asked Jesus, "Who sinned, this man or his parents?" (John 9:2). The presence of affliction and suffering is *not* proof of God's displeasure. Nor is the absence of affliction and suffering proof of God's favor. Rather, affliction and suffering are from God and may or may not occur because of our actions. From this side of heaven, no one can be sure. But we can be sure that God uses all human suffering and affliction for his glory.

V. PRAYER

God, our Father, we praise you for the blessings that you lavish upon us. Your gracious acts on behalf of your people are too numerous to count. We know that every good gift is from above coming down from the Father of lights with whom there is no variation. Truly the Lord is good! In Jesus' name. Amen.

VI. DEEPER DISCOVERIES

A. Oil (29:6)

"Oil" (Heb. *shemen*) is used mostly of olive oil. In its 190 occurrences in the Bible, it is used both in the literal sense and metaphorically, which is the case in this verse. Job used it as a reference to the abundant prosperity he experienced when God was with him (cp. Exod. 32:14; Mic. 6:7). Symbolically, it was often used of prosperity from the hand of God (cp. Deut. 33:24; Ps. 23:5).

B. Comforts (29:25)

"Comforts" (Heb. *naham*) connotes the idea of a person breathing deeply as a physical display of his feelings. Sixty-five times in the Hebrew Bible *naham* is used to speak of comfort and compassion. Perhaps the best known passage that contains *naham,* other than Psalm 23:4, is Isaiah 40:1, "Comfort, comfort my people, says your God." Many passages speak of comforting people in the face of death (Gen. 24:67; 2 Sam. 10:2; Isa. 61:2; Jer. 31:15). Throughout the psalms, *naham* is used to describe the comfort that God gives his people (Ps. 86:17; Isa. 12:1; 52:9). In Hosea 11:8, the word is used to convey God's tender love for Israel.

VII. TEACHING OUTLINE

A. Job's Faith (29:1–6)
  1. He had enjoyed God's protection (29:1–3)
  2. He had enjoyed God's partnership (29:4–5)
  3. He had enjoyed God's provision (29:6)

B. Job's Fame (29:7–17)
  1. He had enjoyed respect from others (29:7–11)
  2. He had earned respect from others (29:12–17)

C. Job's Future (29:18–20)
  1. He expected to live a full life (29:18)
  2. He expected to live a healthy life (29:19–20)

D. Job's Favor (29:21–25)
  1. Men once listened to me (29:21–23)
  2. Men once learned from me (29:24–25)

VIII. ISSUES FOR DISCUSSION

1. Do I recognize and give thanks for God's blessings?
2. Do I demonstrate a spirit of gratitude to God for his goodness?
3. Do I recognize that every good gift comes from God?

Job 30

The Great Depression

Quote

"Everything is needful that He sends. Nothing is needful that He withholds."

John Newton

Job 30

I. INTRODUCTION

All Is Burned Up

Thomas Edison, the prolific American inventor, suffered a devastating loss one night in December 1914. His laboratory and facility were damaged by fire. Most of his projects were destroyed. Almost one million dollars' worth of equipment was lost. In addition, Edison lost the records of much of his life's work.

The next morning, walking about the charred embers of his broken hopes and dashed dreams, the inventor said, "There is value in disaster. All our mistakes are burned up. Now we can start anew."

Job had suffered a devastating personal loss like Thomas Edison—only worse. Both lost valuable personal property when least expected. But even worse, Job lost his children and his health. Yet despite this severe loss, Job initially responded with confident faith in God. He understood that God is free to give and to take away since all belongs to him anyway. But in the days that followed, his faith wavered, and the pain settled in. Weakened and broken, Job poured out his heart to God, seeking relief, even through the escape of death. But no relief was to be found. Nothing could alleviate his pain.

In this chapter, Job lamented his sorrowful condition. Having described his happy days of the past (Job 29), he catalogued the pains he had suffered before God. He recorded his many areas of personal sorrow. This chapter portrays a severely depressed man.

II. COMMENTARY

The Great Depression

MAIN IDEA: *Job bewails his present misery that contrasts starkly with his past happiness.*

A Job's Foes Despise Him (30:1–15)

SUPPORTING IDEA: *Job suffers greatly at the hands of young vagabonds who decry his horrible position.*

30:1–2. "**But now they mock me**," Job declared, referring to men **younger** than he. These were a group of youth who ridiculed Job. Their **fathers** were so despicable that they were not even worth sleeping with Job's **sheep dogs**. Job lamented, "**Of what use was the strength of their hands to me?**" The answer was *none*. They were worthless **since their vigor** (i.e., positive productivity) **had gone from them**. They were parasites on society and even more so in relation to Job.

30:3–4. Like outcasts from society, these men were like wild animals on the prowl, searching for something to get into, looking for trouble. **In the brush** of the wild, **they gathered salt herbs**, probably saltwort, a plant which grew in fertile areas. **Their food was the root of the broom tree**, Job observed. This was a plant that grew in the desert and that only the poorest refugees would eat. They lived a meager existence as they foraged for food.

30:5–6. **They were banished from their fellow men**, expelled from society for the common good. They were **shouted at** by upstanding people **as if they were thieves**. These exiles were berated by society. **They were forced to live in the dry stream beds** like animals, **among the rocks and in holes in the ground**. This was the only habitat suited for these hated outcasts as they were destitute of a home.

30:7–8. Like wild donkeys, **they brayed among the bushes**. With no one else to associate with but themselves, they **huddled in the undergrowth** (i.e., thorn bushes). They wasted their lives in idleness. Job described these no-good nomads as **a base and nameless brood**, not even worthy of names. Further, they did not need names, since no one was around to call upon them. **They were driven out of the land**, the scum of society, exiled from the masses. The lowest of the low were now criticizing Job. This put him at the bottom of the barrel.

30:9–10. "**And now their sons mock me in song,**" Job moaned. They were singing their taunting tunes to deride the fallen patriarch. He had become **a byword** among them. His name had become an object of scorn and ridicule, a symbol of great suffering. Having a great disdain for Job, they detested him and kept **their distance**. They would not approach Job in his cursed state, choosing not to associate with him. Job stated that they did not hesitate **to spit in** his **face**, an act of repudiation and disgust.

30:11. "**God has unstrung my bow,**" Job declared. He believed that God had made him physically weak and demoralized, and had **afflicted** him through all these personal sufferings. In Job's powerless state, people were not afraid to **throw off restraint in** his **presence**. All respect for Job was gone.

30:12. **On my right the tribe attacks**, like an army against a defenseless city, Job observed. They put out **snares** for his feet in order to trap him. They built their **siege ramps** against Job so they could destroy him. Their intent was vicious, seeking to take advantage of Job in his weakened state when he was most vulnerable.

30:13. "**They break up my road,**" moaned Job, as they prevented him from moving forward with his life. They were succeeding in destroying him, doing great damage to a devastated and defeated man. All this was done against Job **without anyone's helping them** in this ruthless attack.

30:14–15. They advanced against Job as through a **gaping breach** in a city wall. **Amid the ruins** of Job's demolished life, they came **rolling in** to attack him like an advancing army surrounding him. In the face of this added injury, **terrors overwhelm me**, Job cried. **My dignity is driven away as by the wind**, swept away. With his prosperity gone, he lamented, **my safety vanishes like a cloud**. All that Job owned, both people and possessions, had disappeared without a trace.

B Job's Body Devastates Him (30:16–19)

SUPPORTING IDEA: *Job lives in physical misery as his fiery trial continues.*

30:16–17. Feeling his strength all but gone, Job cried, "**And now my life ebbs away.**" His sustenance was being poured out of him. **Days of suffering** gripped him, and he was unable to escape this terrible dilemma. Job could not sleep as **night** pierced his **bones**. He could merely lie in bed, but his **gnawing pains** never rested. Day and night, the anguish never left him.

Haunted by constant, nagging, excruciating pain, Job became restless in his frustration.

30:18–19. **In his great power**, bringing this affliction, God became like **clothing** to Job. Job could not escape this trauma which he wore like clothing. This is perhaps an allusion to his skin disorder. He bound Job like the neck of his **garment** and refused to loosen his grip. As one already humbled and humiliated by this ordeal, Job acknowledged, "**He throws me into the mud.**" This pictures disgrace and shame. "**I am reduced to dust and ashes,**" he cried. This symbolized his humiliation and degradation. These three elements—mud, dust, and ashes—would be mentioned again (cp. Job 42:6).

C Job's God Deserts Him (30:20–23)

SUPPORTING IDEA: *Job is devastated that God seems to have deserted him.*

30:20. In the midst of his pain, Job said, "**I cry out to you, O God, but you do not answer.**" It was useless to try to secure God's attention. "**I stand up, but you merely look at me,**" he moaned. God's silence was Job's greatest source of pain.

30:21–22. Accusing God of attacking him, Job charged, **You turn on me ruthlessly** like a fierce hunter pursuing his prey. **With the might of** his **hand** he attacked him, leaving him devoured and devastated. This was not Job's first complaint about his feeling that God was pursuing him (cp. Job 10:3; 16:9,14; 19:22).

30:22. God was like a violent, angry storm that had overwhelmed Job's life. "**You snatch me up and drive me before the wind,**" he declared—this in spite of his pleas for mercy. He tossed him **about in the storm**, reducing Job to nothing.

30:23. Sensing that the end of his life was near, Job moaned, "**I know you will bring me down to death.**" Such an end was now fast approaching, and God, Job believed, was hastening his final day of life. This trial could only lead to an early death, **to the place appointed for all the living**.

D Job's Hope Departs from Him (30:24–31)

SUPPORTING IDEA: *Job chronicles the hopeless emotions he feels as he is wasting away.*

30:24–25. "**Surely no one lays a hand on a broken man,**" Job said, referring to himself as a crushed and shattered person. Yet this is precisely what his three friends did to him. When Job cried **for help**, there was no help offered. Instead, they acted to hurt him. Job himself had **wept for those in**

trouble (cp. Rom. 12:15). Why had the same sympathy not been extended to him by these three counselors? Job's **soul grieved for the poor**. Why had they not done so for him?

30:26. Job had **hoped for good** from them, but he had received only **evil**. The evil came in their misguided counsel that misrepresented both God and Job. He had **looked for light**, hope, and kindness, but he found **darkness**, despair, and rejection.

30:27–28. Job expressed the emotional exhaustion of his soul. He said, **the churning inside me never stops**. This emotional pain was provoked by his constant physical pain. **Blackened** was a term used to denote the disease that was ravaging his body (cp. Job 30:30) or the ash-covered sackcloth that he wore as a symbol of mourning. He would **cry for help**, or relief from the pain, but no relief came.

30:29–30. Because of Job's pain, he wailed like the **jackals** in the wilderness. He had become **a companion of owls**, lonely and rejected (Mic. 1:8). Rejected by humanity, Job made his abode with the animals. His **skin** was peeling and his **body** was burning with intense **fever**. Job was describing the devastating effect of his disease (Job 2:7), which had grown worse.

30:31. As a result, his joy, pictured as a **harp** and **flute**, was **tuned to mourning** and the **wailing** of a funeral dirge. Having held out hope for recovery, Job's fading health caused him to lose all hope of healing. He sank deeper and deeper into despair and depression.

MAIN IDEA REVIEW: *Job bewails his present misery that contrasts starkly with his past happiness.*

III. CONCLUSION

Sustained in Much Sorrow

George Müller, a noted Christian leader in the nineteenth century, founded and directed many orphanages in England. But Müller was also a man who knew tragedy. On February 6, 1870, his wife, Mary, died of rheumatic fever. In deep pain Müller wrote of the tragic event in his diary on the day of her death: "39 years and 14 months ago, the Lord gave me my most valuable, lovely, and holy wife. Her value to me and the blessing God made her to me, is beyond description. The blessing was continued to me till this day, when this afternoon, about four o'clock, the Lord took her to Himself."

Then on February 11 Müller wrote, "Today the earthly remains of my precious wife were laid in the grave. Many thousands of persons showed the deepest sympathy. About 1,400 of the orphans who were able to walk followed in the procession. . . . I myself, sustained by the Lord to the utmost, performed the service at the chapel in the cemetery."

How was George Müller sustained through this most difficult time? Surely the secret is found in the text he preached for her funeral: "You are good, and . . . do . . . good" (Ps. 119:68). It was this truth, the goodness of God, that carried this great man of faith through his darkest hour. So it will be with us as well. God is good and does good. Let us trust him.

IV. LIFE APPLICATION

God Is Good and Does Good

The goodness of God is every believer's strength in the midst of deep suffering. It is found in the truth that God is good and always does good to his people. No matter what fiery trial may come our way, God can only work for good for those who are in Christ Jesus. Even in the midst of deepest personal pain, this is the healing balm for our wounded souls. God is good and does good. Thus, we may kiss the rod that strikes us and believe that God works positively even through our most negative experiences of life.

If you are facing a difficult, painful storm, may you know that God works for your good. This was the hope of George Müller, and it must be the confidence of all believers in their hour of deepest sorrow. Trust him in the dark night of your soul to work for your good. He *is* good and *does* good.

V. PRAYER

Our God and Father, we recognize that often you conform us to the image of your Son by driving us outside the city walls and into deep valleys. In these times of deep despair you mold us and make us. In these refining fires you burn out all dross so that we become pure vessels that can be used for your glory. Lord, we plead with you to continue to make us more holy no matter how bad it hurts. For Jesus' sake we pray. Amen.

VI. DEEPER DISCOVERIES

A. Desolate (30:3)

"Desolate" (Heb. *shoa*) means to be rushed over, as in ruin and swift destruction. It was used to speak of a desert wasteland that is desolate as if it had been destroyed (Job 38:27). It described a consuming storm that brought great destruction (Prov. 1:27; Ezek. 38:9). Thus it was used to speak of divine judgment. Isaiah asked the inhabitants of Israel, "What will you do on the day of reckoning, when disaster comes from afar?" (Isa. 10:3). The impending divine judgment and ruin that awaited Babylon is described as "a catastrophe (*shoa*) you cannot foresee [that] will suddenly come upon you" (Isa. 47:11). The word describes the terrible judgments associated with "the great day of the LORD" (Zeph. 1:14).

B. Attack (30:21)

"Attack" (Heb. *satam*) means to oppose or stand against and was used of animosity or hostility between two people. Job believed God was harboring a grudge against him (cp. Job. 16:9). *Satam* was also used of Esau's hatred of Jacob (Gen. 27:41), the animosity that Joseph's brothers believed he held against them (Gen. 50:15), and the grudge held against David by his enemies (Ps. 55:3).

VII. TEACHING OUTLINE

- A. Job's Foes Despise Him (30:1–15)
    1. Young vagabonds mock me (30:1–8)
    2. Young vagabonds taunt me (30:9–15)
- B. Job's Body Devastates Him (30:16–19)
    1. My soul was poured out (30:16)
    2. My bones were pierced (30:17)
    3. My skin is disfigured (30:18–19)
- C. Job's God Deserts Him (30:20–23)
    1. God has ignored me (30:20)
    2. God has opposed me (30:21–22)
    3. God has harmed me (30:23)
- D. Job's Hope Departs from Him (30:24–31)
    1. I am suffering alone (30:24–26)
    2. I am suffering greatly (30:27–31)

VIII. ISSUES FOR DISCUSSION

1. Do I surrender to God's sovereign will to carry me through difficult times?
2. Do I allow myself to be humbled?
3. Do I ever demonstrate a spirit of bitterness at life's experiences?

Job 31

But I Am Innocent

Quote

"If faith be a jewel, a good conscience is the cabinet in which it is kept."

William Gurnall

I. INTRODUCTION

But I Did Not Do It

A man was traveling on a lonely road in Japan when he was robbed and killed. Two supposed witnesses claimed that Ishimatsu Yoshid, an innocent bystander, committed the crime. One of them grabbed Yoshid and started beating him, yelling, "Confess." "No," Ishimatsu gasped, "I did not do it!" But the incriminating charge was made, and Yoshid was sent to prison for a crime he never committed. For the next twenty-three years, he suffered under great agony that he did not deserve.

Finally released from prison, Ishimatsu Yoshid began to hunt for his two accusers. He soon found one of the witnesses and forced him to admit that his testimony had been false. In fact, the man confided that he himself had committed the crime. Yoshida then hunted for the other witness. Upon finding him, and with all the pent-up emotion of twenty-three years of injustice, he grabbed the man and demanded, "Confess that you committed the murder." The second man admitted he was also guilty. Ishimatsu Yoshida then reopened his case, procured a retrial, and secured an exoneration. Proven innocent, he was able to have his name cleared of any wrongdoing.

This is precisely the frustration that Job was feeling. He knew himself to be an innocent man, undeserving of the charges levied at him by his friends. With mounting frustration, Job pleaded his case before God. In Job 31, his final soliloquy, Job searched his own life to prove that he was not guilty of the crimes assigned to him. He was not claiming perfection but innocence of the charges brought against him by Eliphaz, Bildad, and Zophar.

II. COMMENTARY

But I Am Innocent

MAIN IDEA: *Affirming his sexual purity, Job declares his righteousness in his business dealings, his faithfulness to his wife, his fairness to his workers, and his hospitality to others, all the while longing for God to give him a hearing.*

A Job's Purity (31:1–4)

SUPPORTING IDEA: *Job pledges that his eyes and heart are pure toward other women.*

31:1. Emphatically, Job stated, "**I made a covenant with my eyes not to look lustfully at a girl.**" He had made a firm commitment with his own eyes, mind, and heart to avoid lustful fantasizing about other women. To break this commitment would be to sin (Prov. 6:25; Matt. 5:28), and Job determined not to do so.

31:2–3. **For what is man's lot from God above**, if he should violate this commitment of purity? Surely, his **heritage from the Almighty** would be painful. Sexual sins are followed by heavy consequences. **Is it not ruin for the wicked** that would come to him if he should **do** this **wrong**? The same detrimental fate they suffered would be the fate Job would suffer if he had committed sexual impurity.

31:4. Job asked, **Does** God **not see my ways and count my every step**? The implied answer was *yes*. God sees all and would discipline him if he should entertain lustful thoughts. But Job was innocent of such secret sin.

B Job's Integrity (31:5–8)

SUPPORTING IDEA: *Job declares that his feet have followed the path of just business dealings with others.*

31:5–6. Proceeding to the area of his business dealings, Job stated, "**If I have walked in falsehood or my foot has hurried after deceit.**" Then Job declared metaphorically, **let God weigh me in honest scales** (i.e., meaning judge me by divine, righteous standards) **and he will know that I am blameless**, that is, full of integrity. Dishonest scales are also mentioned in Scripture (cp. Amos 8:5; Dan. 5:27).

31:7. If Job's steps had **turned from the path** of right and fair dealings with others, and if his **heart** had **been led by** his **eyes**, becoming greedy for what he saw, or if his **hands** had **been defiled** with wrongdoing, Job pronounced a curse of self-judgment. Such was Job's confidence in his innocence.

31:8. "**Then may others eat what I have sown**," Job declared—that is, reap and benefit from his labor at his expense. And may his **crops be uprooted**, not for Job to enjoy, if his business dealings were unprincipled. Notice how the punishment fits the crime.

C Job's Fidelity (31:9–12)

SUPPORTING IDEA: *Job declares that his heart is free of any unfaithfulness or adultery.*

31:9. If Job's **heart** had **been enticed by a woman** who was not his wife, causing him to be drawn to his **neighbor's door** in pursuit of his wife, then he should suffer the due consequence. But Job had not been seduced by his neighbor's wife (Prov. 5:8). The penalty for such an act was not what Job was suffering because he had not committed an act of adultery.

31:10–11. Then, pronouncing the penalty he should pay if such an act had occurred, Job said, "**May my wife grind another man's grain.**" That is, may she serve another man as his wife, and **may other men sleep with her** because she would be released from Job because of his unfaithful actions. Such a sin of marital infidelity **would have been shameful** before the eyes of God and others. It would be **a sin to be judged** by God. Sexual sin has built-in consequences which are designed by God (Prov. 6:27–35; 7:24–27).

31:12. Thus, the judgment of God is **a fire that burns to Destruction**. This is a reference to Abaddon (i.e., death and the grave; Prov. 5:5; 7:27). This **fire** would consume a man's soul, marriage, reputation, and hard work, pictured by the phrase **my harvest**.

D Job's Impartiality (31:13–15)

SUPPORTING IDEA: *Job affirms that his dealings with others is marked by justice.*

31:13. With the phrase **If I have denied justice to my menservants and maidservants**, Job shifted the focus of his self-examination to his dealings with others and invited investigation and inquiry into these dealings.

31:14. What will I do when God confronts me? Job, in fact, did have a large number of servants (Job 1:3), and he confessed that they had certain rights. These rights were based, he said, on the creation of all people by God. What would Job answer **when called to account** by God? No excuse could be offered to God, Job said, if he had mistreated any person, no matter how menial a status they occupied.

31:15. Recognizing that God is impartial (Rom. 2:11), Job stated, "**Did not he who made me in the womb make them?**" The implied answer was *yes*. All men are created with dignity and equality by God and are, therefore, deserving of fair and impartial treatment.

E Job's Charity (31:16–23)

SUPPORTING IDEA: *Job refutes the charges of Eliphaz about possible injustices against the wicked as he states that if he has committed the charges he deserves God's judgment.*

31:16. Earlier, Eliphaz had charged that Job had abused the poor and helpless (Job 22:7–9). Here Job refutes this charge, as he had already done previously (Job 24:1–12; 29:12–16). He listed a litany of possible offenses, all of which began with the word *if*, denoting uncertainty. **If I have denied the desires of the poor**, or widows, then Job believed he deserved to suffer as he did.

31:17–18. If I have kept my bread to myself, hoarding it selfishly, Job declared, **not sharing it with the fatherless**, then he had suffered justly. Yet Job's life and deeds had demonstrated just the opposite. To the contrary, Job reared him **as would a father**, showing paternal kindness and compassion to those in need. "**And from my birth I guided the widow**," Job said. He had shown her loving attention that was validated by deeds of love. Job's life was exemplary of deeds done to promote the general welfare of those who could not help themselves.

31:19–20. Or if anyone was lacking **clothing**, and he did not help, Job said, then he was deserving of severe punishments by God. Job's love for others was not demonstrated in word only but also in benevolent deeds. If the **heart** of the needy **did not bless me**, Job said, by giving him **fleece** to warm him, then he should be rebuked and punished by God. But, to his knowledge, he had not committed such sins against the helpless.

31:21–22. If I have raised my hand to do harm **against the fatherless**, Job said, he should suffer. But he maintained that he had not done so. Nor had he misused **influence in court** to throw a case and escape justice. So the suffering he was enduring was unjustified and unprovoked. If guilty, Job pronounced this curse upon himself: **then let my arm fall from the shoulder**. He also asserted that his arms would **be broken off at the joint** by the punishment of the Lord.

31:23. Job had lived with great restraint and fear of mistreating others because he **dreaded destruction from God**. Fear of punishment is a strong deterrent to sin. Fear of God prevented him from doing **such things**.

F Job's Humility (31:24–28)

SUPPORTING IDEA: *Job asserts that he has remained faithful in his allegiance to God.*

31:24. Disclaiming any false trust in idols or any misaligned spiritual priorities, Job claimed, **If I have put my trust in gold**, rather than God for **security**, then certain negative consequences should follow. Earlier, Eliphaz had encouraged Job to let go of his gold and let God become his gold (Job 22:24–25).

31:25–26. If I have rejoiced over my great wealth rather than having delighted in God, Job said, then he should suffer for it. But he had never placed his **fortune** before the Lord. Rather, he was modest and benevolent. **If I have regarded the sun** and **moon** in worshipping the creation rather than glorying in the Creator, Job declared, then he would be an idolater, deserving God's punishment (Deut. 4:19; Ezek. 8:16–17).

31:27. If such idolatry had caused Job's heart to be **secretly enticed**, offering **a kiss of homage**, then he should suffer. Yet Job had never bowed his knee to a foreign idol.

31:28. Then, if such wrong priorities were in place, they were **sins to be judged** by God. Otherwise, he would be **unfaithful to God on high**. Job had been entrusted with great riches (Job 1:3), but he had not succumbed to the temptation of greed and worldliness. Instead, he kept his faith in God first and foremost in his life and thus invited the further blessing of God.

G Job's Hospitality (31:29–34)

SUPPORTING IDEA: *Job notes that he did not gloat over the destruction of his enemies nor did he conceal sin in his life.*

31:29–30. Next Job cleared himself of the sin of gloating over the misfortune of his enemies. **If I have rejoiced at my enemy's misfortune or gloated over the trouble that came to him**, then he would deserve God's discipline (cp. Matt. 5:43–47). But he had not. Further, in regard to his enemies, Job asserted, "**I have not allowed my mouth to sin by invoking a curse against**

his life." Job had not verbally condemned others in this fashion by calling down judgment on them.

31:31–32. Neither had he withheld feeding **meat** to any **stranger** who was in need. His servants, the men of his household, would verify this as fact. His **door was always open to the traveler**. No **stranger** was ever turned away by him **to spend the night in the street**. Job defended his hospitality practices to foreigners.

31:33–34. Neither had hypocrisy or duplicity been an issue in Job's life. **If I have concealed my sin as men do**, covering **my guilt**, within **my heart**, then, by implication, Job would deserve the suffering he was experiencing. But this was not the case. Nor had he attempted to hide his sin from **the crowd** or **the clans**. He had not remained behind closed doors in isolation, living a double life, as one who **would not go outside**. Job did not hide like a hermit. He lived in open view before everyone because he had nothing to hide.

H Job's Activity (31:35–40)

SUPPORTING IDEA: *Job longs for God to hear and answer him by declaring his charges against Job.*

31:35. In a final effort to have God answer him, Job longed for someone to hear him and verify his case before the Lord. **Oh, that I had someone to hear me**! To authenticate his statement of innocence, he stated in a figurative tone, "**I sign now my defense**." Audaciously, he demanded, **let the Almighty answer me**, whether by vindication or punishment. Let his accuser, who was God, **put his indictment in writing** in order to present it to him.

31:36–37. Job desired to **wear** such charges on his **shoulder** for everyone to see. Then he would be able to refute God's indictments against him and prove his innocence. In fact, he boasted that he would wear such charges **like a crown** on his head. He would give God **an account** of his **every step** and await God's verdict of acquittal. There was no area of Job's life hidden from God's scrutinous eye. In fact, **like a prince** filled with great confidence, Job would approach God without hesitation.

31:38–39. Finally, Job returned to one last area of his life that had not been addressed—the stewardship of his land. **If my land cries out against me** to God because of blood guilt, he said, then he should be punished by the Lord. If Job had **devoured its yield without payment**, divine judgment would have consumed his harvest. Not to pay the worker his rightful wages was a grievous sin (Jas. 5:1–6). This would break **the spirit of its tenants** and invite God's curse on his land.

31:40. If Job mistreated the land, **then let briers come up instead of wheat and weeds instead of barley**. This divine judgment should occur. **The words of Job are ended.** The three cycles of speeches between Job and his three friends that began in Job 4 are now completed. Job, who had the first word in Job 3, has had the last word in Job 31.

MAIN IDEA REVIEW: *Affirming his sexual purity, Job declares his righteousness in his business dealings, his faithfulness to his wife, his fairness to his workers, and his hospitality to others, all the while longing for God to give him a hearing.*

III. CONCLUSION

A Thorough Self-Examination

Harry Ironside was the noted pastor of Moody Memorial Church in Chicago for many years. When he was thirteen, he was employed by a cobbler named Dan. His responsibility was to take the leather pelts used in making shoes and beat the water out of them with a wooden mallet, a hard and tedious process. One day he was walking down the street and looked into the window of another shoe shop. There he saw that shoemaker take a leather pelt and shake the water out of it without beating it.

Harry was so intrigued by this that he walked into the cobbler shop and asked the owner why he did not beat the water out as he did. The cobbler answered, "Well, that process is very time-consuming. And the shoes made like this do not last as long, so my customers will come back to buy shoes more often."

Harry walked straight to Dan and told him what the cobbler down the street had told him. Then he asked, "Why do you have me go to such trouble of pounding the water out of the pelts?" Dan took his apron off and hung it on the nail in the wall, and they sat down together. "Harry, I'm a Christian," Dan explained. "I know that one day I will stand before the Lord at the judgment seat of Christ. There, every pair of shoes that I have ever made will be in a large pile. And the Lord will go over every pair of shoes, and he will say, 'Dan, you brought your stitches too close to the sole here. We'll have to discard this pair.' Then, 'This pair, the nails are just right. We'll put this pair over here on this stack.' Or 'Here's one that's made perfectly. We'll put it on the right side. Good job.'"

Then Dan said to young Harry, "I believe that I will see every pair of shoes that I ever made again. So I want to get them right the first time."

This story illustrates why it is so important for us to take careful inventory of our lives in the present. One day we will stand before the Lord, and he will evaluate the work we've done for him. At the judgment seat of Christ, he will sort through our lives and put all our good works—those things built with gold, silver, and precious stones—into one stack. We will be rewarded for those efforts. Then he will put into another stack all our worthless works—those things built with wood, hay, and stubble. Our Lord will burn up those works, and there will be no reward.

Because of this coming day, it is important that each of us evaluate our lives today. Right now counts forever! We must take inventory today and make whatever corrections are necessary because that final day is coming when Christ will audit our lives. Evaluation and corrections made today will bring our Lord's pleasure and approval in that day. Let's prepare for that day—today.

IV. LIFE APPLICATION

A Personal Inventory

Every believer needs to conduct a personal inventory in each of these areas that Job searched out in his own life. What about your *thought life*? You are the only person who can inventory this secret part of your life. Is it pure? Is your mind closed to illicit sights? Do you resist lustful looking at other men or women? What about your *ethics*? Have you padded your expense account? Have you failed to report all your income to the IRS? Is your word your bond? What about your *home life*? Are you singular in your devotion to your spouse? What about your *work life*? Can you say that you treat your secretary fairly? Do you treat your employees with compassion? Would they say the same? Could those who work for you raise a complaint against you? How about those you work for?

What about your *community life*? Do you reach out to widows? Do you help the needy? Do you give to the poor? A real part of our Christian faith is how we treat those who are weak and destitute. What about your *financial life*? What is your attitude toward money? Do you hold your money with an open hand? Are you gripped with a passion to have more of it? Do you have your money, or does it have you? What about your *spiritual life*? What idols do you hold in priority above God? Are you spending adequate time in the Word and prayer? Do you value the creation over the Creator?

What about *the stewardship of your gifts*? What has God entrusted to your care? What spiritual gifts and ministry opportunities? What family responsibilities? What witnessing opportunities? Have you been a faithful steward of these entrustments? Our personal faith must be so integrated into our lives that every area is significantly affected.

V. PRAYER

God, search us and know us, and reveal if there is any hurtful way within us. Turn on your searchlight within our hearts, and make known to us what sin is within us so we may confess it and repent of it. Help us to see what you see as you look within our souls. Prune us that we may grow. In Jesus' name. Amen.

VI. DEEPER DISCOVERIES

A. Covenant (31:1)

A covenant (Heb. *berit*) was a binding pact or agreement between two parties, whether between individuals (Gen. 21:27) or nations (1 Sam. 1:11; Josh. 9:6,15). God often used this word in describing his relationship with Israel, his chosen people. Yet unlike a covenant between people involving a mutual agreement, the covenant between God and his people was a unilateral covenant, or an agreement based upon the faithfulness of God alone. This covenant was initiated and instituted by God to protect and preserve his chosen ones. The one-sided nature of this covenant is evident in the statement, "I will be your God and you will be my people" (Jer. 7:23).

B. Ruin (31:3)

"Ruin" (Heb. *ed*) occurs twenty-two times in the Old Testament and means disaster, oppression, destruction, or ruin. It is found six times in Job (18:12; 21:17,30; 30:12; 31:3,23). It is often used of the day when God's judgment will visit the wicked, rendering just recompense for their evil actions (Prov. 6:15; Jer. 18:17; Obad. 13). Like here, Psalm 18:18 has the righteous sufferer in mind.

VII. TEACHING OUTLINE

A. Job's Purity (31:1–4)
  1. I have covenanted with my eyes (31:1)
  2. I have considered the results (31:2–4)

B. Job's Integrity (31:5–8)
  1. I have evaluated my walk (31:5–6)
  2. I have examined my steps (31:7–8)

C. Job's Fidelity (31:9–12)
   1. I have considered my devotion (31:9)
   2. I have invited God's discipline (31:10–12)
D. Job's Impartiality (31:13–15)
   1. I have weighed my dealings (31:13)
   2. I have weighed God's dealings (31:14–15)
E. Job's Charity (31:16–23)
   1. I have examined my ways (31:16–21)
   2. I have invited God's discipline (31:22–23)
F. Job's Humility (31:24–28)
   1. I have examined my trust (31:24–27)
   2. I have considered the result (31:28)
G. Job's Hospitality (31:29–34)
   1. I have examined my dealings with outsiders (31:29–32)
   2. I have nothing to hide (31:33–34)
H. Job's Activity (31:35–40)
   1. I have pleaded for a hearing (31:35–37)
   2. I have examined my land stewardship (31:38–39)
   3. I have invited God's discipline (31:40)

VIII. ISSUES FOR DISCUSSION

1. Do I live a life of integrity that can withstand God's scrutiny?
2. Do I live a life of sexual purity?
3. Am I faithful to my spouse in all areas of marriage?
4. Do I place the concerns of God's kingdom before the things of this world?

Job 32

A New Voice with a New Message

Quote

"The word of a man is as powerful as himself."

Richard Sibbes

Job 32

I. INTRODUCTION

A Voice from the Crowd

At the famous Speaker's Corner in London's Hyde Park, a man denounced the Christian faith and issued this challenge: "If there is a God, I will give him five minutes to strike me dead!" Before the stunned crowd, he took out his watch and waited. After five minutes, with no thunderbolt thrust down from heaven, he smiled and said, "My friends, this proves that there is no God!" In the crowd that day was a strong Christian who had the presence of mind to respond, "Do you think you could exhaust the patience of God in five minutes?"

In the crowd surrounding Job, there stood one man who could not remain silent. His name was Elihu, a man who had endured this entire dialogue between Job and his three friends. Unlike the terrible trio, Elihu actually spoke what Job needed to hear. What he had to say covered six long chapters (Job 32–37). In these discourses his voice was the only one heard. Elihu shed true light and gave Job the sound counsel he desperately needed. The truthfulness of Elihu's words is later substantiated by the fact that Job's three friends were rebuked by God (Job 42:7–9) but Elihu's words escaped God's correction.

Thus, Elihu correctly explained the character of God. Specifically, he stated that God is gracious and caring (Job 33), just and fair (Job 34–35), great and sovereign (Job 36–37). In his speech Elihu applied these foundational truths to Job's life.

Elihu's approach to Job's suffering was different from that of Job's three friends. Job's counselors had argued that Job needed to repent of sin that he surely had committed before his tragedies. Elihu, on the other hand, said that Job needed to repent of pride that developed during his suffering. The three companions claimed that Job was suffering because he had sinned. But Elihu reasoned that Job was sinning because he was suffering. According to Elihu, Job's suffering had provoked an attitude of self-righteous pride before God as he questioned God's ways.

And what is worse, Job challenged God to appear before his court to argue his case, knowing that he would be put into the right before God. But Elihu's diagnosis cut to the heart of the matter. Sinful attitudes of self-righteousness had swelled up within Job that required his immediate attention and personal repentance. In this first chapter of Elihu's prolonged interruption, he said to Job that God was speaking through him and Job should listen carefully. Elihu was a true friend to Job.

II. COMMENTARY

A New Voice with a New Message

MAIN IDEA: *Elihu becomes angry with Job for refusing to acknowledge his sin of pride and rebukes the three friends for failing to rebut Job's arguments.*

A Elihu's Indignation (32:1–5)

SUPPORTING IDEA: *Elihu, having listened to the three friends, becomes angry toward both Job and the three friends.*

32:1. As this new section begins, **these three men**, referring back to Eliphaz, Bildad, and Zophar, **stopped answering Job**. The reason they stopped was that they had finally exhausted their arguments, all of which had been offered to no avail. Their three rounds of lectures to Job had become increasingly shorter while his responses had become progressively longer. Now on the short end of the debate, Job's three friends finally had nothing left to say. They had been silenced by Job because **he was righteous in his own eyes**. Convinced of his own innocence, Job had been embroiled in defending himself, and he refused to accept their counsel.

32:2. Throughout this long debate, a fourth person had been standing by quietly—a young man named **Elihu**. Having listened to the endless dronings of these men, he felt compelled to speak. Elihu was the **son of Barakel the Buzite, of the family of Ram**. Abraham was probably related to Elihu, since Buz was a brother of Uz. As he endured this seemingly endless harangue, Elihu **became very angry with Job**, upset with his pride and lack of restraint. While Job was initially correct in what he had said, his attitude soon went sour. What he said about God became brazen and distorted.

32:3. Elihu also became **angry with the three friends**. The reason for his infuriation with them was that **they had found no way to refute Job**. Their many words and endless arguments had not been persuasive with Job but had missed the mark in reproving him. They **had condemned him** but not corrected him. So Elihu was angry with everyone involved, with Job as well as his three friends.

32:4. In deference to the advanced age of the three men, **Elihu had waited before speaking to Job**. Because they were older, he showed respect to them by waiting his turn. This was a common practice in the Ancient Middle East. This revealed an important aspect of Elihu's character—respect for one's elders.

32:5. But concluding that they **had nothing more to say** against Job, he was ready to speak, as his pent-up **anger was** greatly **aroused**. Like a ticking time bomb, Elihu was ready to explode and release his anger.

B Elihu's Insight (32:6–14)

SUPPORTING IDEA: *Elihu states that true understanding is found in God.*

32:6. So Elihu addressed Job and the three men by saying, "**I am young in years, and you are old.**" It had been proper for Elihu to wait his turn to speak, the younger deferring to the older. He acknowledged his relative youth and inexperience. Consequently, he was **fearful** and, thus, hesitant **to tell** what wisdom he possessed.

32:7–8. It was Elihu's conviction that, all things being equal, **age should speak** and **teach wisdom**, and his place was to listen and learn. Elihu had patiently waited for the three friends to speak and then at the right time he spoke up. But, in actuality, **it is the spirit in a man**, that is, **the breath of the Almighty**, that brings true wisdom and **understanding**. Prudent insight that leads to successful living comes from God, not from length of years.

32:9–10. Thus, Elihu stated confidently to his elder friends, **It is not only the old who are wise** and **understand**. By implication, Elihu, though younger in age, claimed to be the possessor of wisdom and understanding derived from God. Consequently, Elihu pleaded for an equal hearing with them, saying, "**Listen to me.**" Knowing Job was frustrated, Elihu pleaded for Job to lend him his ear so he could tell Job what he knew to be true.

32:11–12. "**I listened to your reasoning,**" Elihu claimed. Having patiently endured the faulty counsel of the friends, Elihu desired to be given the same courtesy he had extended to them and Job. He said, "**Not one of you has proved Job wrong.**" Their arguments had failed to refute Job and convince him of their rightness, and Elihu knew this to be true.

31:13. Job's three friends were not to say, "**We have found wisdom; let God refute him, not man.**" They should not leave this matter with **God** to do what they could not do. The friends, Elihu reasoned, should have assumed more responsibility than that for their counsel.

32:14. But Job has not marshaled his words against me. Elihu had wanted his opportunity to address Job and succeed where their arguments had failed. He would try a different approach. **I will not answer him with your arguments.** Some important arguments, Elihu felt, had been omitted in their words. Thus, where their limited wisdom had failed, Elihu believed he had the perspective and understanding to supply Job with the truth.

C Elihu's Insistence (32:15–22)

SUPPORTING IDEA: *Elihu declares to Job that he must now speak to him, being under great compulsion.*

32:15. Speaking to Job about his three friends, Elihu exclaimed, "**They are dismayed and have no more to say.**" This fact was apparent because their speeches had grown shorter and shorter, even leaving Zophar without a third speech. Truly, their words had **failed them**, and they had given up in frustration.

32:16–17. "**Must I wait?**" he asked, anxious to speak to Job from his wisdom and understanding. Any more delay would be useless. Now that they were **silent** and had no further **reply**, he must address Job. Elihu confided, "**I too will have my say; I too will say what I know.**" Elihu could no longer keep his thoughts to himself. He must correct the abuses of this long battery of discourses and debates. Like the three friends, Elihu would have his say and speak only what he knew to be true.

32:18–19. Elihu confided that he was **full of words** to speak to Job. In actuality, Elihu noted with earnestness that **the spirit within me compels me**. This is a reference to his own human spirit and not the Holy Spirit. Elihu said that inside he was like **bottled-up wine**. If he did not speak, he would soon explode. He claimed to be like **new wineskins** ready to burst. Old wineskins were brittle and cracked, and they broke easily (cp. Matt. 9:17). But new wineskins were harder to break, pointing to the pressure within Elihu to speak.

32:20–21. Consequently, he **must speak** to Job. For his own **relief**, Elihu had to release his knowledge and use his **lips** to **reply**. As Elihu spoke, he pledged to **show partiality to no one**, not even to Job. Nor would he **flatter** Job with what he had to say. Earlier, Job had accused his three friends of showing partiality toward God against him (Job 13:8,10). Elihu promised he would not do so.

32:22. If Elihu **were skilled in flattery** and used this deceitful ability to address Job, then God, his Maker, would take him away in judgment. Elihu believed that the wrath of God would destroy him if he used flattery. So what followed would be a straight declaration of the truth.

MAIN IDEA REVIEW: *Elihu becomes angry with Job for refusing to acknowledge his sin of pride and rebukes the three friends for failing to rebut Job's arguments.*

III. CONCLUSION

Wisdom Beyond His Years

Oscar Wilde once said, "You're young only once, but you can be immature indefinitely." Unfortunately, some people never grow up, remaining immature all their lives. Rare is the person who is mature when he is young. Elihu proved to be one who was young yet mature. Elihu was the youngest of the voices that spoke to Job, but he proved to be the wisest.

Outwardly, Elihu appeared to be at a disadvantage. The three friends were many years his senior, yet his God-given understanding made his counsel more applicable to Job's situation than the counsel of the older friends. Elihu looked to God, not man, for understanding Job's plight. He listened carefully to Job's arguments, comparing them with what he knew to be true about God. Thus, when Eliphaz spoke, he countered Job's false notions about God with godly counsel.

IV. LIFE APPLICATION

Showing Divine Wisdom

Are there times when you find yourself with a friend who is hurting and feel that you must speak what needs to be said? Surely all believers find themselves in such situations at times. God's people should remember that they are there by divine appointment to be God's representatives. If we are to be used by God, we must be willing to speak the truth in love. In these personal encounters believers should always convey divine wisdom to others.

1. *Speak the truth.* It requires personal courage to speak up to a friend, saying what is difficult to say. Only the Holy Spirit can give the courage to overcome the fear of rejection by a friend.

2. *Be a helpful counselor.* You must have genuine compassion, seeking the highest good of the person to whom you must speak, to be a good counselor. This has nothing to do with winning an argument, but everything to do with helping a hurting friend. True Christians speak to pursue the highest good of the person loved. Our silence is selfishness.

3. *Be a wise counselor.* Helping a friend requires wise counsel. Merely speaking up is not enough. We must know what to say and how to say it. Having divine wisdom is necessary if our words are to prevail. It would be better not to speak at all than to speak unwise words. Thus, we must be people who have divine wisdom if we are to be used by God to point people to the right path when they find themselves in need of divine direction.

V. PRAYER

God, use us in the lives of others who are hurting and in need of your counsel and direction. Make us sensitive to hurting people whom you bring across our path. Make us ready and willing to speak your wisdom and direction. Forgive us for those times when we have not wanted to become involved. May you use us in the lives of those who touch our lives. In Jesus' name. Amen.

VI. DEEPER DISCOVERIES

A. Friends (32:3)

"Friends" (Heb. *rea*) is used 187 times in the Old Testament and is used of both close, intimate friends and of occasional acquaintances. In this case, it speaks of Eliphaz, Bildad, and Zophar, men who presented themselves as close friends within Job's inner circle of relationships.

B. Fearful (32:6)

"Fearful" or "afraid" (Heb. *zahal*) is a word used only three times in the Old Testament. *Zahal* means to draw back or to crawl away in a timed manner. In the two instances outside of Job, it is used in reference to snakes (cp. Deut. 32:24; Mic. 7:17). In Job, the context indicates that Elihu approached Job cautiously and carefully.

C. Full Attention (32:12)

To give "full attention" (Heb. *bin*) means to observe with understanding and insight. The most prominent usage of *bin* is in 1 Kings 3:9 where Solomon asked God to help him "discern between good and evil" (NASB).This keen insight or understanding allows a person to render judgment and is a gift from God (Dan. 2:21). It can be revealed or concealed by God (Isa. 29:14). Found throughout the Old Testament, *bin* is used twenty-three times in Job (cp. 6:24,30; 13:1; 14:21; 23:8; 26:14; 28:23; 42:3)

VII. TEACHING OUTLINE

A. Elihu's Indignation (32:1–5)
   1. Job's heart was arrogant (32:1–2)
   2. Job's friends were ineffective (32:3–5)

B. Elihu's Insight (32:6–14)
   1. He has learned from God (32:6–10)
   2. He has listened to Job (32:11–14)

C. Elihu's Insistence (32:15–22)
   1. I am impelled to speak (32:15–20)
   2. I am impartial in speaking (32:21–22)

VIII. ISSUES FOR DISCUSSION

1. Do I seek godly counsel when I am suffering?
2. Am I equipped to give godly counsel to others who are suffering?
3. Do I make myself available to others when they are suffering?

Job 33

God Is Not Silent

Quote

"God whispers to us in our pleasures, speaks in our consciences, but shouts in our pains."

C. S. Lewis

I. INTRODUCTION

When God Is Silent

During the difficult days of World War II, a young Jewish girl in the Warsaw ghetto of Poland managed to escape over the wall and hide in a cave. Tragically, she died shortly before the Allied army broke into the ghetto to liberate the prisoners. But before she died, she had scratched on the wall some powerful creeds: "I believe in the sun, even though it is not shining. I believe in love, even when feeling it or not. I believe in God, even when he is silent."

This last statement comes close to the problem experienced by Job in his ordeal. Without hearing any audible word from God, Job felt that God was silent. He longed to hear a word from God, but no direct communication was forthcoming. So Elihu, the fourth friend to speak to Job, argued that God had been speaking and had been doing so loud and clear. The problem was that Job had not been listening. Elihu instructed Job that God speaks through dreams, suffering, and messengers. The Almighty had not left himself without a witness. He was speaking—but was Job listening?

Elihu helped Job hear God again. The voice of this young man brought great counsel: Job must recapture a correct view of God. Where Eliphaz, Bildad, and Zophar had failed, Elihu succeeded in helping point Job in the right direction. In the end God rebuked Eliphaz, Bildad, and Zophar but not Elihu because his assessment was on target. Job did not rebut Elihu. His silence indicated that Elihu's words were correct. Each one of Elihu's four speeches was designed to correct Job's wrong view of God. Elihu said that God is not silent (Job 33), unjust (Job 34), uncaring (Job 35), or powerless (Job 36–37). These truths give us a balanced view of God.

II. COMMENTARY

God Is Not Silent

MAIN IDEA: *Elihu declares his anger toward Job but then affirms that true understanding is found in God and that he is compelled to speak what he knows to be true.*

A Elihu's Compulsion (33:1–7)

SUPPORTING IDEA: *Elihu pleads with Job to listen to him as he will speak the truth as given to him by God's Spirit.*

33:1. Elihu began this part of his discourse by pleading for a hearing: **But now, Job, listen to my words**. Elihu, unlike the three friends, addressed Job by name, an indication of his sincerity and concern for Job's welfare. "**Pay attention to everything I say,**" he directed. Elihu pleaded for Job's careful listening.

33:2–3. **I am about to open my mouth** and speak, Elihu declared. He was convinced of the importance and wisdom of his advice about to be given (cp. vv. 31,33). **My words are on the tip of my tongue**. He was compelled to speak and must have a careful hearing with Job. **My words come from an upright heart**. Elihu believed that he spoke without any bias or ulterior motive, stating only what would glorify God and help Job. **My lips sincerely speak what I know**. He was convinced of the truthfulness of what he was about to say. This confidence was grounded in the truth that Elihu was dispensing God's heavenly wisdom, not man's earthly wisdom.

33:4–5. Elihu asserted, **The Spirit of God has made me** and put his **breath** within me. Thus, what Elihu said would come from **the Spirit** within him—from **the Almighty**, who was leading him into what to say. **Answer me then, if you can**. His advice and counsel must be heard and dealt with by Job. **Prepare yourself** to rebut my counsel, if possible, **and confront me**, he instructed. If Elihu said something that was wrong, Job would be under obligation to object. But Elihu was confident that Job would not.

33:6. Seeking to identify with and relate to Job, Elihu stated, **I am just like you before God**. He, likewise, claimed to be **taken from clay**, or made from the dust of the earth. Thus, he considered himself to be equal with Job before God and not superior to him as his three friends had claimed to be. This illustrates Elihu's humility before Job. He had no prideful presumption to uphold.

33:7. As equals before God in creation, Job should not fear what Elihu had to say. **No fear of me should alarm you**. His words were not intended to be so **heavy** upon Job that he could not bear up under them. Rather, his words were intended to build up, not tear down. This was a contrast to the cutting rhetoric of Job's three friends.

B Elihu's Correction (33:8–12)

SUPPORTING IDEA: *Elihu corrects Job's confession that he is free of guilt.*

33:8. Having laid this necessary groundwork to disarm Job's bitterness, Elihu proceeded to quote what Job had earlier said about himself. **But you have said in my hearing—I heard the very words**. In quoting Job, Elihu proceeded to show him where and how he was wrong. Elihu cited evidence to correct Job about what he had heard Job say in his presence.

33:9. Recalling Job's own words in which he had claimed to be blameless, Elihu quoted him as saying, "**I am pure and without sin; I am clean and free from guilt**." But Job never claimed to be sinless. He had actually admitted to being a sinner (Job 7:21; 13:26). Nevertheless, a self-righteous attitude had developed within Job's heart. Although he disclaimed the sins for which he assumed he was being punished, he had overlooked the festering attitude of his own heart. Zophar was the one who had mistaken Job's words to be a claim of perfection—a claim Job had never made (Job 9:20–21).

33:10–11. Elihu quoted Job virtually verbatim as saying, **God has found fault with me**, unjustly so, and treats me as **his enemy**. Job had spoken these words (Job 13:24,27; 16:9; 19:7,11), and they were not true. In fact, Job had wailed, "**He fastens my feet in shackles**," as if he were an enemy treated like a prisoner. Job had stated, "**He keeps close watch on all my paths**," as though he were under constant surveillance in a prison. Believing himself to be incarcerated, Job thought God was after him to take away his freedom.

33:12. Elihu felt that Job needed to be corrected, so he noted, "**But I tell you, in this you are not right, for God is greater than man.**" Elihu reasoned that Job, when compared with God's perfect holiness, was certainly sinful. His railings against God, arising from his soured spirit, were not right. In reality, he should have said nothing against God, no matter how frustrated he was. Job and God were not equals. This fundamental truth had escaped Job.

C Elihu's Contention (33:13–30)

SUPPORTING IDEA: *Elihu contends that God speaks to people in dreams and visions, despite Job's claim that God is silent.*

33:13. Elihu corrected Job's belief that God is silent and does not speak to man. **Why do you complain** to God **that he answers none of man's words**? Further, he corrected Job's tone of fault-finding against God. Such an attitude and words are wrong. Job could not presume that God had not answered his words.

33:14. For God does speak—now one way, now another—though man may not perceive it. Elihu declared that God does communicate to man in different ways. But regardless of the various mediums that God may use to speak to man, man will not always grasp what God is saying. Furthermore, God is consistent when he speaks. The problem is man's inability to hear him.

33:15–16. Elihu maintained that God speaks to man **in a dream** and a **vision of the night**. This had been Eliphaz's earlier experience and contention (Job 4:12–21). God **may speak in their ears** in this manner in order to **terrify** man **with warnings** to correct his errors. Maybe this was why Job was haunted with nightmares (Job 7:14)—to warn him of the consequences of his bad thinking.

33:17–18. The purpose of such divine admonitions, Elihu maintained, was **to turn man from wrongdoing**. God speaks to instill fear within the soul of man and to restrain him from sin, specifically, **pride**—the root and source of all sin. This restraint would **preserve his soul from the pit** (vv. 22,24,28,30), a metaphor for the grave. Such an untimely death would occur by **perishing by the sword**, an act of divine judgment carried out by a human agent who unknowingly carries out God's judgment.

33:19–20. Further, Elihu insisted that God also speaks to man through his pain and suffering. **Or a man may be chastened**, that is, disciplined by God, **on a bed of pain**. This divine correction by God is often a debilitating illness with **constant distress in his bones**. Yes, God was disciplining Job with his pain. God is not silent during times of painful discipline. In fact, God speaks to man in such times of weakness. It is then that man, being sick, **finds food repulsive**.

33:21–22. Concerning fragile man, **his flesh wastes away to nothing** as he lies debilitated on his sickbed and his muscles atrophy. This destructive illness brings him to the point of **death**. Nevertheless, God speaks in such pain, reinforcing what is truly important in **life**. Job could relate to the sickness that confines a person to bed.

33:23. Moreover, Elihu contended that God speaks to man through **an angel**, referring either to a heavenly being or, more probably in this case, to a human being. The word for "angel" means a messenger, one sent from God with a divinely given message. In this context Elihu was likely the angel sent by God to speak to Job. Elihu was **a mediator**, or an arbitrator sent to settle this dispute between God and Job. He would **tell a man**, specifically Job, what was right for him.

33:24. Rather than speaking to Job in harsh tones as the three friends had done, this messenger-mediator would **be gracious to him**. Instead of consigning him to destruction as Eliphaz, Bildad, and Zophar had done, Elihu would say to God on Job's behalf, "**Spare him from going down to the pit**" (i.e., the grave). Representing Job before God, he would say to God, "**I have found a ransom for him.**" This refers to either the repentance of the sick person or a gracious atonement provided by this messenger-mediator.

33:25. The result of his intercession would be effective, for then his **flesh** would be **renewed** like a child's. That is, Job would be delivered from his sickness and would be **restored** to an energetic and youthful state.

33:26. Referring to his own intercessory ministry on Job's behalf, Elihu said, "**He prays to God and finds favor with him.**" He would see God's face in prayer, metaphorically speaking, and would **shout for joy**, knowing that his intercession for Job would prevail. As a result, Job would be **restored by God to his righteous state**. In response to Elihu's message, Job would be restored through repentance to his previous spiritual state before pride entered his heart.

33:27. Then Job should come to **men** and confess his sin of complaining against God. Job should say to them that he had sinned with his self-righteous attitude and had **perverted what was right** in his word against God. Further, Job should humbly state, "**I did not get what I deserved.**" At this point, Job should already be disciplined by God and reduced to the grave, a sin unto death. But Job had not yet reached the breaking point.

33:28. Job should testify to men and say that this messenger-mediator had **redeemed**, or delivered, his soul **from going down to the pit** of death under God's chastening discipline. Thus, Job would live to **enjoy the light** by receiving Elihu's message and confessing that he had sinned. Graciously, God had spared him from the darkness of the pit, allowing him to live in the light of life. This is what Job should say, Elihu declared.

33:29–30. Elihu summarized his words to Job by saying, "**God does all these things to a man,**" both disciplining and delivering him. God does it

twice, even three times, picturing great intensity and completeness so that man will learn the divine lesson. All this God graciously does **to turn his soul from the pit**, away from destruction and death, so **that the light of life may shine on him**, and his years may be extended into the future.

D Elihu's Conclusion (33:31–33)

SUPPORTING IDEA: *Elihu instructs Job to listen carefully to him since he speaks wisdom.*

33:31. Elihu concluded this segment as he started it (vv. 1–7)—with an appeal for Job to listen to what he said because he spoke wisdom. "**Pay attention, Job, and listen to me**," stated Elihu as he desired to **speak** and help, not condemn. Elihu wanted Job to consider carefully what he was saying.

33:32–33. Unlike the three friends, Elihu invited Job to respond to him. **If you have anything to say, answer me; speak up, for I want you to be cleared**. Elihu declared that he was on Job's side and wanted to see him vindicated in his claim of being righteous. Thus, he invited Job's response. But if Job has nothing to say to Elihu, then he should **listen** to him and learn **wisdom** that he wanted to teach him. This wisdom was intended to help Job, not to condemn him or to win theological points in a debate. Therefore for Job's own personal benefit, he should listen to Elihu.

MAIN IDEA REVIEW: *Elihu declares his anger toward Job but then affirms that true understanding is found in God and that he is compelled to speak what he knows to be true.*

III. CONCLUSION

Are You Listening?

A high school class in music appreciation was asked the difference between listening and hearing. At first, there was no response. Finally, a hand went up, and a youngster offered this definition: "Listening is wanting to hear." How true this is. So often we do not listen because we do not want to hear what is being said to us.

This is what Elihu told Job that he needed to do. Job needed to want to hear what God was saying to him. It has been noted that God gave us two ears but only one mouth. Thus, we should listen far more than we talk. This is what Job had to learn to do. Rather than increase his volume, he should increase his listening. Clearly, this is a lesson for every believer. We must sit before an open

Bible and listen to God. What he says to us is infinitely more important than what we say to him. God *is* speaking to you. Are you listening?

IV. LIFE APPLICATION

How to Listen to God's Word

In this hour God speaks to us by his written Word, the Bible. It is incumbent upon us that we listen attentively to what he says. We are responsible to him for what he speaks to us. So the question is: How should we listen to God's Word?

1. *Be humble.* Augustine said many years ago, "When the Bible speaks, God speaks." The authority of Scripture is the same as the authority of God himself. Thus, we must listen with submission and humility, receiving his Word as a royal edict from heaven's throne. It is not to be debated or discussed—only obeyed.

2. *Be alert.* When God is speaking through the words of sacred Scripture, we must be alert to the divine message being conveyed. We are not to be divided in our focus when the Word is being revealed to us, but we should be attentive to what God is saying. A diverted interest will not do when God is speaking.

3. *Be intelligent.* The Word of God is a cognitive message that requires clear thinking, rational thought, and intense study. The true meaning of Scripture is never to be gained through a mystical experience that bypasses the mind. God works through the human intellect when he speaks his truth to us. Thus, our minds must be engaged in careful, critical thought that rightly handles "the word of truth" (2 Tim. 2:15).

4. *Be blameless.* A clear understanding of what God is saying in the Bible requires a pure and blameless life. Unconfessed sin clouds our ability to discern what he is saying in his Word. But when we walk in the light of personal holiness, we are able to see the truths of Scripture. Thus, it is essential in understanding the message of the Bible to walk in purity before the Lord. Believers often do not grasp what God is saying, not because of intellectual limitations, but because of moral failures.

V. PRAYER

God our Father, we thank you that all of life is lived under your sovereign control. We thank you that you have ordained all of our days from of old. Nothing exists outside the reign of your power. Remind us that you have never left us or forsaken us, but we are the ones who often wander from you. In Jesus' name. Amen.

VI. DEEPER DISCOVERIES

A. Confront (33:5)

"Confront" (Heb. *yasab*) means to firmly plant or station oneself. Though *yasab* is used in the physical (Exod. 2:4; 9:13) and figurative senses (Hab. 2:1), here it is used as a term of opposition of those who contend or firmly plant themselves against others. Its most infamous usage is found in Psalm 2:2, "The kings of the earth take their stand (*yasab*) and the rulers gather together against the LORD." Found in various contexts, the word is often associated with victory over an opposing foe (Deut. 7:24; Josh. 1:5; Ps. 5:5). Here Elihu was challenging Job to contend against his advice.

B. Chastened (33:19)

"Chastened" (Heb. *yakah*) means to correct, convince, dispute, rebuke, or reprove. Occurring fifty-seven times in the Old Testament, it is often found in relationship between God and his people (cp. Ps. 6:1; Isa. 2:4; Mic. 4:3). Found throughout Job (cp. 5:17; 13:3,10; 16:21; 22:4), its most familiar usage is Proverbs 3:12: "The LORD disciplines (*yakah*) those he loves."

VII. TEACHING OUTLINE

A. Elihu's Compulsion (33:1–7)
   1. Hear my words (33:1–3)
   2. Heed my words (33:4–7)

B. Elihu's Correction (33:8–12)
   1. I have heard your words (33:8–11)
   2. I now refute your words (33:12)

C. Elihu's Contention (33:13–30)
   1. God speaks through dreams (33:13–18)
   2. God speaks through suffering (33:19–22)
   3. God speaks through a messenger (33:23–30)

D. Elihu's Conclusion (33:31–33)
   1. Listen to me (33:31)
   2. Answer me (33:32)
   3. Learn from me (33:33)

VIII. ISSUES FOR DISCUSSION

1. Do I open myself to criticism from godly counselors?
2. Do I demonstrate a vindictive spirit to those who offer godly counsel?
3. Do I have a teachable spirit?

Job 34

God Will Always Do Right

Quote

"An unjust God would be as unthinkable as a square circle or a round triangle."

Warren Wiersbe

Job 34

I. INTRODUCTION

Are You a Big-Godder?

A former student of Robert Dick Wilson, one of the great professors at Princeton Theological Seminary, was invited to preach in Miller Chapel, twelve years after he had graduated. Dr. Wilson came in and sat down near the front. At the close of the meeting, the old professor came up to his former student, cocked his head to one side in his characteristic way, extended his hand, and said, "If you come back again, I will not come to hear you preach. I only come once. I am glad that you are a big-Godder. When my boys come back, I come to see if they are big-Godders or little-Godders, and then I know what their ministry will be."

His former student asked him to explain. The old professor replied, "Well, some people have a little God, and they are always in trouble with him. He can't do any miracles. He can't take care of the inspiration and transmission of the Scripture to us. He doesn't intervene on behalf of his people. They have a little God, and I call them little-Godders. Then there are those who have a great God. He speaks, and it is done. He commands, and it stands fast. He knows how to show himself strong on behalf of those who fear him. You have a great God, and he will bless your ministry." He paused a moment, smiled, and said, "God bless you," and turned and walked out.

Elihu was a big-Godder. He was one who had a high, transcendent view of God, a knowledge of God that towered over man. Consequently, when he gave counsel to Job, he spoke from the same divine perspective. While Job's suffering may have been greater than Job was, yet in Elihu's estimation God was greater than human suffering. As a result, Elihu sought to put everything in right perspective.

In Elihu's second speech he attempted to answer Job's accusation that God was unjust. The central thrust of this chapter is the righteousness of God—that God will always do what is right. He is incapable of wrongdoing or unrighteousness. If God is truly God, then he is perfect; and if he is perfect, then he cannot do wrong. According to Elihu, what seemed to be unjust to Job was, in reality, just. God is a holy God who can be trusted in every circumstance of life to do what is right. This was a truth that Job needed to hear.

II. COMMENTARY

God Will Always Do Right

MAIN IDEA: *Elihu confronts the false assumptions held by Job and the three friends, defends the justice of God, and encourages Job to look to God with the eye of faith.*

A Elihu's Rebuke (34:1–15)

SUPPORTING IDEA: *Elihu chides Job and his friends for their wrong views of God.*

34:1–2. **Then Elihu said** introduces his next speech, the second discourse he offered. What he said was true, and it needed to be heard by Job. **Hear my words, you wise men**. This is addressed in the plural, indicating that Elihu was speaking to the three friends, who considered themselves to be **men of learning**. In this plea to be heard, Elihu considered himself an authoritative messenger of God whose words should be heeded (Job 32:8; 33:4).

34:3–4. **For the ear tests words as the tongue tastes food** is what Job had said earlier (Job 12:11). That is, his words should be heard with discernment and discrimination, differentiating between good and bad, truth and error. Also, Elihu declared, **Let us discern for ourselves what is right and good** about Job's words. Elihu did not presume to make false assertions about

Job's past, but he evaluated Job on the basis of what he had said in his testimonies to the three friends.

34:5. Elihu next quoted Job in order to refute him and turn him to the truth: **Job says, "I am innocent, but God denies me justice."** This is an accurate representation of Job's words (Job 12:4; 13:18; 27:6), unlike the three friends who misunderstood and often misquoted Job.

34:6. Job had contended all along that he was righteous and that God was punishing him unfairly. **Although I am right**, undeserving this punishment, he had declared, **I am considered a liar**, failing to confess sin. Despite being **guiltless**, God's arrow **inflicts an incurable wound**, one from which, he believed, he would never recover.

34:7–8. What man is like Job, who drinks scorn like water? Job reasoned that man had an unquenchable thirst for the polluted streams of iniquity, consuming it like a thirsty man drinks water. What is more, **he keeps company with evildoers** and **wicked men**. Here is an incriminating charge leveled by Elihu against Job of guilt by association.

34:9. It profits a man nothing when he tries to please God. With these words the discouraged Job was close to buying into Satan's lies. In the opening chapters of the book, the devil had said Job would not worship God if he took away his material prosperity. At this point Job was in peril of crossing an imaginary, theological line and embracing this mind-set—serving God for what he could get from him.

34:10. Still addressing the three counselors, "**So listen to me, you men of understanding,**" Elihu delivered the main burden of his speech by saying, "**Far be it from God to do evil**" (cp. Gen. 18:25). God is always true to his holy, righteous character and can never act in contradiction to it. His righteous actions flow from his righteous character. A holy **God** cannot **do evil**. Neither can **the Almighty** ever **do wrong**. God is incapable of injustice. He can do only what is good and right.

34:11–12. Perfectly and justly, God **repays a man for what he has done**. With equity he rewards righteousness and punishes unrighteousness, never the opposite as Job had supposed. Thus, God **brings upon** a person **what his conduct deserves**. In other words, God gives a person what he has earned. **It is unthinkable** to any enlightened mind **that God would do wrong** or **pervert justice**. God can only do right, Elihu contended. Never would God do what is evil, since he is the source of righteousness and justice.

34:13. Elihu asked Job who had **appointed** him over the earth. He reminded Job that he was not God's judge. No one had appointed Job to rule over the affairs of the world. **Who put him in charge of the whole world?**

Certainly not Job, although his railing words gave the impression that he had put himself in charge of the planet. But God had not appointed Job for this task.

34:14–15. **If it were** God's **intention and he withdrew his spirit and breath**, Elihu said, this would end human life. Yet this was not God's intention toward Job, but much more was at work, much more than Job was aware of. **All mankind would perish together** and **return to the dust** of death. Thus, Elihu was jealous for God's glory as the independent sustainer of life, as the one who had the power to begin and end, to continue or withdraw man's life.

B Elihu's Reproof (34:16–20)

SUPPORTING IDEA: *Elihu rebukes Job and defends God's justice while warning him of God's righteous power.*

34:16. Elihu shifted his address from the three friends and Job to Job himself. This is indicated by the fact that the Hebrew verbs are now in the singular, not in the plural as was used previously. Elihu stated to gain Job's ear, "**If you have understanding, hear this.**"

34:17. Concerned that Job's wrong attitude and misguided apprehension about God's justice could be corrected, he asked, "**Can he who hates justice govern?**" The implied answer was a resounding *no*. God would not be fit to be the sovereign ruler over all if he despised **justice**. Addressing Job, Elihu asked, "**Will you condemn the just and mighty One?**" (cp. Job 40:8). Surely not, yet Job had done so.

34:18–19. **Is** God **not the One who says to kings**, "**You are worthless**"? The implied answer was *yes*. God pronounces kings to be inferior and impotent. With his spoken words he reduces them and their kingdoms to dust. He **shows no partiality to princes**, rendering verdicts against even the wicked in high places as he sees fit. He **does not favor the rich**, for such **partiality** would be unjust and out of line with his character. **They are all the work of his hands** and, therefore, are treated with equal justice by the Lord.

34:20. These powerful rulers **die in an instant**, just as the poor and lowly. Unexpectedly they **pass away** leaving the **people . . . shaken**, or they are removed by divine intervention **without human hand**. They meet the same end in death, just as those over whom they rule. God is no respecter of persons.

C Elihu's Refocus (34:21–37)

SUPPORTING IDEA: *Elihu reminds Job that God is both all seeing and just, and therefore, Job must not seek to make God respond.*

34:21–22. Elihu next affirmed the truth that God is the all-seeing Judge from whom no man's life is hidden. **His eyes are on the ways of men; he sees**

their every step (cp. Prov. 5:21). Actually, Job had made this same affirmation earlier (Job 31:4). **There is no dark place** before God's all-seeing, penetrating vision. He sees even in the **dark** recesses where no human eye has ever seen because nothing in creation is hidden from the face of the Creator.

34:23. God has no need to examine men further, as if cross-examining them in **judgment** would reveal more knowledge to him. He already knows all there is to know as he knows men better than they know themselves.

34:24. There is no need for **inquiry** because he sees all because he knows all and is without need for investigation. Thus, he executes perfect justice based on perfect knowledge. Accordingly, God **shatters the mighty**, punishing their sin. At the same time, God also **sets up others in their place**, rewarding their good.

34:25–26. As God who **takes note of their deeds**, he is able to administer perfect justice. **He overthrows them in the night** based upon his true perception and evaluation. God's knowledge is not skewed like man's. **He punishes them for their wickedness**, correctly levying justice. God renders wrath against the wicked before the eye of the public for **everyone can see them** suffer the due penalty of their wickedness.

34:27–28. Because they turned from following him, they receive divine punishment. The reason they went astray is because they **had no regard for any of his ways**. Because of their failure to follow God, they spurned his commandments. This is sufficient reason for their punishment—their rejection of God. These God-rejecters by their evil actions **caused the cry of the poor to come before him**. God will not turn a deaf ear to such a **cry of the needy**, for he will avenge them.

34:29–30. But if God **remains silent** and does not immediately judge the guilty, **who can condemn him?** Certainly not Job or any human being. Just because God does not act as man thinks, this does not give him the right to condemn God (Rom. 9:20–21). God is **over man and nation alike**, hearing the cry of everyone, whether the affliction is voiced by a single individual or the entire **nation**. No person is beyond his all-seeing eye and all-hearing ear. God will act in perfect righteousness, keeping **a godless man from ruling** and **from laying snares for the people**. Elihu defended the justice of God against Job's accusations.

34:31–32. Elihu applied the truths of the previous verses to Job. **Suppose a man says to God, "I am guilty but will offend no more."** This case was indirectly referring to Job. **Teach me what I cannot see**. In other words, suppose a man requested that God reveal to him sins that he had committed unknowingly. And suppose that man were also to say with a repentant spirit,

If I have done wrong, I will not do so again. Elihu was preparing Job to come to a spirit of repentance.

34:33–34. Elihu then pressed this question to Job's heart: **Should God then reward you on your terms, when you refuse to repent?** Elihu insisted that Job answer, and he underscored his insistence with the challenge, **so tell me what you know.** Directly referencing the words spoken by the three friends, Elihu said, "**Men of understanding declare.**" Elihu now referenced the complaints of the **wise men** (i.e., the three friends) against Job.

34:35–36. These three men had said, "**Job speaks without knowledge.**" Elihu said the same about Job. What Job said was unfounded and wasn't grounded in truth (cp. Job 38:2; 42:3). **His words** lacked the **insight** of divine wisdom and eternal perspective. Elihu, as well as the three friends, felt that Job should be chastened **to the utmost.** He should be punished for **answering like a wicked man.** God was not giving him all the punishment he deserved for his brazen accusations against God.

34:37. To his sin that first brought God's discipline and Job's suffering, Job added **rebellion** against God with his prideful attitude of self-vindication. "**Scornfully he claps his hands among us,**" Elihu charged, treating their advice with contempt as if to silence them. Worse, Job had multiplied **his words against God,** attempting to silence the Almighty. This concluded Elihu's second speech, a discourse delivered to defend the justice of God in the face of Job's cries of divine unfairness.

MAIN IDEA REVIEW: *Elihu confronts the false assumptions held by Job and the three friends, defends the justice of God, and encourages Job to look to God with the eye of faith.*

III. CONCLUSION

Made in Our Image

Voltaire, the famous French author and agnostic, once quipped, "God created man in his image, and man returned the favor." This eighteenth-century French philosopher was belittling the notion that there was one true God who had created mankind in his own likeness. Like other agnostics and atheists, Voltaire believed that man is like a person looking in a mirror and then forming his thoughts about God based on what he sees of himself. Thus, his picture of God, according to Voltaire, was a reflection of himself.

This, unfortunately, was what Job's three friends had done in framing for Job his picture of God. The counsel of Job's three friends was skewed because it came from a false view of God. Only Elihu had an accurate view of God and, thus, only he gave divine counsel and understanding to Job that represented God correctly. The starting point of true, biblical counsel must be an accurate view of God. Elihu noted that God is gracious and concerned with the affairs of men (Job 33). Further, God is faithful, rendering justice with no partiality (Job 34–35). Moreover, God is exceedingly great and sovereign (Job 36–37). These foundational truths about God were the heart of Elihu's counsel to Job.

IV. LIFE APPLICATION

Holding the Tongue

Sometimes, less *is* more. Job would have better served himself by saying as little as possible. The same holds true for God's people today. When suffering, we tend to speak "words without knowledge" (Job 38:2), the charge that God and Elihu (Job 34:35–37) made against Job. During these times of great suffering, a spirit void of understanding and filled with bitterness can emerge. Yet, there is a "time to be silent and a time to speak" (Eccl. 3:7). Many times silence *is* golden.

There is a reason people have two ears and one mouth. Believers must hold their tongue and refrain from making unjust accusations against God. James understood the tongue when he wrote that believers "should be quick to listen, slow to speak and slow to become angry" (cp. Jas. 1:19). No one has a right to call God into court and demand answers of him (cp. Job 9:20–21). "The mouth of the righteous man utters wisdom, and his tongue speaks what is just" (Ps. 37:30). While they are suffering, believers must speak truth when they speak and keep silent when they do not understand what God is doing.

Especially when suffering affliction, a person is in the dark and will have difficulty discerning the moving of God in the midst of the storm. The believer who controls his tongue demonstrates that he is spiritually mature and is able to control his entire body (Jas. 3:2).

V. PRAYER

God, our Father, teach us to consider it joy when we face various trials. Remind us that the testing of our faith develops perseverance that is used to mature us and present us complete in your presence. Lord, teach us to ask for divine wisdom, and help us to ask without doubting your ability to give that for which we ask. May we not be double-minded but stable in all our ways. In Jesus' name. Amen.

VI. DEEPER DISCOVERIES

A. Rebellion (34:37)

"Rebellion" or "transgressions" (Heb. *peshah*) literally means a going away from, departure, or defiance. Rebellion is a willful act against God's sovereign authority and a refusal to acknowledge his right to rule the lives of his people. Rebellion is not merely against other people whom a person may hurt by his sin, but it is always, ultimately, a treasonous act against God (cp. 1 Sam. 12:13; Ps. 51:4).

B. Shatter (34:24)

"Shatter" or "break" (Heb. *raa*) means to dash into pieces or to be broken up (Jer. 15:12). It is used of God afflicting painful judgment on the righteous (Ps. 44:2; Zech. 8:14). Elihu used *raa* in a similar way to demonstrate the punishment of sinners by God.

C. Understanding (34:16,34)

"Understand" (Heb. *sakal*) means to comprehend or to grasp. It was often used to speak of a person's spiritual understanding of God and the things of God. The prophet Isaiah recorded, "They know nothing, they understand (*sakal*) nothing; their eyes are plastered over so that they cannot see, and their minds closed so they cannot understand" (Isa. 44:18; cp. Ps. 14:2; Isa. 41:20). Here, used in the negative, it implies the spiritual blindness of those who are corrupt within their own hearts.

VII. TEACHING OUTLINE

A. Elihu's Rebuke (34:1–15)
  1. Listen to me (34:1–4)
  2. Listen to yourself (34:5–9)
  3. Listen to me (34:10–15)

B. Elihu's Reproof (34:16–20)
  1. Will you condemn God? (34:16–17)
  2. Will you correct God? (34:18)
  3. Will you charge God? (34:19–20)

C. Elihu's Refocus (34:21–37)
  1. God discerns all men (34:21–23)
  2. God deals with all men (34:24–30)
  3. God determines all judgments (34:31–37)

VIII. ISSUES FOR DISCUSSION

1. Do I receive counsel from godly advisers?
2. Do I question the justice of God?
3. Do I have a view of God that is in line with Scripture?

Job 35

When God Refuses to Answer

Quote

"God denies a Christian nothing, but with a design to give him something better."

Richard Cecil

Job 35

I. INTRODUCTION

Unanswered Prayer

Howard Hendricks, distinguished professor at Dallas Theological Seminary, testifies to the blessing of unanswered prayer in his life. When he was a young single man, he was aware that certain mothers had set their minds on him on behalf of their daughters. One mother said to him one day, "Howard, I just want you to know that I am praying that you will be my son-in-law." At that point Dr. Hendricks stopped and asked, tongue-in-cheek, "Have you ever thanked God for *unanswered* prayer?"

At this point in the life of Job, unanswered prayer had been anything but a blessing. The lack of response from heaven, despite his many pleas, had been a heavy burden for him to bear. Job had cried out to God again and again, but there had been no answer. The heavens had been as brass. Job had persistently appealed for an appearance before God, but there was no reply. Time and time again, he had requested a chance to argue his case before God in heaven. But permission had been denied by default. He repeatedly implored God for a change in his circumstances, but there had been no relief from above—only silence. This lack of response from God led Job to conclude that God was indifferent and uncaring toward him.

Elihu addressed this perplexing mystery of unanswered prayer. The silence from heaven that Job had experienced was not because God was indifferent toward his plight. Rather, it was because God's timing is always perfect and cannot be altered by man (vv. 4–8). Thus, Job must wait upon the Lord (v. 14b). Furthermore, Job's pride and his empty words had also caused God to remain silent (vv. 12–16). Not until Job repented of his sinful arrogance and recanted of his accusing words would God hear and answer him. Elihu's words in this chapter explain the enigma of Job's prayers that had gone unanswered during his painful ordeal.

II. COMMENTARY

When God Refuses to Answer

MAIN IDEA: *Elihu answers Job's charge that God did not reward him for his innocence.*

Elihu's Restatement (35:1–3)

SUPPORTING IDEA: *Elihu quotes Job, who has denied the justice of God.*

35:1–2. This chapter begins Elihu's third discourse to Job. He quoted Job and then refuted him, an approach we have seen in previous chapters. Elihu asked, "**Do you think this is just?**" He restated Job's contention that his suffering was not in direct proportion to the righteous life he had lived. By that standard, no, it was not. But the point Elihu made was that God is sovereign and is free to do as he pleases. Job had said, "**I will be cleared by God.**" That is, Job had claimed that once the evidence of his innocent life was presented to God, he would be **cleared** of all charges and released from his suffering.

35:3. Yet you ask him, "What profit is it to me?" Elihu restated Job's complaint that godliness availed him nothing with God. Job's complaint was that there was no advantage in being righteous, a contention he had already voiced (Job 21:15; 34:9). As he was painfully aware, his godliness had resulted only in tragedy and trauma. From Job's perspective, there was no value in serving God. **What do I gain by not sinning**? With these words, Elihu was further quoting Job, who had reasoned that **not sinning** had led only to a life of suffering and shame.

B Elihu's Refutation (35:4–8)

SUPPORTING IDEA: *Elihu refutes Job by insisting that God is sovereign and unaffected by man's sin or righteousness.*

35:4. Having quoted Job's words (vv. 1–3), Elihu now refuted his position, as well as that of the three friends. "**I would like to reply to you and to your friends with you**," Elihu declared. He could not allow their empty words and faulty thinking to remain unanswered. The error of the words must be corrected.

35:5. Pointing above, Elihu said, "**Look up at the heavens**" and "**the clouds so high above you.**" That is, Job should refocus his perspective on the sovereignty of God, who reigns enthroned above. As the skies were higher than Job, Elihu reasoned, so was the supremacy of God far above him. "As the heavens are higher than the earth, so are my ways higher than your ways" (Isa. 55:9).

35:6. **If you sin, how does that affect him?** Elihu's point was that God is so high that nothing human beings do affects his plans. God's holiness remains undiminished regardless of what man does. His eternal purpose moves forward, undeterred even by man's rebellious acts. **If your sins are many, what does that do to him?** The implied answer was *nothing*. God is not affected adversely by man's sin.

35:7. Conversely, neither is God affected by man's righteousness. "**If you are righteous, what do you give to him?**" Elihu asked. Once again, the implied answer was *nothing*. God is so high and lifted up that nothing men do affects him. **Or what does he receive from your hand**? Again, the answer was *nothing*. There is nothing that finite man can do to influence God. By this assertion Elihu was not teaching that God is indifferent to man's sin. Rather, the point he was making is that God's actions toward man are God determined not man initiated. God is not controlled by man, but man is controlled by God.

35:8. The only effect man's sin has is on himself and other people, not God. **Your wickedness affects only a man like yourself**. That is, a person's choices and character do affect his own life. Furthermore, **your righteousness** influences **the sons of men**, Elihu declared. Sinful actions, to one degree or another, always affect others.

C Elihu's Reproof (35:9–16)

SUPPORTING IDEA: *Elihu asserts that God does comfort and care for those who suffer, but this occurs in his perfect timing.*

35:9. Elihu advanced his argument to the ministry of God's comfort for those people, like Job, who are oppressed. **Men cry out under a load of**

oppression, suffering under the heavy blows of life. In their pain, **they plead for relief from the arm of the powerful** God, who alone can lift the heavy burden of adversity.

35:10–11. But no one says, "Where is God my Maker?" In other words, their cry for help is only a selfish plea for relief, not a plea rooted in God-fearing faith and humility. In such a desperate plight, people do not recognize that God is the one **who gives songs in the night**. Further, God **teaches more to us** and **makes us wiser** than all the animals. God graciously gives us more understanding than the various members of the animal kingdom.

35:12. In response to such self-sufficient men, God **does not answer when men cry out**. He does not deliver them from their dangers and distresses. The reason is clear, Elihu asserted: it is **because of the arrogance of the wicked**. Such puffed-up pride by man causes God to turn away with a deaf ear.

35:13. Indeed, God does not listen to their empty plea because it lacks humility and lowliness of heart. The reality is, **the Almighty pays no attention to it**. These prayers lack sincerity and self-denial. God is opposed to those who approach him in pride.

35:14. Applying this principle to Job, Elihu stated, "**How much less, then, will he listen when you say that you do not see him.**" Job's cries were rooted in pride and a demanding spirit, and, thus, would not be heard by God. When **your case is before him** in prayer, Elihu counseled, **you must wait for him** to act in his own time. God would not be hurried by Job's impatient demands.

35:15. Moreover, contrary to what Job thought, God's lack of response to his suffering did not mean he was indifferent to his sin. Job should not suppose, Elihu reasoned, that God's **anger never punishes** sin. Nor should he imagine that God fails to take notice of man's **wickedness**. God takes notice of man's sin and does punish him for it. But he does so in his own perfect time. God's delays in executing his judgment should not be interpreted as divine indifference toward sin.

35:16. In summary, Job had opened his mouth with **empty talk** that was devoid of wisdom. He had multiplied many words against God, but all **without knowledge**. He had spoken what was not true about God, charging him with doing nothing about wickedness (v. 15), an accusation that was simply not true. Job should stop his complaints against God and speak only to confess his sin.

MAIN IDEA REVIEW: *Elihu answers Job's charge that God does not reward him for his innocence.*

III. CONCLUSION

A Smoldering Disobedience

A young boy saw a pack of cigarettes on the ground and decided to try them. He went to a field near his home and, after several fumbling attempts, got one to light up. It burned his throat and made him cough. But it made him feel like an adult. Then he saw his father coming. Quickly he put the cigarette behind his back and tried to be casual. Desperate to divert his father's attention, the young boy pointed to a nearly billboard advertising the circus. "Can we go, Dad? Please, let's go when it comes to town." The father replied, "Son, never make a petition while trying to hide a smoldering disobedience."

This is the exact place where Job had been. While making demands to appear before God and argue his case, he had been harboring a smoldering bitterness, a brewing resentment toward God. For this reason there remained the mystery of unanswered prayer in this painful ordeal for Job. Not until his heart became right with God would he see the circumstances of his life change. His smoldering spirit had to become a sweet spirit of loving fellowship with God. Until this happened, difficulty would continue to reign in his life.

IV. LIFE APPLICATION

Confession and Prayer

The Bible has much to say about unanswered prayer. The psalmist said, "If I regard wickedness in my heart, the Lord will not hear" (Ps. 66:18 NASB). Sin disqualifies prayers of supplication. Prayer goes unanswered when sin is allowed to fester within the heart. A wall of separation is created by sin—a wall that separates the believer and the Lord. Accordingly, husbands are urged to live with their wives in an understanding way "so that nothing will hinder your prayers" (1 Pet. 3:7). Unconfessed sin within the home leads to unheard prayers in heaven. Personal repentance is necessary if there is to be a powerful result to prayer.

Confessing sin is a prerequisite before a person can experience power in his prayers. The apostle John reminded believers, "If we confess our sins, he is faithful and just and will forgive us our sins and purify us from all unrighteousness" (1 John 1:9). If a person will see sin as God sees it by recognizing how sinister it is, God will restore fellowship between himself and his people. But unconfessed sin will cause God to turn a deaf ear to the cries of his people. Confession of sin is a must for the serious believer who wants to have a successful prayer life.

V. PRAYER

God, our Father, teach us to endure with great patience and long suffering the path you have chosen for us to walk. May we learn to look to you, knowing that you work all things after the counsel of your will and for our good. Lord, may you have an open ear to our prayers, for we humbly approach your throne by the righteousness of your Son, the Lord Jesus Christ. In his name we pray. Amen.

VI. DEEPER DISCOVERIES

A. Oppression (35:9)

"Oppression" (Heb. *ashuqim*) refers to tyranny, abuse, or ill treatment brought on by those in authority over lower subjects. Often this oppression was carried out against the weak such as the orphan, the widow, and the poor. Nets of oppression were strictly forbidden by God (Lev. 19:13; Deut. 24:14) yet were often committed by Israel (Ezek. 22:29; Amos 4:1). Here the oppressions (plural in Hebrew) are a general oppression caused by God himself.

B. Case (35:14)

"Case" (Heb. *din*) is found only twenty-three times in the Old Testament. It means judgment, sentence, tribunal, cause, or quarrel. Here it is used of Job's case before God that seemed to Job to be stalled. It is used two other times in Job (19:29; 36:17).

C. Anger (35:15)

"Anger" (Heb. *ap*) is a term that refers to the nose, nostrils, and face. Heavy breathing is often used to express emotion. Often in anger as the rate and intensity of breathing increase, the nostrils dilate. Here it is used of God's anger toward Job that has injured him. It is often used of God's anger as it is demonstrated by divine chastisement (Ps. 6:1; Isa. 12:1) and punishment (2 Sam. 6:7; Jer. 44:6).

VII. TEACHING OUTLINE

A. Elihu's Restatement (35:1–3)

1. Elihu referenced Job's thoughts (35:1–2a)

2. Elihu referenced Job's words (35:2b–3)

B. Elihu's Refutation (35:4–8)

1. Consider the clouds above you (35:4–5)
2. Consider the choices within you (35:6–8)

C. Elihu's Reproof (36:9–16)

1. Men request help from God (35:9)
2. Men receive help from God (35:10–11)
3. Men receive silence from God (35:12–13)
4. You receive silence from God (35:14–16)

VIII. ISSUES FOR DISCUSSION

1. Do I examine my attitude when undergoing severe suffering?
2. Do I allow bitterness toward God to arise in my heart when suffering?
3. Do I understand that my trials are under the sovereign control of God?

Job 36

God Is Great, God Is Good

Quote

"He who feeds His birds will not starve His babes."

Matthew Henry

Job 36

I. INTRODUCTION

Meditating upon God's Goodness

Charles Simeon, rector of Holy Trinity Church in Cambridge, England, for fifty-four years (1782–1836), had a profound effect on his students. Among those converted through Simeon's ministry was Henry Martyn, pioneer missionary to India. Often this noted pastor invited students to his house for tea. Here he encouraged them to question him about spiritual truth. Once he was asked, "How do you maintain a close walk with God?"

This was Simeon's reply: "By constantly meditating on the goodness of God and on our great deliverance from that punishment which our sins deserve. Keeping both of these in mind, we shall find ourselves advancing on our course; we shall feel the presence of God; we shall experience his love; we shall live in the enjoyment of his favor and in the hope of his grace. Meditation is the grand means of our growth and grace."

Job was a man who needed to meditate on the goodness of God. Certainly, he had been focused on the greatness of God. But he needed to realize that divine greatness is mixed with goodness, sovereignty with sympathy, and majesty with mercy. God's supremacy is not arbitrary, inflicting harm on people needlessly. Rather, his control over everything is teamed with compassion for all. In this last portion of Elihu's speech, he offered hope to Job by reminding him of the goodness of God. His suffering was not without divine purpose. Job should learn the lessons that God was teaching for his benefit. The Lord would soon restore his life and soul.

II. COMMENTARY

God Is Great, God Is Good

MAIN IDEA: *Elihu reminds Job of the goodness of God, who works his greatness for Job's benefit.*

A Elihu's Appeal (36:1–4)

SUPPORTING IDEA: *Elihu desires to be heard by Job, knowing that his message is from God.*

36:1–2. **Elihu continued** to speak to Job in this, his fourth and final speech. This was the last appeal Elihu made to Job as he attempted to drive Job to repentance and back to God. Asking for Job's attention, he requested, **"Bear with me a little longer and I will show you that there is more to be said in God's behalf."** More can always be said about the character and attributes of God.

36:3. Claiming to speak divine truth, Elihu proclaimed, **"I get my knowledge from afar,"** that is, from God. His message, unlike the messages of the three friends, did not originate with himself, or from the culture around him. His wisdom was not from this world but from afar—the heights of heaven. **"I will ascribe justice to my Maker,"** Elihu declared. As a God of perfect equity, he can do only what is right. The essential idea of right is used throughout Scripture of a just judgment.

36:4. In order to give credibility to his remarks, Elihu stated, **"Be assured that my words are not false."** They had to be absolutely true because they proceeded from God, the author of truth. Thus, **"one perfect in knowledge is with you,"** Elihu declared. Either this was an arrogant, self-confident claim, or a God-confident claim. Probably the latter was in use here, meaning that Elihu was assured that the source of his message was God.

B Elihu's Argument (36:5–16)

SUPPORTING IDEA: *Elihu affirms the power and justice of God in his dealings with men.*

36:5. With a high view of God's supremacy over everything, Elihu boasted, **God is mighty**, able to order man's circumstances and govern the events of life. Yet, at the same time, God **does not despise men**. He does not abuse his power but uses it for the highest good of his people. Thus, he is both all powerful and all loving, working all things together for the benefit of his people. Therefore, it is a truth to be embraced—the fact that God is **firm in his purpose**. God's eternal decrees and sovereign will are immutable, fixed, and not subject to change by man or circumstances.

36:6. In perfect justice God **does not keep the wicked alive**, Elihu argued. He punishes them for their sin, requiring their death. This statement was made to counter Job's assertion that the wicked were not judged (Job 21:7). Conversely, God **gives the afflicted their rights**, defending and rewarding them for their obedience.

36:7. In so doing, God **does not take his eyes off the righteous** but remains attentive to their needs (cp. Ps. 121:3–8). This argument seems to refute what Job had stated earlier (cp. Job 24:1–17). **He enthrones** these godly ones **with kings** in this life and **exalts them forever** in heaven (cp. 1 Sam. 2:7–8; 1 Pet. 2:9).

36:8–9. But if men are bound in chains, suffering **affliction**, or if they have **sinned arrogantly**, God tells them **what they have done** so they can repent. Thus, God uses their trials to purify them. Elihu probably said this to refute Job's earlier claim that God would not present his charges against him (Job 31:35–36).

36:10. In such hard times, Elihu stated, God makes them listen to **correction**, commanding them to **repent of their evil**. God uses trials to gain man's attention. Never are people more open to divine constructive criticism than when their hearts are melted in the furnace of affliction.

36:11–12. In the fire of adversity, two responses are possible. First, the positive. A person may have a teachable spirit and be ready to repent and obey God. **If they obey and serve him**, they will enjoy **prosperity** and **contentment**. That is, God will reward their obedience and bless them. Second, a negative response is possible. **But if they do not listen** to God and disobey, they will **perish** under divine judgment. They will **die** without knowledge of what they should have gained in this trial.

36:13–14. Some people are **godless in heart**, previously mentioned as those who do not listen to God. These people **harbor resentment**. They become so hardhearted that even when God **fetters** them with affliction, they do not cry out to him for help because their stubborn hearts refuse to repent. Consequently, they receive the just retribution of their disobedience. **They die in their youth**, prematurely cut down in the prime of life, with the ungodly **male prostitutes** of the pagan **shrines**. The godless face the judgment of God in the form of death.

36:15. Elihu concluded this section with penetrating insight. **But those who suffer he delivers in their suffering**, once they have learned the lesson God wants to teach them. **He speaks to them in their affliction**. That is, God uses suffering to discipline them, prune and purify them, and bring repentance.

36:16. Elihu applied all this truth directly to Job. He said, God **is wooing you from the jaws of distress**. Elihu offered this hope to Job, expressing his conviction that an end to his suffering was in sight. With tender compassion God brings his people back to himself. There is an eventual relief to come from God. This relief will be seen as **a spacious place free from the restriction** or escape from this confining adversity. But this will occur only in God's perfect timing. There was a future **comfort** from God that Job would experience, a time coming when he would again eat **choice food** in leisure enjoyment.

 Elihu's Admonition (36:17–23)

SUPPORTING IDEA: *Elihu counsels Job to be patient and learn from his affliction, viewing his trial as God's means of teaching, maturing, and purifying him.*

36:17–19. **But now**, until you repent, Elihu admonished, **you are laden with the judgment due the wicked**. This judgment, the result of God's justice, had taken hold of Job and he could not escape it. God was disciplining him, Elihu declared. One lesson to be learned in this trial was not to trust in **riches** or **a large bribe**. From all indications Job never trusted in his wealth. Job's **wealth** and **efforts** could not sustain him in this ordeal. The implication was that only God could hold him up through this trial.

36:20–21. Job should not **long for the night** of death to avoid what God wanted to teach him in this suffering. Job should learn the life lessons involved in his experiences and not hurry through this difficult time. So, Elihu spoke, **beware of turning to evil** in the midst of this personal crisis. Instead, Job should turn to God in humble repentance rather than resorting to the sin of proud self-reliance that he seemed to prefer to **affliction**.

36:22. Elihu reinforced again the greatness of God over all creation. Ultimately, this is the only true strength for any hurting soul in the midst of trials. **God is exalted in his power**, able to deliver Job out of the pain. But such a rescue would occur only when he had applied the lessons to be learned. **Who**

is a teacher like him? The answer is *no one*. Only God can teach man profound lessons through the tragedies in his life.

36:23. Who has prescribed his ways for him? No one has counseled God about which way he should take. Yet God counsels all people. So how could Job tell God what to do? Likewise, no one can say to God, "**You have done wrong.**" This is because only God can do and say what is right. Therefore, Job should listen to God and learn from him, not try to instruct the Lord.

D Elihu's Affirmation (36:24–33)

SUPPORTING IDEA: *Elihu affirms to Job the greatness and goodness of God, who rules over all and cares for all.*

36:24–25. Elihu continued pointing Job to God's greatness. He said, "**Remember to extol his work**," which is always perfect, just, and purposeful. People have praised God **in song** for such wonderful providence displayed throughout the earth. "**All mankind has seen it**," Elihu affirmed, referring to God's supremacy. They have all gazed at God's amazing works that are visible throughout all creation. It is so majestic that people everywhere can even see if **from afar**.

36:26. The essence of Elihu's counsel was, **How great is God—beyond our understanding**. Although Job might know God personally, the fullness of his divine glory was beyond his ability to grasp. God's ways are infinitely higher than man's ways. **The number of his years is past finding out**. The eternality of God cannot be understood. An infinite God is incomprehensible to finite man.

36:27–28. The infinite greatness of God, Elihu argued, is seen in his power over nature, specifically a rainstorm. But even God's omnipotence is used for man's good. This sovereign ruler **draws up the drops of water, which distill as rain to the streams**. Elihu showed insight into the water cycle with its different stages of evaporation, condensation, and precipitation. Elihu recognized the control of God in the water cycle. **The clouds pour down their moisture and abundant showers fall on mankind**. This is a vivid expression of God's abundant goodness and blessing that is bestowed on humanity.

36:29. Such divine power is mighty and mysterious. **Who can understand how he spreads out the clouds**? The implied answer is *no one*. No single individual can grasp how God's sovereign control works in forming the weather. Or, **how he thunders from his pavilion**? Again, such meteorological operations are beyond man's limited ability to comprehend. Then how could

Job pretend to understand God's operations in the spiritual realm? Of course, he could not.

36:30. See how he scatters his lightning about him, serving his own divine pleasure and plans, **bathing the depths of the sea**. The lightning lights up the depths of the ocean when it flashes across the horizon. God alone controls the natural storm. In the same way, he alone controls the spiritual storms.

36:31. With such power and purpose, **this is the way he governs the nations** as well. His works of providence are great and gracious, mighty and mysterious. They are beyond man's limited ability to comprehend. In so ruling, God **provides food in abundance**. This is the result of rainstorms that provide the needed water for abundant crops. God never misuses his power but uses it for the good of mankind.

36:32. With graphic analogy, Elihu declared that God **fills his hands with lightning** to fulfill his appointed purpose. Thus, he **commands it to strike its mark** precisely by divine decree. Such is the providential power of Almighty God, pinpointing even the **lightning** strikes. The same is true of the storms of life.

36:33. His thunder can be heard in the distance, announcing **the coming storm**. It, too, is sent by divine initiative. **Even the cattle make known its approach**, or perhaps more correctly, are aware of its approaching presence. Should not Job acknowledge the same in his own life?

MAIN IDEA REVIEW: *Elihu reminds Job of the goodness of God, who works his greatness for Job's benefit.*

III. CONCLUSION

Overwhelmed with God's Goodness

About a century ago a missionary named Allen Gardiner suffered a tragic accident and was drowned. When his body was found near his overturned boat along the seashore, his diary was also discovered. It told over and over again of the hunger, privation, persecution, and suffering he had experienced. And yet the very last entry in the book was this: "I am overwhelmed with a sense of the goodness of God!"

Elihu's counsel to Job was that God is good to his people, and he exercises his greatness for his own glory and our good. Despite the many painful experiences through which believers go, overriding it all is the goodness of God. He constantly showers his blessings upon us. God *is* good all the time.

So let us trust him in the midst of life's disappointments. Let us be reminded that he never abuses his power, but always uses it for the betterment and blessing of his people. He is a good God who can always be trusted.

IV. LIFE APPLICATION

Exalting the Righteous

Trials and suffering often distort a person's view of reality and cause him to descend into despair and hopelessness. The sufferer must remember that the best is yet to come because God will enthrone the righteous, exalting them forever (cp. Job 36:7). The Lord promised in Psalm 91:14, "Because he has set his love upon Me, therefore I will deliver him; I will set him on high, because he has known My name" (NKJV). Those who seek refuge in the name of the Lord will be showered with God's love and delivered from their fiery trials. The righteous will be exalted by God. He alone "brings death and makes alive . . . sends poverty and wealth; he humbles and he exalts. . . . He will guard the feet of his saints" (1 Sam. 2:6a,7,9a). God is in control of all the circumstances of your life. No matter what happens—life or death, wealth or tragedy—God will guard you and protect you.

When suffering, the righteous must look to God and remember that he will exalt them. He will, in his timing, lift up the trampled and restore in greater abundance what was lost during the suffering, either in this life (cp. Job 42:10–17) or in the life to come. Therefore, the righteous must humble themselves under God's mighty hand, so that he may lift them up at the time he has determined (1 Pet. 5:6). If you are undergoing great suffering, be of good cheer because God will exalt you. Be assured that God will hear the cry of his people and will deliver them in due time.

V. PRAYER

God, our Father, you are indeed mighty and firm in your purpose. You bless the righteous and judge the wicked. You alone can right all wrongs in justice. You alone hold authority over heaven and earth. Remind us that you do not take your eyes off the righteous and are always aware of your people's plight. Thank you for your righteousness, which has been transferred to us through your Son, the Lord Jesus Christ. In his name we pray. Amen.

VI. DEEPER DISCOVERIES

A. False (36:4)

"False" (*sheqer*) is used of actions or words that are deceptive and false because they are not grounded in truth or fact. The psalmist used this word to speak of those who slandered him without cause (Ps. 69:4). In Proverbs, *sheqer* is used of lying lips and tongues (Prov. 26:28) and food gained by ill means (Prov. 20:17). In the Torah it is used of a false witness (Deut. 19:18) and perjury (Lev. 19:12) and in Zechariah of a lying oath (Zech. 5:4; 8:17). Jeremiah used *sheqer* to indict the false prophets who gave false prophecy (Jer. 5:31; 23:32; 29:9). Here it is used by Job as an indictment of the slanderous, ungrounded allegations of his friends.

B. Affliction (36:8,15,21)

"Affliction" (Heb. *oni*) means misery, depression, or turmoil. This word is used to express the state of pain resulting from affliction. It is found in Job (10:15; 30:16,27) and numerous Old Testament passages (Gen. 16:11; Exod. 3:7; 1 Sam. 1:11; 2 Kgs. 14:26; Ps. 9:13; Lam. 1:7).

C. Hold (36:17)

"Hold" (Heb. *tamak*) is used twenty times in the Old Testament and means to grasp, lay hold of, support, hold up, or maintain. It was often used of moral matters and spiritual truths. Here it is used of the inner support David received from God when he was confronted by his enemies. God would support him in this trial. The word was used by David when he said to the Lord, "In my integrity you uphold me" (Ps. 41:12), meaning he would be strengthened by God to walk in holiness. David used *tamak* in Psalm 17:5, "My steps have held to your paths." The word is even used to represent God upholding the coming Messiah (Isa. 42:1) and upholding Israel with his righteous right hand (Isa. 41:10). These statements convey God's overruling strength. Here it is used by Elihu to speak of God's judgment and justice, which Elihu believed would surely overwhelm Job.

VII. TEACHING OUTLINE

- A. Elihu's Appeal (36:1–4)
  - 1. I have more to say about God (36:1–2)
  - 2. I have more to say from God (36:3–4)
- B. Elihu's Argument (36:5–16)
  - 1. God practices might (36:5)

2. God protects justice (36:6)
3. God promotes righteousness (36:7)
4. God pursues holiness (36:8–16)

C. Elihu's Admonition (36:17–23)

1. You should restrain your impatience (36:17–18)
2. You should abandon your self-trust (36:19–21)
3. You should behold God's supremacy (36:22–23)

D. Elihu's Affirmation (36:24–33)

1. God's greatness is beyond comprehension (36:24–26)
2. God's greatness is seen in nature (36:27–33)

VIII. ISSUES FOR DISCUSSION

1. Do I look to God's Word for comfort when suffering trials?
2. Do I believe that God is concerned about the plight of the righteous?
3. Do I accept the truth that God's plan for my life is a mystery?

Job 37
God Is Still in Control

Quote

"There is no attribute of God more comforting to His children than the doctrine of divine sovereignty."

Charles Haddon Spurgeon

Job 37

I. INTRODUCTION

Who Is in Charge Here?

Ronald Reagan, the fortieth president of the United States, was shot by John Hinckley in an attempted assassination in 1981. In the melee that followed, confusion reigned at the White House. The burning question was: Who was actually in charge? George Bush, the vice president, was not present. At that point, Alexander Haig, the secretary of state and the former military leader of NATO, took it upon himself to fill the leadership vacuum. Stepping in front of a live television camera, Haig uttered those now famous words: "As of this moment, I am in charge here." But he was wrong. The secretary of state was not next in line of command.

This same confusion reigns in the minds of many people today about who is in charge of the universe. Is God governing the affairs of men? Or is man controlling his own lot in life with all its attendant events? Or could it be that Satan is the one who reigns? What about fate? Has some blind, impersonal force fixed the order of circumstances? Who or what is in charge?

Much like Alexander Haig's misguided statement, many people today assign control of the world to everyone and everything but God. But the truth is that God is in charge. He alone is governing this universe, ruling and reigning over the present condition and future destiny of every living person. This is the message of Scripture. Our Lord is controlling all events and circumstances for his glory and the good of his people.

This fourth and final speech of Elihu in Job 37 drove home this monumental truth in the midst of Job's suffering. The same God who governs the storms of nature controls the storms of life. Therefore, Job should put his trust and confidence in God, who causes all things to work together for good (Rom. 8:28). This is the towering truth and source of hope given by Elihu to Job. It is a message that strengthens the hearts of God's people.

II. COMMENTARY

God Is Still in Control

MAIN IDEA: *Elihu declares God's mighty power in nature as a means of teaching God's divine sovereignty over Job's life.*

A God Controls the Electrical Storm (37:1–5)

SUPPORTING IDEA: *Elihu describes God's power in a thunderstorm to indicate his power over the affairs of Job's life.*

37:1. Elihu was gripped with a deep sense of awe at the mighty power of God in nature, specifically in an electrical storm. "**At this**," he said—referring to the thought of God's sovereign control over nature—"**my heart pounds and leaps from its place.**"

37:2–3. **Listen! Listen to the roar of his voice** in **the rumbling** of a thunderstorm (v. 4), Elihu declared. The Hebrew for "listen" is in the plural, indicating that all the three friends, as well as Job, were being addressed here. However, for the most part, these words were addressed to Job. He directed Job to hear and sense God's power in a thunderstorm. In such a storm God **unleashes his lightning beneath the whole heaven**, as if this storm flashed across the skies at his command. He **sends it to the ends of the earth** by his divine decree.

37:4–5. Then, after the lightning, **comes the sound of his roar**—the loud, booming thunder. This ear-splitting blast broadcasts **his majestic voice**, holding **nothing back**. God's voice thunders in this storm, reverberating in man's ears. Such a display of divine might is **beyond our understanding**. The full measure of God's power is incomprehensible to man.

B God Controls the Snowstorm (37:6–10)

SUPPORTING IDEA: *Elihu declares God's power in a snowstorm, heavy rain, or ice storm, revealing his total control over Job's life.*

37:6. Shifting his focus to a winter snowstorm, Elihu demonstrated to Job God's awesome power with yet another object lesson. God says to the snow, "**Fall on the earth**" and the **snow** obeys. He commands the rain shower, "**Be a mighty downpour**," and it is brought to pass. Only God exercises such infinite power over his creation.

37:7–8. A snowfall or heavy rain can stop **every man** from working in their fields, revealing their dependence on God. Mankind must surrender to the weather, which is under God's sovereign control. Even the **animals**, suited to outdoor living, must **take cover** during inclement weather, their lives being disrupted by God's power. The implication for Job was that he, too, should take cover.

37:9–10. **The tempest comes out from its chamber** by divine edict, displaying God's omnipotence, as well as the blistering **cold from the driving wind**. Behind the weather is God, who orders the elements; they obey his command. **The breath of God** is a metaphor for chilling wind that **produces ice, and the broad waters** (i.e., streams and rivers). These frozen conditions of the cold winter reminded Job that the painful seasons of life are directed by God, ultimately, for man's good.

C God Controls the Rainstorm (37:11–13)

SUPPORTING IDEA: *Elihu portrays the rain clouds as being sent by God for the good of man, just as Job has experienced.*

37:11–12. By sovereign directive, God **loads the clouds with moisture**. Further, **he scatters his lightning through them** and empties these same clouds. God fills and drains these clouds by his command. **At his direction they swirl around** in the skies **to do whatever he commands**. The point is that God also controls the storms of life. Like the clouds God fills man's life with sorrow and then empties it of pain. In this was a message of hope for Job. The God who had brought difficulty into his life was the same God who would remove it. This ordeal, Elihu implied, was only for a season and would soon pass.

37:13. The directing of these storms is purposeful, never random. God uses them for his own purposes in man's life, either to **punish** or provide good things. "**He brings the clouds to punish man**," Elihu declared, sometimes to flood the land, ruin the crops, and take human lives. Or, conversely, he **brings** the storm **to water his earth and show his love**, sometimes to cool the summer heat, cause the crops to grow, and provide food for man. Both uses of the storm are from God, whether to blast or to bless.

D God Controls All Storms (37:14–18)

SUPPORTING IDEA: *Elihu presses Job to explain the wonders of God as found in the rich variety of creation.*

37:14. In light of such divine, sovereign power, **Job** should **listen** carefully to this profound truth. He should **stop and consider God's wonders**. Job should be still and contemplate the awesome power of God over man's existence. Job should realize that God is God, working his **wonders** on the earth.

37:15. Elihu asked a series of rhetorical questions (vv. 15–18), each designed to point Job to God and his sovereignty. The implied answer to each of these questions was that God operates beyond the understanding of man. **Do you know how God controls the clouds and makes his lightning flash?** Of course Job did not fully understand these profound phenomena. He saw some of God's awesome deeds, but he did not comprehend them. The same was true of Job's suffering. He witnessed the fact that God ordered his circumstances, but he could not grasp how it was worked out in the plan of God for his life.

37:16. Elihu continued to press, "**Do you know how the clouds hang poised?**" Job did not consider the magnitude of this reality as he should have. He could see the clouds overhead, and he could experience their buffeting and blessing (v. 13). But understand them? Job, with his finite mind, limited and imperfect as it was, could never grasp the awe-inspiring **wonders of him who is perfect in knowledge**. God exercises his sovereign will beyond man's finite comprehension.

37:17–18. Further pressing this point, Elihu addressed Job: "**You who swelter in your clothes when the land lies hushed under the south wind.**" Job baked under the summer sun and sirocco that blew from the desert. Elihu's next probing question was, **Can you join him** (God) **in spreading out the skies, hard as a mirror of cast bronze?** Ancient mirrors were made of bronze and were unbreakable. A bronze, mirrorlike sky pictures sweltering summer heat.

E God Controls Life's Storm (37:19–24)

SUPPORTING IDEA: *Elihu summarizes his lengthy discourse by applying God's sovereignty to Job's life, calling him to submit to God in awe.*

37:19. Elihu concluded his words by telling Job that man could not present his case before God. This is because man lives in the dark about God's ways. If Job were allowed to approach God to present his case, Elihu challenged him to **tell us what we should say to him**. What would Job say to God if he could argue his case before him? **We cannot draw up our case because of our darkness**. Job lived in a world foreign to God and heaven and, thus, could not understand it.

37:20–21. Man is in the dark about the mystery of God's providence. Should God **be told** that man wanted to **speak** with him, man would **be swallowed up**. To challenge or contest God would end in certain death (cp. Exod. 33:20). Elihu compared the audacity of telling God what to do with the blinding experience of staring into the sun. **No one can look at the sun** for long and see clearly. Neither could Job look at God and comprehend him.

37:22. Looking upon and contemplating **God** in his glory who **comes in golden splendor** would be far more blinding than staring at the sun. **God comes in awesome majesty**, exceeding his revelation in creation.

37:23. The Almighty is beyond our reach. We are not able to understand, argue with, or control him. He is **exalted in power**, governing all he has created toward its appointed end. With such absolute sovereignty man should not fear being abused by him but should know that God can do only what is right. **In his justice and great righteousness**, God can be fully trusted. **He does not oppress** needlessly or unfairly but works all things for his glory and the good of his people.

37:24. Therefore, by summation, **men revere him**. They will honor God only to the extent that they understand these truths about his divine majesty. Elihu concluded by asking, "**Does he not have regard for all the wise in heart?**" The implied answer is *yes*. God did have regard for people like Job, who claimed to be wise in heart (Job 9:4). The wise person reverences and fears God, but Job had become puffed up in haughty pride. Before such a sovereign ruler, Job must submit himself and be silent.

MAIN IDEA REVIEW: *Elihu declares God's mighty power in nature as a means of teaching God's divine sovereignty over Job's life.*

III. CONCLUSION

George Müller's Secret

George Müller, famed orphanage director of Bristol, England, was once asked the secret of his service. It was known far and wide that God had met his needs at the orphanage without his making them known. How did he exist like this? The simple answer startled the questioner. Müller replied,

"There was a day when I died, utterly died." As he spoke, he bent lower and lower until he almost touched the floor, displaying his submission before God. "I died to George Müller, his opinions, preferences, tastes, and will," the great man of faith explained. "I died to the world, its approval or censure. I died to the approval or blame even of my brethren and friends. And since then, I have studied only to show myself approved unto God."

This was the place to which Job must come in his relationship with God, Elihu declared. Job must die to all self-interests and all desires. He must die to himself in a decisive act of unconditional surrender to God, who is sovereign over all. After all, Job was only God's lowly servant, a finite creature made in God's image. Job must offer his life afresh to God in total surrender. God is sovereign. Job, as well as all creation, must yield to God.

IV. LIFE APPLICATION

A Knowledge of God

A. W. Tozer once said, "What comes into our minds when we think about God is the most important thing about us." The most important thing about you is who you believe God is. Everything about you is determined by your understanding of who God is. What you think of God is the mainspring from which your entire being flows. Like the foundation of a house that supports the entire structure, your knowledge of God is what upholds your life and gives it direction, purpose, and strength. Deep, intimate, personal knowledge of God is the leading cause of which everything else in your life is the effect. Who you believe God is impacts every area of your life—your attitudes, priorities, choices, and even your destiny. The true knowledge of God is so vast and overreaching that it is the only subject powerful enough to define and determine every aspect of the lives of God's people.

All believers must acquire a high view of God, like Elihu had. The scriptural view of God is weighty and lofty. God is greater and more majestic than we could ever imagine. God is omnipresent, meaning he is everywhere (Ps. 139:7–10), yet invisible since he is spirit (John 4:24). God is personal. He is a Father, friend, and shepherd but not the impersonal pronoun "it." Therefore, he can be intimately known, loved, and adored since he is a personal being.

Further, God knows everything before it happens (cp. Isa. 46:10). Furthermore, God is eternal, meaning he is infinite, without beginning or end (Gen. 21:33; Ps. 90:22). He is also self-existent, meaning he is dependent on nothing (Exod. 3:14). These are just some of God's attributes that demonstrate his greatness. There is no subject more life-changing than God, and there is no greater determinative factor in how you live your life than knowledge of who God really is.

V. PRAYER

God, our Father, you speak to us through your Word. You are actively revealing your greatness throughout all creation. Man pales in comparison with you, who mysteriously control all the wonders of creation. You are clothed in golden splendor and beyond our reach because you are highly exalted in power. Teach us to reverence you with the honor you deserve. In Jesus' name. Amen.

VI. DEEPER DISCOVERIES

A. Earth (37:12)

"Earth" (Heb. *tebel*) is used three different ways in the Old Testament. First, it refers to the physical mass of the earth (1 Sam. 2:8; 2 Sam. 22:16). Second, it refers to the people of the earth (Ps. 96:13; Isa. 13:11). Third, it refers to the habitable part of the land (Ps. 90:2; Nah. 1:5). The first usage is what Elihu had in mind. These two different Hebrew words for earth—*tebel* and *eres*—sometimes appear in parallelism, or in opposition to one another (Ps. 90:2; Isa. 34:1).

B. Wonders (37:14)

"Wonders" (Heb. *pala*) is a reference to something that is wonderful, miraculous, or astonishing. In Psalm 72:18, Solomon wrote, "Praise be to the LORD God, the God of Israel, who alone does marvelous deeds" (*pala*). These wonders of which Elihu spoke are not caused by the actions of men but by the providential interventions of the Lord, who alone can rescue and save. They are called *wonders* because of the effect caused within the heart when God's mighty deeds are observed. In other words, it is astonishment and amazement within when we observe the intervention of God. The word is used throughout Job and Psalms (Pss. 9:1; 71:17; 145:5).

VII. TEACHING OUTLINE

A. God Controls the Electrical Storm (37:1–5)
   1. He unleashes his lightning (37:1–3)
   2. He releases his thunder (37:4–5)

B. God Controls the Snowstorm (37:6–10)
   1. He commands the snow (37:6)

2. He channels the snow (37:7–8)
3. He controls the cold (37:9)
4. He creates ice (37:10)

C. God Controls the Rainstorm (37:11–13)
1. He fills the clouds (37:11)
2. He sends the clouds (37:12)
3. He uses the clouds (37:13)

D. God Controls All Storms (37:14–18)
1. God shines in nature (37:14)
2. God sends the lightning (37:15)
3. God suspends the clouds (37:16)
4. God spreads the skies (37:17–18)

E. God Controls Life's Storm (37:19–24)
1. You cannot approach God (37:19–20)
2. You cannot comprehend God (37:21–23)
3. You must be in awe of God (37:24)

VIII. ISSUES FOR DISCUSSION

1. Do I understand that God has hidden from me his plan for my life?
2. Do I acknowledge that God works in mysteries beyond my comprehension?
3. Do I maintain a proper reverence for God?

Job 38:1–38

Before the Supreme Court

Quote

"Let God be God."

Martin Luther

Job 38:1–38

I. INTRODUCTION

The Judge Brought to Trial

Never before had a Senate hearing drawn the attention that the Clarence Thomas judiciary hearing drew. It started out innocently enough, until the last-minute testimony of a woman by the name of Anita Hill. Instantly, the focus shifted to the moral turpitude of Judge Thomas. One of the highest judges in the land suddenly found himself accused of sexual harassment. The charge was serious. The judge was being condemned as a person unfit to sit on the bench.

As the entire nation watched, the Senate Judiciary Committee sat presiding over the interrogation. Having been nominated to sit as a justice on the highest court of the land, the Supreme Court, Thomas was undergoing an unparalleled character assassination with unsubstantiated innuendoes. This eleventh-hour attack threatened to ruin his life and career while preventing him from sitting on the bench of the Supreme Court. The issue was critical. Did Thomas possess the personal character necessary to sit in judgment of others? Thomas was eventually cleared of all wrongdoing and found to be competent to serve on the highest court in the land.

The story of Job is one of high drama. Job had been accusing God, the Judge of heaven and earth, of injustice and had demanded his day in court to present his case against God. Having charged God with being unfit to sit on his throne, the issue at stake was the Judge's competency to rule the universe. Is God qualified to preside over all creation? That was the issue. The Creator had been charged with wrongdoing by one of his creatures and must defend his own glory and honor.

But near the end of the proceedings the case took an unexpected turn. Rather than God himself taking the witness stand as Job had hoped, God chose to put Job, the plaintiff, on the stand and examine him. No other witness was brought forward. No other evidence was submitted. No more cross-examination was needed. God himself was in control of this entire court scene. Job had asked for a hearing with God so he might present his case before him (Job 31:35). He wanted God to present a bill of indictment with specific charges, which he believed himself to be adequately prepared to answer.

But when Job got what he wanted—a day in court with God—he did not want what he got. God suddenly burst on the scene and spoke to Job out of a whirlwind, asking him over seventy questions. What follows is the longest conversation in the Bible in which God speaks. If you can learn about someone by his words, there is much for us to learn about God here. The theophany, or appearance of God, that Job had asked for finally arrived.

II. COMMENTARY

Before the Supreme Court

MAIN IDEA: *God breaks his silence and speaks to Job, overwhelming him with a display of his sovereign majesty.*

A God Rules over Job (38:1–3)

SUPPORTING IDEA: *God confronts Job about his competency to call God into question.*

38:1. God suddenly broke his long silence and spoke to Job in anger. Directly. Audibly. Powerfully. **Then the LORD answered Job out of the storm.** A fierce whirlwind blew across the landscape where Job was standing, dramatizing the awesomeness of this divine encounter. In like manner God spoke to Moses out of a turbulent storm (Exod. 19:16–17). He also spoke to his prophets in a similar fashion (1 Kgs. 19:11–13; Ezek. 1:4). This turbulent twister conveyed the awesome power and infinite force of God and his spoken words.

38:2. God spoke, "**Who is this that darkens my counsel with words without knowledge?**" Job's words had only confused the truth about who God is. The more Job had spoken, the more he had obscured the reality of

God's person and work. Job's words and discourses were constructed in a mind devoid of knowledge.

38:3. Abruptly, God warned, "**Brace yourself like a man.**" This was a military command that called a soldier to prepare for a fierce battle. It was Job's time to appear before God, but it would be a heated cross-examination, more than Job could have ever imagined. **I will question you; and you shall answer me**. It would not be Job who would be questioning God but conversely. God would be in the dominant position as Job's questioner. This was a challenge for Job to teach God (cp. Job 40:7). Job would be put on the defensive, led about by the sovereign initiative and dominion of God. God is here represented as the sovereign Lord who guides and governs all and who will submit to no mere mortal.

B God Rules over the Earth (38:4–7)

SUPPORTING IDEA: *God humbles Job by asking him an array of questions about his creation of the physical world, none of which Job can answer.*

38:4. What God said to Job was put in the form of a series of questions, all intended to reveal the sovereignty of the Lord and the absurdity of Job's challenges to him. With disarming profundity, God asked, "**Where were you when I laid the earth's foundation?**" The questions posed were intended to put Job in his proper place—a humble position before God. Clearly, Job was nowhere to be found at the time of creation. If Job did not create the world, what made him think he could run it? "**Tell me, if you understand,**" God declared. But, of course, Job did not understand the genius of God in creation. So how could he possibly counsel or correct God about the governance of his life?

38:5. As if measuring a building, God asked about the earth, "**Who marked off its dimensions?**" Challenging Job, he pressed, "**Surely you know!**" This was intended to quiet Job, who had assumed to know so much about creation. **Who stretched a measuring line across it?** In other words, who was able to measure the earth? The implied answer is *no one but God.* The same was true about the affairs of Job's life.

38:6. Representing creation as a building project, God asked, "**On what were its footings set, or who laid its cornerstone?**" Could Job explain how God suspended the earth in midair? No, and because he could not, neither could he explain how God governed the affairs of the earth, especially the affairs of men.

38:7. God's act of creation took place **while the morning stars sang together**, clearly a reference to **the angels** (Job 1:6) who rejoiced in the founding of the earth. Should not Job also rejoice in the works of God in his life?

C God Rules over the Sea (38:8–11)

SUPPORTING IDEA: *God questions Job about the creation of the sea with the purpose of revealing Job's lack of knowledge.*

38:8. Shifting his line of questioning to the earth's oceans, God asked, "**Who shut up the sea behind doors?**" This pictures the ocean as being restrained by closed doors, kept in its place by divine decree. This sovereign placement first occurred **when it burst forth from the womb**. Here, the creation of the ocean is pictured as the earth giving birth. This is a reference to the depths below the earth's substance from which waters flowed—the flood (Gen. 7:11; cp. Gen. 49:25).

38:9–10. At that critical time God **made the clouds its garment and wrapped it in thick darkness**, like clothing a newborn baby in swaddling clothes. The sea is not a ferocious force independent of leadership but is under the sovereign direction of God. It was at this time of creation that God **fixed limits** for the shoreline. The ocean could not go beyond these fixed points because God **set its doors and bars in place**, as if bolted shut and held in place. The sea is restrained in its appointed place by God, who controls all of his creation.

38:11. Addressing the ocean, God said, "**This far you may come and no farther; here is where your proud waves halt**" (cp. Jer. 5:22). If the arrogant ocean knew its place and boundaries, then why did Job not know his limits?

D God Rules over the Sun (38:12–15)

SUPPORTING IDEA: *God continues to humiliate Job by interrogating him with questions he cannot answer about God's ways with the wicked.*

38:12. Shifting his questioning to the rotation of the earth's sphere, God pressed Job harder. **Have you ever given orders to the morning**? That is, had Job ever commanded the morning to appear? **Or shown the dawn its place**? Had Job ushered in the evening even one time? The implied answer is *no*. Only God has done this. Thus, only God had the right to order and command the events of Job's life, and only he could do so with precision.

38:13. Such divine directives were issued so the ocean **might take the earth by the edges**, like a person grasping the corners of a blanket. This describes the removing of darkness by God, as dawn is unveiled. This was an act which seemingly uncovered the wicked, leaving them no place to hide.

38:14. Describing the rotation of the earth, God said, "**The earth takes shape like clay under a seal.**" The earth is pictured as a document written on a clay tablet. Its surface is changed when a seal is rolled, or impressed, upon it. So it is when the sun rises and the light of day causes the earth's surface to stand out and appear different. Thus, the earth's globe is represented as turning, causing the night to change to day. Just as the surface of the earth is unveiled, so the wicked are exposed as each new day dawns.

38:15. **The wicked are denied their light.** The night is when the wicked are active and carry out their heinous acts. But when denied the night, they are hindered from carrying out their deeds of darkness, as if **their upraised arm is broken.** Job could not control the plight of the wicked. God answered Job's questions about the seemingly prosperous plight of the wicked (Job 9:22–24; 12:5–6; 21:7) by noting that he exposed them.

E God Rules over the Deeps (38:16–18)

SUPPORTING IDEA: *God challenges Job, asking if he knows the various enigmas surrounding death and the deep.*

38:16. God proceeded to question Job about the subterranean waters under the earth. **Have you journeyed to the springs of the sea** beneath the earth's surface **or walked in the recesses of the deep?** Such acts were beyond Job's ability to perform. **Have the gates of death been shown to you?** Job did not know what awaited man following death. Thus, his comments about death were spoken in ignorance. Such knowledge was inaccessible to Job. It was in these deep places where the realm of death was believed to exist.

38:17. **Have you seen the gates of the shadow of death?** Again, a negative answer was anticipated, the implication being that such things were too deep for Job. The mystery of divine providence is too deep for man to grasp.

38:18. **Have you comprehended the vast expanses of the earth?** The point here was that Job had not grasped the deep things of God's physical creation. There were countless enigmas and mysteries of which Job was ignorant; yet God was not. In an argument from the lesser to the greater, the implication is that neither had Job understood the deep matters of God's spiritual kingdom. Mockingly, God chided Job, "**Tell me, if you know all this.**" Job remained silent, dumbfounded by the profound workings of God's providence in creation.

F God Rules over the Light (38:19–21)

SUPPORTING IDEA: *God continues his cross-examination with probing questions designed to remind Job that God alone is the Creator and thus is superior to Job.*

38:19. This science exam next proceeded to the subject of **light** and **darkness**. God cross-examined Job, "**What is the way to the abode of light?**" Where did the light of the sun go at night? **And where does darkness reside?** Or where did the darkness go during the day?

38:20. And even if Job knew where, God asked, "**Can you take them to their places?**" That is, did Job have the power to command them to their respective places? **Do you know the paths to their dwellings?** Again, a negative response was anticipated by God from Job.

38:21. If Job was in the dark about simple matters of God's physical creation, how could he possibly be in the light about God's spiritual kingdom? "**Surely you know,**" God challenged, "**for you were already born**" at the time of creation. Job's arrogant demands of God seemed to assume that Job, too, predated creation. The point God was making is that he alone preceded creation. Job's various assertions in earlier chapters were presumptuous because he was ignorant of creation and, therefore, ignorant of how creation works.

G God Rules over the Snow (38:22–23)

SUPPORTING IDEA: *God continues to overload Job with questions, reminding him that he is ignorant of both snow and hail.*

38:22. Moving to the subject of the mysterious origin of snow, God queried Job, "**Have you entered the storehouses of the snow?**" This is, do you know where snow comes from? (cp. Deut. 28:12; Jer. 10:13). Have you ascended to the heights above and **seen the storehouses of the hail**? Could Job grasp such a lofty subject as the making of hail? Of course not. Snow and hail are mysteries known only by God.

38:23. Snow and hail were to be used in **times of trouble**. In the **days of war and battle**, God unleashed these elements to defend against his enemies (cp. Isa. 30:30). Even so, the affairs of God's providence are far over man's head, lofty and unfathomable.

H God Rules over the Rain and Lightning (38:24–28)

SUPPORTING IDEA: *God interrogates Job with questions about lightning and rain.*

38:24. Furthermore, the same enigmatic origin can be said about lightning. **What is the way to the place where the lightning is dispersed?** In other words, Job, can you find the birthplace of lightning? No, for such is too transcendent for earthbound man. Or did Job know **the place where the east winds are scattered over the earth?** Apparently not. Only God knows such mystery.

38:25. **Who cuts a channel for the torrents of rain?** The answer was *God*, not Job. And who opens **a path for the thunderstorm, to water a land where no man lives.** Only the sovereign pleasure of God moves the rain about, and this is done without consulting Job. This was a response to Job's claim that God used water for destructive purposes (cp. Job 12:15).

38:26–27. God may even cause it to rain in the **desert** for no apparent reason to man. Yet such an act is a demonstration of God's goodness as even the desert rains make their way to other bodies of water in inhabited places. Who is able to **satisfy a desolate wasteland** and cause it to **sprout with grass?** Only God could do this, not Job. God has his reasons, which are unknown to man.

38:28. In a slight shift, the focus is on the origin of the various phenomena of the natural order. God probed deeper: **Does the rain have a father? Who fathers the drops of dew?** In other words, What is their beginning? How are they begun?

I God Rules over the Ice (38:29–30)

SUPPORTING IDEA: *God reminds Job that the source of frozen precipitation is God, who controls water in its various forms.*

38:29–30. **From whose womb comes the ice?** Or **the frost?** They come from God, but man does not understand its origin. Neither did Job grasp the beginning of his trials before God's throne in heaven. The same is true of **the waters** that are **frozen** and turned into sleet, causing it to **become hard as stone.** Accordingly, Job could not understand the birth of his troubles that were conceived by divine initiative.

J God Rules over the Planets (38:31–33)

SUPPORTING IDEA: *God continues to pepper Job with questions, specifically asking if Job can manage the various celestial bodies and galaxies.*

38:31. Pointing to the vast expanse of outer space, God further interrogated Job, "**Can you bind the beautiful Pleiades**" or "**loose the cords of Orion?**" That is to say, "Job, can you control the movement of the clusters of nebulae above?" No, of course, Job could not. Only God the Almighty could do this.

38:32. **Can you bring forth the constellations in their seasons?** This refers to a group of stars. Again, the answer is *no*. Or, could Job **lead out the Bear with its cubs?** This is perhaps a reference to the constellation known as Ursa Major. Once more the answer was so obvious that God need not answer it. Puny man cannot orchestrate the galaxies. The implication was that neither could he control God, who controls all things.

38:33. **Do you know the laws of the heavens?** This means the laws and powers that regulate the courses of the planets and celestial bodies. At this point Job had not answered a single question. Of course, he did not know the governing courses that God had set into motion. **Can you set up God's dominion over the earth?** Job, in no way, could control the weather. Neither could he control God. Rather, God controls all things.

K God Rules over the Clouds (38:34–38)

SUPPORTING IDEA: *God pushes Job to answer his questions that deal with the control of the meteorological forces.*

38:34. Each set of questions became increasingly absurd. God mocked, "**Can you raise your voice to the clouds,**" as if to affect them, "**and cover yourself with a flood of water?**" The answer by this point was predictable. Job could not. So why would he counsel or correct God?

38:35. **Do you send the lightning bolts on their way?** No, Job had no such control over the elements. **Do they report to you,** as if to do Job's bidding and seek his approval, saying, **Here we are?** Absolutely not. Then, by reasoning, how did Job think he could exercise control over God, who is greater than the weather?

38:36. Driving to the heart of the real issue behind the act of creation, God declared, "**Who endowed the heart with wisdom?**" The implied answer is that God himself put within man the wisdom to face life successfully. And who **gave understanding to the mind?** Surely, only God bestowed such insight to man. The **wisdom** of God that created and sustains the world was the same divine genius at work in Job's suffering (cp. Job 28).

38:37. The wisdom needed to create and sustain the universe is infinitely beyond man and belongs to God alone. This is the point that God established when he asked, "**Who has the wisdom to count the clouds?**" Certainly no man has such intellectual capacity. Thus, no mortal man has the power to call God to account about his work of providence in man's suffering. Further, God probed, "**Who can tip over the water jars of the heavens?**" In other words, who could cause the rain to fall?

38:38. This rain would come when it was most needed—**when the dust becomes hard and the clods of earth stick together** (i.e., drought conditions). Only God can control the rainstorm in such a way. Therefore, only God can control the storms of life, or trials and sorrows.

MAIN IDEA REVIEW: *God breaks his silence and speaks to Job, overwhelming him with a display of his sovereign majesty.*

III. CONCLUSION

God Gets 100; You Get 0

A college student went to class to take a final exam at the end of the semester. To his amazement he did not know the answer to any of the questions. Not one! He knew that he had no possibility of passing the exam, so he attempted to win his professor's favor with humor. Across the top of the exam page he wrote, "Only *God* knows the answer to these questions. Merry Christmas!" He turned in the paper and went home for the Christmas break. During the holidays, the student received in the mail his exam that had been graded by the professor. At the top, it read in big red letters, "Then *God* gets 100, and *you* get 0. Happy New Year!"

Like that student Job had flunked God's exam. He had scored a big, fat zero. He had not answered one of God's questions—not one. The same would be true for each of us. None of us would have fared any better. All of us need God's grace in order to stand with acceptance before his throne. And what we need, God provides through his Son, Jesus Christ. Although we have all sinned and fallen short of God's glory (Rom. 3:23), the Lord Jesus can cause us to stand faultless before God.

IV. LIFE APPLICATION

Creator and Creation

Job's assumptions were derived from a false perspective about the positions of God and man. Forgotten by Job was the truth that God was the Creator and he was the creation—not the other way around. Never must the righteous lose sight of the lofty, exalted position that God occupies. A loss of the heavenly perspective can lead to catastrophic results in the life of a believer. The prayer of Nehemiah reminds believers of God's high position as Creator: "You alone are the LORD. You made the heavens, even the highest heavens, and all their starry host, the earth and all that is on it, the seas and all that is in them. You give life to everything" (Neh. 9:6). Only God created all there is, and he alone gives life.

By virtue of his position as Creator, God is Lord over all his creation. He has the divine right to do with it whatever he pleases. The Lord is the Potter; we are the clay. He is the Shepherd; we are the sheep. He is the Master; we are the slaves. He is the Father; we are his children. Never must the believer lose sight of the position of God, as he reigns and rules in the heavens doing whatever he pleases.

Do you have a proper heavenly perspective? Do you submit to God as Creator and understand that you are a part of his creation? Only when you understand God's lofty position will you understand your humble position before him. Then you will relate to your Creator in the right way as you see him as he truly is.

V. PRAYER

God, our Father, forgive us for questioning your ways. We are a very ignorant people. What is man that he dares to answer back at you? May we remain silent when we do not understand. May we humbly submit to your sovereign will in all things. May we kiss the rod that has afflicted us. In Jesus' name we pray. Amen.

VI. DEEPER DISCOVERIES

A. Laid the Earth's Foundation (38:4)

The root word "founded" (Heb. *yasad*) means to fix firmly, to build up, to lay a foundation, or to set. The real or literal sense of the word is used to refer to the foundation of a structure (Josh. 6:26; Ezra 3:6,10,12; Zech. 4:9). *Yasad* may be used in a figurative or metaphorical sense of that which is fixed and cannot be moved (Ps. 104:5; Isa. 54:11). This is how it is used here by the Lord.

B. Know (38:21,33)

"Know" (Heb. *yada*) means to acknowledge or to make known. It emphasizes the clear recognition and convincing declaration of a fact that is an intimately known reality. This is one of the most important Hebrew words in the Old Testament, a word used 944 times. It means to acquire a deep and thorough knowledge of someone or something, such as a husband would know his wife in a sexual relationship (Gen. 4:1). Here it means to make a full disclosure of something about which a person has an intimate knowledge.

VII. TEACHING OUTLINE

A. God Rules over Job (38:1–3)
   1. He appeared in the storm (38:1)
   2. He answered from the storm (38:2–3)
B. God Rules over the Earth (38:4–7)
   1. He created the earth (38:4)
   2. He calculated the earth (38:5)
   3. He constructed the earth (38:6–7)
C. God Rules over the Sea (38:8–11)
   1. He made the sea (38:8–9)
   2. He fixed the sea (38:10–11)
D. God Rules over the Sun (38:12–15)
   1. He orders the rising sun (38:12–13)
   2. He rotates the earth (38:14–15)
E. God Rules over the Deeps (38:16–18)
   1. He created the deeps (38:16–17)
   2. He comprehends the deeps (38:18)
F. God Rules over the Light (38:19–21)
   1. He created the light (38:19)
   2. He comprehends the light (38:20–21)
G. God Rules over the Snow (38:22–23)
   1. God creates the snow (38:22)
   2. God uses the snow (38:23)
H. God Rules over the Rain and Lightning (38:24–28)
   1. He creates the wind (38:24)

2. He sends the rain (38:25–28)

I. God Rules over the Ice (38:29–30)

1. He creates the ice (38:29)
2. He controls the ice (38:30)

J. God Rules over the Planets (38:31–33)

1. He controls the planets (38:31–32)
2. He controls heaven's laws (38:33)

K. God Rules over the Clouds (38:34–38)

1. He creates the clouds (38:34–36)
2. He controls the clouds (38:37–38)

VIII. ISSUES FOR DISCUSSION

1. Do I understand that God's ways are not my ways?
2. Do I submit to the sovereignty of God over my life?
3. Do I maintain a humble attitude when suffering?

Job 38:39–39:30

Sobering Sovereignty

Quote

"How should finite comprehend infinite? We shall apprehend Him, but not comprehend Him."

Richard Sibbes

Job 38:39–39:30

I. INTRODUCTION

It Was God's Idea

H. G. Wells, the English writer, once visited the home of his friend Henry James, the American novelist. As they talked in the drawing room, filled with many of James's artifacts, Wells noticed a large stuffed bird in the drawing room. "What is that?" asked Wells.

"This is a stork," replied James.

"Humph," snorted Wells. "That's not my idea of a stork."

"Perhaps not," James replied, "but apparently it was God's idea."

This is the lesson that God needed to teach Job. Regardless of what Job's idea was about the running of his life, all that mattered was what God thought. God *is* God, and Job was not. That is, God is free in his sovereignty to act however he pleases. Being infinitely wise and absolutely good, God does everything perfectly, regardless of what man may think. As Job had been accusing God with the mismanagement of his life, it was time that he received a crash course in divine sovereignty. In a review of the animal kingdom, God examined Job about the peculiarities of many of his animals. God was driving home the truth that it was his idea to create each creature as he had done. All that God does, he does with perfect genius and brilliance. Job needed to realize this and rest in this truth.

In order to get the point across, God asked Job many questions about the created order and providential care of the animal kingdom. His power over these animals demonstrates his sovereignty over all. God's questions focused upon ten animals—six beasts and four birds. The questions were intended to show God's greatness and Job's littleness. This would be the turning point for Job. The point God was making was that he is sovereign and was capable of governing Job's life and circumstances. God created all, sustains all, and governs all with precision.

II. COMMENTARY

Sobering Sovereignty

MAIN IDEA: *The Lord humbles Job by exposing his ignorance of the animal kingdom.*

A God Rules over the Lion (38:39–40)

SUPPORTING IDEA: *God implies that Job should trust him as much as the lion does for its food.*

38:39. God launched into this second phase of his interrogation of Job by focusing on lions. God asked Job, "**Do you hunt the prey for the lioness and satisfy the hunger of the lions?**" That is, "Job, do you concern yourself with feeding these chief predators?" The implied answer is *no*.

38:40. God takes care of lions **when they crouch in their dens**, waiting to be fed, **or lie in wait in a thicket**. Job did not feed these animals, but God did (cp. Ps. 147:9). If God cares for their needs, how much more must he provide for Job (cp. Matt. 6:25–33)?

B God Rules over the Raven (38:41)

SUPPORTING IDEA: *Job should trust God as the raven does to provide for its young.*

38:41. **Who provides food for the raven when its young cry out to God and wander about for lack of food?** Job was incapable of feeding the raven and its young, but not God (cp. Matt. 6:26). The Lord was able to supply the needs of this helpless bird and, thus, should be trusted. If the bird could rely on God, why could Job not do the same? The bird's dependence on God was in stark contrast to Job's arrogant demands of God.

C God Rules over the Goat (39:1a)

SUPPORTING IDEA: *God queries Job about the birthing process of the mountain goat, showing his sovereignty over all.*

39:1a. God continued interrogating Job by asking, "**Do you know when the mountain goats give birth?**" The anticipated answer is *no.* Job did not know this. In the absence of his understanding, he should trust God, even for what he did not comprehend about his own life.

D God Rules over the Doe (39:1b–4)

SUPPORTING IDEA: *God examines Job about the birthing process and development of deer, something as mysterious as God's providence in his life.*

39:1–2. **Do you watch when the doe bears her fawn?** Again, it is assumed by this question that Job did not know the answer. Such knowledge was beyond him. So God's providential working in Job's life was beyond his comprehension. **Do you count the months till they bear?** No, Job did not. The deer gave birth without him knowing the length of their gestation period. **Do you know the time they give birth?** Job did not have such knowledge. Such animals are hidden from man, living in the wild. Innumerable events in creation were beyond Job's knowledge, especially the mysterious workings of God's providence in his life.

39:3. Mountain goats **crouch down** so as to deliver **and bring forth their young**. After their delivery, **their labor pains are ended**. But Job did not see this act because he was not all-seeing like God.

39:4. **Their young thrive and grow strong in the wilds** away from the watching eyes of civilization. **They leave** the place of their birth **and do not return**. Did Job see where they went? No; such knowledge was beyond him. In like manner, so was the knowledge of the mystery of God's will above and beyond him. Also, God protects and provides for the animals in their most vulnerable time. God would protect Job in the same way.

E God Rules over the Donkey (39:5–8)

SUPPORTING IDEA: *God questions Job about the donkey, showing how little Job really knows.*

39:5–6. God continued his questioning of Job with mounting force. **Who let the wild donkey go free? Who untied his ropes?** That is, from whom did the wild donkey receive its natural instinct to live in the desert? Did Job instill this instinct? God claimed this work, saying, "**I gave him the wasteland as his home, the salt flats as his habitat.**" It was God, not Job, who put this animal in its habitat. The same was true of Job's life. God had put him in his assigned place, including this experience of suffering.

39:7–8. The wild donkey **laughs at the commotion in the town**, not desiring to live with people but in the desert. **He does not hear a driver's shout** because he does not submit to a human rider. **He ranges the hills for his pasture**, looking for food. Refusing to be domesticated, he **searches for any green thing** without any human assistance. God made the wild donkey so it could care for itself. Its instinct for survival is instilled by God, not man.

F God Rules over the Ox (39:9–12)

SUPPORTING IDEA: *God challenges Job about the stubbornness of the ox, a characteristic that Job himself has developed toward God.*

39:9. God pressed Job, "**Will the wild ox consent to serve you?**" Can you humble and subdue this animal to come under your authority? If not, what had made Job assume that he could tame the ox's Creator? **Will he stay by your manger at night?** If Job could not control the creation, he surely could not control its Creator.

39:10. This wild ox refused to yield to the authority of any man. **Can you hold him to the furrow with a harness?** That is, did Job have the ability to tame this wild animal and cause it to plow his field? **Will he till the valleys behind you?** The implied answer is *no*. The implication is that if Job could not tame this animal, it was insane to assume he could do so with God, its Creator.

39:11. Pressing the point further, God asked, "**Will you rely on him for his great strength?**" This implied answer is *yes*. It could be trusted to do its work for man's benefit. **Will you leave your heavy work to him?** This question assumes the positive answer *yes*. Although the wild ox could not be tamed, this animal could be relied on to assist man. The implication is clear: Job could not tame God, but instead must rely on him. If man could trust animals to help, then surely God could be trusted.

39:12. **Can you trust him to bring in your grain?** The assumed answer is *yes*. This animal could be trusted to serve the needs and best interests of man. Likewise, could Job trust him to gather the grain to his **threshing floor**? The expected answer is *yes*. Therefore, Job should do the same with God. He should trust God implicitly rather than attempt to correct the Almighty.

G God Rules over the Ostrich (39:13–18)

SUPPORTING IDEA: *God uses the ostrich as an illustration of the mystery of God's great wisdom.*

39:13. God next described the ostrich, an odd-looking bird with bizarre features and behavior. Rather than asking a series of rhetorical questions, this section instead contains declarative statements. The point is that Job could not explain the ostrich. Neither could he explain God, who created the ostrich. **The wings of the ostrich flap joyfully**, but, oddly enough, it cannot fly. The wings simply fan the air. These wings **cannot compare with the pinions and feathers of the stork**, being covered with down instead of feathers.

39:14–15. Other birds build their nests in trees, but the ostrich **lays her eggs on the ground and lets them warm in the sand**. This bizarre bird camouflages the eggs from predators and hunters. The ostrich conveys that it is **unmindful that a foot may crush them**, or **that some wild animal may trample them**. The idea is, had Job observed the incubating habits of ostriches?

39:16–17. By outward appearance the ostrich **treats her young harshly as if they were not hers**. Abandoning her young only adds to the unusual nature of this bird. She acts as if her young are not her own. This gives the impression that **she cares not that her labor was in vain**, delivering them only to abandon them. It can only be concluded that **God did not endow her with wisdom or give her a share of good sense**. Her stupidity is clearly seen, since she forgets where she has buried her eggs.

39:18. Yet, in spite of this lack of smarts, **when she spreads her feathers to run, she laughs at horse and rider**. This odd bird, although inferior in intelligence, is superior in speed. Remarkably, she represents the mystery of God's sovereignty which is past human comprehension. The God who has created such a silly bird also has designed a strange providence that exceeds man's ability to understand. In God's genius, he has created a bird that cannot fly, a fact that is an enigma to man. The mystery of what God was doing in Job's life was also past Job's finding out.

H God Rules over the Horse (39:19–25)

SUPPORTING IDEA: *God reverts back to questioning Job, using the horse to reveal Job's inferiority to God.*

39:19. God shifted the focus of his discourse to **the horse**, an animal quite unlike the ostrich. Rather than being the object of ridicule like the strutting ostrich, the horse was admired for its strength and valor, especially in the face of danger. Returning to the form of rhetorical questions, God asked Job, "**Do you give the horse his strength or clothe his neck with a flowing mane?**" No, Job did not create the horse, nor could he endow it with might and majesty.

39:20. Do you make him leap like a locust, bounding aggressively forward, even in the face of great danger? Clearly, Job, though superior to the horse, could not make it do this. Neither could Job make the horse strike **terror with his proud snorting**. It was God, not Job, who made this animal so full of courage in the face of adversity. The implication was that God could also make Job confident as he faced his devastating trials.

39:21–22. Preparing to charge into battle, the horse **paws fiercely**, ready to run, **rejoicing in his strength**. Expectant of victory, this warhorse **charges into the fray**, without regard for its own life. In spite of being surrounded by danger on all sides, **he laughs at fear, afraid of nothing**. In the day of battle, **he does not shy away from the sword** of opposing soldiers because he has unflinching courage.

39:23–24. The rider's **quiver**, full of arrows, **rattles against his side** as the horse gallops headlong into conflict. **The flashing spear and lance** are also courageously carried by the warhorse into the skirmish. Not with fearful hesitation but **in frenzied excitement**, the horse **eats up the ground**, charging forward. **He cannot stand still when the trumpet sounds**, but must advance into battle.

39:25. At the blast of the trumpet sounding the charge, the horse **snorts** through flared nostrils. He is invigorated and stimulated in the face of combat. As if looking and longing for war, **he catches the scent of battle from afar**. Eagerly, with an insatiable desire for war, he is drawn into the battle by **the shout of commanders and the battle cry**. Because Job is inferior to this courageous animal, he is infinitely inferior to its Creator, whom Job has been audaciously calling into account.

I God Rules over the Hawk (39:26)

SUPPORTING IDEA: *In another effort to expose Job's ignorance, God asks Job if the hawk looks to him for direction and instruction.*

39:26. God's review of the animals concluded with two birds, **the hawk** and the eagle, both of which are known to soar at incredible heights. God asked, "**Does the hawk take flight by your wisdom and spread his wings toward the south?**" The intent of this probing question was, once again, to put Job in his proper place. It was an inquiry intended to show that God, not Job, was in charge of the universe. The migrating instinct is placed within this bird by God, directing its flight south. Mysteriously, this animal is led about by God. So does God also mysteriously govern events and people according to divine purpose.

J God Rules over the Eagle (39:27–30)

SUPPORTING IDEA: *God challenges Job with an inquiry about the eagle, showing that some things are too lofty for Job to discover.*

39:27–29. **Does the eagle soar at your command and build his nest on high?** Quite obviously, Job did not direct the eagle in its activities. That power and ability belong to God alone, Creator, Sustainer, and Ruler of all. So did God also order the events of Job's life. God noted that the eagle **dwells on a cliff** high above **and stays there at night**. Far beyond Job's vantage point, **a rocky crag is his stronghold**. From there, at high altitudes, **he seeks out his food**. He sees what no man can see. **His eyes detect it from afar** with extraordinary eyesight that is given by God.

39:30. **His young ones**, baby eagles, **feast on** the **blood** of dead animals. Eagles do all this because God made them this way. Thus, because God has so ordered his creation, everything works according to his design. The same was true with the circumstances of Job's life. It was unfolding as God had purposed it.

MAIN IDEA REVIEW: *The Lord humbles Job by exposing his ignorance of the animal kingdom.*

III. CONCLUSION

The Painful Inquiry

Throughout this divine examination, Job was jolted by God's relentless assault. He once thought he had *all* the answers, but now, such arrogant presumption was rapidly slipping away. Job was beginning to realize that he had *none* of the answers. In fact, he did not even know the right questions to ask God. Why did God put Job through this painful exam? So he could reveal his greatness to Job. Through this divine interrogation, God taught Job that he alone created everything, the heavens and the earth, and all that is in them. But what is more, he alone controls all that he created. The powerful truth of divine sovereignty is clear through this examination.

God has the right to do with his own as he pleases. He is under no obligation to explain his actions to his creation. He alone is sovereign and, thus, not accountable to man. "But who are you, O man, to talk back to God? Shall what is formed say to him who formed it, 'Why did you make me like this?'"

(Rom. 9:20). This is the lesson revealed to Job by the Lord. In the absence of knowing why, Job needed to be quiet and submit to God. Only in seeing and knowing God would he find the relief for which he was searching.

IV. LIFE APPLICATION

Discovering God's Greatness

1. *See God's greatness.* The purpose of this exam of the animal kingdom was to impress on Job the greatness of God, his majesty as sovereign Creator, and his creative genius and providential care of all things. Making all the animals as he has done displays his perfect wisdom. Likewise, God has made you with the gender, race, physical size, and intelligence that you have. He has made you with perfect design, giving you a unique personality and temperament. Do you see the greatness of his plan toward you?

2. *Submit to God's greatness.* We must yield our lives to the supremacy of God. How could we ever be impressed with our "greatness" after beholding God's true grandeur? The only proper response to God's infinite majesty is to bow before him in total humility, giving him priority in our lives. Will you submit your will to him? Will you surrender your dreams and ambitions to him? The more we humble ourselves before God, the more he will exalt us.

V. PRAYER

God, you alone reign over all creation that you have created for yourself. As Creator you exercise supreme authority over all things. From you and through you and to you are all things. To you be the glory forever. In Jesus' name. Amen.

VI. DEEPER DISCOVERIES

A. Mountain Goats (39:1)

The mountain goat is a species of goats that can still be found in the high cliffs of En Gedi (cp. 1 Sam. 24:1–2).

B. Wild Ox (39:9)

The wild ox is an undomesticated animal (cp. Num. 24:8; Deut. 33:17). Assyrian royalty hunted wild oxen for sport.

VII. TEACHING OUTLINE

A. God Rules over the Lion (38:39–40)
  1. Do you feed the lioness? (38:39a)
  2. Do you feed the lions? (38:39b–40)
B. God Rules over the Raven (38:41)
  1. Who provides food for the raven? (38:41a)
  2. Who feeds its young? (38:41b)
C. God Rules over the Goat (39:1a)
  1. Who delivers the goats? (39:1a)
  2. When do they give birth? (39:1a)
D. God Rules over the Doe (39:1b–4)
  1. Do you see the doe give birth? (39:1b)
  2. Do you know when the doe delivers? (39:2)
  3. The doe gives birth to its young (39:3)
  4. The doe's young develop and mature (39:4)
E. God Rules over the Donkey (39:5–8)
  1. Who made the donkey wild? (39:5)
  2. God gave the donkey its home (39:6–8)
F. God Rules over the Ox (39:9–12)
  1. Who made the ox wild? (39:9–10)
  2. Will the wild ox serve you? (39:11–12)
G. God Rules over the Ostrich (39:13–18)
  1. The ostrich seems so strange (39:13–17)
  2. The ostrich runs so fast (39:18)
H. God Rules over the Horse (39:19–25)
  1. Do you give the horse strength? (39:19)
  2. Do you give the horse swiftness? (39:20)
  3. The horse possesses great courage (39:21–25)
I. God Rules over the Hawk (39:26)
  1. Does the hawk soar by your wisdom? (39:26a)
  2. Does the hawk fly south by your wisdom? (39:26b)
J. God Rules over the Eagle (39:27–30)
  1. Does the eagle soar by your command? (39:27)
  2. The eagle acts in a special way (39:28–30)

VIII. ISSUES FOR DISCUSSION

1. Do I look to God to understand my suffering?
2. Do I have a God-centered worldview?
3. Am I dependent on God to supply all my needs?

Job 40

Speechless, Spitless, and All Shook Up

"Absolute sovereignty is what I love to ascribe to God. God's sovereignty has ever appeared to me a great part of His glory"

Jonathan Edwards

Job 40

I. INTRODUCTION

High and Lifted Up

The Sears Tower in Chicago, Illinois, is a magnificent structure that rises majestically above the downtown skyline, dwarfing the other skyscrapers. Built with 76,000 tons of steel and 6,000 bronze-tinted windows, this modern-day marvel stands 110 stories tall and climbs to a staggering height of 1,400 feet. Containing a total of 4.5 million gross square feet, it weighs 222,500 tons. Standing on the sidewalk and looking straight up can strike awe into the heart of the onlooker. The building seems to rise up forever until it disappears into the clouds. The clouds moving behind the tower give an eerie illusion that the building is swaying. A person's head begins to spin. The knees shake as one stares at its imposing height.

This is precisely what Job had been feeling—reduced in size. In the towering presence of God, Job was overwhelmed and made painfully aware of his smallness. In previous chapters he had pressed God to present his case and prove his innocence. But now, looking upward at God's greatness, he realized that he was only a speck of dust. Job saw God for who he really is and discovered that God is far greater than he had ever imagined. He was awestruck by the magnitude of God's supremacy.

In Job 40, God continues his interrogation of Job, a cross-examination that exposes Job for what he truly is—a finite creature. Having quizzed Job about the inner and outer workings of planet Earth (Job 38) and the animal kingdom (Job 39), God now will press Job further. God will chide Job, challenging him to do a better job than he at being God and running the world. Through all this Job will be reduced to a state of humility before Almighty God.

II. COMMENTARY

Speechless, Spitless, and All Shook Up

MAIN IDEA: *God hammers Job by asking him unanswerable questions about creation, himself, and the behemoth.*

A God Traumatizes Job (40:1–5)

SUPPORTING IDEA: *God humbles Job about his inferior wisdom.*

40:1–2. With devastating directness, God concluded his first speech to Job (Job 38–39) by issuing a direct challenge. This challenge left Job humbled. **Will the one who contends with the Almighty correct him?** In these strong words God accused Job of charging him with wrongdoing. Job had slandered God's holy character. So the Almighty called Job to account for such a reckless attack. Then God pressed Job further: **Let him who accuses God answer him!** God had presented his overwhelming case (Job 38–39), and now he called on Job to present his case. Would Job actually reprove God? Job now had the hearing for which he had lobbied. Face-to-face with God, would Job charge him with injustice?

40:3. Reluctantly and repentantly, Job answered the Lord. This was a new posture for Job to assume. Undoubtedly, Job regretted his persistence in asking God for his day in court.

40:4. Job answered, "**I am unworthy—how can I reply to you?**" Having been confronted with God's parade of power in creation, nature, and the animals (Job 38–39), how could he continue his arguing with God? Job realized that he was inferior to God in knowledge and power. He was unable to control God's creation. So how could he possibly control the Creator? Recognizing his own unworthiness before this awesome God, he confessed his sin and withdrew his complaint. **I put my hand over my mouth.**

This was a strong gesture of humiliation before a superior. No longer would Job, the faultfinder, argue with God. He recognized his inability to respond to the Almighty. Reduced to silence, he had nothing to say against God. He was finally unwilling to speak another word of complaint against God.

40:5. Job confessed, "**I spoke once, but I have no answer—twice, but I will say no more.**" He realized that he had already spoken far more than he should have. He had spoken once, even twice—but no more.

B God Threatens Job (40:6–8)

SUPPORTING IDEA: *God humbles Job about his puny charges.*

40:6. God had more to say to Job because he was not yet fully broken. So **the LORD spoke to Job out of the storm**. This was another devastating experience for Job. The storm represented the fury of God's words—words that were powerful and irrefutable.

40:7. God further challenged Job, "**Brace yourself like a man.**" That is, prepare for conflict, gird your loins for action. "**I will question you, and you shall answer me,**" God said. This was the total opposite of what Job, once brazenly sure of himself, had anticipated. He now found himself on the defensive, with God acting as the prosecuting attorney. Job was on the receiving end of this direct confrontation with God.

40:8. Speaking with the power of a destructive whirlwind, God interrogated Job. **Would you discredit my justice?** That is, would Job continue to accuse God of injustice? Surely not. Would he condemn God to justify himself? Would Job continue to put God in the wrong in order to put himself in the right? Such a position was spiritual insanity.

C God Taunts Job (40:9–14)

SUPPORTING IDEA: *God taunts Job by asking if he has the attributes of the Almighty.*

40:9. Putting Job further in his place, God asked, "**Do you have an arm like God's?**" The arm was a symbol of strength (Ps. 89:13; Isa. 53:1). The piercing question was, Do you have power like God to run the universe? Of course, Job did not. Then God pressed, "**Can your voice thunder like his?**" Could Job speak with the sovereign authority of Almighty God and order the universe? He could not.

40:10. Pushing this confrontation further, God spoke with biting sarcasm and challenged Job to assume his role as God. **Then adorn yourself with**

glory and splendor, and clothe yourself in honor and majesty. The challenge here was for Job to become God and see if he could do a better job at running the universe. *Glory, splendor, honor,* and *majesty* are divine attributes of infinite superiority that belong to God alone.

40:11. Taunting Job more, God said, **Unleash the fury of your wrath** against rebellious humanity. **Look at every proud man and bring him low.** If God was to act like God (cp. 2 Kgs. 8:11; Isa. 13:11), he must humble the self-asserting, arrogant people of this world. This is what God must do every day. Could Job perform all the functions of deity? If so, the implication was that Job should start with himself.

40:12. God would not back off. He pressed Job harder: **Look at every proud man and humble him** with an all-penetrating gaze. Then, having peered through their external façade of self-righteousness, Job was challenged, **crush the wicked where they stand** with furious judgment. Earlier Job had charged that God did not take notice of the crimes of the wicked and therefore refused to act in judgment (cp. Job 12:6; 24:1–2).

40:13–14. Challenged to act as if he were God, Job was asked to bury the wicked **in the dust together.** If Job was so wise, he should administer divine judgment and unleash justice on the wicked. Job should execute justice like God. "**Shroud their faces in the grave,**" God added. Job should demolish the proud and hide them out of sight in an act of judgment. If he could do this, then God would praise Job as his superior. **Then I myself will admit to you that your own right hand can save you.** God would yield to Job in such a case, if he could execute perfect justice. This was the virtue Job had said was missing in God. He should try to run the universe and do a better job than God. Then Job could save himself.

D God Teaches Job (40:15–24)

> **SUPPORTING IDEA:** *God uses the behemoth to demonstrate that he alone is the Creator and has the power to harness this powerful creature.*

40:15. God pressed Job further: **Look at the behemoth, which I made along with you.** God spoke as if he and Job were cocreators of the behemoth. Apparently, Job was not yet fully humbled to the point of repentance. So the interrogation continued, aimed at Job's pride. The term *behemoth* describes an extraordinarily large animal, possibly a hippopotamus or an elephant, or even a dinosaur. Job was challenged to consider this massive animal and learn again about his own insignificance.

40:16–17. Pointing to the power of the behemoth's mid-stomach section, God noted, "**What strength he has in his loins, what power in the muscles of his belly**!" This animal far surpassed man in its might. Focusing next upon the animal's power, God said, "**His tail sways like a cedar.**" This animal was extremely strong and overpowering. The **sinews** of his thighs were **close-knit**, stocky and sturdy.

40:18–19. **His bones** were **tubes of bronze**, unbending and unbreakable, able to carry and support the heaviest load. **His limbs** were **like rods of iron**, durable and strong. This imposing animal ranked **first** among the **works of God**, foremost in size and strength. Thus he was the mightiest animal of the animal kingdom. But in spite of his towering stature, **his Maker** could approach him with his **sword**. Only God dared to draw near this beast. No man could approach it.

40:20–21. Thus, **the hills bring him their produce**. As a grass-eating animal (v. 15), the hippopotamus grazes the fields by night but hides submerged in lakes, rivers, swamps, and marshes by day. **All the wild animals play nearby** without fear of being consumed. **Under the lotus plants he lies**, submerged beneath the water during the day. There he rests, **hidden among the reeds in the marsh**, relaxing in its natural habitat. Only its ears, eyes, and nostrils are raised above the water level.

40:22–23. **The lotuses conceal him in their shadow**, hidden from view. **The poplars** (i.e., trees growing by the river's edge) **surround him**, concealing his form. **When the river rages, he is not alarmed**. His size and strength enable him to withstand the pull of the current. **He is secure** in the rushing river, able to remain anchored in his position, **though the Jordan should surge against his mouth**. This beast could ingest a great amount of water, seemingly as much as the Jordan River contained. This is a form of hyperbole intended to convey the behemoth's enormous size and power.

40:24. God concluded this section of questions by asking Job, **Can anyone capture him by the eyes** when he is peering out of the water? Can anyone **trap him and pierce his nose** with a spear as it extends above the river level, breathing air? The answer was that no man could **capture** or **trap** such a powerful beast. If not, then what made Job think he could control this animal's Creator? Neither did Job have the ability to administer the world as he claimed in his charges against God.

MAIN IDEA REVIEW: *God hammers Job by asking him great, unanswerable questions about creation, himself, and the behemoth.*

III. CONCLUSION

Who Made All This?

One evening a group of Napoleon Bonaparte's officers began discussing the existence of God. Caught up in the atheistic spirit of the times, the officers were unanimous in their denial of God's existence. Finally, someone suggested they ask Napoleon if there was a God. Napoleon raised his hand, pointed to the starry sky, and simply asked, "Gentlemen, who made all that?"

Creation *does* point to the existence of a Creator, the one who made all things. Further, this same Creator continues to sustain and control all he has made. As a result, all people should humble themselves before the God who has made them. This is the thrust of what God had been teaching Job in this discourse. Job could not control the behemoth. Then what made him think he could control the Creator of the behemoth? Job must submit himself to God, who made all and controls everything. This is the point that God was trying to get across to Job. All creation must bow before the Creator and yield their lives to him.

IV. LIFE APPLICATION

Contending with God

Whenever a person passes through the dark storms of life or when he understands that God is behind his suffering, there is a possibility that he might become embittered toward God. Such a disposition gripped Job for a time and provoked him to contend with God. Believers today face this same temptation. But God's people must guard their hearts against such evil thoughts. When Paul wrote of the weighty matters about God's sovereignty, he asked, "Who has known the mind of the Lord? Or who has been his counselor?" (Rom. 11:34). The implied answer is *no one*. God is not like man. He does not lack wisdom and knowledge. He does not stand in need of a counselor.

For the believer to contend with God implies that God is in need of knowledge and wisdom. For any believer to question God demonstrates that the person, *and not God,* lacks knowledge and wisdom. Further, it demonstrates that the inquisitor is failing to trust God and is guilty of unbelief. If you are struggling with an embittered spirit, you must go to God, humbling yourself while pleading for him to intervene and remove your prideful attitude. Honesty and openness before God about your feelings and frustrations are wise actions. God's lovingkindness will grant to his people a peace that passes all understanding (Phil. 4:7). This peace, Paul asserted, will guard and protect the hearts and minds of Christians.

V. PRAYER

God, our Father, who are we to contend with you? You are the Potter, and we are the clay. You are the Shepherd, and we are the sheep of your pasture. You are the Master, and we are your servants. You are our Father, and we are your children. Lord, we are eternally grateful for salvation that is ours through your Son and our Savior, the Lord Jesus Christ. Amen.

VI. DEEPER DISCOVERIES

Behemoth (40:15)

"Behemoth" is the transliteration of a Hebrew word that means "superbeast." It is difficult to be certain about the exact identity of this creature in this context. Some scholars believe it may have been a dinosaur or an elephant, but it was probably a hippopotamus. The description of the animal supports this view. Whatever it was, it was an imposing creature.

VII. TEACHING OUTLINE

A. God Traumatizes Job (40:1–5)
   1. God spoke in majesty (40:1–2)
   2. Job submitted in humility (40:3–5)

B. God Threatens Job (40:6–8)
   1. Brace yourself for conflict (40:6–7)
   2. Brace yourself for correction (40:8)

C. God Taunts Job (40:9–14)
   1. Are you my equal? (40:9)
   2. Act like my equal! (40:10–14)

D. God Teaches Job (40:15–24)
   1. Consider the behemoth's size (40:15–18)
   2. Consider the behemoth's superiority (40:19–20)
   3. Consider the behemoth's sphere (40:21–23)
   4. Consider the behemoth's strength (40:24)

VIII. ISSUES FOR DISCUSSION

1. Do I ever contend with God?
2. Do I ever question God's ways?
3. Do I maintain a proper understanding of my insignificance before God?

Job 41

Unconditional Surrender

Quote

"Let God have your life; He can do more with it than you can."

D. L. Moody

Job 41

I. INTRODUCTION

Your Sword First

The British admiral Horatio Nelson always treated his vanquished opponents with kindness and courtesy. One defeated admiral, knowing Nelson's reputation for courtesy, advanced across the quarterdeck with arms outstretched as if he were advancing to shake hands with an equal. Nelson's hand remained by his side. "Your sword first," he said, "and then your hand."

Job was learning a similar lesson from God. He was learning the terms of the unconditional surrender of his life to almighty God. Unfortunately, Job, in his mounting frustration, had become increasingly demanding toward God. With audacious arrogance Job charged God with punishing him unjustly. He argued that the punishment did not fit the crime. Whatever the crime might be, Job did not know, but it could not merit such a harsh infliction of suffering upon him. He wanted his day in court to present his case before God. But in the process, Job had pitted himself against God with a self-righteous attitude. So God finally interrupted Job's pity party and taught him a lesson in humility and submission. What God was calling for in Job's life was unconditional surrender.

In chapter 41 of Job, God asked Job if he could control the leviathan (v. 1). The word *leviathan* is basically a transliteration of the Hebrew word for "sea monster" or "sea serpent." Its exact identity is disputed. The traditional view is that it was the crocodile. The description of the leviathan begins as a detailed description of a formidable beast. But as the description unfolds, the leviathan becomes a fire-breathing dragon. This term appears four other times in the Old Testament (Job 3:8; Pss. 74:14; 104:26; Isa. 27:1). In each text, *leviathan* refers to some mighty creature that can overwhelm man. But it is, obviously, no match for God. This creature lives in the sea among ships (Ps. 104:26). Thus, a sea monster, or possibly a marine dinosaur, is intended here.

The point is: Could Job control such a monster? The answer is *no*. If Job could not stand against the leviathan, what made him think he could contend with God? Job would be far better off fighting a sea monster or dinosaur than fighting against God. God created this terrifying creature, along with the behemoth of the previous chapter (Job 40), which no man could control. If Job could not master the creation, why was he contending with the Creator?

Job could not control the leviathan, but he wanted to tell the monster's Creator what to do. Not a wise decision! The leviathan was mighty, but God is infinitely more powerful. Until Job could manage the leviathan, he had no business tackling God. What follows is God's direct challenge of Job as he calls for his unconditional surrender.

II. COMMENTARY

Unconditional Surrender

MAIN IDEA: *God points out the inability of Job to control or subdue the mighty sea creature known as the leviathan.*

A Leviathan's Autonomy (41:1–11)

SUPPORTING IDEA: *God illustrates his greatness over Job by asking him if he can harness the great leviathan.*

41:1. Without any break in this divine interrogation, God continued his long confrontation with yet another object lesson, the leviathan. With relentless pursuit, God asked Job, **"Can you pull in the leviathan with a fishhook?"** While some have attempted to identify the leviathan as a mythological sea monster, the details given in this account suggest otherwise. No doubt, this was an actual creature known to Job, possibly a crocodile, a whale, a great white shark, or a marine dinosaur. This question for Job was:

Could he catch or control such a large creature? Could he **tie down his tongue with a rope**? The description that follows indicates that the leviathan was even more terrifying than the behemoth (Job 40).

41:2–3. Could Job **put a cord through his nose** to capture him? Or could he **pierce his jaw with a hook** to capture him like a fish? The implied answer was that no man could do this. Once caught, would the leviathan keep begging Job for **mercy**? Again the answer was *no*. An animal this powerful would not be submissive to man. God asked, **"Will he speak to you with gentle words?"** Certainly not. This mighty creature would not appeal to man in kind communication.

41:4–5. God asked, **"Will he make an agreement with you for you to take him as your slave for life?"** In other words, could Job tame this animal and domesticate it? Could he **make a pet of him like a bird** for his enjoyment and entertainment? Or could he **put him on a leash** for his girls to play with? Of course, the answer was *no*. Such a thought was absurd. It would be far more likely that the leviathan would have Job on a leash.

41:6. Would **traders barter for him** like a commodity easily bought and sold? Would they divide the leviathan up among the **merchants** like a product that is bought at the discretion of others? Again, the implied answers were *no*. This creature was too big and powerful to be at man's disposal.

41:7–8. Even if Job had large and effective fishing equipment, could he **fill his hide with harpoons or his head with fishing spears**? No matter how sharp the harpoons and spears, this creature could not be captured by man as if he were a mere fish. In fact, if Job laid **a hand on him**, he would **remember the struggle and never do it again**. This dramatic encounter would prove to be so dangerous and unsuccessful that no man would attempt it a second time—that is, if he lived through the first encounter.

41:9. Any hope of **subduing** the leviathan, no matter how strong the equipment, was **false**. In other words, the hope of caging the leviathan was an expectation never to be fulfilled. If the **sight of him** was **overpowering**, how much more the actual attempt to capture him?

41:10. No one was able to **rouse him** out of his place as long as he chose to remain there. This is a reply to Job's desire that the animal be roused (cp Job 3:8). The point was that if this reptile was this autonomous, how much more must its Maker be who was greater than all? If neither Job nor any man was able to control the leviathan, then surely no one could control God, the maker of this beast. Thus, God drove home the point by asking, **"Who then is able to stand against me?"** Of course, the answer was *no one*. God, the sovereign Lord of heaven and earth, would do as he pleased (Ps. 115:3) because no one could resist his will.

41:11. **Who has a claim against me that I must pay?** Again, the answer was *no one*. God is no man's debtor. No person is owed anything from God except judgment. Yet Job believed he was to be rewarded for his righteousness (cp. Job 34:5–8). **Everything under heaven belongs to me.** Thus, no person can give anything to God because everything is already his.

B Leviathan's Anatomy (41:12–30)

SUPPORTING IDEA: *God continues to demonstrate his greatness and man's weakness by noting the anatomical qualities of the leviathan.*

41:12–13. God next detailed the powerful body of this reptile. **I will not fail to speak of his limbs, his strength and his graceful form.** This animal combined power and beauty and agility. **Who can strip off his outer coat?** Of course, the answer was that no mere man could do so. Apparently, his **outer coat** of skin was valuable to man and, thus, coveted. **Who would approach him with a bridle**, attempting to harness and saddle him?

41:14–16. **Who dares open the doors of his mouth** in an attempt to pry it open? No one in their right mind would attempt to open his ringed mouth **with his fearsome teeth**. No one would intentionally get up close to this formidable creature. Regarding his impenetrable outer protection, God said, "**His back has rows of shields tightly sealed together.**" His scales were closely fit together, forming a tough, almost impenetrable outer skin. **Each is so close to the next that no air can pass between.** That is how closely connected his shields had been placed together by the Creator.

41:17–18. **They are joined fast to one another; they cling together and cannot be parted.** They were inseparable and impenetrable. Thus, any attempt to hunt and kill the animal was useless. The leviathan's nose, eyes, and mouth put fear into people. **His snorting throws out flashes of light.** This portrays water projected out of his nostrils when sneezing, giving the appearance of **flashes of light**, as it gleamed in the bright sun. **His eyes** were **like the rays of dawn.** The thin eyes were the first part of the animal to appear when it emerged from the water, giving the appearance of the sun's rays shining over the horizon.

41:19–20. **Firebrands stream** as it gleams **from his mouth; sparks of fire shoot out.** This highly figurative, exaggerated poetic language represents the reptile's breath as saliva was spewed from its mouth, looking like a stream of fire being shot forth. In what resembles fire and smoke from a dragon's mouth, God said that **smoke pours from his nostrils as from a boiling pot over a fire of reeds**. This smoke was probably the spray of water shot from his nostrils with the sun reflecting on it.

41:21. **His breath sets coals ablaze, and flames dart from his mouth.** Here is depicted the expelling of water and hot breath into the air. This resembled a stream of fire as it left the leviathan's mouth.

41:22. Describing that area above his upper shoulders, God noted that **strength resides in his neck**. Extremely powerful and able to overwhelm and overpower any who attempted to capture him, **dismay goes before him**. Frightened people run away from this reptile in terror, fearing for their lives.

41:23–24. **The folds of his flesh are tightly joined; they are firm and immovable.** That is, the leviathan's vulnerable areas around his chin are made of impenetrable hide. This animal has no soft spot where he can be struck and killed. **His chest is hard as rock, hard as a lower millstone**, suggesting a bone-hard underside like rock. The leviathan was not susceptible to the hunter's weapon.

41:25. An animal this large and powerful made quite an impression when it began to move. When he rose up out of the water, the **mighty** were **terrified**. Even the strongest of men were fearful and retreated before his **thrashing** of the water.

41:26. Regarding how impenetrable his outer hide was, God said, "**The sword that reaches him has no effect, nor does the spear or the dart or the javelin.**" The hunter or warrior who would come against him could not conquer this creature, even with the most lethal weapons.

41:27–28. **Iron**, used in these weapons, he treated **like straw and bronze like rotten wood**. That is, they did not harm him, and he could break them easily. He was virtually impregnable with no vulnerable points. **Arrows** fired at him did not make him **flee** in self-defense. **Slingstones** were like **chaff to him**, unable to drop him to the ground.

41:29. **A club seems to him but a piece of straw**, all to no avail. **He laughs at the rattling of the lance** that holds the sharp, two-edged sword. The thought of such an instrument subduing him was so absurd that the leviathan laughed.

41:30. Further describing the leviathan's protective hide, God declared, "**His undersides are jagged potsherds.**" This reptile's outer covering was jagged and sharp like broken pieces of pottery. As he moved about in his natural habitat, a swamplike basin in a river area, he left **a trail** of marks **in the mud like a threshing sledge**.

C Leviathan's Agility (41:31–34)

SUPPORTING IDEA: *God continues to intimidate Job by noting that the powerful leviathan is greater than the haughty.*

41:31–32. The leviathan made the depths **churn like a boiling caldron** when he swam to the bottom of the water. He stirred up the sea **like a pot of ointment**, causing the mud and sediment to rise to the surface in a foam. **Behind him** he left **a glistening wake** in the water that was swirled up in a path created by the undertow of his movements. The moving of the water was so pronounced that **one would think the deep had white hair**. That is, white-caps arose in the wake created by this reptile as it swam through the water, giving the appearance of white hair. This majestic creature could not move even slightly without being noticed.

41:33. As a result of all that had been stated about the leviathan, God concluded, "**Nothing on earth is his equal—a creature without fear.**" He was incomparable with any other creature on earth. He was so powerful and well-protected that he lived without any fear of man or animal. At the same time everyone lived in terror of him.

41:34. The leviathan looked down on all who were **haughty**, possessing an exalted position of supremacy over all other creatures. He was **king over all** that were **proud**, even Job himself who had become puffed up with pride in defending himself before God.

MAIN IDEA REVIEW: *God points out the inability of Job to control or subdue the mighty sea creature known as the leviathan.*

III. CONCLUSION

I Am a Little Servant

Years ago, the moderator of a church gave J. Hudson Taylor a flattering introduction. When Taylor, founder of the China Inland Mission, stepped into the pulpit, he quietly said, "Dear friends, I am a little servant of an illustrious master." Is this not the testimony of every Christian? We are all little servants of an illustrious master.

That is what Job learned as God challenged him in this final divine speech. The fact is that Job could not control the leviathan. How much less could he confront God, the Creator of the leviathan? Job needed to realize that he was not as big as he thought himself to be. He had expected God to answer him. But instead, Job was answerable to God. Like Hudson Taylor, Job realized that he was only a little servant of an illustrious and awesome God.

IV. LIFE APPLICATION

Man's Weakness

Like Job, all believers are weak and pitiful. Jesus Christ understood the weakness and helplessness of mankind when he said, "Apart from me you can do nothing" (John 15:5). So impotent is fallen man that outside of divine enablement he can do nothing. People are dependent on God for their very breath. Without God we would cease to exist.

John stated in his Gospel, "A man can receive only what is given him from heaven" (John 3:27). Everything given to man is sent from God, and nothing is received that is not given by God (cp. Jas. 1:17). Paul remarked, "Not that we are competent in ourselves to claim anything for ourselves, but our competence comes from God" (2 Cor. 3:5). The secret to living life is understanding our weakness and helplessness. God's greatness and power "is made perfect in weakness" (2 Cor. 12:9). To be used by God, believers must understand their powerlessness.

V. PRAYER

God, our Father, we are by nature a haughty people who are proud and rebellious. We need to be reminded of our weakness and frailty. Help us to remember that we are dust and apart from you we can do nothing. Only you are great. Only you are sovereign. Teach us to realize your greatness and our insignificance. In Jesus' name. Amen.

VI. DEEPER DISCOVERIES

Leviathan (41:1)

"Leviathan" is the transliteration of a Hebrew word that means sea monster or sea creature. It was used to describe sea monsters in the deep that supposedly inhabited the Mediterranean Sea. The word was used to describe Israel's enemies (Isa. 27:1), especially Egypt (Ps. 74:13–14). In ancient mythology, the leviathan was a many-headed monster that ruled the waters and feared no man. Some scholars believe this mysterious creature may have been a marine dinosaur. Others believe it may have been a crocodile.

VII. TEACHING OUTLINE

A. Leviathan's Autonomy (41:1–11)
   1. He cannot be captured (41:1–10a)
   2. God cannot be controlled (41:10b–11)

B. Leviathan's Anatomy (41:12–30)
   1. His body is powerful (41:12–17)
   2. His breath is potent (41:18–21)
   3. His backside is protected (41:22–30)

C. Leviathan's Agility (41:31–34)
   1. He glides through the water (41:31–32)
   2. He governs over the earth (41:33–34)

VIII. ISSUES FOR DISCUSSION

1. Do I attempt to control God?
2. Do I acknowledge and understand that everything under heaven belongs to God?
3. Do I have unconfessed pride?

Job 42

Nowhere to Look but Up!

Quote

"I will take my repentance to the gates of heaven."

Philip Henry

Job 42

I. INTRODUCTION

Mature Heads Bend Low

Two brothers grew up on a farm. One went away to college to make a name for himself. He earned a law degree and became a partner in a prominent law firm in the state capital. The other brother stayed on the family farm, running his father's business. One day the ambitious brother visited his brother on the farm. He asked, "Why don't you go out and make a name for yourself? Why don't you be somebody in this world so you can hold your head up high like me?"

The brother who stayed home said, "See that field of wheat out there?"

The attorney brother answered, "Yes. What about it?"

"Those heads that are most mature and well-filled bend low to the ground," the farmer brother answered. "Only the *empty* heads stand up tall."

The empty heads of men stand tallest, while the full heads stoop lowest. This is a spiritual lesson that Job had learned the hard way. Throughout the course of this painful interrogation, he had been greatly humbled by God. His heart has been emptied of pride before God. Yet it had been in this lowering process that Job's faith had been turned upward to God with a new attitude. Hearts full of God are always bent low before him in humility. Man is never more devoid of true grace than when he is trying to elevate himself before God. And he is never more growing in grace than when he humbles himself before the Lord.

That is exactly the place where Job had finally found himself. He was, at last, made a humble man, bent low before the throne of God with nowhere to look but up. Either we humble ourselves, or God will humble us. This had been a painful lesson for Job to learn. Ever since his friends began accusing him of wrongdoing, he had been panic-stricken. But God put Job flat on his back, only to look up into the face of God. In that moment Job knew everything was going to be well with his soul. Job saw God as the sovereign Creator of heaven and earth. With a new awareness beyond his previous understanding, he realized that God was greater than all his trials. God was above and beyond his ability to grasp or understand.

God still had not told Job why he was suffering. All Job knew was that God was there with him—and that God alone was sufficient. Job didn't have to know *why.* All he needed to know was *who.* Can you relate to this? Are you going through a trial and struggling to see behind a curtain? God could explain everything to us about his workings behind the scenes of our trials. But we wouldn't be able to understand it. How can his infinite wisdom fit into our finite brains? All we need to know is that God is in control of our lives and that he loves us very much.

Maybe you need to come to that place in your life. If so, I urge you to stop your squirming and simply look up. Look up and see the face of God. When there are no answers, there is still comfort for your troubled heart. Peace is found in knowing the God who is there and who is sovereign. Strength is found in knowing the God who controls the universe. As we come to the end of the book, Job looks up and sees God in a new and fuller way. He realizes that God is perfectly orchestrating all the events of his life. He can trust God with his life. God is God. Job is finally brought to the end of himself. The end of ourselves is the beginning of God. Notice Job's response of faith.

II. COMMENTARY

Nowhere to Look but Up!

MAIN IDEA: *Broken and humbled, Job repents of his low view of God, restores his three friends back to God, and is abundantly blessed by God with more than he had before the great tragedies struck.*

A Job's Repentance (42:1–6)

SUPPORTING IDEA: *Job repents of his arrogance, acknowledging God's sovereignty and power, all while acknowledging his ignorance and renewed sight of God.*

42:1. Having been shown the divine power and majesty in creation by God himself (Job 38–41) and, thus, overwhelmed, Job **replied to the LORD**. He repented and humbled himself before Almighty God as a broken man who had been brought to the end of himself. He responded to God with a new realization and appreciation of God's sovereignty.

42:2. Job confessed, "**I know that you can do all things.**" He saw, at last, that God's purposes are supreme. God will do *as* he pleases, *when* he pleases, *how* he pleases, with *whom* he pleases. Furthermore, no plan of his **can be thwarted**. Job realized that all his sovereign purposes will be fully carried out. He came back to the single, most fundamental truth of theology—that God rules over all. Implied in this strong declaration by Job was a new submission to the God whose eternal purposes cannot be resisted or altered. Thus, it was insane for Job to question the Lord's verdicts or oppose his decrees. God is supreme, not Job.

42:3. Referring to God's words spoken to him earlier (Job 38:2), Job said, "**You asked, 'Who is this that obscures my counsel without knowledge?'**" By quoting these words of God, Job confessed his own guilt. Job had spoken wrongly about God and, thus, had covered over divine counsel with his foolish talk. **Surely I spoke of things I did not understand**. That is, as Job had spoken of God and his purposes, he said things which were beyond his ability to process and comprehend. These things were **too wonderful** for him to know. Where previously the ways of God were disturbing to him, the **knowledge** of his sovereign ways was now wonderful to his soul.

42:4. Quoting God's earlier words to him (Job 38:3; 40:7), Job admitted that he had said, "**Listen now, and I will speak; I will question you, and you shall answer me.**" By citing these previous words spoken by God, Job admitted that these divine words had been heard and heeded. He understood God's judicial authority as the supreme sovereign to demand answers from him. So Job did listen to God speak. Subdued and silenced, he had sat under the scrutiny of God's questions and now was ready to answer, not rebut. By quoting God's words verbatim, Job showed that he had carefully weighed the divine rebuke.

42:5. With deepening repentance, Job confided, "**My ears had heard of you but now my eyes have seen you.**" Through his ordeal Job had been confronted with a deeper realization of God's wisdom, power, and providential care. What little Job had known about God was now eclipsed by a deeper understanding of his divine attributes. What his **eyes** had **seen** of God refers not to a physical vision, such as a theophany, but to spiritual insight. Job now had a greater understanding of God's awesome character than before his suffering began. In this sense his agonizing trial had been worth the suffering. His eternal, spiritual gain outweighed his temporal, physical loss.

42:6. As a result of this deepening knowledge of God, Job confessed, "**Therefore I despise myself and repent in dust and ashes.**" Self-denial and deep sorrow filled Job's life. He despised himself, hating the self-righteous attitude that had filled his heart. He renounced the reckless accusations that he had voiced against the flawless character of God. He was deeply grieved over his blatant sin. Having seen God in his holiness (Job 38–40; 42:5), Job finally saw himself in his unholiness. The sovereignty of God exposed the sinfulness of his heart. Job was a sorrowful, subdued, and submissive man, yielded to God with humility.

B Job's Reconciliation (42:7–9)

SUPPORTING IDEA: *God rebukes Job's three friends in anger, ordering them to give a burnt sacrifice and directing Job to pray for them.*

42:7. **After the LORD had said these things to Job**, God turned his attention to the three friends who also needed correction. He said to Eliphaz the Temanite, "**I am angry with you and your two friends.**" Righteous indignation caused God to be angry with them. These remarks were directed to **Eliphaz** because he probably was the oldest and, thus, the leading spokesman. Eliphaz had spoken first in each of the three rounds of speeches (Job 4–5; 15; 22).

God was angry **because you have not spoken of me what is right, as my servant Job has.** They spoke inaccurately about God. In their effort to champion God's justice, they had restricted his sovereignty. They taught that all suffering is the direct result of sin. But such theology is not true. Although much of what they said about God was true, not all their words were accurate. God was angry with Job's three friends because they had misrepresented him. Job alone had spoken the truth about God by insisting that his suffering was not a punishment from God.

42:8. In order to make a covering for the sins committed by Job's friends, God ordered the friends to **take seven bulls and seven rams and go to my servant Job and sacrifice a burnt offering for yourselves.** This was precisely the number of sacrifices specified in Numbers 23:1 by Balaam, indicating this was probably a standard burnt offering to atone for sin. God continued, "**My servant Job will pray for you, and I will accept his prayer and not deal with you according to your folly.**" Job the servant became Job the intercessor, praying on behalf of his friends.

Reiterating their sin that needed divine forgiveness, God stated, "**You have not spoken of me what is right, as my servant Job has.**" This is not to say that everything they had said about God was incorrect. Rather, it means they had misrepresented God to Job. This, in turn, caused them to bring wrong charges against Job, stating that God was punishing him for his sin, which was not the case.

42:9. **So Eliphaz the Temanite, Bildad the Shuhite and Zophar the Naamathite did what the LORD told them.** They brought the burnt offerings to Job and sought his prayer on their behalf. They fully obeyed and did as God requested. As a result, **the LORD accepted Job's prayer** and restored these three friends to himself and reconciled them to Job.

C Job's Restoration (42:10–17)

SUPPORTING IDEA: *God restores to Job the great abundance of health, children, and possessions that he had before his tragedy.*

42:10. Job interceded on behalf of his friends. **After Job had prayed for his friends, the LORD made him prosperous again and gave him twice as much as he had before.** This was the turning point for Job. After he prayed for his three friends, God restored Job's fortune and family to him.

42:11. **All his brothers and sisters and everyone who had known him before came and ate with him in his house.** Earlier all who saw Job had despised his presence (cp. Job 16:2; 19:13). But now his family gathered around him and fellowshipped with him. **They comforted and consoled him over all the trouble the LORD had brought upon him.** In this Job's siblings and friends encouraged him. Further, **each one gave him a piece of silver and a gold ring** as expressions of their love for him.

42:12. In an amazing display of divine grace, **the LORD blessed the latter part of Job's life more than the first**. As greatly as he had been favored by God before his tragedy (Job 1:2–3), God gave him more than what had been taken from him. In fact, Job gained more than he had lost. **He had fourteen thousand sheep, six thousand camels, a thousand yoke of oxen and a thousand donkeys.** These possessions were twice as much as he had previously owned. Such was the infinite goodness of God.

42:13. **And he also had seven sons and three daughters.** This doubled the number of Job's children, replacing the children he had lost (Job 1:3). This made a total of twenty children, ten on earth and ten in the presence of God.

42:14. Regarding their names, **the first daughter he named Jemimah, the second Keziah and the third Keren-Happuch.** "Jemimah" means dove or daylight, "Keziah" means cinnamon or sweet smelling, and "Keren-Happuch" means container of antinomy—a beautiful color that was often used by women in cosmetics as eyeshadow. These names represent the joyful new beginning for Job that he experienced in the addition of these children.

42:15. **Nowhere in all the land were there found women as beautiful as Job's daughters.** They were strikingly beautiful, both internally and externally. Job was a blessed man, and he **granted them an inheritance along with their brothers**. This was contrasted with Numbers 27:8 which called for an inheritance to be given to daughters only when there were no sons. But in Job's case he extended his inheritance to both his sons and daughters. This gesture of kindness expressed the generosity of his heart.

42:16. After his repentance and restoration, **Job lived a hundred and forty years**. Thus, he lived to be around 200 years old, or possibly 210 years—140 years after the tragedies and 60 to 70 before they happened. This long life span was not unusual for a patriarch at this time (cp. Exod. 6:16). **He saw his children and their children to the fourth generation**. This was a blessing from the Lord. Great was Job's legacy on the earth.

42:17. And so Job died, **old and full of years**, enjoying abundant favor with God and man. This long, full life was an expression of God's goodness toward Job, as he was allowed to live many years with his new family and wealth. Did God ever explain to Job why all this tragedy had occurred? He did if Job himself was the author of this inspired book.

MAIN IDEA REVIEW: *Broken and humbled, Job repents of his low view of God, restores his three friends back to God, and is abundantly blessed by God with more than he had before the great tragedies struck.*

III. CONCLUSION

Saving the Best for Last

Timothy Dwight was a brilliant learner. Born in 1752, he advanced rapidly in his studies and at eleven was taught Latin and Greek. He entered Yale College at the age of thirteen and graduated in four years. As he continued his graduate studies, he was hired as a tutor for the college. But these rapid advancements came at a great cost to the young man. His rigorous study habits left little time to eat, sleep, or get physical exercise. These unhealthy habits led to a life-threatening sickness from which he never fully recovered. After months of agonizing suffering, Dwight was debilitated. Nearly blind because of the devastating effects of his illness, he could never again read without experiencing headaches.

Dwight's long, personal suffering fitted him for the future God had prepared for him. With the onset of the American Revolution, he became a chaplain to the Continental Army and labored over the souls of soldiers with the Word of God. Then in 1783, he entered the pastorate of the church in Greenfield, Connecticut. While pastoring there, he taught Bible in an academy and began to battle against the influence of Deism in the United States. In 1795, his alma mater, Yale College, called him as the new president. For Dwight this would be his life-defining crucible. Nowhere had French deistic thought made more headway than in the new colleges of America, and Yale College was no exception.

From the beginning of his tenure, Dwight faithfully preached the Word of God. Then after seven years, the Spirit of God greatly moved, and proud hearts began to melt. As revival broke out, one-third of the college's students were brought into the knowledge of Christ. Many of these students were involved in the revival that began to spread from New England. The zeal of Timothy Dwight for reform and revival led to what is now called "the Second Great Awakening." God had saved the best for last in his life.

Life's great tragedies are designed to be a preparation for future blessings. God delights in showing his great power through weak, earthly vessels. This is the lesson that Job learned, and it is a reality that we must experience as well. We stand tallest when there is nowhere to look but up.

IV. LIFE APPLICATION

How to Deal with Tragedy

When tragedy strikes, believers must rely on certain truths about their relationship with God. Trusting him can enable us to go through the deep waters triumphantly.

1. *Recognize God's sovereignty.* Have you come to realize God's sovereignty over your life? He chose to place you in the family in which you were born. He gave you the parents he desired. He had you born where it pleased him. He had you born with the gender, physical size, health, and appearance you have. The same is true of the circumstances in our lives. It is his divine right to make and mold us as he chooses. This is the first key in enduring any trial successfully.

2. *Realize God's inscrutability.* We must accept divine mysteries in the Christian life. Much that occurs in our lives is beyond our understanding. The lines of divine providence intersect far above our heads. The apostle Paul came to this conclusion when he wrote, "Oh, the depth of the riches both of the wisdom and knowledge of God! How unsearchable are his judgments and unfathomable His ways! For WHO HAS KNOWN THE MIND OF THE LORD, OR WHO BECAME HIS COUNSELOR?" (Rom. 11:33–34 NASB). We need to be cautious of others who offer themselves as interpreters about the why and wherefore of all that is happening. Be wary of those who say, "God let this happen so you might learn such and such lesson." The fact is, we do not fully *know* what God is doing through a particular set of circumstances or events.

3. *Reflect on God's superiority.* Suffering makes students of all believers. Charles Spurgeon once said, "The doorstep to the temple of wisdom is the knowledge of our own ignorance." Job is standing at the very threshold now, ready to learn life's most important lessons.

4. *Refocus on God's intimacy.* Christianity is a personal, abiding relationship with God and Jesus Christ (John 17:3), a communion in which we are to grow closer to him and know him more intimately. Are you growing in your knowledge of God?

5. *Repent of all sin.* One mark of a great person is not that he or she never sins. But when the person does sin, he or she is sorrowful and broken over that sin. King David was a man after God's own heart not because he never sinned. He was a godly man because when he sinned he was deeply broken over it and chose to turn back to God. That was the case with Job. Job sinned

against God with prideful rebellion. But once God revealed his sin to him, Job was quick to repent.

What about you? Is your heart quick to repent when God points out your sin? Do you take full ownership of your sin by confessing it? Too many believers sin retail and confess wholesale. God's people must humble themselves and confess their sin, holding nothing back.

V. PRAYER

God, we bow before you and acknowledge that you can do all things and that no plan of yours can be thwarted. Lord, as we have heard of you with the hearing of our ears, may you enlighten our eyes with your Word so we may see you more clearly. Give us clearer understanding of your character and attributes so we may glorify you. In Jesus' name. Amen.

VI. DEEPER DISCOVERIES

A. Seen (42:5)

"Seen" (Heb. *raa*) means to understand as if one would see intellectually what had not been previously understood; other denotations are to behold, perceive, or view with right understanding. Here it means to be made to see and understand with divine enlightenment that only God can give (Num. 8:4; 2 Kgs. 8:10,13; Jer. 24:1; Amos 8:1).

B. Despise (42:6)

"Despise" (Heb. *maas*) means to disdain or reject. It is often used in reference to the Lord as men despise his Word (1 Sam. 15:23,26; Jer. 8:9) and his law (Amos 2:4). This word was also used to describe Israel's rejection of the Lord for a king (1 Sam. 10:19).

C. Inheritance (42:15)

"Inheritance" (Heb. *nahala*) is a reference to that which is passed on by right. It was often used as it is here to designate an estate or portion that was inherited as a permanent possession (cp. Gen. 31:14).

VII. TEACHING OUTLINE

A. Job's Repentance (42:1–6)
   1. He recognized God's sovereignty (42:1–2)
   2. He realized God's inscrutability (42:3)

3. He reaffirmed God's supremacy (42:4)
4. He refocused on God's intimacy (42:5)
5. He retracted his own sin (42:6)

B. Job's Reconciliation (42:7–9)

1. God was angered by the three friends (42:7)
2. God advised the three friends (42:8)
3. God accepted the three friends (42:9)

C. Job's Restoration (42:10–17)

1. God restored his fortune (42:10–12)
2. God restored his family (42:13–15)
3. God restored his future (42:16–17)

VIII. ISSUES FOR DISCUSSION

1. Have you come to the place where you are knocked flat on your back and look up into the face of God?
2. Do you see a sovereign God who is in control of all your circumstances?

Glossary

affliction—A severe trial that causes the sufferer to be bowed down under the weight of its heavy burden

blameless—The quality of being spiritually and morally upright, not being sinless but morally whole and complete, maintaining personal integrity

confession of sin—The agreement with and acknowledgment to God of one's sin

deity—A reference to God and all the divine attributes that belong to him

demons—Fallen angels who now perform evil deeds under the leadership of Satan

despair—A feeling of hopelessness that produces deep anguish

divine attributes—The characteristics of God that describe his divine being

divine glory—The sum total of all the divine greatness, grandeur, and splendor revealed to man

divine holiness—The infinite transcendence of God along with his moral perfection that sets him apart from his creation

divine judgment—The perfect assessment of one's life by God, resulting in either reward or retribution

divine justice—The perfect equity by which God gives to man exactly what is due him, no more and no less

divine majesty—The greatness and glory of God

divine omnipotence—God possesses all power to do everything he wants to accomplish

divine omniscience—God knows all things that can be known perfectly, immediately, and intuitively

divine sovereignty—The unlimited freedom and absolute right of God to speak and act as he pleases; the free exercise of God's will and authority over all things

divine wrath—God's holy hatred and punishment of all sin

divine wisdom—The inscrutable genius of God by which he chooses the best means to accomplish the highest ends for all creation

evil—That which is morally bad, being contrary to God and his holiness

faith—A belief and confidence in God that trusts him explicitly, even in tumultuous circumstances

fellowship with God—A personal relationship between a believer and God that involves their sharing a common life, concerns, and interests

heaven—The perfect place where God lives, along with his angelic beings and all the redeemed

hell—The real place of eternal torment, reserved for the devil, his fallen angels, and all unbelievers

hope—The positive expectation of a glorious future that gives strength to the believer in his present difficulty

humility—The quality of lowering oneself before God and others

mediator—One who goes between two parties in an attempt to bring about their reconciliation

perseverance—The God-given ability to endure and press on in the midst of severe trials

providence—God's active, continual involvement in guiding all people, events, and circumstances, whether good or evil, toward their divinely appointed ends

punishment—God's inflicting of suffering, pain, or loss to a person as retribution for wrongdoing

reverence for God—The respect, awe, and honor given to God for who he is and what he does

salvation—The divine act of rescuing the person who believes in God through his Son, Jesus Christ, from divine wrath and estrangement from God

sanctification—The divine act of making the believer holy

Satan—Literally, the adversary or the accuser. Originally created to be the highest of angelic beings, this archangel rebelled against God and was expelled from heaven to the earth, where he is now the prince of darkness, the head of the demons, and the leader of all opposition against God

Savior—Jesus Christ, by his atoning death, became the deliverer from sin and hell of all who believe on him

sin—Any act or attitude that fails to conform to the holiness of God or that violates his Word.

temptation—The act of man being lured into sin by Satan and his demons through their deception, seduction, and lies

theodicy—The attempt to defend God's involvement in man's calamity by showing that he is not responsible for evil

worship—The act of believers offering to God the praise and honor due his name

Bibliography

Commentaries

Anderson, Francis I. *Job: An Introduction and Commentary.* The Tyndale Old Testament Commentaries. Downers Grove: InterVarsity Press, 1976.

Barnes, Albert. *Barnes' Notes.* Vol. 3. Grand Rapids: Baker Books, 1983.

Calvin, John. *Sermons on Job.* Edinburgh: Banner of Truth Trust, 1993.

Clines, David J. A. *Job 1–20.* Word Biblical Commentary. Vol. 17. Dallas: Word Publishing, 2002.

Delitzsch, Franz. *Keil-Delitzsch Commentary on the Old Testament.* Vol. 4. Peabody, MA: Hendrickson Publishers, 2001.

Dyer, Charles, and Eugene Merrill. *The Old Testament Explorer.* Dallas: Word Publishing, 2001.

Hartley, John E. *The Book of Job.* The New International Commentary on the Old Testament. Grand Rapids: Eerdmans Publishing Co., 1988.

Henry, Matthew. *Matthew Henry Commentary.* Vol. 3. Peabody, MA: Hendrickson Publishers, 1991.

Lawson, Steven J. *When All Hell Breaks Loose.* Colorado Springs: NavPress 1993.

Smick, Elmer B. *Job.* The Bible Expositor's Commentary. Vol. 4. Grand Rapids: Zondervan Publishing House, 1988.

Spurgeon, Charles. *The Suffering of Man and the Sovereignty of God: 25 Selected Sermons on the Book of Job.* Oswego, IL: Fox River Press, 2001.

Swindoll, Charles. *Job: A Man of Heroic Endurance.* Nashville: Thomas Nelson Publishing, 2004.

Thomas, Derek. *The Storm Breaks: Job Simply Explained.* Darlington, UK: Evangelical Press, 1996.

Unger, Merrill. *Unger's Commentary on the Old Testament.* Vol. 1. Chattanooga: Amy Publishers, 2002.

Wiersbie, Warren W. *Old Testament Wisdom and Poetry.* Old Testament Commentary. Vol. 3. Ontario: Cook Communications, 2004.

Williams, Peter. *From Despair to Hope: Insights into the Book of Job.* Leominster, UK: DayOne Publications, 2003.

Zuck, Roy. *Job.* The Bible Knowledge Commentary of the Old Testament. Ontario: Cook Comunications, 1985.

——— *Job.* Everyman's Bible Commentary. Chicago: Moody Publishers, 1995.

Zuck, Roy, ed. *Sitting with Job*. Eugene, OR: Wipf & Stoch Publishers, 2003.

Hebrew Tools

Armstrong, Terry A., Douglas L. Busby, and Cyril F. Carr. *A Reader's Hebrew and English Lexicon of the Old Testament*. Grand Rapids: Zondervan Publishing House, 1989.

Brown, Francis, Samuel R. Driver, and Charles A. Briggs. *A Hebrew and English Lexicon of the Old Testament*. Peabody, MA: Hendrickson Publishers, 1996.

Even-Shoshan, Abraham. *A New Concordance of the Old Testament*. Jerusalem: Kiriyat sefur, 1985.

Harris, R. Laird, Gleason L. Archer Jr., and Bruce K. Waltke. *Theological Wordbook of the Old Testament*. 2 vols. Chicago: Moody Publishers, 1980.

Owens, John Joseph. *Analytical Key to the Old Testament*. 4 vols. Grand Rapids: Baker Books, 1989.

Ringgaren, Butterweck, ed. *Theological Dictionary of the Old Testament*. 13 vols. Grand Rapids: Eerdman's Publishing Co., 1977.

The Englishman's Hebrew and Chaldee Concordance of the Old Testament. Peabody, MA: Hendrickson Publishers, 1996.

Torrey, R. A. *Treasury of Scripture Knowledge*. Peabody, MA: Hendrickson Publishers, 1983.

VanGameren, William A., ed. *New International Dictionary of Old Testament Theology and Exegesis*. 5 vols. Grand Rapids: Zondervan Corp., 1997.

Weingreen, Jacob. *Practical Grammar for Classical Hebrew*. London: Oxford University Press, 1959.